BIOETHICS AND DISABILITY

Bioethics and Disability provides tools for understanding the concerns, fears, and biases that have convinced some people with disabilities that the health care setting is a dangerous place and some bioethicists that disability activists have nothing to offer bioethics. It wrestles with the charge that bioethics as a discipline devalues the lives of persons with disabilities, arguing that reconciling the competing concerns of the disability community and the autonomy-based approach of mainstream bioethics is not only possible, but essential for a bioethics committed to facilitating good medical decision making and promoting respect for all persons, regardless of ability.

Through in-depth case studies involving newborns, children, and adults with disabilities, *Bioethics and Disability* proposes a new model for medical decision making that is mindful of and knowledgeable about the fact of disability in medical cases. Disability-conscious bioethics will bring together disability experts and bioethicists to identify and mitigate disability bias in our health care systems.

Alicia Ouellette is a Professor of Law at Albany Law School and a Professor of Bioethics in the Union Graduate College/Mt. Sinai School of Medicine Bioethics Program. Her recent publications include *Shaping Parental Authority over Children's Bodies* and *Growth Attenuation, Parents' Choices, and the Rights of Disabled Children*. She is also a coeditor (with Laurence McCullough and Robert Baker) of the *Cambridge Dictionary of Bioethics* (2011).

Before joining the law faculty, she served as an Assistant Solicitor General for the State of New York. As ASG, she briefed and argued more than 100 appeals on issues ranging from termination of treatment for the terminally ill to the responsibility of gun manufacturers for injuries caused by handguns. She continues her advocacy work in select cases and was lead counsel on the law professors' brief submitted in support of same-sex couples who sought the right to marry in New York State.

Disability Law and Policy Series

The *Disability Law and Policy* series examines these topics in interdisciplinary and comparative terms. The books in the series reflect the diversity of definitions, causes, and consequences of discrimination against persons with disabilities, while illuminating fundamental themes that unite countries in their pursuit of human rights laws and policies to improve the social and economic status of persons with disabilities. The series contains historical, contemporary, and comparative scholarship crucial to identifying individual, organizational, cultural, attitudinal, and legal themes necessary for the advancement of disability law and policy.

The book topics covered in the series also are reflective of the new moral and political commitment by countries throughout the world toward equal opportunity for persons with disabilities in such areas as employment, housing, transportation, rehabilitation, and individual human rights. The series will thus play a significant role in informing policy makers, researchers, and citizens of issues central to disability rights and disability antidiscrimination policies. The series grounds the future of disability law and policy as a vehicle for ensuring that those living with disabilities participate as equal citizens of the world.

Books in the series

Ruth Colker, *When Is Separate Unequal? A Disability Perspective*, 2009

Larry M. Logue and Peter Blanck, *Race, Ethnicity, and Disability: Veterans and Benefits in Post–Civil War America*, 2010

Lisa Vanhala, *Making Rights a Reality? Disability Rights Activists and Legal Mobilization*, 2010

Alicia Ouellette, *Bioethics and Disability: Toward a Disability-Conscious Bioethics*, 2011

Eilionoir Flynn, *From Rhetoric to Action: Implementing the UN Convention on the Rights of Persons with Disabilities*, 2011

BIOETHICS AND DISABILITY

Toward a Disability-Conscious Bioethics

Alicia Ouellette

CAMBRIDGE
UNIVERSITY PRESS

CAMBRIDGE UNIVERSITY PRESS
Cambridge, New York, Melbourne, Madrid, Cape Town,
Singapore, São Paulo, Delhi, Mexico City

Cambridge University Press
32 Avenue of the Americas, New York NY 10013-2473, USA

Published in the United States of America by Cambridge University Press, New York

www.cambridge.org
Information on this title: www.cambridge.org/9781107610651

First published 2011
First paperback edition 2013

A catalogue record for this publication is available from the British Library

Library of Congress Cataloging in Publication data
Ouellette, Alicia.
Bioethics and disability: toward a disability-conscious bioethics / Alicia Ouellette.
p. cm. – (Disability law and policy series)
Includes bibliographical references and index.
ISBN 978-0-521-11030-3 (hardback)
1. People with disabilities – Legal status, laws, etc. – United States. 2. Discrimination
against people with disabilities – Law and legislation – Moral and ethical aspects – United
States. 3. Medical ethics – United States. I. Title.
KF480.O94 2011
174′.957–dc22 2011000624

ISBN 978-0-521-11030-3 Hardback
ISBN 978-1-107-61065-1 Paperback

To Jacob, Molly, and Sam. You give me reason to believe.

Contents

Contents

Contents

Preface

Much has changed during the years in which I have been working on this book. For one thing, disability is no longer a shadow issue in bioethics. When I first started my work, I rarely heard the phrase "disability perspective" in discussions with bioethicists. A three-day conference might include a single sparsely attended session on disability issues. Disability is now part of the conversation. More and more often, articles by disability experts appear in bioethics journals and texts. In the past year alone, I have participated in several national bioethics conferences devoted exclusively to disability issues. These developments give me hope that the field is ripe for change. Nonetheless, the transformative change I'd like to see – a movement toward a bioethics that incorporates disability as a central issue and engages disability experts in the enterprise – will take more than a series of conferences and articles. The real work will take place on the ground floor – in medical education, in hospitals, in the courtroom, in law schools, in government – wherever the work of bioethics is done. This book is my contribution to that work.

In the end, this is a book about collaboration, which is especially fitting given the teamwork that went into its creation. Although the mistakes and omissions are mine alone, I share credit for the worthwhile sections with many people. I am enormously grateful to my colleagues at Albany Law School, especially Dede Hill and Christine Chung who provided invaluable feedback and support in every possible form and at all times of day and night. I am also grateful to Dale Moore and Kathy Katz for convincing me I had something worthwhile to say; to James Gathii for being my constant sounding board; and to Tim Lytton, who always asks the hardest questions. From outside the law school, I owe special thanks to Bob Baker, who took a chance in giving me my first position in bioethics, to William Peace, whose challenging feedback shaped my arguments, and to Kathy Cerminara, Elizabeth Pendo, Jane Greenlaw, Jennifer Bard, Amy Campbell, Sean Philpott, and all the others who have commented on drafts, pushed my ideas forward, or simply disagreed with me. This project would have been impossible without the incredible efforts of Fredd Brewer and Laurie Dayter who kept me on task through the years. A special thanks to Fredd for refusing to let me sweat the small stuff during the last, final push. I have been fortunate to have the help of many capable student research assistants over the years. Jessie Cardinale, Alaina Bergerstock, and Ashley Torre deserve special note for their enormous contributions to this book.

Sadly, two of the people who taught me most of what I know about life with disability, Harriet McBryde Johnson and Paul Longmore, died while I was writing the manuscript. This would not have been the same book, and I would not be the same person, had I not been lucky enough to have crossed their paths. Their written contributions and life examples will continue to educate and inspire generations to come, but I mourn their early deaths and will forever regret that they did not live long enough to see how far I've come, and to explain the ways I still don't get it.

Finally, I thank my family. You gave me the space and strength to carry on. You are my everything. I hope I've done you proud.

Introduction

AS AN APPELLATE ATTORNEY WORKING IN THE NEW YORK State Attorney General's office, I was assigned a case that involved an adult woman with profound physical and mental disabilities. The woman was terminally ill and unable to digest any food or water. After consulting with her doctors, her family requested that she be allowed to die without being provided any further nutrition or hydration, which could be administered – if at all – through an intravenous catheter. Although the provision of nutrition and hydration would extend her life, the treatment would not change the fact that she was dying. Instead, it would increase her pain through an extended dying process. Everyone directly involved in the woman's medical case – the doctors, family, and ethics consultants – agreed the plan for palliative care and the termination of the intravenous nutrition and hydration was in the patient's best interest. In most states, the treatment plan would have been carried out and the patient allowed to die peacefully in a matter of days. Because the patient was in a New York State hospital, however, and because she had never had capacity to express her own wishes with respect to end-of-life treatment, the case ended in litigation, which prolonged her life for several excruciating months.

At the time, New York law did not permit family members or doctors to withhold nutrition or hydration from a person who never had the capacity to make her own decisions. The state agency charged with advocating on behalf of persons with mental disabilities sought representation by the State's attorney to enforce the law. The client agency was adamant in its demand that the law requiring the provision of nutrition and hydration be enforced. In its view, the patient's family and doctors wanted to do something that was not legal in New York, and allowing for any exception to the rule would open the door to the slippery slope of euthanasia or even a new eugenics. My role was to support the trial attorney in his representation of the agency and then to handle any appeal arising after a trial court decision. My job was to keep the patient alive.

Despite the clear New York rule requiring life-prolonging treatment, there was nothing straightforward about application of the law in this particular woman's case. The patient's family and doctors submitted evidence that although providing nutrition and hydration would extend her life, the treatment was medically inappropriate. The woman's body was no longer able to digest or metabolize caloric intake. As a result, her body bloated; her organs deteriorated; her skin stretched to the point where it fell off; and her condition made pain relief impossible. The doctors documented the patient's excruciating journey toward death in her medical chart. They argued that applying the law as written was morally wrong, even inhumane. Eventually the trial court judge was persuaded to put the law aside and issue an order allowing the doctors to stop the treatment. The woman at the center of the litigation suffered for months before finally dying, just as an appellate court was ready to hear arguments.

By the time I wrote the appellate brief and prepared my arguments for the appellate court, it was clear to me and everyone else on the legal team that New York's rigid law was having unintended – even tragic – consequences. We saw that the patient at the center of our case was in intractable pain because of the very treatment that was prolonging her life. In our brief to the appellate court, we modified our position from the one taken at the trial court, where we vigorously advocated application of New York's law, to one tempered by recognition that the presence of iatrogenic harm caused by the life-extending treatment might justify an exception to the rule. It was too little too late. The case was dismissed without a written decision.

After leaving the Attorney General's office to begin teaching at a law school, I wrote a law review article that put together the ideas and arguments I had been thinking about since my involvement in the case.[1] The paper criticized New York's end-of-life law for its insistence that people who had not specifically expressed a desire to forgo life-prolonging treatment be given life-prolonging treatment. My intent was to use principles from bioethics to make an argument for disability rights at the end of life. Specifically, I argued that New York's law was especially harmful to people with cognitive disabilities who could never express their wishes regarding end-of-life care because the law made them particularly vulnerable to the horrific death experienced by the patient in my case. It seemed clear to me that New York's law hurt people who never had decision-making capacity because they could never access medically appropriate comfort care without artificial nutrition and hydration. I saw the barriers to comfort care as a form of disability discrimination. In short, I thought I'd written a pro–disability rights paper.

Although it seems naïve in retrospect, I was shocked and upset when I received angry e-mails from disability rights activists following publication and even angrier responses in person after I presented my argument at conferences. The activists charged that by advocating for a change in New York's laws to allow people with disabilities to die without the use of all available life-prolonging treatments, I was promoting the myth that life with disability is not worth living. I was cast as someone complicit in a new eugenics that would kill off people with disabilities as "useless eaters."

[1] Alicia Ouellette, *When Vitalism Is Dead Wrong: The Discrimination Against and Torture of Incompetent Patients by Compulsory Life-Sustaining Treatment*, 79 IND. L. J. 1 (2004). *See infra* Chapter 7.

Introduction

The response I got paled in comparison to the disability community's attacks against Michael Schiavo, triggered by his decision to withhold artificial nutrition and hydration from his wife, Terri Schiavo, who had been kept alive in a persistent vegetative state for more than ten years.[2] In response to the Schiavo case, the disability rights community engaged in a desperate battle for the life of a woman they viewed as representative of the lives of all people with disabilities.[3] The Schiavo case pitted disability rights activists against bioethicists who emerged in defense of Michael Schiavo on a very public stage.

The activists confronted bioethicists directly in my hometown when a bus full of members of the activist disability group Not Dead Yet took over in vocal protest the plenary session of a large national conference I had helped organize with my local bioethics institute. Their message was clear: Laws that facilitate dying, whatever their form, discriminate against and hurt people with disabilities. People who advocate such laws are enemies to people with disabilities.

In the years following the publication of my first article, I immersed myself in the teachings of people who study about and advocate for people with disabilities. My feeling was that I could no longer hold myself out as an advocate for people with disabilities until I understood a perspective I had never considered. I have learned a great deal from that course of study as well as from the people I've met along the way. I now understand on a much more fundamental level the history that drives that branch of the disability rights community most vocally opposed to laws that allow for choice in dying. I also see more clearly why and how bioethics is a discipline largely vilified by many disability rights activists. But my immersion into disability studies has not shaken my belief that laws like New York's are more harmful than

[2] The Schiavo case is discussed at length in Chapter 7.

[3] For a comprehensive overview of the disability community's response to the Schiavo case, *see* Kathy L. Cerminara, *Critical Essay: Musings on the Need to Convince Some People with Disabilities That End-of-Life Decision-Making Advocates Are Not Out to Get Them*, 37 LOY. U. CHI. L. J. 343 (2006).

helpful to the very people they are designed to protect. Nor has my immersion into disability studies shaken my belief that application of the core principles of bioethics – autonomy, beneficence, nonmalefi- cience, and justice – is fundamental in a health care system that best respects individuals as human beings.

Although my analytic orientation remains rooted in bioethics, I have taken more from my immersion in disability studies than a schol- arly understanding of an alternative worldview. My study of disability scholarship and activism has fundamentally altered my understanding of life with disability and has convinced me that as a field, bioethics is often indifferent to and sometimes insensitive about disability issues. Although I frequently disagree with disability rights activists about what it means to advance the interests of individuals with disability in the health care system, I have come to believe that bioethics would be richer – and more effective in promoting respect for all persons – were it deliberately conscious of disability issues.

This book is the result of my ten-year journey toward disability- consciousness. It draws on materials from bioethics, law, and disability studies to make the case that health care professionals, policy makers, and bioethicists can and should be both mindful of and knowledgeable about the issue of disability in medical cases. In other words, they need to develop an informed disability consciousness. Being disability con- scious does not need to undermine patient self-determination, as feared by some bioethicists, nor does continued respect for self-determination and surrogate decision making need to result in disability discrimina- tion, as feared by some disability rights activists. Instead, becoming disability conscious will require bioethicists, policy makers, and health care professionals to engage the work of disability scholars and partic- ipate in civil discourse with disability experts. If successful, this book will serve as a useful resource in facilitating that cross-disciplinary conversation and study.

In addition to presenting disability and bioethics perspectives on a wide range of cases, the book proposes an analytic framework for a disability-conscious bioethics. The framework is a starting point for a much-need conversation about how to promote respect for people of all abilities in the health care setting, but it is by no means a panacea. Even if it is successful in moving bioethics toward disability-consciousness, my proposal will not eliminate the distrust and fear expressed by many disability activists toward medicine and bioethics. Nor will it provide answers to vexing issues in health care. But moving toward a disability-conscious bioethics should allow scholars, practitioners, and activists on both sides of the divide to come together to place individuals with disabilities at the center of the decision-making process with a full and accurate awareness of the realities of life with disability, including its gifts. If nothing else, I hope this book makes room for nuanced discourse beyond the angry rhetoric that characterizes and stunts the current debate.

Before I begin, some disclosures and caveats are in order. First, I am an American lawyer by training and profession. Like many people who write or think about bioethical issues, I am not credentialed in bioethics. Nor am I a philosopher, historian, social worker, clinician, or theologian. This disclosure is important in several respects. As a "naked JD," my formal training and practical experience are limited, as is my analytical approach to bioethical disputes. My training in legal analysis (and lack of training in other disciplines) shows throughout the book. Like any good lawyer, I start with some factual background, move into rules, and then apply those rules to the specific facts of individual cases. And like most lawyers and legal academics, I am a firm believer in the case-study method for nuanced understanding of legal doctrine and policy. For that reason, most of this book focuses on case studies rather than abstract theory or debate.

Also, I have a U.S. bias. My primary focus as a practitioner and academic has been and remains American law and its relationship to the provision of health care. Although I consider international perspectives in analyzing issues (specifically I draw from the United Nations Convention on the Rights of Persons with Disabilities in addressing

what a disability-conscious bioethics might look like), and I have
included international perspectives about some of the cases that make
up this work, the book relies heavily on U.S. cases and U.S. law. In
some respects, the U.S. bias in the book might be explained as reflective of the field's origins. Although bioethics has spread to countries
around the globe where it has taken on decidedly local dimensions,
the recent histories of the field recognize bioethics as a discipline with
American origins,[4] and the U.S. legal system as a major player in its
development.[5] Moreover, many of the case studies I've included are
seminal cases that are indispensible to any study of the tension between
bioethics and disability. I have no doubt, however, that the main reason
I rely so heavily on American cases is that I am familiar with them.

Next, I have no visible disabilities. I have a neurological condition that is completely disabling when it strikes, chronic struggles
with blood sugar, a damaged shoulder, and an arthritic hip. But I am
physically and genetically lucky. In other words, I have no condition
so immediately apparent as to give me the presumed authority to talk
about life with disability that sometimes comes with a visible disability. I provide this bit of information to answer the question that has
inevitably arisen whenever people are considering whether to invite
me to participate in a panel or debate about disability. I've learned that
to many people, my lack of visible disability is a disqualifier as real as
the lack of any other professional credential. Although I would like to
think that I have something to offer in discussions of disability despite
my relative physical and genetic luck, I know my approach to problems
is shaped by my experience in the body I inhabit. I understand and
respect the people who have been forthright about their belief that

---

[4] Even Spanish medical historian Diego Gracia, who takes issue with those who claim
bioethics is essentially American, acknowledges that "bioethics had its first development in the US." Diego Gracia, *History of Medical Ethics, in* BIOETHICS IN A
EUROPEAN PERSPECTIVE, at 44–45 (2001).

[5] Renee C. Fox and Judith P. Swazey provide an excellent summary of the various
theories offered to explain the origins of the field in *Observing Bioethics* (2008).

only those who have had the lived experience of visible disability have standing in disability-related discussions. For that reason, I acknowledge at the outset my limitation in experience and my position as an interested outsider.

Finally, I have excluded from this book some of the most contentious issues in bioethics and disability studies. By starting my study of the human life span at the moment of birth rather than the moment of conception, I avoid discussion of prenatal screening, abortion, and genetic manipulation of embryos. Those omissions are obviously not trivial. The treatment of embryos with disabilities ranks with the treatment of seriously disabled newborns and end-of-life decision making as among the most disputed in the conflict between disability rights advocates and bioethicists. I decided to exclude cases raising questions about the treatment of embryos with disabilities for practical and substantive reasons. As a practical matter, addressing life before birth would require a thorough analysis of unresolved questions about the moral and legal status of the embryo and the role of abortion politics in the debate – discussions so complicated that they could easily overwhelm the book.[6] As a matter of substance, the debate about embryos with disabilities is, in my view, conceptually distinct from the others I address because of the interdependent nature of the maternal-fetal relationship. Excluding discussions about life before birth, therefore, seemed a reasonable way to keep the book focused, as intended, on documenting and reconciling the views of disability and bioethics experts in a manner that will be useful both inside and outside the United States. In any event, if it is successful, the model of disability-conscious bioethics I propose here should be applicable to issues that arise during human gestation, but my explanation of how the model applies before birth will have to wait for another day.

---

[6] For a thorough discussion of these issues, *see* Hasting Center Studies in Ethics, PRENATAL TESTING AND DISABILITY RIGHTS (Erik Parens & Adrienne Asch eds., Georgetown University Press 2000).

Introduction

Even though this book does not address prebirth issues, it does address issues that arise throughout the rest of the human life cycle: in infancy, childhood, the reproductive years, the adults years, and at the end of life. It is a book about perspectives, debate, and respect. And, as a book written to follow the advice I constantly give students – "show, don't tell" – it is a book of stories. Chapter 1 shows how the conflicting perspectives and conflicts between the bioethics and disability rights communities have developed, as a result of various social, legal, and cultural events that have influenced the thinking and advocacy in bioethics and the disability rights communities.

Chapter 2 serves two purposes. First it tests the depth of conflict between disability studies and bioethics by comparing, at an introductory level, the methodology and teachings of both fields. To illustrate the contrasting perspectives and illuminate practical points of tension, the chapter contrasts the perspectives of each group on the case of Elizabeth Bouvia, a young healthy woman with disabilities who sought and ultimately received court authority to refuse artificial nutrition and hydration. The Bouvia case is heralded within bioethics as a triumph for autonomy and by the disability rights community as a key example of disability discrimination in action. It is as clear an example as any of a case subject to different interpretation depending on one's perspective. Having identified the points of tension central to the conflict, the chapter makes the case for and proposes a methodology of reconciliation.

The next five chapters do the major work of the book. Focusing on different stages of the human life cycle, they use case studies – stories from people's lives – as a platform for looking beyond the rhetoric, and building a more nuanced understanding of the interests, concepts, biases, and fears that inform discussion within the disability and bioethics communities. Each chapter begins with two or three case studies. In first describing the cases, I try to report objective facts. I then compare the reactions and analysis to the cases from a disability rights perspective with analysis and reaction from a bioethics perspective.

Where possible, I rely on the words of members of the bioethics or disability rights community to highlight the different approaches. In some cases, I offer my own analysis from one or the other perspective. At the end of each of these chapters, I include a section entitled "Observations." The Observations sections are intended to highlight the features of the debate emerging from the case studies that inform the development of a disability-conscious bioethics in Chapter 8. The chapters are organized to take the reader through the human life span from birth to death.

I found two things especially challenging as I wrote each of the chapters containing case studies. First, choosing the cases was difficult. I ultimately decided to include cases about which there have been significant and public disagreements between members of the disability rights movement and bioethicists, in order to best illustrate conflicting perspectives and leave room for finding common ground. Of course, that decision affected the story the book tells. Most of the case studies involve a decision that had the effect of hastening a person's death. Although such cases are in the eye of the stormy dispute between disability rights activists and bioethicists, they do not represent the everyday challenges faced by people with and without disabilities in the health care system. They are extraordinary cases. The focus on the extraordinary cases that cause extraordinary disputes tends to exaggerate the divide between the bioethics and the disability rights communities. Indeed, there is much common ground between the camps, which brings me to my second area of difficulty.

As I emphasize repeatedly throughout the book, there is neither a single bioethics nor a single disability rights perspective. Even knowing that, I present "views from bioethics" and "views from the disability community" for each case study. In choosing the representative "views," I sorted through the internal debates among bioethicists and the internal debates among disability rights advocates and scholars to ferret out what can be fairly characterized as mainstream or representative views from each camp. If there was no apparent mainstream view on a particular issue (for example, as among bioethicists, there is simply no agreement about the treatment of newborns with catastrophic disability), I present a view that represents the point of dispute or concern from the disability rights or bioethics perspective. I want to acknowledge, however, that the divide between the fields is not always as clear as the case studies suggest. Indeed, on many issues, several individuals from each community agree with positions taken by individuals from the other community. Although I have taken care to refer in the text or footnotes to alternative perspectives from within each field, describing the full range of perspectives is a task beyond the scope of this book.

Following the case studies, in the final chapter, is a call to action. In it, I argue that bioethicists have good reason to work with members of the disability community to resolve ongoing conflicts. Toward that end, I propose a path toward reconciliation, with the ultimate goal of generating new, mutually beneficial relationships. The chapter engages the necessary first steps toward reconciliation by synthesizing the materials provided in the case studies to identify, among other things, how and when bioethics as a field has been indifferent about or insensitive to disability. I then propose a framework for a disability-conscious bioethics in which bioethicists are sensitive to and sensible about disability in their academic and clinical work. Finally, I revisit the cases to illustrate how disability-consciousness will affect the work of bioethicists.

At the end of the day, application of disability-conscious bioethics will not eliminate debate. If it is successful, however, it will go a long way toward allowing two groups with a common commitment to ensure respect for all persons in the health care setting and empower them to work together to achieve their goals.

1

The Struggle: Disability Rights versus Bioethics

A DISABILITY RIGHTS ACTIVIST ONCE CHARGED, "IF I WERE listing the most dangerous people in the U.S. today, bioethicists, aka medical ethicists, would top my list – way above skinheads, whose beliefs they appear to share."[1] A different activist testified in a hearing on health reform that the bioethics think tank, the Hastings Center, and the "movement for bioethics ... directly continue the eugenics movement that organized Hitler's killing of patients, and other costly and supposedly unworthy people."[2] The activists' sentiments are not unusual. For the last three decades, an escalating conflict has pitted disability rights activists against bioethics.[3] Despite a common

---

[1] Alice Mailhot, *Introduction to Theories from Hell*, Mouth Magazine, 1994, *available at* http://www.notdeadyet.org/bioethic.html.

[2] Remarks of Anton Chaitkin, transcript of the Department of Health and Human Services, Federal Coordinating Council for Comparative Effectiveness, Listening session, Wednesday June 10, 2009, at 151–2.

[3] *See* http://www.notdeadyet.org; Kathy L. Cerminara, *Tracking the Storm: The Far-Reaching Power of the Forces Propelling the Schiavo Cases*, 35 STETSON L. REV. 147, 159–77 (2005) (tracking procedural and substantive effects post-Schiavo); Mark Kuczewski & Kristi Kirschner, *Bioethics and Disability: A Civil War?*, 24 THEORETICAL MED. 455 (2003). *See also*, Independent Living Institute, The Right to Live and be Different, (Feb. 2000), *available at* http://www.independentliving.org/docs1/dpi022000.html (position paper by representatives of disability groups from

interest in facilitating good medical care, disability rights activists and bioethicists differ sharply in their approach to such issues as how to treat newborns with disabilities, the stunting of growth in children with disabilities, and the removal of life support from patients in persistent vegetative states. These differences manifest in political action, disruptive protests launched at scholarly meetings, and in scholarly papers deeming bioethics "a disabling project."[4]

The fact of conflict between members of the disability rights and bioethics communities is at the same time surprising and predictable. On the one hand, both bioethics and disabilities studies are disciplines that share a common core commitment to respect for persons and ethical and fair medical decision making. On the other hand, disability experts often approach the same issues from a very different perspective than that of bioethicists. In a nutshell (and speaking in very broad strokes), bioethics promotes informed individual choice in medical care, even when the choice leads to the death of a patient. Disability experts promote the protection of people with disabilities as a group, even when the community interest might conflict with the choice of an individual member.

The resulting disputes have generated distrust and protest among disability rights activists who sincerely view positions taken by bioethicists as a direct threat to the social and physical well-being of people with disabilities. Disability rights activists use all available avenues to spread their message – the internet, political protest, the courts, the media, and legislative agendas. Their consistent message resonates: We are better off alive than dead, and efforts to promote choice in dying or to allow others to choose death for someone with disabilities are a form of disability prejudice.

twenty-three countries charging that bioethical debates "have prejudiced and negative views of our quality of life. They have denied our right to equality and therefore denied out human rights.")

[4] Christopher Newall, *Disability, Bioethics, and Rejected Knowledge*, 31 J. MED. & PHIL. 269, 276 (2006).

Bioethics and Disability

The response by bioethicists to charges of disability prejudice ranges from "reflexive scorn,"[5] to polite dismissal, to calls for discourse. The most public cases raising charges of disability discrimination – Schiavo, Ashley X, and even American health reform efforts – have triggered occasional public or academic rebuttal from the bioethics community.[6] And there have been collaborative projects on specific issues, such as the Hastings Center projects on surgically shaping children[7] and prenatal testing.[8] It is fair to say, however, that except for a small corner of bioethics inhabited by people with disabilities, experts in disability studies, and disability rights advocates, there is no well-developed disability-conscious approach to bioethics.

To understand what a disability-conscious bioethics might look like, it is helpful to compare the history, theoretical underpinnings, and perspectives of bioethics and the disability rights movements. This chapter begins that comparison by outlining the historical evolution of bioethics and the disability rights movement. The descriptions touch only the surface of two rich fields with rich histories. The goal here is not to replicate already existing treatises and histories; the case studies set forth in Chapters 3–7 provide a more nuanced picture of the perspectives of each field through in-depth study of particular cases. What follows is intended to provide readers new to either field with enough background information about the fields, their origins, and relevant players to understand the historical roots of conflict between the two.

---

[5] Carl Schneider used the term "reflexive scorn" to describe the reaction to disability activists' arguments against the removal of Terri Schiavo's feeding tube. Carl E. Schneider, *Hard Cases and the Politics of Righteousness*, 35 HASTINGS CTR. REP., May–June 2005, at 24, 26.

[6] *See infra* Chapters 4 and 7; Mark Kuczewski & Kristi Kirschner, *Bioethics and Disability: A Civil War?*, 24 THEORETICAL MED. 455 (2003).

[7] SURGICALLY SHAPING CHILDREN: TECHNOLOGY, ETHICS, AND THE PURSUIT OF NORMALITY (Erik Parens ed., Johns Hopkins University Press 2006).

[8] *Id.*

I. AN INTRODUCTION TO AND SHORT HISTORY OF THE DISABILITY-RIGHTS COMMUNITY[9]

To the extent it can be defined as a single entity, the disability rights community consists of activists and scholars who focus on the social, political, legal, and philosophical implications of disability. As a whole, the community contests the social oppression of people with disabilities and the prevailing cultural perceptions of life with disability.[10] Rejecting the notion that life with disability is inherently tragic, the disability community constructs a narrative of meaningful life with disability in which it "isn't necessarily bad to be disabled, but it is bad to be discriminated against, unemployed, poor, and blocked by bad laws, architecture, and communication."[11] Neither disability activists nor disability scholars speak with one voice or purport to speak for every person with a disability.[12] Instead, the community "is a fluid entity that includes people with a range of different disabilities (and even people with no disability at all), different life experiences, different material needs, and different ideological perspectives."[13] Its members

---

[9] Much of the material in this chapter was first published in Alicia Ouellette, *Disability and the End of Life*, 85 OR. L. REV. 123 (2006) © University of Oregon and is reprinted here with permission.

[10] Gareth Williams, *Theorizing Disability, in* HANDBOOK OF DISABILITY STUDIES, 124 (Gary L. Albrecht et al. eds., Sage Publications, Inc. 2001).

[11] LENNARD J. DAVIS, BENDING OVER BACKWARDS: DISABILITY, DISMODERNISM, AND OTHER DIFFICULT POSITIONS 5 (NYU Press 2002).

[12] *See* Adrienne Asch, *Distracted by Disability*, CAMBRIDGE Q. HEALTHCARE ETHICS, 77, 81 (Jan. 1988). Asch explains the difficulties with defining a disability rights community, but asserts that:

> what people with disabilities share is the experience that their departure from what is species typical makes them the objects of unequal treatment such as denial of employment or education for which they qualify ... [M]ore than half of the respondents [to a 1994 survey] perceived themselves to be a member of a minority and accepted the notion that they were indeed members of a disability rights community.

[13] SAMUEL R. BAGENSTOS, LAW AND THE CONTRADICTIONS OF THE DISABILITY RIGHTS MOVEMENT 3 (Yale University Press 2009).

include Marxists, feminists, postmodernists, and poststructuralists.[14] Nonetheless, as explored more deeply in Chapter 2 and several of the case studies, the community presents a remarkably coherent message about the medicalization of disability and the impact of the medical view of disability on positions taken by bioethicists.[15] A brief review of the history of the treatment of people with disabilities with particular focus on the historic relationship between the medical establishment and people with disability sheds light on why some members of the community distrust bioethics and contest the role of bioethicists in policy making for people with disabilities.[16]

The story of disability is one of both oppression and empowerment. Since antiquity, people in power have treated people with disabilities as

---

[14] For example, James I. Charlton analyzes disability oppression and activism from an international perspective in JAMES I. CHARLETON, NOTHING ABOUT US WITHOUT US: DISABILITY OPPRESSION AND EMPOWERMENT (University of California Press 1998). Joseph Shapiro traces the history of the movement in his book, *No Pity*. JOSEPH P. SHAPIRO, NO PITY: PEOPLE WITH DISABILITIES FORGING A NEW CIVIL RIGHTS MOVEMENT (Three Rivers Press 1994). Michelle Fine and Adrienne Asch explore disability from a feminist perspective in *Women with Disabilities* (Temple University Press 1988). Nancy L. Eisenland applies disability theory to liberation theology in *The Disabled God: Toward a Liberatory Theology of Disability* (Abingdon Press 1994). Stanley Herr et al., explore human rights issues in *The Human Rights of Persons with Intellectual Disabilities: Different but Equal* (Oxford University Press 2003). *See also* JULIE SMART, DISABILITY, SOCIETY, AND THE INDIVIDUAL (Aspen Publishers 2001); SHARON L. SNYDER, DISABILITY STUDIES, ENABLING THE HUMANITIES (Modern Language Association of America 2000).

[15] The loudest dissenting voice from within the disability rights community was that of the recently deceased Andrew Batavia. Batavia started an organization called Autonomy that stands out in the disability rights community. "AUTONOMY represents persons with disabilities who expect choice in all aspects of their lives, including choice at the end of life." *See* Autonomy, http://www.autonomynow.org. His work was also published in prestigious journals such as the *New England Journal of Medicine*. *See* Andrew I. Batavia, *Disability and Physician Assisted Suicide*, 336 N.E. J. M. 1671 (1997).

[16] Of course one could compile the history of disability from many perspectives. "Different disabilities make for different individual and group histories." PAUL K. LONGMORE, WHY I BURNED MY BOOK 51 (Temple University Press 2003).

outcasts, curiosities, idiots, objects of pity, and harbingers of evil cursed by the divine. In 355 B.C., for example, Aristotle said that people "born deaf become senseless and incapable of reason."[17] In the eighteenth century, people with epilepsy were punished for witchcraft. In 1756, the Pennsylvania Hospital in Philadelphia created a special section for the treatment of mental illness and mental retardation, where patients were chained to the walls of the basement and put on display for a fee. Throughout the twentieth century, circuses, carnivals, and so-called freak shows displayed people whose bodies deviated from species normal. Until recent decades, children with disabilities were not educated. Adults with disabilities have relied on charity for survival.[18]

Perhaps the ugliest chapter in the history of disability involves the eugenics movement of the late nineteenth and early twentieth centuries.[19] In 1883, Sir Francis Galton coined the term "eugenics" to describe a process of improving the qualities of the human population by discouraging reproduction by people believed to be defective because of an inheritable trait, and encouraging reproduction by persons presumed to have inheritable desirable traits. Eugenics became a social movement around the world. In the United States, proponents held "best baby" contests at country fairs and advocated laws that would ban reproduction of "inferiors." Indiana passed the nation's first eugenic sterilization law in 1913. In 1915, eugenics proponent Dr. Harry Haiselden allowed a disabled newborn to die and then promoted the practice as a way to reduce the disabled population. Eugenicists produced the movie "The Black Stork" in 1916 to encourage other doctors to allow "defective" newborns to die. The eugenics message took hold. By the late 1930s, "more than half the

---

[17] KENNETH W. HODGSON, THE DEAF AND THEIR PROBLEMS: A STUDY IN SPECIAL EDUCATION, 62 (Watts and Co. 1953).

[18] PAUL K. LONGMORE, THE NEW DISABILITY HISTORY: AMERICAN PERSPECTIVES (Laura Umansky ed., NYU Press 2001).

[19] PAUL A. LOMBARDO, THREE GENERATIONS, NO IMBECILES: EUGENICS, THE SUPREME COURT, AND BUCK V. BELL (The Johns Hopkins University Press 2008).

states in [the United States] had laws on the books encouraging sterilization of people with disabilities, usually those with developmental disabilities including epilepsy, but also those who were blind or deaf, because they were viewed as so burdensome as to be unqualified for parenting."[20]

Nazi Germany took eugenics to a new extreme. After Hitler came to power in 1933, the government required German physicians to report "unfit" citizens to "Hereditary Health Courts" that examined and approved patients for sterilization. Under the program, the German government authorized the sterilization of more than 400,000 German citizens.[21] Eventually, Nazi medical centers killed a quarter-million people because they were considered "useless eaters."[22]

Before revelation of its radical extermination program, however, the German eugenics program drew public praise from the medical establishment in the United States. The *New England Journal of Medicine*, for example, referred in an editorial to Germany as "the most

---

[20] ANITA SILVERS ET AL., DISABILITY, DIFFERENCE, DISCRIMINATION: PERSPECTIVES ON JUSTICE IN BIOETHICS AND PUBLIC POLICY 42 (Rowman & Littlefield Publishers, Inc. 1998).

[21] Lombardo, *supra* note 19, at xii.

[22] Steven L. Mikochik, *Individual Rights and Reasonable Accommodations under the Americans with Disabilities Act:Assisted Suicide and Disabled People*, 46 DEPAUL L. REV. 987, 999 (1997); *see generally* HUGH G. GALLAGHER, BY TRUST BETRAYED: PATIENTS, PHYSICIANS, AND THE LICENSE TO KILL IN THE THIRD REICH (Henry Holt & Co1990). Mikochic points to a quote from Leo Alexander, chief medical consultant at Nuremberg, who observed the Nazi atrocities:

Whatever proportions these crimes finally assumed, it became evident to all who investigated them that they had started from small beginnings ... at first were merely a subtle shift in emphasis in the basic attitude of physicians. It started with the acceptance of the attitude, basic in the euthanasia movement, that there is such a thing as a life not worthy to be lived. This attitude in its early stages concerned itself merely with the severely and chronically sick. Gradually, the sphere of those to be included in this category was enlarged to encompass the socially unproductive, the ideologically unwanted, the racially unwanted and finally all non-Aryans. But it is important to realize that the infinitely small wedged-in lever from which this entire trend of mind received its impetus was the attitude toward the non-rehabilitable sick.

progressive nation in restricting fecundity among the unfit."[23] In 1934, the American Public Health Association praised Germany's example of a modern health program and mounted an exhibit on Germany's sterilization program at its annual meeting.[24]

Justice Holmes most famously confirmed that the United States viewed people with disabilities as the problem when he sanctioned the forced sterilization of Carrie Buck:

> We have seen more than once that the public welfare may call upon the best citizens for their lives. It would be strange if it could not call upon those who already sap the strength of the State for these lesser sacrifices, often not felt to be such by those concerned, in order to prevent our being swamped with incompetence. It is better for all the world, if instead of waiting to execute degenerate offspring for crime, or to let them starve for their imbecility, society can prevent those who are manifestly unfit from continuing their kind. The principle that sustains compulsory vaccination is broad enough to cover cutting the Fallopian tubes. Three generations of imbeciles are enough.[25]

Even after the horrors of Nazi Germany came to light, the United States continued its practice of forced institutionalization, sterilization, and eugenics.[26] More than 60,000 people with disabilities were

Joan R. Bullock, *Abortion Rights in America*, 1994 BYU L. REV. 63, 70 (1994) (quoting Leo Alexander, *Medical Science Under Dictatorship*, 241 NEW ENG. J. MED. 39, 44 [1949]).

[23] Lombardo, *supra* note 19, at 203.

[24] ROBERT WHITAKER, MAD IN AMERICA: BAD SCIENCE, BAD MEDICINE, AND THE ENDURING MISTREATMENT OF THE MENTALLY ILL 64 (Basic Books 2002).

[25] Buck v. Bell, 274 U.S. 200, 207 (1927). Questions existed not only about the heritability of conditions, but whether the patients actually had the suspect conditions. For example, research indicates that Carrie Buck, the focus of Buck v. Bell, 274 U.S. 200 (1927), was not in fact mentally handicapped. *See* Roberta M. Berry, *From Involuntary Sterilization to Genetic Enhancement: The Unsettled Legacy of Buck v. Bell*, 12 NOTRE DAME J.L. ETHICS & PUB. POL'Y 401, 420–21 (1998).

[26] The American experience, at least as to sterilization, preceded the National Socialist Programs. *See* PHILIP R. REILLY, THE SURGICAL SOLUTION: A HISTORY OF INVOLUNTARY STERILIZATION IN THE UNITED STATES, 30–40 (The Johns Hopkins University Press 1991).

involuntarily sterilized because of real or perceived disabilities pursuant to state laws in the United States.[27]

Justice Marshall later compared this country's treatment of the disabled to the Jim Crow regime.[28] People with disabilities were denied access to education, housing, and jobs. Immigration policy was crafted to keep people with disabilities from entering the country. Laws reflecting the widespread belief that persons with disabilities drain valuable societal resources were on the books in the United States until the 1970s.

Opposition to practices and policies that oppressed people with disabilities arose on many fronts. People with physical disabilities mobilized against oppressive practices during the Great Depression, when they joined together in New York City to form the League of the Physically Handicapped.[29] The League protested poor relief programs in the United States because they exempted people with disabilities from the obligation to work. League members argued that such seemingly charitable programs "stigmatized and segregated" people with disabilities, "codifying job market discrimination into law."[30]

Veterans also organized to press for programs that would allow veterans with disabilities to participate meaningfully in society. Among other things, veterans advocated passage of the Smith-Sear Veterans Vocational Rehabilitation Act of 1918, which established the first federal vocational program for soldiers with disability. Later, in 1972, advocacy group Paralyzed Veterans of America was a lead plaintiff in a landmark lawsuit that forced the Washington

---

[27] Michael G. Silver, *Eugenics and Compulsory Sterilization Laws: Providing Redress for the Victims of a Shameful Era in United States History*, 72 GEO. WASH. L. REV. 862, 867 (2004).

[28] Mikochik, *supra* note 22, at 1000 (citing City of Cleburne v. Cleburne Living Ctr., 473 U.S. 432, 461–2 (1985) (Marshall, J., concurring in part and dissenting in part).

[29] Bagenstos, *supra* note 13, at 13.

[30] *Id.*

Metropolitan Area Transit Authority to incorporate access for the disabled into their design for a new, multibillion-dollar subway system in Washington, DC.

The Federation for the Blind was founded in 1940 to promote independence and opportunity, not charity. The Federation successfully advocated for the white-cane and guide-dog laws that allow people who need canes or service animals to move about independently in public streets, and enter and use public buildings and restaurants.

Whereas the Paralyzed Veterans of America and the Federation for the Blind advocated for societal changes that would facilitate full participation of persons with disabilities in society, other groups have united around their particular physical condition as marker of a cherished cultural identity. The most prominent example is the Deaf Community, which views itself as a cultural or linguist minority group. Members of the Deaf Community see deafness as a kind of gift, an entry into a rich and valuable culture.[31] They often chose to live together in communities in which signing is the primary means of communication. Deaf advocates reject the notion that being deaf is disabling and insist on the value of Deaf identity.[32] Gallaudet University in Washington, DC, became the focus of the Deaf pride movement in 1988, when students engaged in a "Deaf President Now" protest.

Although disability activism emerged in different forms and on different fronts, the various groups came together in the 1970s, 1980s, and 1990s to support federal legislation that would facilitate full inclusion of persons with disabilities in society. These activists oversaw the passage of pro-disability legislation like the Rehabilitation Act and the Americans with Disabilities Act.[33] The pro-disability laws placed responsibility on social structures for excluding people with disabilities. Public schools, employers, churches, hospitals, and other places

---

[31] *See infra* Chapter 4 for an in-depth discussion of the role of deaf culture in medical decision making.

[32] Davis, *supra* note 11, at 37.

[33] Laura L. Rovner, *Disability, Equality, and Identity*, 55 ALA. L. REV. 1043 (2004).

of public accommodation became responsible for accommodating the needs of people with disabilities.

The disabilities movement took on a more radical form – what I call a new activism – in the late 1980s and early 1990s. The original focus of the new activists was the Jerry Lewis Muscular Dystrophy Association Telethon. New activists consider telethons that feature a disabled child as a mascot "demeaning and exploitive of disability as tragic and catastrophic."[34] Evan Kemp, Jr., former chair of the federal Equal Employment Opportunity Commission, presented the earliest public critique of telethons in a 1981 *New York Times* editorial, stating that "[b]y arousing the public's fear of the handicap itself, the telethon makes viewers more afraid of handicapped people.... [T]he telethon's critical stress on the need to find cures supports the damaging and common prejudice that handicapped people are sick."[35] A decade after Kemp's critique was published, the early activists began to demonstrate against the telethons.[36] The activists' message was angrier than Kemp's.[37] One activist protested, "It's all about stirring up pity, when we don't want pity. And Jerry Lewis ought to be fired. He actually called people in wheelchairs 'half persons.'"[38]

---

[34] Sharon Barnartt et al., *Advocacy and Political Action, in* HANDBOOK OF DISABILITY STUDIES, at 441 (Sage Publications, Inc. 2001) (referring to eighteen protests against telethons in 1992 and ten protests in 1993).

[35] Evan J. Kemp, Jr., Op-Ed., *Aiding the Disabled: No Pity, Please*, N.Y. TIMES, Sept. 3, 1981, at A19, *quoted in* Shapiro, *supra* note 14, at 23–4.

[36] *See* Shapiro, *supra* note 14, at 24–6.

[37] *See* Harriet McBryde Johnson, *Honk If You Hate Telethons, in* TOO LATE TO DIE YOUNG: NEARLY TRUE TALES FROM A LIFE 3, 45–5 (Henry Holt and Co. 2005). Johnson explains her reaction to telethons:

> Together in the crip ghetto, my friends and I watched the annual parade of our little doppelgängers being publicly sentenced to death.... Later, having moved on to the mainstream world, I wanted to go to law school, qualify for scholarships, start a business. But dying children aren't allowed to do such things; they can't be trusted to fulfill their obligations.

Id. at 50.

[38] *Id.* at 48.

Having organized against telethons, the new activists turned their attention to court actions involving medical decision making in the wake of the so-called Baby Doe cases.[39] Baby "John Doe" was born in 1983, in Bloomington, Indiana. He had Down syndrome and an esophageal blockage. The blockage was treatable with a relatively minor surgical correction, but his parents opted against the surgery because of advice given to them by their physician about the dismal prospects for a person living with Down syndrome. The baby died of starvation six days after being born.[40] In a similar case, the parents of "Baby Jane Doe" declined surgery for their daughter, who had been born with spina bifida and hydrocephalus, based on the advice of their physicians.[41] Both babies were denied treatment that could have alleviated certain of their medical problems because they had permanent disabilities that no medical treatment could cure. The denial of treatment in the Baby Doe cases "represented a kind of discrimination against people with disabilities by the medical profession and frightened parents who were unable to imagine having a child with a disability as anything but a tragedy and a disaster...."[42]

---

[39] Adam A. Milani, *Better Off Dead than Disabled?: Should Courts Recognize a "Wrongful Living" Cause of Action When Doctors Fail to Honor Patients' Advance Directives?*, 54 WASH & LEE L. REV. 149, 210 (1997) (describing intervention by activists on behalf of Kenneth Bergstedt, a Nevada man who became quadriplegic and dependent on a ventilator as a result of a swimming accident at age ten. At age thirty-one, faced with the imminent death of his ill father, Kenneth petitioned the Court to allow his father to turn off his respirator.). *See* McKay v. Bergstedt, 801 P.2d 617, 624–5 (Nev. 1990).

[40] Doe v. Bloomington Hosp., 464 U.S. 961 (1983) (denying certiorari).

[41] Weber v. Stony Brook Hosp., 467 N.Y.S.2d 685 (App. Div. 1983). The Baby Doe cases were explored by a Presidential commission, which issued a report in 1983 that would disallow denial of surgery to "an otherwise healthy Down Syndrome child whose life is threatened by a surgically correctable complication." *See* Adrienne Asch, *Disability, Bioethics, and Human Rights, in* HANDBOOK OF DISABILITY STUDIES 303 (quoting President's Commission 6–7).

[42] *Id.* at 304.

Scholars and activists used the Baby Doe cases to illustrate the community's long-simmering distrust of and disagreement with the medical community's understanding of disability. As discussed in more depth in Chapter 2, disability scholars took issue with the medical view of disability, the view that says that a person with a disability is flawed and needs cure. Such a view, they claimed, is responsible for past abuses and present practices that cause people with disabilities to be isolated, overmedicated, and even killed as a means of solving the "problem" of disability. The dangers of the medical model of disability, they argued, were particularly pronounced in cases like the Baby Doe cases, in which an individual with disabilities was allowed to die because of the assumption inherent in the medical view of disability that disabled lives are not worth living.[43]

In advocating for policies to protect children with disabilities from death at the hands of a medical system that failed to appreciate the value of life with disability, disability advocates found themselves in an uneasy alliance with various pro-life groups. Many members of the disability rights community supported abortion rights. Moreover, the arguments voiced in favor of laws and policies that would have protected Baby John Doe were ideologically distinct from those voiced by pro-life groups. Nonetheless, the alliance between the new activists and pro-life groups proved to be enduring.

For example, the disability rights group Not Dead Yet found itself on the same side as pro-life advocates in its battle to save Terri Schiavo's life. Not Dead Yet is a major player in the public fight against the legalization of assisted suicide, euthanasia, and the termination of life-sustaining treatment. The group stages noisy demonstrations; its members arrive at courtrooms, lecture halls, and rallies in a mass of wheelchairs. Members carry signs that say "Health Care Not Death Care" and "Medical Ethicists Are Not Ethical."[44] They submit briefs

---

[43] Chapter 3, *infra*, presents two modern-day "Baby Doe" cases.

[44] Diane Coleman, *Not Dead Yet, The Resistance Meets Success*, MEMPHIS CTR. FOR INDEP. LIVING, http://www.mcil.org/mcil/mcil/ndy.htm (last visited Sept. 9, 2006).

in court cases[45] and lobby heavily in state legislatures.[46] Members of Not Dead Yet have actively opposed laws that permit people or their surrogates to terminate life-sustaining treatment since 1983, when Californian Elizabeth Bouvia obtained a court order that required a hospital to remove a "nasogastric tube inserted and maintained against her will and without her consent by physicians who so placed it for the purpose of keeping her alive through involuntary forced feeding."[47]

The group began its public activities in 1996, when Jack Kevorkian started providing assisted suicide to the public.[48] In a 1997 rally, 500 people with disabilities gathered to chant "Not Dead Yet" in protest of Kevorkian's acquittal on criminal charges.[49] The group's purpose is to prevent disability discrimination in end-of-life cases. It frames the issue of assisted suicide as follows: "Though often described as

[45] *See, e.g.,* Brief for Not Dead Yet et al. as Amici Curiae Supporting Petitioners, Gonzales v. Oregon, 126 S. Ct. 904 (2006) (No. 04–623); Brief for Not Dead Yet et al. as Amici Curiae Supporting Appellants, Schiavo ex rel. Schindler v. Schiavo, 916 So. 2d 814 (Fla. 2d DCA 2005) (No. 2D05–968); Brief for Not Dead Yet et al. as Amici Curiae Supporting Appellants, Oregon v. Ashcroft, 368 F.3d 1118 (9th Cir. 2004) (No. 02–35587); Brief for Not Dead Yet et al. as Amici Curiae Supporting Respondents, Wendland v. Wendland, 28 P.3d 151 (Cal. 2001) (No. S087265).

[46] *See, e.g.,* Disability Rights Education & Defense Fund, http://www.dredf.org/ (last visited Sept. 14, 2006) (describing various state initiatives and explaining the organization's mission as "dedicated to protecting and advancing the civil rights of people with disabilities through legislation, litigation, advocacy, technical assistance, and education and training of attorneys, advocates, persons with disabilities, and parents of children with disabilities"). *But cf.* Press Release, Not Dead Yet, Disability Advocates: Texas "Futile Care" Law Should Be Euthanized, http://www.notdeadyet. org/docs/TXfutilecarelawPR0506.html (last visited Sept. 14, 2006) (calling for a "halt to the backroom lobbying by special interest groups" related to Texas' "futile care" statute).

[47] Bouvia v. Superior Court, 179 Cal. App. 3d 1127, 1127, 225 Cal. Rptr. 297, 297 (Ct. App.1986).

[48] Not Dead Yet, About Not Dead Yet, http://www.notdeadyet.org/docs/about.html (last visited Sept. 23, 2006) (explaining the composition of the group and the reason for its existence).

[49] *Id.*

compassionate, legalized medical killing is really about a deadly double standard for people with severe disabilities, including both conditions that are labeled terminal and those that are not.... [C]ountless people with disabilities have already died before their time. For some, a disabled person's suicidal cry for help was ignored, misinterpreted, or even exploited by the right-to-die movement. For others, death came at the request of a family member or other health care surrogate. This is not compassion, it's contempt."[50]

The organized activity against choice in dying reached fever pitch in the case of Terri Schiavo, a case discussed at length in Chapter 7. One of the most powerful voices in the Schiavo case was Harriet McBryde Johnson's. McBryde Johnson was a disability rights lawyer and activist who suffered from a neuromuscular degenerative disease that left her, in her words, "a jumble of bones in a floppy bag of skin."[51] She was not able to walk, stand, lift heavy objects, or swallow solid foods.[52] To keep herself upright in her chair, she leaned forward, "rest[ed] her ribcage on [her] lap, plant[ed] elbows beside her knees."[53] She ate pureed food, lacked the physical strength to get out of bed on her own, and knew from a young age that she would eventually need to eat through a feeding tube.

Johnson was anything but weak. Her mind had the strength and agility her body lacked.[54] Her writing was wicked: sharp, insightful, and funny.[55] Her oral presentations were equally compelling. She used personal stories and insights strengthened by her physical weakness to

---

[50] *Id.*

[51] Harriet McBryde Johnson, *Unspeakable Conversations*, N.Y. TIMES, Feb. 16, 2003, (Magazine), § 6.

[52] *Id.*

[53] *Id.*

[54] She has a B.S. in history from Charleston Southern University, a Master's in Public Administration from the College of Charleston, and a J.D. from the University of South Carolina. Biography of Harriet McBryde Johnson, http://www.nd.edu/~ndr/issues/ndr8/johnson/bio.html (last visited Sept. 6, 2006)

[55] *See, e.g.,* Johnson, *supra* note 51.

advocate her positions on issues involving life and death.[56] Specifically, she used the strongest sort of identity politics, legal acumen, and powerful straight talk to argue against choice in medical decision making. Her message resonates.

Harriet McBryde Johnson brought the tension between persons with disabilities and bioethicists to national prominence when she published a cover story in the *New York Times Magazine*.[57] In the article, Johnson described her experience at Princeton University in which she confronted ethicist Peter Singer. She saw the debate with Singer as personal, stating "[Peter Singer] doesn't want to kill me. He simply thinks it would have been better, all things considered, to have given my parents the option of killing the baby I once was, and to let other parents kill similar babies as they come along and thereby avoid the suffering that comes with lives like mine and satisfy the reasonable preferences of parents for a different kind of child."[58]

Johnson first met Singer when she attended a lecture entitled "Rethinking Life and Death" in the spring of 2001 at the College of Charleston.[59] She confronted him during the question-and-answer session, and their dialogue continued by e-mail over the next year. Eventually, Singer invited Johnson to debate him at Princeton. They worked out an arrangement for two presentations by Johnson. She detailed and reflected upon her talks in an article titled "Unspeakable Conversations," in which she skewers Singer's abstract philosophical

---

[56] *Id.*

[57] *Id.*

[58] *Id.* Johnson's description of Singer's position is accurate. *See generally* PETER SINGER, RETHINKING LIFE AND DEATH: THE COLLAPSE OF OUR TRADITIONAL ETHICS (St. Martin's Griffin 1994); PETER SINGER & HELGA KUHSE, SHOULD THE BABY LIVE? THE PROBLEM OF HANDICAPPED INFANTS iii (Oxford University Press 1985); Peter Singer, *Making Laws about Making Babies*, 15 HASTINGS CTR. REP. 5 (1985); Peter Singer & Helga Kuhse, *Ethics and the Handicapped Newborn Infant*, 52 SOC. RES. 505, 527–34 (1985); Peter Singer, *Which Babies Are Too Expensive to Treat?*, 1 BIOETHICS 275 (1987).

[59] Johnson, *supra* note 51.

thinking with her lived experience.[60] The article became regular reading in bioethics, philosophy, and disabilities law classes across the country.

Johnson continued to argue against Singer's radical position in the years that followed. She presented numerous lectures and continued her work as a disability rights lawyer. She showed up on the national stage again during the Schiavo debacle, where she made arguments that paralleled those made by Not Dead Yet and other new activists in briefs to courts[61] and in lobbying efforts. The results of the legal and lobbying work of McBryde Johnson and the new activists were stunning.

The lobbying effort helped achieve state legislation, federal and state court litigation, federal legislation, executive action, and twenty-four-hour media coverage for weeks on end.[62] Through its involvement in the case, Not Dead Yet raised the profile of the disability rights movement and its message to a national stage in a very real way.[63] Suddenly, the public was engaged in debates about persistent vegetative states, advance directives, and artificial nutrition and hydration. Even after the furor over Schiavo subsided, disability activists continued to voice opposition to laws that allow people or their surrogates choice in dying. Viewing decisions that lead to the death of someone with disabilities

---

[60] *Id.*

[61] Brief for Not Dead Yet et al. as Amici Curiae Supporting Appellants, Schiavo ex rel. Schindler v. Schiavo, 916 So. 2d 814 (Fla. 2d DCA 2005) (No. 2D05–968), *available at* http://www.notdeadyet.org/docs/schaivobrief.html.

[62] George J. Annas, "*Culture of Life" Politics at the Bedside – The Case of Terri Schiavo*, 352 NEW ENG. J. MED. 1710, 1710–1715 (2005); Lois Shepherd, *Terri Schiavo: Unsettling the Settled*, 37 Loy. U. Chi. L.J. 297 (2006) (contemplating potential shift in decision making by health care and judicial entities irrespective of statutory modifications); Cerminara, *supra* note 3; Tom Mayo, *Living and Dying in a Post-Schiavo World*, Jurist, December 3, 2005, http://jurist.law.pitt.edu/forumy/2005/12/living-and-dying-in-post-schiavo-world.php (discussing unsettling changes concerning the medical treatment resulting from the Schiavo case).

[63] *See* Cerminara, *supra* note 3.

as perpetuating the notion that a disabled person's life is not worth living, some activists lobbied for a Model Starvation and Dehydration of Persons with Disabilities Prevention Act. The Act would effectively take away the power of surrogate decision makers to withhold life-sustaining treatment, especially nutrition and hydration, in the absence of a written living will.[64] Some members of the community have also protested against reform of the health insurance industry in the United States out of fear that reform will necessarily deprive people with disabilities of the health care they need. Those opposing health reform have particularly targeted bioethicists who have supported health reform as part of medical establishment long complicit in overt and subtle policies designed to eliminate people with disabilities from the population. These charges of disability discrimination do not sit well within bioethics, a field in which respect for persons of all abilities is a first principle.

II. INTRODUCTION TO AND A BRIEF HISTORY OF BIOETHICS

Bioethics is a broad interdisciplinary field that employs ethical analysis to explore, predict, and resolve issues raised by the use of medical and biological technology. It draws from and touches on philosophy, medicine, medical ethics, law, public health, religion, and public policy to confront issues that range from the very personal, like the resolution of specific conflicts between a single patient and her doctor, to the very public, like how to set up systems to allocate donated organs. Some bioethics is clinical: Ethicists are employed as hospital consultants, or serve on institutional committees, or review panels to help resolve specific disputes. Much of bioethics is academic, involving rigorous in-house debate and argument, teaching, explaining, and empirical

---

[64] *See infra* Chapter 7 (discussing the Model Act in detail).

research. Much is also policy-oriented. Bioethicists serve on presidential commissions, work for state and local governments, and advise policy makers in all branches of government. The field is multidimensional. There are feminist, Jewish, pragmatic, utilitarian, deontological, virtue theory, narrative, and casuist schools of thought. Inevitably, the many internal perspectives and nature of the issues faced means there is no one bioethics and no one right answer to the difficult issues it confronts.

Despite its many faces, bioethics has at its core a central concern with respect for persons through respect for individual autonomy and good medical care. Numerous historians have offered various "origin stories" – stories of technological advancements, issues as catalyst, timelines of events, organizational changes, and linguistic moments – to explain the development of the field.[65] What follows is one version of the story, a brief overview of events, phenomena, and legal developments that played a role in the rise of modern bioethics and its broad emphasis on autonomous choice. The overview is necessarily superficial. Reference to historical texts is necessary for other than a fairly superficial understanding of the origins of a complex field.[66]

The notion that health care providers have ethical or legal obligations to respect patients' choice is decidedly modern. Traditionally,

[65] For an excellent overview, *see* RENEE C. FOX & JUDITH P. SWAZEY, OBSERVING BIOETHICS 3532 (Oxford University Press 2008); BEN A. RICH, STRANGE BEDFELLOWS: HOW MEDICAL JURISPRUDENCE HAS INFLUENCED MEDICAL ETHICS AND MEDICAL PRACTICE (Kluwer Academic 2001); ROBERT M. VEATCH, THE BASICS OF BIOETHICS (2d ed., Prentice Hall 2003); Robert Baker, *Getting Agreement: How Bioethics Got Started*, 35 HASTINGS CENTER REPORT 50 (May–June 2005); DAVID ROTHMAN, STRANGERS AT THE BEDSIDE (Basic Books 1992); ALBERT JONSEN, THE BIRTH OF BIOETHICS (Oxford University Press 1998); JOHN EVANS, PLAYING GOD (University of Chicago Press 2001); THE STORY OF BIOETHICS: FROM SEMINAL WORKS TO CONTEMPORARY EXPLORATIONS (Jennifer K. Walter & Eran P. Klien eds., Georgetown University Press 2003).

[66] *See* ROBERT B. BAKER & LAURENCE B. MCCULLOUGH, THE CAMBRIDGE WORLD HISTORY OF MEDICAL ETHICS, Part VII, 475–530 (Cambridge University Press 2009); ENCYCLOPEDIA OF BIOETHICS (W. T. Reich ed., Macmillan, 1978); RUTH R. FADAN & THOMAS L. BEAUCHAMP, A HISTORY AND THEORY OF INFORMED CONSENT (Oxford University Press 1986).

doctors issued orders that were to be obeyed by patients and staff.[67] Hiding information from and making choices for patients was standard practice – supported by then-applicable codes of ethics designed to protect patients from bad news and difficult decisions.[68] Before the advent of modern bioethics, medical paternalism – the notion that doctor knew best – was the rule of the day.[69] That paradigm shifted gradually to today's patient-centered model largely in response to abuses of people involved – often against their will or without their knowledge – as subjects in scientific experimentation.

Although bioethics did not emerge as a field until decades after the end of World War II, Nazi experiments on death camp prisoners were a focus of some of the earliest bioethical thinking. In fact, bioethicist Arthur Caplan claims that "bioethics was born from the ashes of the Holocaust."[70] As is well documented elsewhere, Nazi doctors conducted horrific experiments on death camp prisoners. They submerged them in freezing water to see how long they would survive, tested mustard gas on prisoners, and inoculated prisoners with spotted fever to test vaccines. During the trial of Nazi doctors at Nuremberg, a code of permissible research was promulgated that contained as its first principle: "the voluntary consent of the human subject is absolutely essential."[71] The Nuremberg Code continues to influence the direction of research ethics policy and practice, as it essentially embodies the doctrine we now call informed consent.

But the Nuremberg Code had little direct impact on research practices in the United States.[72] Public attention turned to U.S. research

---

[67] Veatch, *supra* note 64, at 11–13 (discussing the Hippocratic tradition).

[68] Rich, *supra* note 65.

[69] Laurence B. McCullough challenges this historical understanding. *See* Laurence B. McCullough, *Was Bioethics Founded on Historical and Conceptual Mistakes About Medical Paternalism*, 25 BIOETHICS 66 (2011).

[70] *Id.* at 44 (quoting Arthur Caplan).

[71] *Id.* at 62.

[72] *Id.*

practices only after Harvard Medical School physician Henry Beecher published a 1966 article entitled "Ethics and Clinical Research" in the *New England Journal of Medicine*.[73] The article detailed and challenged twenty-two mainstream research programs as patently unethical for their use of unknowing human subjects or their exposure of subjects to extreme risk for the sole purpose of advancing scientific knowledge. Most famously, Beecher wrote about the Willowbrook hepatitis study in which children with cognitive disabilities were intentionally infected with hepatitis so that researchers could test a vaccine on the now-infected children. Admittance into the school depended on parental consent for participation in the research, and the researchers publicly defended the study on the ground that its resulting scientific discovery would serve the public good.

The public outcry against the Willowbrook study was intense, as was the reaction to another research project, the Tuskegee Syphilis study.[74] Starting in the early 1930s, U.S. government researchers recruited 400 black men infected with syphilis into a study designed to determine the incidence of syphilis in rural populations. The men were denied treatment for their disease, even after penicillin was introduced in 1947. The men were told they had "bad blood" and were observed throughout their lives or until the 1970s when the study was finally exposed. Over the course of the forty years of this "life history" research, dozens of subjects died of syphilis and hundreds more suffered complications and infected their wives and partners, who in turn infected their children. Over the years, government reparations and recognition of the legacy of Tuskegee have done little to

---

[73] Beecher had two earlier publications that also expressed his concern with unethical research practices. *See* Henry K. Beecher, *Experimentation of Man*, 169 JAMA 461–478 (1959). It was the later article, *Ethics and Clinical Research*, 274 New Eng. J. Med. 1354–60 (1966), that is widely cited as the document that triggered public outrage and played an important role in creation of the National Commission for the Protection of Human Subjects in 1974.

[74] James H. Jones, Bad Blood: The Tuskegee Syphilis Experiment (Free Press 1993).

rebuild the eroded trust of many African Americans regarding research involving human subjects.

In response to the public outrage that followed Beecher's article and revelations about Willowbrook, Tuskegee, and other studies, the Nixon administration formed the National Commission for the Protection of Human Subjects of Biomedical and Behavioral Research. The commission was a multidisciplinary group of scientists, moral theologians, ethicist-philosophers, and policy experts. Its charge was to "identify the basic ethical principles that should underlie the conduct of biomedical and behavioral research involving human subjects and to develop guidelines which should be followed to assure that such research is conducted in accordance with those principles."[75] In 1979, the Commission promulgated the *Belmont Report*, which described three fundamental principles of biomedical research ethics: respect for persons, beneficence, and justice.[76] These principles entailed, respectively, informed consent, the weighing of risks and benefits, and the equitable selection of subjects for research. The *Belmont Report* also emphasized that people with diminished capacity and vulnerable populations such as children or prisoners should receive special protection from research abuses.

The doctrine of informed consent emphasized in the *Belmont Report* was developed and expanded beyond the research context in the courts. In 1914, the New York State Court of Appeals decided *Schloendorff v. Society of New York Hospital.* The case was brought by an unhappy patient against a doctor who performed surgery to remove a tumor without the patient's consent. The removal of the tumor was medically indicated, but the court held for the patient, recognizing that when a doctor acts without a patient's consent, he or she commits a

---

[75] National Research Act of 1974.

[76] THE BELMONT REPORT: ETHICAL PRINCIPLES AND GUIDELINES FOR THE PROTECTION OF HUMAN SUBJECTS OF BIOMEDICAL AND BEHAVIORAL RESEARCH, 44 FED. REG. 23, 192 (Apr. 18, 1979).

tort. In analyzing how the surgery harmed the patient, Judge Benjamin Cardozo famously explained: "Every human being of adult years and sound mind has a right to determine what shall be done with his own body; and a surgeon who performs an operation without his patient's consent, commits an assault, for which he is liable in damages."[77]

Although the previously quoted language may be the most oft-cited passage in medical jurisprudence, the doctrine of informed consent did not get much further attention from courts until the early 1970s. At the same time that the public and federal government were focusing on research abuse, state courts began examining more closely what it meant for a person to give informed consent in the clinical context. For example, in *Canterbury v. Spence*,[78] a California court held that physicians have a duty to disclose risks of procedures so that patients can make informed choices. The case involved nineteen-year-old Canturbury who had laminectomy, a kind of back surgery in which posterior arch of the vertebra is removed, as a treatment for chronic back pain. During his recuperation, Canterbury fell from his bed and became paralyzed. Canterbury sued several defendants, including his surgeon, against whom he alleged negligence in the performance of the surgery and failure to inform him beforehand of the risks involved. The court recognized that Canterbury had a cause of action against the doctor even if the doctor was not negligent in his performance of the procedure. The court explained: "True consent to what happens to one's self is the informed exercise of a choice, and that entails an opportunity to evaluate knowledgeably the options available and the risks attendant upon each. The average patient has little or no understanding of the medical arts, and ordinarily has only his physician to whom he can look for enlightenment with which to reach an intelligent decision. From these almost axiomatic considerations springs the need, and in turn the requirement, of a

---

[77] Schloendorff v. Society of N.Y. Hosp., 105 N.E. 92, 129–30 (1914).

[78] Canterbury v. Spence, 464 F.2d 772 (D.C. Cir. 1972).

reasonable divulgence by physician to patient to make such a decision possible."[79] The court further defined the physician's legal obligations in terms of the patient's rights: "The patient's right of self-decision shapes the boundaries of the duty to reveal. That right can be effectively exercised only if the patient possesses enough information to enable an intelligent choice."[80] The court's reliance on patient rights to define legal parameters for physician's behavior foreshadowed the approach bioethicists would take in defining the ethical parameters of the physician-patient relationship.

Questions about the scope of patient's rights of self-decision took on new dimensions with the advent of the ventilator, a machine that moves air in and out of the lungs of patients who cannot breathe on their own. The ventilator changed the practice of medicine. Patients who would surely die before its invention could be saved, but the results of its use were mixed. Some patients "could be tided over by this miraculous machine until they could breathe again … [but] some patients failed ever again to breathe on their own and some patients slipped into deep unconsciousness, kept alive only by the pumping respirator."[81] The results troubled physicians who began to question their ethical and moral obligations with respect to use of the ventilator on patients who would not again breathe on their own,[82] and with respect to patients in deep unconsciousness whose circulation was maintained through artificial respiration.

---

[79] *Id.* at 780.
[80] *Id. See also* Cobbs v. Grant, 8 Cal. 3d 229, 104 Cal. Rptr. 505, 502 P.2d 1 (Cal. 1972) (holding that "the patient's right of self-decision is the measure of the physician's duty to reveal. That right can be effectively exercised only if the patient possesses adequate information to enable an intelligent choice. The scope of the physician's communications to the patient, then, must be measured by the patient's need, and that need is whatever information is material to the decision. Thus the test for determining whether a potential peril must be divulged is its materiality to the patient's decision.")
[81] ALBERT R. JONSEN, THE BIRTH OF BIOETHICS 236 (Oxford University Press 1998).
[82] *Id.* at 236–37.

Specifically, physicians questioned the then-prevailing definition of death – the permanent cessation of heart and lung function. That definition did not apply to patients maintained on ventilators, even those who had suffered grave trauma to the brain that caused deep and apparently permanent unconsciousness and central breathing paralysis. Should these patients be considered dead despite the presence of circulation? Harvard Medical School convened a group of physicians and other scholars to answer that question. The Harvard group published its findings in the 1968 *Journal of the American Medical Association*[83] in a paper that sought "to define irreversible coma as a new criterion for death."[84] Although the paper was subjected to criticism for its lack of citation to scientific evidence and its conflation of permanent unconsciousness with lack of brain stem activity,[85] the report "canonized the concept of brain death, gave physicians guidance in diagnosing this condition, and gave transplanters fresh access to fresh organs."[86]

By the time the Harvard paper was published, philosophers, theologians, clinicians, and lawyers were actively engaged in "the study of the ethical dimensions of medicine and the biological sciences,"[87] an emerging field some called bioethics.[88] Many of the field's pioneers began examining bioethical issues in the 1960s, after a *Life* magazine article told the story of hospitals' ethics committees it called "God squads" – hospital-based groups charged with making life-and-death choices about who would get kidney dialysis, then a rare resource.[89]

---

[83] *Id.* at 238 (citing Report of the Ad Hoc Committee at Harvard Medical School to Examine the Definition of Brain Death, "*A Definition of Irreversible Coma,*" 205 JAMA [1968], at 337–40).

[84] *Id.,* at 1.

[85] *See* Jonsen, *supra* note 81, at 240.

[86] *Id.*

[87] THE ENCYCLOPEDIA OF BIOETHICS xix–xx (Warren T. Reich ed., The Free Press 1978).

[88] Dan Callahan, *Bioethics as a Discipline,* 1 HASTINGS CENTER STUDIES 66, 66–7 (1973).

[89] Jonsen, *supra* note 81, at 212–213.

These early ethics committees often grounded their allocation decisions in value-laden, social-worth criteria. A group of philosophers and theologians gathered in what has been called the first bioethics conference to discuss the issues raised in the article.[90] The participants reached consensus that social-worth criteria were not appropriate and that a rigorous analysis based on established principles should govern. That consensus influenced national policies on organ allocation and set the stage for bioethics' next great debate – end-of-life decision making.

The early bioethicists found ethically problematic the implication of the *Harvard Report* that persons in irreversible coma should be treated as if they were dead.[91] They struggled to define "the human functions that define human life and how are their presence and absence recognized"[92] as a starting point for defining death. Some of that work took place on a national stage after the President's Commission for the Study of Ethical Problems in Medicine and Biomedical and Behavioral Research – the body that succeeded the National Commission on Human Subjects of Biomedical and Behavioral Research[93] – received its first mandate: to study "the ethical and legal implications of the matter of defining death."[94] The Commission's final report, *Defining Death*,[95] proposed a uniform definition of death that included criteria for brain death more specific and narrow than those contained in the Harvard study. Specifically, the proposed definition of brain death required cessation of function of the entire brain, including the brain

---

[90] *Id.* at 213.

[91] *E.g.*, Robert M. Veatch, *The Definition of Death: Ethical, Philosophical and Policy Confusion, in* BRAIN DEATH (1978).

[92] Jonsen, *supra* note 82, at 242.

[93] For a history of Presidential Commissions and their work, *see* http://www.bioethics.gov/reports/past_commissions/index.html

[94] 42 U.S.C. 1395a, § 1802 (1978).

[95] President's Commission for the Study of Ethical Problems in Medicine and Biomedical and Behavioral Research, *Defining Death: A Report on the Medical, Legal, and Ethical Issues in the Determination of Death* (1981).

stem. The Commission's proposed definition became law in almost every state in the country.[96]

Reaching apparent consensus on the definition of death did little to address the other issues raised by the advent of the ventilator, such as whether a competent patient or a family of a person who lacked decision-making capacity could demand its withdrawal. The courts played a pivotal role in resolving these questions. Having already recognized that the right to informed consent encompassed a right to refuse medical treatment,[97] the courts confronted the first right-to-die cases when family members sought orders requiring doctors to turn off the ventilators that were keeping their loved ones alive. In the 1976 case of Karen Ann Quinlan,[98] for example, a father sought a court order to allow the withdrawal of a ventilator that was pumping air into the lungs of his twenty-one-year-old daughter. Quinlan suffered cardiac arrest after ingesting a combination of drugs and alcohol, and was declared permanently unconscious by doctors. Applying the constitutionally recognized right to privacy that supported a woman's right to an abortion, the court held that the right to privacy included a patient's right to refuse medical treatment in some situations, and that "Karen's right of privacy may be asserted on her behalf by her guardian under the peculiar circumstances here present."[99] The court explained, "We have no doubt … that if Karen were herself miraculously lucid for an interval (not altering the existing prognosis of the condition to which she would soon return) and perceptive of her irreversible condition, she could effectively decide upon discontinuance of the life-support apparatus, even if it meant the prospect of natural death." The court

---

[96] "An individual who has sustained either (1) irreversible cessation of circulatory and respiratory functions, or (2) irreversible cessation of all functions of the entire brain, including the brain stem, is dead. A determination of death must be made in accordance with accepted medical standards." *Id.* at 14.

[97] *See, e.g.,* Lane v. Candura, 6 Mass. App. Ct. 377 (1978).

[98] *In re* Quinlan, 70 N.J. 10, 355 A.2d 647 (1976).

[99] *Id.* at 41.

recognized that the State has valid interests in preserving the life of its citizens, but found "that the State's interest … weakens and the individual's right to privacy grows as the degree of bodily invasion increases and the prognosis dims. Ultimately there comes a point at which the individual's rights overcome the State's interest."

The *Quinlan* decision was "the stimulant and fulcrum"[100] of a decade of debate over the ethical and legal implications of withdrawing life-sustaining treatment. In its wake, the President's Commission turned its attention to decisions to forgo life-sustaining treatment. The literature produced by bioethicists during that debate informed the Commission. Its report, "A Report on Deciding to Forego Life-Sustaining Treatment,"[101] concluded that:

> Neither criminal nor civil law precludes health care practitioners or their patients and relatives from reaching ethically and medically appropriate decisions about when to engage in or to forego efforts to sustain the lives of dying patients. Applying the findings of our earlier study on informed consent, we have concluded that the authority of competent, informed patients to decide about their health care encompasses the decision to forego treatment and allow death to occur. We note, however, that all patients, including those who reject various forms of life-support should receive other appropriate medical care to preserve their dignity and minimize suffering to the greatest extent possible. When patients are incompetent to make their other own decisions, others must act on their behalf. The Commission found that existing legal procedures can be adapted for the purpose of allowing people while competent to designate someone to act in their stead and to express their wishes about treatment.[102]

Justice Sandra Day O'Connor cited the report, along with a number of other papers that employed bioethical analysis,[103] in her critical

---

[100] Jonsen, *supra* note 82, at 259.

[101] http://www.bioethics.gov/reports/past_commissions/deciding_to_forego_tx.pdf

[102] *Id.*

[103] She cited, for example, Council on Ethical and Judicial Affairs, American Medical Association, AMA Ethical Opinion 2.20, Withholding or Withdrawing

concurrence in the first so-called right-to-die case to reach the U.S. Supreme Court. *Cruzan v. Director, Missouri Department of Health*[104] pitted the family of an adult woman against the State of Missouri. Nancy Beth Cruzan suffered massive trauma in a car accident in 1983. After the accident, she slipped into a coma and then into a persistent vegetative state, a condition in which a person is completely unaware of herself or her environment, "show[s] no evidence of sustained, reproducible, purposeful, or voluntary behavioral responses to visual, auditory, tactile, or noxious stimuli; show[s] no evidence of language comprehension or expression; ha[s] bowel and bladder incontinence; and ha[s] variably preserved cranial-nerve and spinal reflexes."[105] Cruzan was breathing on her own but unable to swallow voluntarily.[106]

Life-Prolonging Medical Treatment, Current Opinions 13 (1989); The Hastings Center, Guidelines on the Termination of Life-Sustaining Treatment and the Care of the Dying 59 (1987); and Major, The Medical Procedures for Providing Food and Water: Indications and Effects, in By No Extraordinary Means: The Choice to Forgo Life-Sustaining Food and Water 25 (J. Lynn ed., Indiana University Press 1986)

[104] Cruzan v. Dir., Mo. Dep't of Health, 497 U.S. 261 (1990).

[105] The Multi-Society Task Force on PVS, *Medical Aspects of Persistent Vegetative State,* 330 New Eng. J. Med. 1499 (1994).

[106] The trial court described Cruzan's condition: "[H]er respiration and circulation are not artificially maintained and are within the normal limits of a thirty-year-old female; (2) she is oblivious to her environment except for reflexive responses to sound and perhaps painful stimuli"; (3) she suffered anoxia of the brain resulting in a "massive enlargement of the ventricles filling with cerebrospinal fluid in the area where the brain has degenerated" and [her] "cerebral cortical atrophy is irreversible, permanent, progressive and ongoing"; (4) "her highest cognitive brain function is exhibited by her grimacing perhaps in recognition of ordinarily painful stimuli, indicating the experience of pain and apparent response to sound"; (5) she is a spastic quadriplegic; (6) her four extremities are contracted with irreversible muscular and tendon damage to all extremities; (7) "she has no cognitive or reflexive ability to swallow food or water to maintain her daily essential needs" and ... "she will never recover her ability to swallow sufficient [sic] to satisfy her needs." In sum, Nancy is diagnosed as in a persistent vegetative state. She is not dead. She is not terminally ill. Medical experts testified that she could live another thirty years." Cruzan v. Harmon, 760 S.W.2d 408, 411 (Mo. 1988) (en banc).

Doctors surgically implanted a feeding tube (a gastrostomy tube) into her stomach to ensure she received adequate nutrition and hydration. After it became clear that her condition was permanent, Cruzan's family sought to terminate the tube feeding that kept her alive. The hospital refused to comply unless so ordered by a court. The trial court granted the family's request based on evidence that Nancy Cruzan had told her roommate that she would not want her life to continue "unless she could live at least halfway normally."[107] The Missouri Supreme Court reversed. Unpersuaded that the conversation with her roommate was sufficient evidence of Nancy's wishes to justify ending her life, the Court considered the family's argument that it had a right to make decisions for Nancy. The Court concluded that no person has the right to choose to order the termination of medical treatment "for an incompetent in the absence of the formalities required under Missouri's Living Will statutes or the clear and convincing, inherently reliable evidence absent here."[108]

The Supreme Court granted certiorari to consider "whether Cruzan has a right under the United States Constitution which would require the hospital to withdraw life-sustaining treatment from her under these circumstances." Chief Justice William Rehnquist wrote the majority opinion for a deeply divided Court. Surprising some conservatives, Rehnquist acknowledged "the principle that a competent person has a constitutionally protected liberty interest in refusing unwanted medical treatment,"[109] and was willing to "assume that the United States Constitution would grant a competent person a constitutionally protected right to refuse lifesaving hydration and nutrition."[110] But Rehnquist also explained that even if it exists, the right to refuse life-saving nutrition and hydration does not apply to people who lack

---

[107] *Id.* at 433.
[108] *Id.* at 425.
[109] *Cruzan*, 497 U.S. at 278.
[110] *Id.* at 279.

competence to make their own decisions. "An incompetent person is not able to make an informed and voluntary choice to exercise a hypothetical right to refuse treatment or any other right. Such a 'right' must be exercised for her, if at all, by some sort of surrogate."[111] Given its strong interest in preserving life, Missouri was free to demand clear and convincing evidence – the most stringent evidentiary standard available in civil cases – of the patient's wishes before it approved a request to terminate life-sustaining treatment.

In her concurrence, critical to the five-to-four majority vote, Justice O'Connor wrote separately to make clear her view that "the liberty guaranteed by the Due Process Clause must protect, if it protects anything, an individual's deeply personal decision to reject medical treatment, including the artificial delivery of food and water." Citing the American Medical Association (AMA) Ethical Opinion and guidelines published by the bioethics think tank, the Hastings Center,[112] she explained that "artificial feeding cannot readily be distinguished from other forms of medical treatment. Whether or not the techniques used to pass food and water into the patient's alimentary tract are termed 'medical treatment,' it is clear they all involve some degree of intrusion and restraint. Feeding a patient by means of a nasogastric tube requires a physician to pass a long flexible tube through the patient's nose, throat and esophagus and into the stomach.... Requiring a competent adult to endure such procedures against her will burdens the patient's liberty, dignity, and freedom to determine the course of her own treatment."[113]

Although Justice O'Connor disagreed with the dissenters' conclusion that Nancy's rights could be protected only if her parents were allowed to speak for her, she went out of her way to endorse positions taken by bioethicists in favor of surrogate decision-making statutes.

---

[111] *Id.*

[112] *See, e.g.,* AMA Ethical Opinion 2.20, *supra* note 104, at 13; *Guidelines on the Termination of Life-Sustaining Treatment and the Care of the Dying, supra* note 104, at 59.

[113] *Cruzan,* 497 U.S. at 289 (internal citations and quotations omitted).

Missouri did not have surrogacy laws, and no issue about the effect of such laws was before the court. Nonetheless, Justice O'Connor wrote that laws that allow people to act as a surrogate or proxy for someone who has decision-making capacity "may be a valuable additional safeguard of the patient's interest in directing his medical care. Moreover, as patients are likely to select a family member as a surrogate, ... giving effect to a proxy's decisions may also protect the 'freedom of personal choice in matters of ... family life.'"[114] Even more remarkable for a judge known for writing narrowly focused opinions, Justice O'Connor strongly suggested that states may have a constitutional obligation to respect the wishes of a duly appointed surrogate.

In the years following *Cruzan*, every state in the country has adopted some procedural mechanism – a living will, a health care proxy, a durable power of attorney – that allows a competent person some measure of control in medical decision making in the event he or she loses competence to make his or her own decisions. Although the specifics of those laws are subject to debate, their passage was a triumph for bioethics.

Bioethicists have not limited their focus to treatment-refusal cases. Indeed, they are vocal opponents of practices that allowed health care providers to make unilateral decisions to deny care. For example, bioethicists Allen Buchanan and Dan Brock condemned the "Purple Dot Affair," the details of which "came to light because of a lawsuit against a large hospital in New York State":[115]

> A patient went into cardiac arrest in his hospital room during a visit by several members of his family. The resuscitation unit rushed into the room, but stopped short, then retreated, after one member of the team remarked that this patient was a "No Code." The outraged family, who apparently had not been consulted, demanded to know how this could be, since there was no DNR order in the patient's

---

[114] *Id.* at 291.

[115] ALLEN E. BUCHANAN & DAN W. BROCK, DECIDING FOR OTHERS: THE ETHICS OF SURROGATE DECISIONMAKING 273 (Cambridge University Press 1990).

chart. It soon became known that a DNR order was marked in the patient's chart by affixing a purple dot to the chart, that nurses did this, and that purple dots were available in the hospital gift shop, where anyone could purchase them.

In another institution, instead of a purple dot, a red circle on the hospital room door next to the room number served as secret code for "No Code" status – known only to hospital personnel, not to patients or their families.[116]

Buchanan and Brock argued that such policies carry an "utter disregard for the rights of patients and families and enormous potential for gross abuses (including murder)." Instead, they and others advocated for DNR policies like that passed into law by New York State in 1988 in response to the Purple Dot Affair. New York's DNR law put the decision of whether to forgo cardiopulmonary resuscitation in the hands of patients and their families.

Bioethicists also spoke out against another secret practice of physicians after the publication of a letter in a major medical journal in 1988 brought the issue of euthanasia to the attention of the public. The letter, entitled "It's Over, Debbie,"[117] was submitted by an anonymous author who described a late-night visit to the room of a twenty-year-old patient named Debbie, who was dying of ovarian cancer. The author claimed to be a gynecology resident working the late shift, who met a patient for the first time at night, assessed her suffering, and administered a lethal injection of morphine in the presence of her family.[118] Many people criticized the publishers of the unsourced and

---

[116] *Id.*

[117] Anonymous, *It's Over, Debbie, 250* JAMA 259 (January 8, 1988).

[118] "The patient was tired and needed rest. I could not give her health, but I could give her rest. I asked the nurse to draw 20 mg of morphine sulfate into a syringe. Enough, I thought, to do the job. I took the syringe into the room and told the two women I was going to give Debbie something that would let her rest and to say good-bye. Debbie looked at the syringe, then laid her head on the pillow with her eyes open, watching what was left of the world. I injected the morphine intravenously and watched to see if my calculations on its effects would be correct. Within

unverifiable letter for failure to verify sources and endorsing an illegal practice, but bioethicists focused on the ways in which the author's conduct, if true, violated principles of autonomy and nonmaleficience.

The question of the physician's role in helping patients die moved from academic circles to the public stage in 1990, when Michigan doctor Jack Kevorkian began a public crusade to make physician-assisted suicide available to all comers, and again in 1991, when Dr. Timothy Quill published an article in the *New England Journal of Medicine* detailed his long-term relationship with Diane, a patient who asked for and received his help in committing suicide. It was around the issue of physician-assisted suicide that bioethicists came into direct conflict with disability activists. That the conflict started on this issue is somewhat ironic, as the issue of physician-assisted suicide divided bioethicists. Most condemned the reckless Kevorkian, but some supported Quill's actions as those of a devoted physician who respected the autonomous choice of a long-time patient. By the time the issue of the existence of a constitutional right to suicide got to the Supreme Court in companion cases *Quill v. Vacco* and *Glucksburg v. Washington*, one could find a range of analysis on the ethics of physician-assisted death. Although there are members of the bioethics community who staunchly support physician-assisted suicide under certain circumstances, the bioethicists' brief submitted to the Supreme Court in regard to these two cases argued against the practice.[119]

In recent years, the scope of bioethical inquiry has expanded well beyond research and clinical ethics to new technologies, environmental ethics, and neuroethics. The broadened focus of the field does not signal resolution of the "old" questions that arise in the clinical and research setting. To the contrary, bioethicists continue to debate all

seconds her breathing slowed to a normal rate, her eyes closed, and her features softened as she seemed restful at last."
    Id.
[119] Brief of Amicus Curiae Bioethicists, Vacco v. Quill, No. 95. 1858, U.S. Sup. Ct. (Oct. term 1996).

kinds of issues and often reach different conclusions about the ethical resolution of specific cases. Despite the internal debates, bioethics and bioethicists have a well-established and important place at the table in public and academic discussions of issues concerning the use of biomedical technology. Ethics committees, consultants, and experts are now permanent fixtures in hospitals, medical school faculties, and health care facilities. Lawmakers and the media consult bioethicists before proceeding. Presidential committees speak on national policy. Medical schools require various courses in ethical principles founded in bioethics. Without question, the field's emphasis on autonomy and patient choice has shaped health policy, law, and the provision of health services – a development not entirely welcome within the disability rights community.

2

Clashing Perspectives and a Call for Reconciliation

THE EVENTS AND ISSUES THAT HAVE PRECIPITATED AND explain the emergence of bioethics as a scholarly field and a social movement differ in a fundamental way from the events and issues that have inspired and explain the emergence of disability studies as a scholarly field and disability activism as a social movement. As detailed in Chapter 1, the field of bioethics emerged largely in response to the perceived mistreatment of individuals by researchers and health care providers: experiments conducted without individual consent, medical procedures forced on or denied to individual patients, the denial of an organ to a particular person. To be sure, emerging technologies triggered a great deal of discussion and continue to broaden the scope of bioethical inquiry well beyond the realms of research and clinical medicine, but the focus of much bioethical discussion was and remains the appropriate use of particular medical interventions for particular individuals. By contrast, the disability rights movement formed largely in response to perceived mistreatment of the community as a whole: the purposeful elimination of people with disabilities from the human race, the systematic exclusion of persons with disabilities from employment and education, and the systematic devaluation of people with disabilities in popular culture. It is hardly surprising, then, that the movement's primary focus was and remains on community concerns. That is not to say that members of the disability community are not concerned with what happens to individuals – they are. Independent living – and the individual autonomy it provides – is one of the twin pillars of the disability rights movement. The other is protection of community members from abusive practices: eugenics, isolation, institutionalization, and the like. Thus, the focus of inquiry among disability experts is often what a particular policy, law, or incident means for people with disabilities generally. The different focal points of the bioethics and the disability communities help explain their differing perspectives on particular issues of common interest, and why points of friction manifest where the bioethics perspective appears to threaten the disability community.

This chapter has two purposes. First, it begins to explore the depths of the conflict between the disability and bioethics communities to identify the points of friction in what some have deemed a "civil war."[1] It then makes the case for reconciliation. The exploration of the various methodologies and teachings of bioethics and disability studies presented in the first part of this chapter is just deep enough to identify the most contentious issues. In summarizing perspectives, I make no claim that there is a single bioethics or a single disability rights position on any issue. To the contrary, much of the writing in both fields reflects internal disputes on particular issues. Nonetheless, it is possible to identify the common threads of inquiry and major teachings of each group that explain where and why the group members tend to take contrary positions. The introductions to bioethics and disability studies provided here do not do justice to the emerging threads of inquiry that make both bioethics and disabilities studies far richer fields than I can describe in an introductory chapter.[2] Indeed, many of the emerging threads of bioethics and disabilities studies blur any superficially

---

[1] Mark Kuczewski & Kristi Kirschner, *Bioethics and Disability: A Civil War?*, 24 THEORETICAL MED. 455 (2003); *See also*, Christopher Newall, *Disability, Bioethics, and Rejected Knowledge*, 31 J. MED. & PHIL. 269, 276 (2006) (deeming bioethics a "disabling project").

[2] For an in-depth guide to the nuanced discourse taking place in bioethics, *see generally* THE OXFORD HANDBOOK OF BIOETHICS (Bonnie Steinbock ed., Oxford University

sharp difference between the fields. For example, feminist bioethicists emphasize context and community in much the same way that traditional disability scholars do,[3] and the Autonomy Now branch of the disability community emphasizes the importance of individual choice in language virtually identical to that used by many bioethicists.[4] That said, a direct comparison of perspectives in bioethics and disability studies reveals stark differences. To help illustrate, the chapter introduces the paradigmatic case of Elizabeth Bouvia, about which there is a significant disagreement. It then argues that reconciliation between disability and bioethics experts will benefit both disciplines.

I. PERSPECTIVES AND TEACHINGS IN BIOETHICS

Although no one theory or model unifies bioethics, its defining feature from its earliest days has been the rejection of paternalistic medical practices in favor of patients' rights, often framed as respect for the principle of autonomy.[5] The rejection of paternalism can be traced in part to the problems posed to the field's founders. As described in Chapter 1, doctors practicing in the days of doctor-knows-best medicine understood

Press 2007) and A COMPANION TO BIOETHICS (Helga Kuhse & Peter Singer, eds., Wiley-Blackwell 2007). For an in-depth guide to the nuanced discussion taking place in disabilities studies, *see* HANDBOOK OF DISABILITY STUDIES (Gary L. Albrecht et al. eds., Sage Publications, Inc. 2001) and THE DISABILITY STUDIES READER (Lennard J. Davis ed., 2d ed., Routledge 2006).

[3] *See, e.g.*, Susan Sherwin, *Wither Bioethics?: How Feminism Can Help Reinvent Bioethics*, 2 INT'L. J. OF FEMINIST APPROACHES TO BIOETHICS 134 (2009); RELATIONAL AUTONOMY: FEMINIST PERSPECTIVES ON AUTONOMY, AGENCY, AND THE SOCIAL SELF (Catriona MacKenzie & Natalie Stoljar eds., Oxford University Press 2000).

[4] For example, *see*, Andrew I. Batavia, *The Relevance of Data on Physicians and Disability on the Right to Assisted Suicide: Can Empirical Studies Resolve the Issue?*, 6 PSYCH. PUB. POL'Y & L. 546 (2000).

[5] Laurence B. McCullough argues that this view is a historical mistake. *See, Was Bioethics Founded on Historical and Conceptual Mistakes About Medical Paternalism*, 25 BIOETHICS 1467 (2011).

themselves to have a professional obligation to act in what they perceived to be their patient's best interest. When that paternalistic tradition collapsed, the interdisciplinary discourse about the ethical use of biotechnology, clinical decision making, and research involving human subjects that is today's bioethics emerged. As discussed later in the chapter, bioethical discourse takes place on many levels but tends to be unified around the notion that decisions about whether to use or refuse medical treatment should be the province of individuals and their families.

From the beginning, bioethical discussion involved the search for general values and principles that should be brought to bear on the moral difficulties and issues presented in health policy and the health professions. Early discussions imported from the Nuremberg Code and the Belmont Report the notion that informed consent and respect for individual autonomy are critical components of sound ethical theory. This emphasis on informed consent and respect for individual autonomy permeates all methods of bioethical inquiry.

Among the most prominent methods for resolving bioethical disputes is priniciplism. Often attributed to Tom Beauchamp and James Childress, principlism holds that bioethical dilemmas can be resolved by application of certain number of unranked moral principles. Beauchamp and Childress name four: beneficence, autonomy, nonmaleficence, and justice. In a nutshell, the principle of beneficence requires agents to take positive steps to help others. Beneficence requires physicians, for example, to aim to do good and promote the interests of their patients. Autonomy is the state of being self-governed, or the right to live one's life in one's own way. Beauchamp and Childress state that autonomy is "the personal rule of the self that is free from both controlling interference by others and from personal limitations that prevent meaningful choice.... The autonomous individual freely acts in accordance with a self-chosen plan."[6] Respect for autonomy

---

[6] Tom L. Beauchamp & James F. Childress, Principles of Biomedical Ethics 99 (6th ed., Oxford University Press 2009).

requires health care professionals to accept the decisions of competent adults about their medical care, including decisions to refuse seemingly beneficial medical treatment. Nonmaleficence imposes an obligation not to inflict harm on others. Nonmaleficence would prohibit a doctor from intentionally harming or killing a patient. And the principle of justice requires fairness, that equals be treated equally, and that burdens be distributed according to justified norms. The principle of justice would prohibit the allocation of scarce resources based on subjective social worth criteria. Beauchamp and Childress derive rules from the principles. The rules include informed consent, veracity, fidelity, privacy, and confidentiality. Beauchamp and Childress say the principles and rules are all presumed to be binding. Each is mandatory and of no greater importance than the other, and one can only give way to another when the context demands it.[7]

Principlism is not without its critics. Some complain that it is not theoretical enough, as it does not explain where principles come from and does not provide guidance for resolving disputes when principles collide. For example, when a patient requests a doctor to administer a harmful treatment, two ethical principles collide. The provider cannot administer the treatment without violating the principle of nonmaleficence, but the provider who denies the patient the requested treatment may violate the principle of respect for patient autonomy. Resolving the conflict may require a deeper understanding of the meaning of autonomy or its theoretical underpinnings than simple application of principles allows.

Some in bioethics turn to moral philosophy to resolve such theoretical questions.[8] Tom Beauchamp and James Childress identify five

---

[7] *Id.*

[8] For more thorough expositions on theory, *see* John D. Arras et. al, *Moral Reasoning in the Medical Context, in* ETHICAL ISSUES IN MODERN MEDICINE (John D. Arras & Bonnie Steinbock eds., 7th ed., McGraw-Hill 2009); Beauchamp & Childress, *supra* note 6; ROBERT M. VEATCH, THE BASICS OF BIOETHICS (2d ed., Prentice Hall 2003).

discrete moral theories at play in contemporary bioethics: utilitarianism, Kantianism, liberal individualism, communitarianism, and the ethics of care.[9] Although theoretical discourse has influenced bioethics since its inception, many bioethicists find theory less than useful. Philosopher John Arras, for example, says the "theory driven ethicist could offer advice in the vein of a 'Consumer Reports' Service: 'well, in this situation a Kantian would do X, a utilitarian would promote Y, and natural rights theorist would advocate Z. Needless to say, such 'advice' might not prove enormously helpful to those doctors, nurses, and social workers who haven't quite figured out where they stand in the ongoing debate between partisans of Kant, Mill, and Locke." As Tom Beauchamp explains:

> Many individuals in law, theological ethics, political theory, the social and behavioral sciences, and the health professions carefully address mainstream issues of bioethics without finding ethical theory essential or breathtakingly attractive. This is not surprising. Moral philosophers have traditionally formulated theories of the right, the good, and the virtuous in the most general terms. A practical price is paid for theoretical generality. It is often unclear whether and, if so,

---

[9] Utilitarianism holds that best state of affairs among any set contains the net balance of human pleasure, or happiness, or satisfaction. Rule utilitarianism specifies what rules are morally preferable based on their utility-producing consequence. Kantianism rejects utilitarianism in favor of the notion that one should follow a general principle of moral action. An important Kantian principle is respect for persons, which Kant constructed as a categorical imperative that one person should never treat any person as a means, but that all people should be treated as ends. Liberal individualism refers to the notion, deeply embedded in the American legal system, that individuals in society have various personal rights that may not be interfered with by others, especially the state. In contrast to liberal individualism, communitarianism focuses on the good of the community and places special emphasis on community traditions and cooperation. Like communitarianism, the ethics of care rejects the centrality of individualism to moral practice. Rather than focusing on the good of community, however, the ethics of care focuses on the creation, sustenance, and transformation of relationships between particular actors. These descriptions are, of course, gross simplifications of highly developed and nuanced moral theories.

how theory is to be brought to bear on dilemmatic problems, public policy, moral controversies, and moral conflict – which I here refer to as problems of practice. By "problems of practice" I mean the actual moral difficulties and issues presented in health policy and the health professions when decisions must be made about a proper action or policy.[10]

In any event, it is the work of practical ethicists – doctors, lawyers, nurses, and policy makers who confront the "problems of practice" – that draws the fire of members of the disability rights community. For that reason, this book focuses on the methods of bioethical inquiry used on the ground level by clinicians, clinical ethicists, and lawyers.

In addition to principlism, an important approach to problems of practice is casuistry – a case-based approach to resolution of bioethical problems. Casuistry works much like the common-law method of legal analysis. It starts from the proposition that similar cases should be treated similarly, and relies on the comparison of new cases to paradigm cases. Paradigm cases are those on which there is widespread agreement. They offer relatively clear moral solutions. Casuistry holds that if a new case shares morally relevant features with a paradigm case, the cases should be treated alike. When the new case differs from a paradigm case, the inquiry goes deeper to consider how the maxim or principles associated with the paradigm sheds light on the case at hand. "According to Albert Jonsen and Stephen Toulmin, the prime movers of casuistry as a rival method to principlism, the primary locus of moral justification and certitude is the paradigm case. Modelling their vision of ethics on the common law, these authors assert that moral knowledge results from the slow accretion of cases and our efforts to distil principles out of them. 'Moral principles are just so many afterthoughts trailing behind our intuitive responses to paradigm cases. If we are looking for normativity, we will find it,' asserts Toulmin, 'in the

---

10 Tom L. Beauchamp, *Does Ethical Theory Have a Future in Bioethics?*, 32 J. L. MED. & ETHICS 209, 209 (2004).

paradigm case – not in principles distilled post hoc, and certainly not in abstract ethics theory.'"[11]

As a practical matter, bioethical discourse continues on many levels, and many people in the field employ a combination of principlism, casuistry, and metaethics to resolve disputes. As Robert Veatch observed, what is critical for a full and consistent approach to bioethics is not resolution of methodological disputes, but that all levels of moral discourse be brought into "equilibrium."[12] In other words, the goal of bioethical inquiry is to use various methods of inquiry to reach a full and consistent position at all levels of moral discourse: "If one begins with a case intuition and discovers that that intuition cannot be brought in line with firmly held beliefs about moral rules and principles, then something must give. Either one adjusts the case intuition, or, if the case judgment is firm and unrelenting, then maybe the commitments at the higher level will have to be adjusted."[13]

The complexity of bioethical methodology helps explain the many and varied positions taken within the field on specific issues. Despite the methodological and substantive disputes, bioethics has reached consensus on some issues. There is widespread agreement, for example, that competent adults have the right to refuse medical treatment; that patients have a right to make decisions about their medical care and to be given all available information relevant to such decisions; and that medically administered nutrition and hydration is a form of medical treatment. These teachings were all at play in the case of Elizabeth Bouvia.[14]

---

[11] John D. Arras, *The Way We Reason Now, in* OXFORD HANDBOOK OF BIOETHICS 54 (Bonnie Steinbock ed., Oxford University Press 2009).

[12] Veatch, *supra* note 8, at 10.

[13] *Id.*

[14] Bouvia v. Superior Court, 225 Cal. Rptr. 297 (Cal. Ct. App. 1986). Disabilities scholars frequently cite two other cases to make the same point: McKay v. Bergstedt, 385 S.E.2d 801 (Nev. 1990); Georgia. v. McAfee, 259 Ga. 579 (Ga. 1989). McAfee is discussed in depth in Chapter 6.

Elizabeth Bouvia was twenty-eight years old when she asked a California Court to issue an order requiring her doctors to remove a nasogastric tube and allow her to die of starvation. Bouvia was not terminally ill. She had cerebral palsy and arthritis. Her physicians objected to her request, but the court granted her wish.[15] The court rejected the argument that withdrawing treatment was a form of suicide. Finding Bouvia competent, and tube feeding a form of medical treatment, the court emphasized the importance of the right to self-determination: "Elizabeth Bouvia's decision to forego medical treatment or life-support through a mechanical means belongs to her. It is not a medical decision for her physicians to make. Neither is it a legal question whose soundness is to be resolved by lawyers or judges. It is not a conditional right subject to approval by ethics committees or courts of law. It is a moral and philosophical decision that, being a competent adult, is hers alone."[16]

Within bioethics, where respect for autonomy had become the dominant principle guiding medical decision making, *Bouvia* was hailed as a landmark victory. The case affirmed the teaching of principlists – then the dominant voice in the field – that even those who are not terminally ill can decline treatment, and that artificial nutrition and

---

[15] Elizabeth Bouvia chose not to end her life after the court granted her wish to die. She explained her decision during a *60 Minutes* segment broadcast on September 7, 1997 ...

> Mike Wallace: (*voiceover*) After several attempt[s] at starvation, Elizabeth told us, it just became physically too difficult to do. She didn't want to die a slow, agonizing death, nor to do it in the spotlight of public scrutiny. And she told us, with great regret, she quietly chose to live.
> Ms. Bouvia: Starvation is not an easy way to go.
> Wallace: Oh, no.
> Ms. Bouvia: You can't just keep doing it and keep doing it. It really messes up your body. And my body was already messed up.

JERRY MENIKOFF, LAW AND BIOETHICS: AN INTRODUCTION 262 (Georgetown University Press 2001).

[16] *Bouvia*, 225 Cal. Rptr. at 305.

hydration is medical treatment.[17] Bouvia's case became paradigmatic in bioethics. Casuists on the ground level – clinicians, ethics consultants, and lawyers – resolved new cases involving treatment decisions by competent adults by analogizing to Elizabeth Bouvia's case and applying its maxim that decisions about whether to accept or continue medical treatment belong to the patient, even if the treatment is life-saving or -prolonging.

Of course, Bouvia's case is morally and legally distinguishable from cases involving adults who lack decision-making capacity. The maxim that medically administered nutrition and hydration is a form of medical treatment may apply, but the rule that decisions should be made by the patient him or herself cannot be applied directly to people who lack decision-making capacity. Bioethicists take different tacks in resolving the question of who decides for a patient who cannot decide for oneself, but most agree that decisions for people who lack decision-making capacity should approximate as closely as possible decision making for someone with capacity. Advance directives have widespread support as useful tools for effectuating autonomous choices of individuals who once had decision-making capacity. Advance directives are an exercise of what some in the field call precedent autonomy,[18] and are widely respected as the best evidence about what the now incapacitated patient would choose if he or she had the current capacity to make a decision.

In the absence of an advance directive, bioethicists still endeavor to respect the choices the individual would have made if he or she had capacity, and where that is not known, to apply the principle of beneficence to do what is in the best interest of the patient. To best approximate individual decision making for a patient who lacks decisional

---

[17] *See, e.g.,* Jerry Menikoff, *Demanded Medical Care,* 30 ARIZ. ST. L. J. 1091, 1091 (1998); Elizabeth W. Malloy, *Beyond Misguided Paternalism Resuscitating the Right to Refuse Medical Treatment,* 33 WAKE FOREST L. REV. 1035, 1037 (1998).

[18] Ronald M. Dworkin, *Autonomy and the Demented Self,* 64 MILBANK Q. 4, 10 (Supp. 2 1986).

capacity and an advanced directive, bioethicists generally look to some-one close to the person for whom the decision must be made – usually a spouse or a family member as a surrogate decision maker. There is general consensus that a surrogate decision maker should have the authority to make any decisions for the incompetent person that the incompetent person could once make, including decisions to refuse or withdraw treatment. Bioethics teaches that, where possible, the surrogate decision maker should make the decision that the incapacitated patient would have made if he or she could make the decision. Clinical ethicists are trained to help surrogates assess what an incapacitated would have decided by evaluating not only specific statements made by the patient when competent, but the patient's values, goals, prognosis, and available alternatives. When it is not possible to determine what an incapacitated person would decide, bioethics teaches that the surrogate should make decisions that are in the best interest of the patient. Often, but not always, the patient's best interests are viewed as a matter of medical efficacy: what choice will restore this person to health or functionality. As a field, however, bioethics is cognizant of the burdens of medical care and supportive of the notion of a good death, one characterized by comfort care and support of family. Thus, the notion that a decision to terminate or withhold life-sustaining treatment can be in person's best interest is well embedded in bioethical thinking.

The nuances of these teachings will be fleshed out in the study of specific cases, but the overview – when contrasted with an overview of disability scholarship – helps identify the points of friction between the bioethics and disability communities.

II. PERSPECTIVES AND TEACHINGS FROM THE DISABILITY-RIGHTS COMMUNITY

Like bioethics, the disability rights community is not a monolith. It consists of activists and scholars, many of whom take contrary positions on specific issues. No one faction or group speaks for every person with a disability, but many disability rights activists speak for what they have defined as the disability rights community. With respect to the medical view of disability, the activists present a remarkably coherent message that is clearly informed by the work of disability studies scholars.

Disabilities scholars deconstruct the myth of the tragic life of the person with disabilities. As a field, disability studies emphasize the social oppression of people with disabilities and the correct cultural perceptions of life with disability.[19] Its central tenet is the rejection of the medical model of disability as a foundation for effective understanding of impairment or disability:[20] "The medical view of disability ... treats the individual as deficient and inherently inferior because she falls below an arbitrary physiological standard that delineates social acceptance and that can only be 'normalized' and incorporated into society through a medical cure."[21] Falling below the physiologic standard is problematic, in the medical view of disability, because "impairment of normal species functioning reduces the range of opportunity open to the individual ... [to] construct a plan of life or conception of the good."[22] Thus, the medical view of disability essentially locates the problems caused by disability in the disabled individual.

---

[19] Gareth Williams, *Theorizing Disability, in* HANDBOOK OF DISABILITY STUDIES, at 124 (Sage Publications, Inc. 2001).

[20] *Id.*

[21] Jonathan C. Drimmer, Comment, *Cripples, Overcomers, and Civil Rights: Tracing the Evolution of Federal Legislation and Social Policy for People with Disabilities*, 40 UCLA L. REV. 1341, 1348 (1993); *see also* Adrienne Asch, *Disability, Bioethics, and Human Rights, in* HANDBOOK OF DISABILITY STUDIES 297–301 (Gary L. Albrecht et al. eds., Sage Publications, Inc. 2001) (stating that "the first right of people with disabilities is a claim to life itself, along with the social recognition of the value and validity of the life of someone with a disability").

[22] N. L. DANIELS, JUST HEALTH CARE: STUDIES IN PHILOSOPHY AND HEALTH POLICY 27 (Cambridge University Press 1985).

Instead of a medical view of disability, disability scholars view disability as "a socially constructed condition, through which the 'problem' is defined as 'a dominating attitude by professionals and others, inadequate support services when compared with society generally, as well as attitudinal, architectural, sensory, cognitive and economic barriers.'"[23] As stated by one scholar:

> [T]he "socio-political" model of disability views disability as "a product of interaction between health status and the demands of one's physical and social environment," and 'locates' disability in the interface between the individual and her environment. In doing so, the socio-political model of disability (and a related construct – the minority model) stand in stark contrast to the medical model of disability, "which regards disability as a defect or sickness which must be cured through medical intervention," and which expressly locates the 'problem' in the disabled person.[24]

The classic example of the social view of disability is a paralyzed person who cannot get into a building because the entrance is at the top of the stairs. That person is not "disabled" by his or her physical impairments. The disability results from the social failure to provide wheelchair-accessible ramps. Thus, "the culprit is not biological, psychic, or cognitive equipment but the social, institutional, and physical world in which people with impairments must function – a world designed with the characteristics and needs of the nondisabled in mind" in which "an impaired arm becomes a manual disability or social handicap only

---

[23] Laura L. Rovner, *Disability, Equality, and Identity*, 55 ALA. L. REV. 1043, 1043–44, (2004) (citing Deborah Kaplan, *The Definition of Disability:Perspective of the Disability Community*, 3 J. HEALTH CARE L. & POL'Y 352, 352–353 [2000]); Michelle Fine & Adrienne Asch, *Disability Beyond Stigma: Social Interaction, Discrimination, and Activism*, 44 J. SOC. ISSUES 3 (1988).

[24] Rovner, *supra* note 23, at 1044 (citing Deborah Kaplan, *The Definition of Disability: Perspective of the Disability Community*, 3 J. HEALTH CARE L. & POL'Y 352, 352 [2000]); Richard Scotch, *Understanding Disability Policy*, 22 POL'Y STUD. J. 170, 172 (1994) (reviewing EDWARD D. BERKOWITZ, DISABLED POLICY: AMERICA & PROGRAMS FOR THE HANDICAPPED [Cambridge University Press, 1987]).

because of the interaction of a particular physiology with a specific social, legal, and attitudinal environment."[25]

The prevailing message in disability scholarship is that life with disability is not tragic.[26] Rather, the tragedy is the failure of social institutions to help people with physical impairments lead productive lives. Thus, disability scholars argue that "rules, laws, means of communication, characteristics of buildings and transit systems, the typical eight-hour work day, and aesthetic preference[s] all exclude some people from participating in school, work, civic, or social life."[27] Given appropriate accommodation by society, a disabled person can have a rewarding life.[28]

Disability scholars have supported their theoretical positions through empirical studies that reveal that "people who experience disability – whether it be congenital or acquired, whether sensory, cognitive, motor, or other – can find considerable reward and satisfaction in their lives."[29] Indeed, studies have consistently shown that the number of people with disabilities who found satisfaction in their lives far exceeds predictions by health professionals.[30]

[25] Asch, *supra* note 21, at 300.

[26] *Id.*

[27] *Id.* Thus Adrienne Asch criticizes bioethics:

[B]ioethics insists that individuals should be able to determine the situations under which they find life intolerable but has never challenged them to ask themselves what they found intolerable. Nor has bioethics suggested that what was unacceptable might not be inherent in quadriplegia, stroke, or a degenerative neurological disorder but instead could result from the social arrangements facing people living with such conditions.

Asch, *supra* note 21, at 299.

[28] *Id.* The Americans with Disabilities Act was a major victory for disability scholars and activists. It adopted as law the rule that society had the obligation to offer people with disabilities a better quality of life and the opportunity to contribute meaningfully to society.

[29] *Id.* at 301. The evidence shows that "even those who work most closely with the disabled underestimate their quality of life." Mark G. Kuczewski, Disability: An Agenda for Bioethics, 1 AJOB 39 (2001).

[30] *See* Asch, *supra* note 21, at 302 (citing eleven such studies); *see also* NATIONAL ORGANIZATION ON DISABILITY, NOD/HARRIS SURVEY OF DISABLED AMERICANS

Disability scholars also use personal narratives to counter the medical view of disability. For example, Alison Davis countered the early (and infamous) work by bioethicists Peter Singer and Helga Kuhse that argued that some infants with severe disabilities should be killed with the following narrative: "I was born with severe spina bifida, and am confined to a wheelchair as a result. Despite my disability and the gloomy predictions made by doctors at my birth, I am now leading a very full, happy and satisfying life by any standards. I am most definitely glad to be alive."[31]

Disability scholars view court cases involving medical decision making as statements about the tragedy of life with disability. According to the literature, courts have accepted and perpetuated two incorrect assumptions in allowing people to forgo medical treatment and choose death over life with disability: "First, the life of someone with a chronic illness or disability ... is forever disrupted,.... Second, if a disabled person experiences isolation, powerlessness, poverty, unemployment, or low social status, these are inevitable consequences of biological limitation."[32]

Consider again the case of Elizabeth Bouvia.[33] Disability scholars read *Bouvia* very differently from the bioethicists who heralded it as a triumph of the principle of autonomy. Disability scholars saw Elizabeth Bouvia as a person with disabilities who lacked the social support necessary to allow her life to have meaning.[34] They pointed out that she demanded the right to starve herself only after she had a miscarriage, her husband left her, her family abandoned her, the county failed to

---

(1994); S. Saigal et al., *Self-Perceived Health Status and Health-Related Quality of Life of Extremely Low Birthweight Infants at Adolescence*, 276 J. AM. MED. ASS'N 492 (1996).

[31] Alison Davis, *Yes the Baby Should Live*, NEW SCIENTIST at 54 (1985)

[32] Asch, *supra* note 21, at 300.

[33] *See e.g.*, *Bouvia*, 225 Cal. Rptr. 297; *McKay*, 801 P.2d 617 at 623.

[34] *See e.g.*, Paul K. Longmore, *Elizabeth Bouvia, Assisted Suicide, and Social Prejudice*, 3 ISSUES L. MED. 141, 144 (1987).

find a suitable place to house her, and she was forced to withdraw from graduate school because the dean believed her disability made her an inappropriate student.[35]

Disability scholars saw Bouvia's plight as a classic case of society failing a person with disability. The appropriate answer to Bouvia's plight, argued disability scholars, was social support and intervention, not acquiescence to her demand for death.[36] The community saw the court's decision to allow Bouvia to starve herself as judicial confirmation that lives with disability are not worth living.

The judge who authored *Bouvia* gave the disability scholars many reasons to believe that the decision was not about autonomy, but about disability discrimination.[37] The court went to great lengths to describe in painstaking detail the physical elements of Bouvia's disability. It then explained that her decision that her life had no meaning was reasonable: "Her mind and spirit may be free to take great flights but she herself is imprisoned, and must lie physically helpless subject to the ignominy, embarrassment, humiliation and dehumanizing aspects created by her helplessness."[38] Thus, the judge asserted that disability had ruined Bouvia's life: "such life has been physically destroyed and

---

[35] Asch, *supra* note 21, at 311.

[36] Alicia Ouellette, *Disability and the End of Life*, 85 OR. L. REV. 123, 135 (2006) (citing Paul K. Longmore, *Elizabeth Bouvia, Assisted Suicide and Social Prejudice*, 3 ISSUES L. & MED. 141 [1987]).

[37] The 1996 decision in Washington v. Glucksberg that supported physician-assisted suicide also portrayed life with disabilities as hopeless. The court referred to people with physical impairments as existing in "a childlike state of helplessness" exemplified by physical immobility or by their use of diapers to deal with incontinence. Compassion in Dying v. Washington, 79 F.3d 790, 814 (9th Cir. 1996); *see also*, *McAfee*, 385 S.E.2d at 651 (describing the plaintiff, a ventilator-dependent man who been needlessly housed in a hospital ICU for months as being "incapable of spontaneous respiration, and ... dependent upon a ventilator to breathe. According to the record, there is no hope that Mr. McAfee's condition will improve with time, nor is there any known medical treatment which can improve his condition.")

[38] *Bouvia*, 225 Cal. Rptr. at 3051.

its quality, dignity and purpose [are] gone."[39] Without exploring the implications of the social changes in Bouvia's life, the judge characterized extending her life as "monstrous."[40]

The functional limitations faced by Bouvia mirrored those of many disability rights leaders who could live productively for decades with the assistance of medical treatment and technology.[41] Thus, unlike the earlier cases that involved decision making for people who were permanently unconscious or terminally ill,[42] the case got the attention of disability scholars.

Following *Bouvia*, disability scholars started to question whether such cases were really about autonomy – a principle cherished by the community – or about a new eugenics.[43] They argued, "[The nondisabled public] readily concludes that the disabled person's wish to die is reasonable because it agrees with their own preconception that the primary problem for such individuals is the unbearable experience of a permanent disability.... If permanent disability is the problem, death is the solution."[44] The disability scholars further observed that "when the nondisabled say they want to die, they are labeled as suicidal; if they are disabled, it is treated as 'natural' or 'reasonable.'"[45]

The willingness of courts and the bioethicists cited by the courts to accept as reasonable the wish to die exemplified, in the view of the disability scholars, a lack of social recognition for the value and validity of

[39] *Id.* The "monstrous" language was quoted by the court in *McKay*, 385 S.E.2d 801.

[40] *Id.*

[41] Asch, *supra* note 21, at 312.

[42] *See, e.g., in re* Quinlan, 353 A.2d 647 (1976) (allowing family to terminate treatment for permanently unconscious patient); Satz v. Perlmutter, 362 So. 2d 160 (Fla. App. 1978) (allowing terminally ill patient to refuse life-sustaining treatment).

[43] *See* Stanley S. Herr et al., *No Place to Go: Refusal of Life-Sustaining Treatment by Competent Persons with Physical Disabilities*, 8 ISSUES L. & MED. 36 (1992).

[44] Carol J. Gill, *Suicide Intervention for Persons with Disabilities: A Lesson in Inequality*, 8 ISSUES L. & MED. 37, 39 (1996).

[45] Compassion in Dying v. Wa., 49 F.3d 586, 593 (9th Cir. 1995).

a disabled life.[46] From a disability perspective, courts failed by focusing on limitations created by physical impairment instead of focusing on the ways in which "law, medicine, bioethics, and government programs failed to help traumatically disabled patients discover the financial technological, social, and psychological resources that could sustain them and provide the opportunity for rewarding life."[47] And bioethicists were held responsible. It was, after all, their scholarly worked cited by judges to justify decisions that devalued disabled lives.

In response to this perceived threat to the existence of people with disabilities, the first right of people with disabilities became "a claim to life itself."[48] Laws that allow the refusal of treatment became suspect. Disability scholarship came to question the emphasis in current law and bioethics on autonomy as the paramount concern in end-of-life cases.[49] The skepticism became especially pronounced when the nation turned its attention to the question of physician-assisted suicide.[50] Disability scholars strongly opposed physician-assisted

---

[46] Asch, *supra* note 21, at 301.

[47] Adrienne Asch, *Recognizing Death While Affirming Life: Can End of Life Reform Uphold a Disabled Person's Interest in Continued Life?, in* IMPROVING END OF LIFE CARE: WHY HAS IT BEEN SO DIFFICULT, A HASTINGS CENTER SPECIAL REPORT, at S34 (2005) [hereinafter. *Recognizing Death While Affirming Life: Can End of Life Reform Uphold a Disabled Person's Interest in Continued Life?*].

[48] Asch, *supra* note 21, at 301.

[49] *Recognizing Death While Affirming Life: Can End of Life Reform Uphold a Disabled Person's Interest in Continued Life?, supra* note 47, at S33 (pointing to the "danger of relying on a simple notion of patient autonomy when deciding to withdraw life-sustaining treatment.")

[50] *See* M. Cathleen Kaveny, *Proper Honoris Respectum: Managed Care, Assisted Suicide and Vulnerable Populations,* 73 NOTRE DAME L. REV. 1275 (1998) (discussing the dangers of physician-assisted suicide in American health care institutions and its repercussions on vulnerable populations); *Conference of Transcript Socially-Assisted Dying: Media, Money & Meaning,* 7 CORNELL J. L. & PUB. POL'Y 267 (1998) (illustrating views of "proponents and opponents from the disability community" concerning assisted death); Stephen L. Mikochik, *Assisted Suicide and Disabled People,* 46 DEPAUL L.REV. 987, 999 (1987); Yale Kamisar, *Against Assisted Suicide – Even a Very Limited Form,* 72 U. DET. MERCY L. REV. 735 (1995).

suicide, arguing expressly that right-to-die cases "reflect a societal prejudice that devalues the worth of disabled persons' lives."[51] As a result, scholars urged "clinicians and policy makers to question how truly autonomous is anyone's wish to die when living with changed, feared, and uncertain physical impairments...."[52]

In time, scholars criticized laws that allow family members to withhold treatment.[53] As one scholar noted, "Even a demonstrably loving and involved family may be unable to put aside its own view of how limited life with disability is to imagine such a life from the vantage point of someone without impairment."[54] In keeping with its position, disability scholars applauded the New York Court of Appeals when it refused to allow the mother of a man with profound mental retardation the option of declining treatment for her son's cancer.[55] The mother had provided good care to her son throughout his life but was concerned that the treatments were unduly upsetting. The court held that no one, not even a loving family member, could decline life-saving treatment for someone who has not expressed his or her own wish to refuse treatment.[56]

---

[51] Gill, *supra* note 44, at 39; Pamela Fadem et al., *Attitudes of People with Disabilities Toward Physician-Assisted Suicide Legislation: Broadening the Dialogue*, 28 J. HEALTH POL. POL'Y & L. 977 (2003); Longmore, *supra* note 36; Adam A. Milani, *Better Off Dead than Disabled?: Should Courts Recognize a "Wrongful Living" Cause of Action When Doctors Fail to Honor Patients' Advance Directives?*, 54 WASH & LEE L. REV. 149, 198 (1997).

[52] *Recognizing Death While Affirming Life: Can End of Life Reform Uphold a Disabled Person's Interest in Continued Life?, supra* note 47, at S33.

[53] Asch, *supra* note 21, at 310 (citing Dresser & Robertson, *Quality of Life and Non-Treatment Decisions for Incompetent Patients*, 17 L. MED. & HEALTH CARE 234–44 (1989)).

[54] Asch, *supra* note 21, at 309.

[55] *In re* Storar, 52 N.Y. 363, 380–81, *cert. denied*, 454 U.S. 858 (1981).

[56] *Id.; see also In re* Westchester County Med. Ctr. (O'Connor), 531 N.E.2d 607, 613 (N.Y. 1988) ("[N]o person or court should substitute its judgment as to what would be an acceptable quality of life for another."). The *Storar* and *O'Connor* decisions have been roundly criticized by people who advocate for self-determination as the

In addition to questioning the ability of family members to make decisions for their disabled loved ones, some disability scholars questioned the notion of precedent autonomy. Precedent autonomy is the concept that supports living wills.[57] It allows people to decide in advance what medical decisions they would want if they become unable to later express their wishes, and requires health care providers to act on those decisions. Disability scholars are suspicious of such directives, believing that people who are not disabled cannot imagine that life with a disability would be rewarding.[58] According to the scholars, rather than blindly following advance directives, decision makers should evaluate treatment decisions from the viewpoint of the recently disabled individual.[59] If a person appears to take pleasure in her current state of disability, that current state should be maintained regardless of what the person may have expressed in the past about wanting to avoid life in a disabled state.

Thus, disability scholarship calls into question the role of autonomy, families, and advanced directives in end-of-life decision making. The bottom line, argues scholar Adrianne Asch, is that "it is crucial for anyone seeking to advance the dignity and worth of people with all disabilities to promote their participation in life-and-death decisions and to circumscribe family decisionmaking on behalf of those who have less than full legal authority to make their own decisions."[60]

---

paramount concern. *E.g.*, Stewart F. Hancock, Jr., *The Role of the Judge in Medical Treatment Decisions*, 57 ALB. L. REV. 647 (1994). Obviously, someone who has never been competent to express his wishes could never refuse medical care.

[57] Leslie Pickering Francis, *Decisionmaking at the End of Life: Patients with Alzheimer's or other Dementias*, 35 GA. L. REV. 539, 551, 569–576 (2001) (citing Ronald M. Dworkin, *Autonomy and the Demented Self*, 64 MILBANK Q. 4, 10 [Supp. 2. 1986]).

[58] Asch, *supra* note 21, at 310 (citing Dresser & Robertson, *Quality of Life and Non-Treatment Decisions for Incompetent Patients*, 17 L. MED. & HEALTH CARE 234–44 (1989)).

[59] *Id.*

[60] Asch, *supra* note 21, at 311.

III. POINTS OF FRICTION

In sum, bioethics and disability studies share a common concern with respecting all persons and ensuring fair treatment of all individuals in the health care system. Indeed, the two fields focus on many of the same problems: access to care, end-of-life decision making, advance directives, and physician-assisted suicide. Their members, however, come at the problems from different perspectives. At times, the groups appear to be talking past each other, even shouting at each other, in what has become "a toxic and contentious environment."[61]

The dispute is most heated over critical issues on which disability and bioethics experts have opposing perspectives. The particular points of tension include:

- the wisdom of allowing people with disabilities to refuse medical treatment that will extend their lives;
- the proper role of families in medical decision making for people with disabilities;
- the validity of advanced directives;
- the status of medically administered nutrition and hydration as basic human right or dispensable medical treatment;
- the best response to disabling physical impairments: fix the impairment or provide societal accommodations;
- the status of persistent vegetative state as a disability; and
- the importance of evaluating social and community costs as part of risk benefit analyses conducted in individual cases.

Chapters 3–7 will explore how these points of friction play out in particular cases arising at different points in the human lifespan: infancy, childhood, the reproductive years, middle age, and the end

---

[61] Kuczewski & Kirschner, *supra* note 1, at 456.

of life. The discussion of the cases adds important nuance and reveals far more common ground – and certain internal contradictions – that helps explain both how the groups might work together and why the groups appear to be talking past each other. Before getting to the case studies, I should explain why reconciliation will be worth the effort, and propose a process through which collaborative work may emerge.

IV. A CALL FOR PEACE

In scholarly articles,[62] international documents,[63] activist magazines,[64] on blogs,[65] and in deliberately disruptive protests of national bioethics meetings,[66] disability experts demand to be "included in all debates and policy-making regarding bioethical issues."[67] The protesters accuse bioethicists of deliberately excluding people with disabilities in furtherance of an agenda that includes the devaluation of people with disabilities.[68] To the dismay of disability experts and a handful of bioethicists, the dominant response in bioethics to the

---

[62] Christopher Newall, *supra* note 1, at 276 (deeming bioethics a "disabling project"); Asch, *supra* note 21, at 297.

[63] Independent Living Institute, *The Right to Live and be Different* (Feb. 2000), *available at* http://www.independentliving.org/docs1/dpi022000.html (position paper by representatives of disability groups from twenty-three countries charging that bioethical debates "have prejudiced and negative views of our quality of life. They have denied our right to equality and therefore denied out human rights.")

[64] *See, e.g.,* The Disability Rag, and Ragged Edge Online, at http://www.ragged-edge-mag.com/.

[65] *See, e.g.,* www.notdeadyet.org.

[66] *See, e.g.,* http://notdeadyetnewscommentary.blogspot.com/search/label/alicia%20ouellette (describing one such protest).

[67] Independent Living Institute, *supra* note 63.

[68] *See, e.g.,* http://notdeadyetnewscommentary.blogspot.com/2009/04/monday-media-interview-on-whats-up-with.html; Independent Living Institute, *The Right to Live*

disability perspective is inattention,[69] deliberate dismissal,[70] or out-right rejection.[71]

It is my position that bioethicists who dismiss the disability perspective are making a mistake. By taking disability seriously, bioethicists will be better equipped to do the work of bioethics. Drawing on the knowledge of experts who have deep knowledge of the meaning of disability in society, they will learn about important data that is directly relevant to bioethical inquiry. They will operate from positions of trust in discussions of equity and justice issues surrounding resource allocation and health reform. They also will be better positioned to diffuse the distrust of the medical system at the heart of so many bioethical cases. If the evidence is that the story of disability need not be the story of tragedy, and that biased and disproven assumptions about life with disability are at play in medical decision making, then it is the business of bioethics to work with disability experts to figure that out and to work to eliminate that bias.

Working with disability experts can be a challenge. Some of the leaders in the disability community are very angry and – despite chants of "nothing about us without us" – greet invitations to participate in bioethics projects with the hostility apparent in this blog posting written by Stephen Drake in response to my invitation to Not Dead Yet's President Diane Coleman to participate in a conference designed to find common ground between disability and bioethics:

Give me a break.

First of all, there have been several single-shot events by different entities over the years that accomplished nothing – except perhaps for the bioethicists who sponsored the events to pat themselves on the back for their one-time exercise in inclusion. And, having

---

and be Different, (Feb. 2000), *available at* http://www.independentliving.org/docs1/dpi022000.html.

[69] *See,* Kuczewski, *supra* note 29, at 36.

[70] Kuczewski & Kirschner, *supra* note 1, at 456.

[71] Newall, *supra* note 1.

done that, return to exclusion as a matter of standard operating procedure....

...

If the past is any good indicator of the future, that is what this will be. One more entity that can pat itself on the back for a moment of inclusiveness – and go back to the real business of marginalizing disability advocates and activists. They'll co-opt those things that they approve of and attempt to understand how better to undermine us in the future.

The reality is that this "discourse" around bioethics is more than just an exchange of philosophies, ideas, and experiences. At the core, this is a political struggle over public policy – a struggle between those who have power and seek to hold onto it and those directly affected by the policies who want to take power,

And no one knows it better than the bioethicists who are hosting this event.[72]

Overcoming the anger and distrust evident in the blog post will take work. The skepticism and fear that permeate the movement are deeply rooted and well founded. Having lived for years feeling isolated and marginalized, disability experts have had to shout to be heard, and even then the reception is less than welcoming.

In my view, it is in the interest of bioethics to earn the trust of disability experts – including the new activists – and cultivate trust between the disability community and the medical community more generally. Lack of trust erodes the doctor-patient relationship, the ability to develop sound policies regarding the provision of health care, and can harm individual patients and their family who make fear-based defensive decisions. Trust is an essential component of the doctor-patient relationship, especially in this era of evidence-based medicine. Art Caplan put it bluntly, "Without trust, outcome-based medicine is doomed.... When patients do not trust what physicians say – not for want of evidence about prognosis and benefit but because patients do

[72] http://notdeadyetnewscommentary.blogspot.com/search/label/alicia%20ouellette

not believe that physicians are their advocates, because physicians do things that are ... insensitive – the prognosis for trust is poor.... When the prognosis for trust is poor, so are the prospects for guiding treatment by means of data."[73] Defensive decision making by a patient or family will likely generate more requests that "everything be done," even when professional judgment of the treating team is that treatment should not be continued. To the extent bioethics is concerned with overtreatment and its negative consequences (the bad death, suffering, waste of resources), bioethics has a role to play – and work to do – to create an environment of trust and collaboration with the disability community.

Reconciliation will take work. Ideally, the process of reconciliation involves participation of all parties to a conflict and requires at least three steps: listening and understanding; acknowledging fears, alliances, and values; and identifying points of consensus and an agreeable framework for future collaborations.

Unable to insist that all parties to the conflict come together and thoughtfully listen to one another, I have tried to start the process on paper. Turning to the written words of various stakeholders, I have presented throughout the next five chapters the views of various stakeholders on a series of controversial cases as I've come to understand them. Where possible, I quote directly to avoid spinning or misrepresenting positions. As hundreds of articles and complete books have been written on many of the cases I examine, the presentations are not complete but provide enough information to allow the reader to "listen" and explore what one group might learn from the other. In addition, the case studies reveal a great deal about the fears, alliances, and values at play in the debates, as well as several important points of consensus. In this way, they provide the raw materials for building a disability-conscious bioethics.

---

[73] Arthur Caplan, *Odds and Ends: Trust and the Debate over Medical Futility*, 125 ANNALS OF INTERNAL MED. 688 (1996).

3

Infancy

A NEWBORN BABY IS A TINY BUNDLE OF POTENTIAL WHOSE arrival is often met with joy and wonder. The arrival of a baby born with a disability or a health condition that may result in disabilities can generate more complicated reactions. To be sure, some parents welcome a baby with disabilities with the same joy and wonder as they would any other child. Indeed some parents celebrate the arrival of a child with traits like deafness and achondroplasia as special blessings foretelling a life that will be enriched by the special trait. For many families, however, the realization that an infant has or might develop disabilities brings with it concern, fear, even grief. Whatever the parental reaction, the presence or potential for disability in an infant often means the need for medical decision making. Most decisions made for infants with disabilities are about routine matters, but some are quite literally a matter of life or death. As is evident in the case studies that follow, making decisions about when to use or refuse life-saving treatments for infants with disabilities can be wrenching regardless of parental or analytic perspective.

The law provides some guidance. The advent of the modern neonatal intensive care unit (NICU) in the 1970s brought with it an ever-increasing ability to save the lives of babies facing life-threatening crises. As options for saving imperiled newborns increased, the public's interest in medical protocols that allowed babies to die also increased. Questions arose not just about whether we could save a particular baby, but whether we should. For many years, medical practitioners deferred to parental choices for their babies, including, in some cases, decisions to allow premature or potentially disabled newborns to die. In 1973, for example, two pediatricians from the Yale-New Haven Medical Center published an article in which they admitted that they had accepted parental decisions to forgo treatment for infants with disabilities in forty-three cases.[1] A 1977 study found that an overwhelming majority of pediatricians and pediatric surgeons in the United States would honor a parent's decision against surgery to save the life of an infant with Down syndrome.[2] A film entitled *Who Should Survive? One of the Choices on our Conscience*[3] was produced by the Kennedy Family Foundation to bring to light issues raised in two cases from Johns Hopkins University Hospital in which babies with Down syndrome were allowed to die in the NICU at the request of the parents. The film presents a dramatization of an actual case involving a baby with a blockage between the higher duodenum and the lower stomach that prevented passage of food and water.[4] The parents were informed that the baby would die if they did not consent to surgery, and the parents refused to consent. Pediatric surgeons at Hopkins honored the request. The film captures discussions by clinicians and ethicists about the decision to withhold care as it shows dramatization of a young baby slowly starving to death

---

[1] Raymond S. Duff & A. G. M. Campbell, *Moral and Ethical Dilemmas in the Special-Care Nursery*, 289 NEW ENG. J. MED. 890, 894 (1973).

[2] *See* Shaw et al., *Ethical Issues in Pediatric Surgery: A National Survey of Pediatricians and Pediatric Surgeons*, 60 PEDIATRICS 588, 590, Table 4 (1977).

[3] Videotape: "Who Should Survive?: One of the Choices on Our Conscience" (Joseph P. Kennedy Foundation,. 1972) (distributed by Bono Film & Video Services), http://virgobeta.lib.virginia.edu/catalog/u3630315.

[4] For a thorough background on the Johns Hopkins case, *see* Armand Antommaria, *"Who Should Survive?: One of the Choices on Our Conscience": Mental Retardation and the History of Contemporary Bioethics*, 16 KENNEDY INST. OF ETHICS J. 205–4 (2006).

over the course of fifteen days.[5] The baby's bassinet is marked with a sign directing "nothing by mouth."[6]

Public disclosures of cases in which (in the parlance of the times) "defective" newborns were allowed to die provoked controversy and prompted calls for legal action. In 1982, the first so-called Baby Doe case reached the courts.[7] The infant was born in Bloomington, Indiana, with Down syndrome and tracheosohageal fistula, a life-threatening blockage in the esophagus. The blockage was correctable with surgery, but Down syndrome, a condition caused by a particular genetic config-uration, was permanent. The referring obstetrician told the parents that "some people with Down syndrome are 'mere blobs' and that 'the life-time costs of caring for down syndrome would almost surely be close to one million dollars.'"[8] After considering the doctor's dire predictions, the parents decided against the operation, and decided to keep the baby comfortable while he died. Hospital administrators and pediatricians opposed the decision and went to court. At the hearing, the obstetri-cian asserted that even if the surgery was successful, "the possibility of a minimally adequate quality of life was nonexistent" because of "the child's severe and irreversible mental retardation." The court ruled that the parents had the right to make the decision about whether or not to treat their child.[9] The case was appealed through the Indiana courts. At each stage, the court ruled for the parents.[10] The baby died before the U.S. Supreme Court decided whether to become involved.

---

[5] GREGORY E. PENCE, CLASSIC CASES IN MEDICAL ETHICS: ACCOUNTS OF CASES THAT HAVE SHAPED MEDICAL ETHICS, WITH PHILOSOPHICAL, LEGAL AND HISTORICAL BACKGROUNDS 218 (McGraw-Hill Humanities/Social Sciences/Languages 4th ed. 2003).

[6] Antommaria, *supra* note 4, at 214.

[7] "Baby Doe cases" are cases in which an infant, usually a newborn, is denied medical treatment that could save its life.

[8] Pence, *supra* note 5, at 220.

[9] *Id.* at 200.

[10] Infant Doe v. Bloomington Hosp., 464 U.S. 961 (1983).

Intense media coverage of the Indiana case prompted the Reagan administration to promulgate regulations that would require treatment of all infants, regardless of disability. The so-called Baby Doe Rules had several iterations.[11] First, the Department of Health and Human Services promulgated regulations under the authority of Section 504 of the federal Rehabilitation Act of 1973. The regulations interpreted the Act to prohibit the denial by federally funded institutions of medical treatment to handicapped infants on the basis of their handicap. These rules encouraged hospitals to establish Infant Care Review Committees and required them to post large notices in the NICU stating that "Discriminatory Failure to Feed and Care for Handicapped Infants in This Facility Is Prohibited by Federal Law."[12] The posters had a phone number for a hotline to which reports of discrimination could be made. When a report came in, "Baby Doe squads" were dispatched to investigate. "As long as they existed, the Baby Doe squads were ready on an hour's notice to rush to airports, fly cross country, and suddenly arrive…. Like outside accountants doing a surprise bank audit. Records were seized, charts were taken from attending Physicians, and all night investigations took place. The attitude of the squads was that time was of the essence because an innocent baby's life may be at stake."[13] While they existed, the Baby Doe squads did intervene in some cases to save the life of babies that had a fair chance of living useful lives. In other cases, the squads insisted on "extraordinary surgical measures" that gave babies no more than a few days of extra life at enormous financial and emotional costs…. In a few instances, parents had to give up custody of their children to the state after they refused to permit surgery."[14]

[11] *See* Pence, *supra* note 5, at 221.

[12] *Id.*

[13] *Id.* at 221–2.

[14] *Id.* at 222; see also JOHN LANTOS & WILLIAM MEADOW, NEONATAL BIOETHICS: THE MORAL CHALLENGES OF MEDICAL INNOVATION, 70 (Johns Hopkins University Press 2009).

The raids by the Baby Doe squads were not well received by physicians and hospital groups who challenged their authority, as well as the validity of the Baby Doe rules, in court. Ultimately, the regulations creating the Baby Doe squads were invalidated by the U.S. Supreme Court, which held that the Secretary of Health and Human Services was not authorized to "give unsolicited advice to either parents, to hospitals, or to state officials who are faced with difficult treatment decisions about handicapped or disabled children."[15]

Undeterred, the Reagan administration turned to Congress, which promulgated another set of Baby Doe Rules. These rules, which remain on the books today, were adopted as amendments to the federal Child Abuse Prevention and Treatment Act (CAPTA). They represent something of a compromise between positions advanced by proponents and opponents of the first Baby Doe Rules. This second set of Baby Doe Rules conditioned the grant of federal funds for any state's child protective services program on the state's assurance that it can respond to reports of medical neglect, which may include the withholding of medical treatment from disabled infants with life-threatening conditions. The rules require states receiving federal funds for their child welfare programs to have procedures for responding to reports of potential "medical neglect" of infants. States are permitted to fit these procedures into whatever framework the state has for responding to any other potential case of child abuse or neglect. The rules do not directly impose substantive obligations on hospitals or individual physicians. Nor do they impose civil or criminal liability on doctors or hospitals who fail to treat infants. They merely obligate states to set up protective procedures in order to receive federal child abuse funds, and they leave enforcement to the states. Nonetheless, the rules have been interpreted to create a legal presumption in favor of treating infants regardless of disability or health status.

[15] Bowen v. Am. Hosp. Ass'n 476 U.S. 610, 611 (1986).

The Baby Doe Rules define "medical neglect" as including the "withholding of medically indicated treatment from disabled infants with life-threatening conditions."[16] "Medically indicated treatment" includes treatment that, in a physician's reasonable medical judgment, would most likely be effective in "ameliorating or correcting" all of the infant's life-threatening conditions.[17] Medical treatment is not medically indicated under the rules in three situations: when the infant is "chronically and irreversibly comatose"; when the treatment would "merely prolong dying," would not be "effective" in ameliorating or correcting the conditions, or would be "otherwise futile in terms of the survival of the infant"; and when the provision of treatment "would be virtually futile in terms of the survival of the infant and the treatment itself under such circumstances would be inhumane."[18]

Had they been in effect, the Baby Doe Rules would have required aggressive treatment of the Indiana and Johns Hopkins babies. In fact, the rules require aggressive treatment for most infants. But application of the rules in cases involving extremely premature and marginally viable newborns is a matter of debate. In some hospitals, they are interpreted to require aggressive care in all cases. In others, hospitals do not require aggressive treatment for very low birth weight babies, when the burden on the baby is overwhelming and its chance of survival is bleak.[19] In such cases, the rules probably do not require aggressive treatment, but that has never been determined by a court. Nor are the rules helpful in determining when treatment is futile, or virtually futile. In large measure, under the Act, the determinations of medical effectiveness and futility are left to physicians.

---

[16] 45 C.F.R. § 1340.15(b)(1) (1990).

[17] 45 C.F.R. § 1340.15(b)(2) (1990).

[18] 45 C.F.R. § 1340.15(b)(2)(i–iii) (1990).

[19] J. J. Paris et al., *Ethical and Legal Issues, in* Assisted Ventilation of the Neonate 81 (Jay P. Goldsmith & Edward Karotkin eds., 4th ed. 2003).

As a result of ambiguities inherent in medical decision making and in the law, physicians sometimes make determinations that are different from the ones parents make. This chapter presents two such cases. In the first, the doctors provided aggressive treatment to save the life of an imperiled newborn, despite her parents' refusal to consent to the treatment. In the second, providers refused to provide treatment they deemed medically ineffective despite the pleas for treatment by the infant's mother. Because the cases presented in this chapter involve life-and-death decisions for babies, they are among the most divisive among and between the bioethics and disability communities, and may be the most ethically and emotionally challenging cases in the whole book. Despite that, they come first because they involve the first minutes and months of life.

I. THE CASE OF SYDNEY MILLER

Sydney Miller was born at twenty-three weeks gestation on August 17, 1990.[20] Her mother, Karla, had been admitted to the Woman's Hospital of Texas in premature labor. An ultrasound revealed that her fetus weighed about 629 grams, or 1.25 pounds. Karla's doctors administered drugs that stopped her labor, but Karla's condition worsened. Her temperature and heart rate increased. Her obstetrician determined that Karla had an infection that could endanger her life if labor were further postponed. He therefore advised Karla and her husband Mark that the best course of action was to induce labor. Neither a caesarean section nor an abortion was an option because of the infection.

The obstetrician and a neonatologist advised the couple that the fetus had little chance of surviving delivery. A full-term pregnancy is

---

[20] Case facts are taken from the decision of the Supreme Court of Texas, Miller v. HCA, Inc., 118 S.W.3d 758 (2003); and petition for review submitted to the Supreme Court of Texas by Sydney Miller and her parents, *available at* 2001 WL 34378193.

thirty-eight to forty-two weeks. Babies born before thirty-eight weeks gestation have a characteristic set of problems resulting from immaturity of organ and tissue functions.[21] Babies born at twenty-three weeks gestation rarely survive birth, and those that do are critically ill. Their lungs are too undeveloped to function normally at birth. They must be resuscitated and placed on mechanical ventilators to have any chance of survival. Those who are resuscitated experience complex problems in the first weeks of life, including respiratory distress syndrome, intracerebral hemorrhage, and necrotizing enterocolitis. "Their skin is thin and leaks body fluid; the flesh is jellyish and bruises easily. Liver, kidneys, heart, and glands perform poorly: the babies have great difficulty even maintaining normal body warmth."[22]

The Millers were advised that if the fetus did survive, the baby would likely suffer "severe impairments, including cerebral palsy, brain hemorrhaging, blindness, lung disease, pulmonary infections, and mental retardation." Mark testified the doctors told him "that anything done to sustain a life that premature would be experimental."[23] At trial, Karla said that she understood resuscitation would mean a "huge amount of suffering" for the baby, and that "pain would be a way of life" for the child.[24]

After the lengthy consultation with the doctors, Karla and Mark Miller "opted for compassionate care based on the recommendation that the alternative aggressive treatments would almost certainly

---

[21] *See* Sadath A. Sayeed, *The Marginally Viable Newborn: Legal Challenges, Conceptual Inadequacies, and Reasonableness*, 34 J. L. MED. & ETHICS 600 (2006); Craig A. Conway, *Baby Doe and Beyond: Examining the Practical and Philosophical Influences Impacting Medical Decision-Making on Behalf of Marginally-Viable Newborns*, 25 GA. ST. U. L. REV. 1097 (2009).

[22] Neil Campbell, *When Care Cannot Cure: Medical Problems in Seriously Ill Babies*, *in* BIOETHICS: AN ANTHOLOGY 303, 304 (Helga Kuhse & Peter Singer eds., Wiley-Blackwell 2d ed. 2006).

[23] Petition for Review, Miller v. HCA, Inc., No. 01–0079, 2001 WL 34378193, at *8 (Tex. April 12, 2001).

[24] *Id.*

cause painful, life-long illness and disability."[25] They asked that the doctors refrain from resuscitating the baby and instead place her in her mother's arms so that Karla could hold and comfort the baby as nature took its course. Mark testified that the decision not to resuscitate the baby was "the most difficult decision (he) ever made in (his) life."[26] The obstetrician recorded the Millers' decision in the medical records: "Parents requested no extra-heroic measures be done at this point." He also informed the nursing staff that no neonatologist would be needed at the delivery. On the doctor's advice, Mark left the hospital to make funeral arrangements.

While Mark was gone, a nurse informed other hospital staff about the Millers' situation. A meeting was held in which it was decided that hospital policy required the presence of a neonatologist in the delivery room, as well as the resuscitation of any baby who weighed more than 500 grams at birth. At trial, questions were raised about the legitimacy of the claims that such a policy was in place. Some of the testimony suggested that, at best, the "policy" was an informal one. In any event, the decision was made that a neonatologist would be present and the fetus would be resuscitated. The hospital advised Mark of the change of plans and asked him to sign a consent form authorizing resuscitation. He refused and asked how he could prevent resuscitation. He was told he would have to take his wife out of the hospital. Given the state of Karla's health, checking out was not an option.

Later that evening, Karla's condition worsened. The health team decided that labor should be induced and augmented to prevent further complications. They administered drugs to start the labor and help it proceed quickly. Sidney was born approximately eleven hours after her parents first declined consent to "heroic measures." She weighed 615 grams and had a heartbeat. She gasped for air, cried spontaneously, and showed no visible sign of disability. Without asking for the

---

[25] Mark Miller, "Letters," 35 HASTINGS CENTER REP. 4 (Jan./Feb. 2005).
[26] *Id.*

consent of the parents, the attending neonatologist manually ventilated and incubated Sydney. He then placed her on a mechanical ventilator. He explained his actions:

> [T]his baby is alive and this is a baby that has a reasonable chance of living. And again, this is a baby that is not necessarily going to have problems later on. There are babies that survive at this gestational age that – with this birth weight, that later on go on and do well.[27]

At first, Sidney responded well to the treatment, and she was admitted to the NICU. On the fourth day after birth, however, Sydney suffered the complications predicted by the doctors. Her brain hemorrhaged, causing permanent destruction. Clotted blood from the hemorrhagic area of the brain blocked circulation of the cerebrospinal fluid within the brain's ventricles, causing a condition called hydrocephalus. In the weeks that followed, the Millers consented to various forms of treatment for Sydney, including surgical insertion of other lines, and the insertion of a cerebroventricular shunt to relieve hydrocephalus. They claim that no one discussed with them the possibility of forgoing these interventions.

After two months in the NICU, Sidney was transferred to Texas Children's Hospital. At six months, she was released from the hospital to her parents, who have cared for her at home since her discharge. She has had numerous surgeries to repair or replace the shunt. At seven years old, Sidney "could not walk, talk, feed herself, or sit up on her own.... [She] was legally blind, suffered from severe mental retardation, cerebral palsy, seizures, and spastic quadriparesis in her limbs. She could not be toilet-trained and required a shunt in her brain to drain fluids that accumulate that and needed care twenty-four hours a day."[28] At fourteen, her condition had not improved.[29] She did not

---

[27] *Miller*, 118 S.W.3d at 763.

[28] *Id.* at 764.

[29] John A. Robertson, *Extreme Prematurity and Parental Rights after Baby Doe*, 34(4) HASTINGS CENTER REPORT 32, 35 (2004).

walk or talk, was blind and incontinent. According to one report, "She smiles and appears to interact with parents to some extent, although she seems to lack the capacity for symbolic interaction. With good care she could live to age seventy."[30]

Sydney's parents sued the hospital and its parent company, HCA, for battery and negligence. Both claims stemmed from allegations that Sydney was treated without their consent and that, despite their instructions to the contrary, the hospital resuscitated Sydney, performed experimental procedures, and administered experimental drugs without which Sidney would not likely have survived. The Millers did not sue the physicians. They placed blame with hospital officials and the institutional policies they enforced. During a two-week trial that took place in January 1998, the parents presented evidence that it was the treatments used to keep Sydney alive that caused the brain hemorrhage that resulted in her blindness and mental retardation.

After hearing testimony from the parents, the attending physicians, hospital administrators, and a slew of experts, a jury concluded that the hospital performed resuscitative treatment on Sidney without the consent of the Millers, and that the hospital's and HCA's negligence "proximately caused the occurrence in question."[31] The jury further concluded that HCA and the hospital were grossly negligent and that the hospital acted with malice. The jury awarded the Millers $29,400,000 for medical expenses, $17,503,066 in interest on those expenses, and $13,500,000 in punitive damages.

The mid-level Texas appellate court reversed the jury verdict and ordered that the Millers take nothing. Among other things, the court held that Texas Legislature, which had passed an act that allowed parents of terminally ill children to withhold medical treatment, had never given parents the authority to withhold medical treatment from "children with non-terminal impairments, deformities, or disabilities, regardless of their

[30] *Id.*
[31] *Miller*, 118 S.W.3d at 764.

severity."[32] Nor could the court locate any other authority "allowing a parent to withhold urgently-needed life sustaining medical treatment from a nonterminally ill child." The court thus concluded that when an infant's condition is not terminal, "a health care provider is under no duty to follow a parent's instructions to withhold urgently-needed life-sustaining medical treatment."[33] The health care provider can override the parent's refusal to consent without a court order because a court cannot decide "between impaired life versus no life at all."[34]

A dissenting judge would have required a court order to override the Millers' refusal to consent. That judge asserted that under the circumstances of the Miller's case, "a court must decide the most important issue: What is in the best interest of the child?"[35]

The Texas Supreme Court also held against the parents, but for different reasons. The high court framed the case as one that requires a determination of "the respective roles that parents and healthcare providers play in deciding whether to treat an infant who is born alive but in distress and is so premature that, despite advancements in neonatal intensive care, has a largely uncertain prognosis."[36] It then reviewed established law. First, the court noted that as a matter of constitutional law, "the custody, care, and nurture of an infant resides in the first instance with the parents."[37] That general rule includes the presumption that parents have the right to consent to or refuse medical treatment for their children. That right is not unlimited, noted the court. The state has the authority to protect children. It may punish parents for child abuse or neglect and "supervene parental decisions before they become operative to ensure that the choices made are not so detrimental to a child's interests as to amount to neglect and abuse,"

---

[32] *Id.* at 765.
[33] *Id.*
[34] *Id.*
[35] *Id.*
[36] *Id.* at 766.
[37] *Id.* at n.19 (citing Prince v. Mass., 321 U.S. 158 (1944)).

but "as long as parents choose from professionally accepted treatment options the choice is rarely reviewed in court."[38] The court noted that the state legislature had recognized the limitations on parental power when it provided the courts the power to modify the rights and duties of parents or appoint a conservator to consent to medical treatment refused by a child's parent.

The court went on to consider the rule that a physician who provides treatment without consent commits a battery.[39] The rule is based on the patient's right to receive information adequate to exercise an informed decision to accept or refuse the treatment. There are exceptions, said the court. Consent is implied, for example, when a person is "unconscious or otherwise unable to give express consent and an immediate operation is necessary to preserve life or health."[40]

As to children, the court acknowledged that a physician commits a legal wrong by operating on an infant without parental consent, except when there are "emergent circumstances": "[A] physician, who is confronted with emergent circumstances and provides life-sustaining treatment to a minor child, is not liable for not first obtaining consent."[41] The court did not hold that consent is implied in such circumstances – indeed it could not have so held in the Millers' case because the providers had actual notice of a lack of consent – but that there is "an exception to the general rule that a physician commits a battery by providing treatment without consent."[42] "Emergent circumstances" exist when there is no time to consult the parents or seek court intervention. In emergent circumstances, said the court, a physician may treat a child even over the objection of a parent.[43]

---

[38] *Id.* at 766–7.
[39] *Id.* at 767 (citing Gravis v. Physicians & Surgeons Hosp., 427 S.W.2d 310, 311 (Tex. 1968)).
[40] *Id.*
[41] *Id.*
[42] *Id.*
[43] *Id.*

The court rejected the Millers' argument that because the hospital had eleven-hours notice that the parents had refused consent, there was plenty of time to seek a court order. The court explained that in cases like Sidney's, involving extreme prematurity, parental decisions made before birth "would necessarily be based on speculation."[44] Thus a decision made before birth could not control "whether the circumstances facing [the neonatologist who treated Sidney] were emergent."[45] Sidney could only be properly evaluated when she was born. The court went on to stress that the best medical practice in cases of premature delivery is to obtain parental consent before birth for evaluation and "warranted medical treatment."[46] Ultimately, however, "when emergent circumstances exist, a physician cannot be held liable under either battery or negligence theories solely for providing life-sustaining medical treatment to a minor child without parental consent."[47]

In 2009, "Sidney Miller [was] eighteen, yet she [could not] walk, talk, feed herself, or sit up on her own. She [was] legally blind in one eye, and [had] a range of vision of only a few feet in the other. She suffer[ed] from cerebral palsy, seizures, and spastic quad paresis in her limbs. She ha[d] severe mental retardation and [would] have the mental capacity of an infant for the remainder of her life. She ha[d] a surgically implanted shunt in her skull to drain fluid leaking from her brain. She periodically require[d] hospitalization to clean or replace the shunt. And her family provide[d] twenty-four hour care to change her diapers, feed and clothe her, and take care of her needs. Sidney's condition [would] never improve."[48]

---

[44] *Id.* at 769.

[45] *Id.*

[46] *Id.* at 770.

[47] *Id.* at 771–2.

[48] William J. Winslade, *Personal Reflections on Extremely Premature Newborns:Vitalism, Treatment Decisions, and Ethical Permissibility*, 25 GA. ST. U. L. REV. 931, 938 (2009).

A. Views from the Disability Community

Disability advocates made their views on the Miller case loud and clear. Dozens of activists protested outside the courtroom when judges heard arguments on appeal, and twenty disability rights groups from around the nation submitted a friend-of-the-court brief in the case. John Hoffman, a member of the disability rights group ADAPT, explained the position of the advocates in blunt terms: "It's not right to allow disabled children to die."[49] The legal brief framed the case as one about discrimination based on disability. It opened:

> This case is about disability. It is not about medical malpractice, or the common law of negligence, or about advance directives, or about the validity of consent. This case is about an assessment of an unborn or newborn's potential quality of life as viewed through a societal prism in common use by a substantial portion of the medical community and many potential parents and which at its fundamental core devalues the worth of children and adults with severe disabilities.
>
> This case is about whether medical treatment can be withheld from a premature infant at birth *solely because* the infant may be or become disabled. It is about whether a hospital's accepted medical protocol – to treat equally *all* newborns over a minimum weight, to not discriminate against premature infants who may develop disabilities, to provide all newborns the appropriate medical care and treatment – will be upheld. This case is about discrimination based on disability. [50]

Having thus framed the case, the advocates argued that children with disabilities have the right to receive the same medical care as all other

---

[49] Dave Reynolds, *Protesters Rally Outside Courtroom in Sydney Miller Hearing,* INCLUSION DAILY EXPRESS, April 5, 2002, *available at* http://www.inclusiondaily. com/news/advocacy/sidneymiller.htm#040502.

[50] Brief for Not Dead Yet et al. as Amici Curiae Supporting Respondents, Miller v. HCA, Inc., 118 S.W.3d 758 (2003) (No. 01–0079), 2002 WL 32349030 at *2–3.

children, that all children are entitled to life-saving medical care, and that Sydney's parents had no right to deny her that care. The brief questioned the degree to which the Millers' decision to refuse treatment was based on their own and their doctors' erroneous, if not prejudiced, understanding of life with disability:

> Many parents, like the Petitioners, know very little about disability at the time they first learn that their child may have or does have a severe disability. They might be terribly guilty that they are the cause of their child's disability and probably are very confused when they are told by a doctor that their newborn will be or will likely become disabled. Naturally they rely on the doctor's opinion and judgment, and at least unconsciously they rely on their own stereotypes of and prejudices toward people who have disabilities. They may never have met or spoken with children who have disabilities or their parents.
>
> Most obstetricians are no different than the Petitioners in their lack of experience with and knowledge of disability, other than the general stereotypes society presents. They may not have friends who have disabilities, have never gone to watch a professional basketball game with a disabled teenager, or talked to severely disabled adults about whether they perceive their lives have quality. Their medical treatment of newborns ends at the delivery, without any on-going experience with how the newborn grows into an infant, adolescent and young adult. Consequently many treating health providers give "medical" opinions based primarily on non-medical experiences, but on the same societal stereotypes that non-medical persons have.[51]

The brief argued that these stereotypes biased medical judgments against the use of life-saving medical procedures for the disabled, and likely affected the information the Millers received and the choice they made against life-saving treatment. The brief also asserted that medical stereotypes about life with disability were wrong: "[M]ost adults with disabilities, including those who have had a disability since birth,

---

[51] *Id.* at *8.

choose life and have quality in their lives. Most parents of children with disabilities value and believe their children's lives have quality."[52]

Although the specific case was about Sidney Miller, the brief claimed that the case was really about all people with disabilities. The claim was that upholding the jury verdict would perpetuate the debunked myth that life with disability was worse than death, which would have tragic consequences for people with disabilities. Thus the advocates concluded their brief: "We represent people with disabilities of all ages and families of children with disabilities, throughout Texas and across the nation, and we call upon this Court to unequivocally affirm the equal value of our lives under the law."[53]

The arguments made in the advocate's brief in the Miller case represent the standard disability rights critique of cases in which doctors and parents have denied medical care to newborns with disabilities. According to disability scholar Joseph P. Shapiro, medicine has long been complicit in practices that devalue and underestimate life with disability:

> Throughout U.S. history, doctors have routinely starved or ended the lives of infants born with Down Syndrome or various birth defects, although those children were in no danger of dying. The practice was given national exposure in 1983, when the Reagan Administration opposed the parents of "Baby Jane Doe," a Long Island infant born with spina bifida. The baby's mother and father chose to withhold medical treatment, agreeing with their doctors that it was more humane for the severely disabled child to die.... In 1973, two doctors, writing in the *New England Journal of Medicine*, revealed that forty-three infants with various disabilities had been allowed to die in the special care nursery of the Yale-New Haven Hospital "rather than face lives devoid of meaningful humanhood."

---

[52] *Id.* at *10.

[53] *Groups Support Rights of Children with Disabilities in "Wrongful Life" Case*, INCLUSION DAILY EXPRESS, March 22, 2002, *available at* http://www.inclusiondaily.com/news/advocacy/sidneymiller.htm#032202.

A California state court in 1979 ruled in favor of the parents of Philip Becker, a thirteen-year-old with Down Syndrome, who wanted to withhold life-saving heart surgery, arguing that his life was not worth living.[54]

Disability experts maintain that these practices reflect discriminatory attitudes that permeate medical culture. For example, in a brief to the Supreme Court filed in a challenge to the Baby Doe regulations, the Association of Retarded Citizens argued that the "difference in the treatment of handicapped and non-handicapped children directly reflects the physician's judgment that the life of handicapped infant is of significantly less value than is the life of the non-handicapped infant."[55] The physician bias is said to constrain parental choice. Parents who must make treatment decisions for newborn children with disabilities must rely on specialized knowledge and experience of physicians. The parents "are mentally and emotionally vulnerable, and they are often told that they must make their decisions quickly."[56] Their choices are thus suspected to be the result of subtle or not so subtle pressure from doctors who devalue life with disability.

Scholar Adrienne Asch stresses the failure of society to view disability as a public problem as contributing factor in nontreatment cases:

People with disabilities may need medical care at higher levels and with greater frequency than people without them. They may need support services in the form of interpreters if they are deaf, readers if they are blind, attendants if they are unable to perform manual tasks …

And the families of people with disabilities need support – emotional, financial and sometimes professional – to assist them in working

---

[54] JOSEPH P. SHAPIRO, NO PITY: PEOPLE WITH DISABILITIES FORGING A NEW CIVIL RIGHTS MOVEMENT 273–4 (Three Rivers Press 1993).

[55] Brief for the Ass'n for Retarded Citizens et al. as Amici Curiae Supporting Petitioner, Bowen v. Am. Hosp. Ass'n, 476 U.S. 610 (1986) (No. 4–1529), 1985 WL 669102 at *7.

[56] SAMUEL R. BAGENSTOS, LAW AND THE CONTRADICTIONS OF THE DISABILITY RIGHTS MOVEMENT 100 (Yale University Press 2009).

with and caring for a child who needs physical, occupational, speech or other therapy.

If those services existed routinely, and if society were much more serious about thinking of people with disabilities as genuinely part of the community, then we would be making decisions about ... newborns with disabilities in a vastly different climate.[57]

The current climate "allows parents to decide that a new life with impairments is not one worth living."[58] Thus, Asch argues, "quality of life" should not be a matter for discussion by parents and doctors: "*If the infant can live*, albeit disabled, then it should be helped to do so."[59] Asch distinguishes cases in which infants will surely die within weeks or month, regardless of what medical technology does. Those infants, she says, should not be "forced to undergo treatment."[60] Ultimately, Asch argues, "the needs of the disabled must be met simply because they are human beings. The most basic need is the chance at life. If disabled children could be seen as truly valuable, we would not have situations requiring intervention against parent and doctor; everyone would strive to provide for the lives of all citizens."[61]

Opposition to the nontreatment of newborns runs deep in the disability community. Even Sam Bagenstos, a disability scholar who is fairly skeptical of the disability rights critique, concedes that "the critique of the nontreatment of infants with disabilities stands on its own ... Although the disability rights critique of selective nontreatment has the same structure as the critiques of assisted suicide and selective abortion (with which Bagenstos takes issue) – and it has a similar resonance with antiabortion advocates – the selective nontreatment critique is quite distinct."[62] He explains that prohibiting the selective

---

[57] Adrienne Asch, *On the Question of Baby Doe*, Health PAC Bull. 8 (1986).
[58] *Id*. at 9.
[59] *Id*.
[60] *Id*.
[61] *Id*.
[62] Bagenstos, *supra* note 56, at 114–15.

nontreatment of infants does not undermine the autonomy of persons with disabilities, because "[i]nfants, unlike fetuses, are clearly 'persons,' but unlike adults who seek assistance in suicide they have no say over the nontreatment decision."[63]

Thus from a disability perspective, the decision rendered by the Supreme Court of Texas in Sydney Miller's case appears to be a clear victory. It rejected the notion that life with disability is worse than death and gave Sidney Miller and other children like her a chance at life. In so doing, it will likely prevent parents and doctors from refusing to treat newborns with disabilities in future cases, a result the disability community has long sought. Bioethics is more conflicted about cases like Sidney Miller's.

B. Views from Bioethics

The conclusion of the Supreme Court of Texas in *Miller* that physicians may disregard parental preference for comfort care and unilaterally initiate resuscitation when faced with the birth of an extremely preterm but potentially viable newborn meets more resistance in bioethics than it did in the disability community. The reactions within bioethics to issues raised in the *Miller* case are not uniform, however. Indeed, questions about the respective role of parents and health care providers in deciding whether and how to treat severely premature infants whose prognosis is uncertain have long vexed bioethics.[64] In an article on *Miller*, George Annas deemed the issues "intractable."[65]

Before considering specific reactions to the Miller case, it may be helpful to review the background debate. As a general matter, bioethics

---

[63] *Id.*

[64] Robertson, *supra* note 29, at 35; Sayeed, *supra* note 21; Conway, *supra* note 21; Duff & Campell, *supra* note 1.

[65] George J. Annas, *Extremely Preterm Birth and Parental Authority to Refuse Treatment – The Case of Sidney Miller*, 351 NEW ENG. J. MED. 2118 (2004).

is far more supportive of parental decisions to withhold or withdraw treatment from imperiled newborns than is the disability community.[66] Bioethicists look to parents to make medical decisions for their children in consultation with physicians, and generally presume that parents will act in their child's best interests by choosing from among a menu of medically acceptable alternatives. Bioethics is comfortable with the notion that in a limited number of cases, nontreatment can be a medically acceptable choice in the best interest of a child. Indeed, the primary focus of bioethical discussions about seriously ill or imperiled newborns is overtreatment, and the burdens overtreatment places on dying babies: "Sometimes limiting or stopping life support seems most appropriate, especially if treatment only preserves biological existence or if the overall goal of therapy has shifted to the maintenance of comfort."[67] Thus, as a starting point, bioethicists instinctively resist efforts to intrude into family decision making about how aggressively to treat imperiled newborns.[68]

That said, bioethicists recognize that parents do not always act in the best interests of their newborns, and that infants have interests independent of their parents that sometimes obligate medical providers to override parental choices. Much of the work of the more conceptual or philosophically trained bioethicists involves identifying those interests and establishing ethical frameworks for distinguishing treatments that are obligatory from those that require the consent of parents, and those that are themselves morally impermissible.

---

[66] See *generally,* Lantos & Meadow, Neonatal Bioethics, *supra* note 14.

[67] *See* Committee on Bioethics, *Guidelines on Forgoing Life-Sustaining Medical Treatment,* 93 PEDIATRICS 532 (1994) [hereinafter Forgoing Life-Sustaining Medical Treatment].

[68] See, e.g., A President's Commission for the Study of Ethical Problems in Medicine and Biomedical and Behavioral Research, Deciding to Forgo Life-Sustaining Treatment 215 (U.S. Gov't Printing Office 1983) ("Public Policy should resist state intrusion into family decision making unless serious issues are at stake and intrusion is likely to achieve better outcomes without undue liabilities.").

With respect to treatment of newborns with conditions similar to those at the center of the original Baby Doe cases – babies with Down syndrome or spina bifida whose lives are threatened by independent and entirely treatable conditions – the overwhelming bioethical consensus is that treatment is obligatory.[69] Arguments for the obligatory treatment of cognitively or physically disabled neonates with correctable life-threatening conditions take many forms. They include concessions to legal requirements imposed by the Baby Doe rules,[70] sanctity-of-life arguments,[71] and various applications of quality-of-life judgments.[72] Whatever their form, arguments for obligatory treatment reflect an evolution in societal understanding of the capacity for meaningful life with Down syndrome or other physical disabilities from that which infected the decision-making process in the Johns Hopkins cases depicted in the film "Who Should Survive?"[73] Even as the Baby Doe Rules were being promulgated, clinicians of all stripes had a newfound awareness that children with Down syndrome and spinal defects could go on to live meaningful adult lives. The change in societal attitudes is further reflected in clinical practice where it is now "unheard of for an infant to have standard treatment withheld simply because the child has Down Syndrome, or spina bifida, another common birth defect."[74]

The harder question, and the one that is unresolved within bioethics, is when, if ever, is treatment obligatory for extremely premature newborns? Unlike the original Baby Doe infants – newborns with Down syndrome or spinal defects and secondary but correctable

[69] Richard A. Mccormick, *To Save or Let Die:The Dilemma of Modern Medicine*, 229(2) JAMA 172 (1974).

[70] Robertson, *supra* note 29.

[71] Mccormick, *supra* note 69.

[72] Arthur Caplan & Cynthia Cohen, *Standards of Judgment for Treatment, in* LIFE CHOICES: A HASTINGS CENTER INTRODUCTION TO BIOETHICS 214 (Georgetown University Press 2d ed. 2000).

[73] *E.g.,* Antommaria, *supra* note 4.

[74] Norman Fost, *quoted in* Christopher Mims, *The Pillow Angel Case–Three Bioethicists Weigh In,* http://www.scientificamerican.com/article.cfm?id=the-pillow-angel-case-th.

life-threatening conditions that could be effectively ameliorated with treatment – extremely premature newborns have complex medical needs and highly uncertain prognoses. Even with aggressive medical treatment, many extremely premature newborns will die and others survive with profound cognitive and physical disabilities that may cause life-long physical suffering and prevent meaningful human interaction.[75] Bioethics takes seriously the suffering of newborns caused by aggressive technology. It counters narratives of the miracle babies with the all-too-common story of the long-suffering, long-dying baby. One of its paradigm cases is that of "Baby Andrew."[76] Andrew was born in the early 1980s at twenty-five weeks gestation. At that time, 95 percent of babies born at that stage of prematurity died. Despite evidence that he would almost certainly die, and against his parents' wishes, Andrew's doctors treated him aggressively over the course of six months for brain hemorrhage, respiratory failure, necrosis of the right leg, gangrene, rickets, multiple bone fractures, retolental fibrosis, blindness, and pulmonary hypertension. The aggressive treatment did not save Andrew but it did cause him excruciating suffering, which was detailed by his parents in a book entitled *The Long Dying of Baby Andrew*. Bioethicists took note, and the case became central to the decades-long search for an ethical framework that appropriately protects imperiled newborns from the harm of overtreatment, while ensuring that those newborns that could go on to have meaningful lives are not wrongfully denied life-saving treatment.[77] The search is

[75] "At the margins of viability, twenty three to twenty four weeks gestation, mortality occurs in half or more of the cases, and survivors often have significant physical and mental handicaps, including blindness, hydrocephalus, cerebral palsy, limited use of language, and learning disabilities." Robertson, *supra* note 29, at 35.

[76] *See* ROBERT & PEGGY STINSON, THE LONG DYING OF BABY ANDREW (Little Brown & Co. 1983).

[77] *See generally,* THOMAS H. MURRAY & ARTHUR L. CAPLAN, WHICH BABIES SHALL LIVE? HUMANISTIC DIMENSIONS OF THE CARE OF IMPERILED NEWBORNS (Humana Press 1985); Caplan & Cohen, *supra* note 72, at 6–19; Charity Scott, *Baby Doe at Twenty-Five*, 25 GA. ST. U. L. REV. 801 et seq. (2009) (exploring the modern-day

not over. Devising an ethically appropriate framework for medical decision making about extremely premature newborns is complicated by the uncertainty surrounding their care and long-term prospects. That uncertainty is morally significant to bioethicists, but its implications are a matter of intense debate.

The case of Sydney Miller brought to the fore the problematic uncertainty faced by parents and providers who must make medical decisions in cases of extremely premature newborns. The Texas Supreme Court's decision in *Miller* ended a five-year period in Texas (that began with the jury's verdict in *Miller*) during which medical providers faced the prospect of lawsuits and huge damage awards if they saved the lives of extremely premature newborns against the wishes of parents. In its ruling, the court transferred to physicians the power to provide treatment regardless of parental assessment of the quality of life, and raised stark questions about notions of suffering and the centrality of quality-of-life assessments in protecting the best interests of children.

Prominent bioethicists John Robertson and George Annas published separate articles on the Miller case.[78] Although they employed different analytic frameworks, both Robertson and Annas supported the Court's decision in favor of the hospital and the decision to resuscitate. In this respect, at least some bioethicists aligned with the disability community.

On the question of whether treatment is required immediately after birth, John Robertson's position is absolute: resuscitate fist and ask the hard questions later. He wrote:

[P]arents' directions not to resuscitate at birth should not be given effect until a medical assessment of the child's condition and

significance of the "Baby Doe Rules" twenty-five years after their enactment); GEOFFREY MILLER, EXTREME PREMATURITY: PRACTICES, BIOETHICS, & THE LAW (Cambridge University Press 2006) (examining the contentious concerns associated with clinical administration of premature neonates).

[78] *Id.;* Robertson, *supra* note 29; Annas, *supra* note 65.

prognosis justifying nontreatment has been made. Doctors and hospitals should be legally free to have neonatologists resuscitate and treat for a limited period after birth to assess the child's capacity regardless of parental consent or orders not to resuscitate. Under this standard, the initial medical response in the *Miller* case – resuscitation at birth if the child is alive – was reasonable.[79]

He explains that a rule requiring resuscitation of all newborns is necessary to "uphold the general principle that all children born alive are to be treated equally regardless of disability,"[80] but he also recognizes that competing concerns for parental autonomy weigh against the equal-treatment principle. In Robertson's view, parental autonomy "is not so robust that parents have the right to deny a disabled child the medical resources necessary for life regardless of the child's interests in living or ability to interact with others."[81]

Annas is more circumspect about initial treatment decisions. He ultimately concludes the "split second" decision to resuscitate Sidney Miller was reasonable. However, Annas is more ready than Robertson to support parental decisions against resuscitation made before birth so long as the medical reasonableness of the decision is confirmed by a neonatologist exercising medical judgment after birth.[82] In this respect, Annas's view on the initial resuscitation decision is consistent with the "individualized approach" endorsed by a special Hastings Center project on neonatal ethics. The individualized approach encourages discussion among parents and physicians and informed decision making prior to birth based on predelivery assessment of gestational age and weight. Then, after the birth of the infant, the parents and physicians jointly reevaluate the infant's prognosis as compared to the predicted one so that parents can make an informed decision based on their

---

[79] Robertson, *supra* note 29, at 38.
[80] *Id.* at 36.
[81] *Id.* at 38.
[82] Annas, *supra* note 65, at 2121.

child's best interest. When the parent can make an informed decision against resuscitation on the spot, and the decision is not medically unreasonable, parental wishes control. Where time is needed to make the evaluation, an override of parental wishes is justified. The Hastings Center report explains that "an individualized approach that seeks a high degree of moral probability rather than certainty can be embraced with some confidence. As time goes on, physicians do gain more information about the probable outcome for very premature babies, though of course in an individual case they can be wrong. The possibility of error should, we believe, be reason for caution, not an excuse for mandating aggressive treatment until the bitter end."[83]

Not all bioethicists agree that the physicians were on sound moral ground when they treated Sydney Miller against her parents' wishes. William Winslade, the bioethicist who served as the expert on the Miller case, reevaluated the case in 2009 and concluded:

[I]t was ethically permissible for the Millers, on the basis of the information provided by their physicians, to choose not to have a neonatologist present and not to attempt resuscitation or LST. I think it was also ethically permissible for the physicians to accept the Millers' decision. The Millers did not want to put their unborn child at risk for the predicted disabilities, pain, and suffering that did in fact ensue. They relied in good faith on what indeed was reliable information and a prediction about outcomes. Given the uncertainty of survival and the probability of severe disability, it was reasonable and responsible for the Millers to opt for no resuscitation which they understood to be "heroic measures."

However, if the Millers had listened carefully to their physicians and then after deliberation said, "Well, if our baby is born alive, we want you to resuscitate her at birth," that would also have been ethically permissible. The Millers might have based such a decision on vitalism, religious faith, hope, or gambling against the odds that she would not suffer severe impairments. If the Millers had chosen

---

[83] Caplan & Cohen, *supra* note 72, at 13.

resuscitation at birth, it would have been medically and ethically obligatory for a neonatologist to be present.[84]

Thus, Winslade advocates that treatment decisions be individualized and contextualized, and emphasizes the right of parents to make the decisions.[85]

Similarly, ethicist Loretta Kopelman has forcefully advocated against the view that maximal treatments cannot be withheld or withdrawn unless an infant is dying or comatose.[86] Kopelman articulates a flexible, individualized version of the best-interests standard that employs a benefit/burden analysis and allows a surrogate to choose comfort care rather than life-sustaining treatment for a patient, including a newborn, who is experiencing pain and suffering.

Where bioethicists and disability experts appear to part ways completely is about the scope of parental power to terminate treatment for those extremely premature infants who survive birth but face life with profound disabilities. Unlike the disability advocates who rail against decisions to terminate treatment based on an infant's perceived quality of life, bioethicists employ a number of ethical frameworks that necessarily rest on quality-of-life assessments to define when treatment can be terminated. Annas and Robertson posit two such frameworks to argue that after the initial crisis of birth, Sydney's parents should have been permitted to terminate or withhold life-saving treatment once it became apparent that even if she did survive, she would live with profound cognitive and physical disabilities.

Robertson and Annas both distinguish treatment decisions made before or at birth from those made in the NICU during the weeks

---

[84] Winslade, *supra* note 48, at 945.

[85] See also, Kenneth Kipnis, *Harm and Uncertainty in Newborn Intensive Care*, 28 THEORETICAL MEDICINE AND BIOETHICS 393 (2007) (arguing for deference to parental choices).

[86] Symposium, *Baby Doe at Twenty-Five*, 25 GA. ST. U. L. REV. 801 (2009) (discussing ethical perspectives on the Baby Doe Rules).

following the birth of an extremely premature infant. Although they supported the override of parental choice at Sydney Miller's birth, Robertson and Annas would have given her parents legal and moral authority to decide against treatment once it became clear that she had suffered a devastating brain hemorrhage. As a conceptual matter, Robertson would place stricter limitations on parental discretion than would Annas.

Robertson argues that after resuscitation and evaluation, parents have the presumptive right to make decisions against treatment for an infant if the infant "lacks or is reasonably certain to lack the mental capacity for symbolic interaction or relationship."[87] In other words, Robertson's view is that treatment can and should be obligatory regardless of parental consent whenever the child possesses a minimal level of cognitive ability.

Robertson's view is a variant of the relational potential standard proposed in 1974 by theologian and bioethicist Robert McCormick and advocated by bioethicists Arthur Caplan and Cynthia Cohen.[88] The position incorporates the child's best interest standard supported by many bioethicists,[89] and adopted by the President's Commission in 1983.[90] The child's best interests standard holds that an appropriate ethical framework for imperiled newborn cases is one that "focuses exclusively on the interests of imperiled children, not the interests of

---

[87] Robertson, *supra* note 29, at 38.

[88] Caplan & Cohen, *supra* note 72.

[89] *See, e.g.*, Paris et al., *supra* note 19 at 81 ("There is now strong consensus in the medical, legal, and ethical literature that it is the best interests of the infant – not the desires of parents or the determination of the physician – that must prevail in the care of newborns.... Translated into practice, this means that if the burden on the infant is overwhelmingly bleak, as is true in the presence of a lethal abnormality, there is no obligation to subject the infant to further procedures.").

[90] President's Commission for the Study of Ethical Problems in Medicine and Biomedical Research, *Deciding to Forego Life-Sustaining Treatment* (1983) 197–230, http://www.bioethics.georgetown.edu/pcbe/reports/past_commissions/deciding_to_forego_tx.pdf.

their families or of the community as a whole."[91] The focus on the interests of the child requires that life-preserving treatment be administered to infants except in three situations: "when (1) the infant is dying, (2) treatment is medically contraindicated, ..., and (3) continued life would be worse for the infant than an early death."[92] The third condition necessitates quality-of-life judgments but consciously seeks to prevent adult decision makers from imposing their own personal values about life with disability by requiring that the quality-of-life assessment be made from the infant's point of view.[93] From the infant's point of view, the interests that matter are life and comfort; thus a decision maker could consider severe and intractable pain that would be experienced by the infant in determining whether to terminate treatment.

The relational potential standard would also allow adult decision makers to withhold life-saving treatment in a fourth situation: when a child is so neurologically impaired as to lack any potential for human relationships. The argument is that when a child lacks capacity for human relationships, the child's only interest is to avoid suffering. In such cases, treatment can be discontinued without harming the infant. Robertson struggles to define what it means "to have potential for human relationships."[94] He explains:

> Under such a standard, treatment would still be required for premature infants who have suffered or might suffer intraventricular hemorrhaging and severe brain damage because such infants are still capable of some interaction with others. Despite their severe physical and mental disabilities, such children do respond to stimuli and appear to experience pleasure when touched or rubbed – arguably a form of "interaction or relationship" because it leads to further touching or rubbing. In the *Miller* case, for

[91] Caplan & Cohen, *supra* note 72, at 31.
[92] *Id.* at 15.
[93] *Id.*
[94] Robertson, *supra* note 29, at 37.

example, there was evidence that Sidney smiled and responded favorably to physical contact.

If interaction or relationship is taken to mean the human capacity for meaningful symbolic interaction or communication, then some greater mental capacity would be required than such severely damaged children have. If one lacks altogether the capacity for meaningful symbolic interaction, then one lacks the characteristics that make humans the object of moral duties beyond that of not imposing gratuitous suffering on them. We value humans in large part because of the capacity to have conscious interests and experiences, including meaningful symbolic interaction with others.[95]

Thus Robertson would have allowed Sydney Miller's parents to refuse aggressive interventions once it was established that she was never likely to have the minimum cognitive ability for symbolic relationships.

Annas joins many bioethicists who would give parents more latitude to determine whether to terminate treatment for imperiled newborns: "Giving parents the right to make treatment decisions for their extremely premature newborns in the NICU not only is consistent with basic legal principles, but also accords with good medical practice."[96] Parents should make decisions after they discuss the child's condition with the treatment team to determine if their therapeutic goals are reasonable or achievable: "Defining a therapeutic goal depends on a combination of the medical prognosis, the family's circumstances, and the quality of life of the child, and no one-size-fits-all legal or medical rule is possible."[97] Rather, says Annas, parents must engage in a benefit/ burden analysis, which is inherently ambiguous. The important thing, says Annas, is "clear, regular, and honest discussions with the parents about the health of and prognosis for their child, as well as trials of therapy that have realistic stopping points."[98]

[95] *Id.*
[96] Annas, *supra* note 65, at 2122.
[97] *Id.*
[98] *Id.* at 2123.

Annas's inclusion of "family circumstance" as a factor to be considered in setting therapeutic goals suggests he joins those ethicists who argue that parental interests may appropriately be considered in determining a child's best interests. Among the most adamant of this school are Hilde Lindemann and Marian Verkerk, who published an article defending the framework employed in the Netherlands to allow doctors to euthanize certain babies. The Groningen Protocol allows doctors to end the life of three categories of babies: (1) those who have no chance of survival; (2) those who may survive after a period of intensive treatment but face such a grim future that it is "judged to be better off dead than forced to endure the only kind of life it can ever have";[99] and (3) babies with an extremely poor prognosis "who do not depend on technology for physiologic stability and whose suffering is severe, sustained, and cannot be alleviated."[100] In defending the protocol as morally justified in the Dutch context for "tragically impaired infants," Lindemann and Verkerk sharply criticized the American view that "family members must not consider anything but the interests of the patient":[101]

> When parents make decisions about the treatment of babies who are very badly damaged …, they do not and should not decide on the basis of some impersonal and impartial best-interests standard. They do it out of an intermingling of selves that marks this particular baby as nested within these particular parents, uniquely situated to judge what quality of life their child would find unacceptable.[102]

It is important, they argue, to "take parents' interests, wishes, and fears very seriously."[103] From this perspective, parents should have wide deference in the face of medical uncertainty.

---

[99] Hilde Lindemann & Marian Verkerk, *Ending the Life of a Newborn: The Groningen Protocol*, 38 HASTINGS CENTER REPORT 42, 44 (2008).

[100] *Id.* (citing E. Verhagen & P. J. J. Sauer, *End-of-Life Decisions in Newborns: An Approach from the Netherlands*, 116 PEDIATRICS 736, 736–9 [2005]).

[101] *Id.* at 50.

[102] *Id.* at 49.

[103] *Id.* at 50.

Certain academic bioethicists take the argument for parental autonomy to an extreme. Most notorious are utilitarians Peter Singer and Helga Kuhse who argued in their 1985 book, *Should the Baby Live: The Problem of Handicapped Infants*, that "some infants with severe disabilities should be killed"[104] and proposed that it be made legal to kill a child within approximately the first twenty-eight days of life. Although Singer's position has little support, and no traction whatsoever outside academia, it is included here because of the response it gets from the disability community. The following is a sample from Singer's 1993 book, *Practical Ethics*:

A Bioethical View: When It's Right to Kill an Infant

Suppose that a newborn baby is diagnosed as a hemophiliac. The parents, daunted by the prospect of bringing up a child in this condition, are not anxious for him to live. Could euthanasia be defended here? Our first reaction may well be a firm 'no', for the infant can be expected to have a life that is worth living, even if not quite as good as that of a normal baby. The "prior existence" version of utilitarianism supports this judgment. The infant exists. His life can be expected to contain a positive balance of happiness over misery. To kill him would deprive him of this positive balance of happiness. Therefore it would be wrong.

On the "total" version of utilitarianism, however, we cannot reach a decision on the basis of this information alone. The total view makes it necessary to ask whether the death of the hemophiliac infant would lead to the creation of another being who would not otherwise have existed. In other words, if the hemophiliac child is killed, will his parents have another child whom they would not have if the hemophiliac child lives? If they would, is the second child likely to have a better life than the one killed?

Often it will be possible to answer both these questions affirmatively. When the death of a disabled infant will lead to the birth of another infant with better prospects of a happy life, the total amount of

---

[104] HELGA KUHSE & PETER SINGER, SHOULD THE BABY LIVE? THE PROBLEM OF HANDICAPPED INFANTS (Oxford University Press 1985).

happiness will be greater if the disabled infant is killed. The loss of happy life for the first infant is outweighed by the gain of a happier life for the second.

Therefore, if killing the hemophiliac infant has no adverse effects on the others, it would, according to the total view, be right to kill him. The main point is clear: killing a disabled infant is not morally equivalent to killing a person. Very often it is not wrong at all.[105]

Singer's argument depends entirely on subjective assessments about an individual's prospects for quality of life. Those assessments do not need to be based on evidence or experience.

The lack of analytic rigor and potential for biased decision making that plagues Singer's argument troubles certain clinical ethicists who demand that ethical analysis be supported by good evidence. These same ethicists also reject frameworks that depend on imprecise or ambiguous terminology, such as "best interests of the patient," "tragically impaired infants," and "unbearable suffering."[106] They argue that the better ethical reasoning buttresses the legal removal of decision-making discretion entirely from parents and physicians in favor of a rule that says it is "always *unreasonable* to prefer (and choose) the peaceful death of a peri-viable newborn unless the case fits into some pre-categorized form of futility."[107] This evidence-based approach to ethics has traction in institutions that deny treatment to certain premature babies based on their gestational age,[108] and is defended by some bioethicists.[109]

---

[105] PETER SINGER, PRACTICAL ETHICS 185–186, 191 (Cambridge University Press 1999).

[106] Frank A. Chervenak & Laurence B. McCullough, *Are Their Babies Different from Ours?*, Letter to the Editor, 38 HASTINGS CENTER REPORT 6 (2008).

[107] Sayeed, *supra* note 21, at 604.

[108] *See, e.g.*, J. W. Kaempf et al., *Counseling Pregnant Women Who May Deliver Extremely Premature Infants*, 123(6) PEDIATRICS 1509 (June 2009) (describing experiences "implementing consensus medical staff guidelines used for counseling pregnant women threatening extremely premature birthweights" and providing "an account of family preferences and the immediate outcome of their infants").

[109] Ken Kipnis, *Harm and Uncertainty in Newborn Intensive Care*, 28 THEOR. MED. BIOETH. 393, 393–12 (2007).

If this primer on the bioethical perspectives on cases involving extremely premature newborns proves anything, it is this: Bioethical argument about the treatment of imperiled newborns is complex and nuanced. For most points, there is a counterpoint, and the range of proposed analytic frameworks is overwhelming. As discussed, some of those frameworks turn on findings of futility, a concept expressly incorporated in the Baby Doe Rules. The next case demonstrates the complexity of applying and defining futility as a useful concept for medical decision making.

II. THE CASE OF EMILIO GONZALEZ

Emilio Gonzalez was born in Austin, Texas, at thirty-five weeks gestation on November 3, 2005.[110] In the weeks following his birth, Emilio started exhibiting neurological abnormalities. His doctors diagnosed Emilio with Leigh's disease – a rare, progressive neurometabolic disorder that collapses the central nervous system. As happened in Emilio's case, Leigh's disease usually presents in very young infants. The first signs are often poor sucking ability, loss of head control, and generalized weakness. In addition, there may be loss of appetite, vomiting, irritability, continuous crying, and seizures. As the disorder progresses, those afflicted experience episodes of lactic acidosis (the body becomes more acidic than usual), leading to respiratory and kidney function impairment. There is no definitive test for Leigh's disease. It is diagnosed by the steady progression of symptoms, and it is uniformly fatal. Treatment options are limited. Thiamine and Vitamin B1 may help slow the destruction of the central nervous system – some children have survived as many as six or seven years with Leigh's – but most infants who are afflicted die by age three.

---

[110] Harris C. Jacobs, *The Texas Advance Directives Act – Is It a Good Model?*, 33 SEMINARS IN PERINATOLOGY 384, 388 (2009).

By his first birthday, it was clear that Emilio's case was progressing rapidly. Emilio had significant "global developmental delay and decreased muscle tone and reflexes."[111] He was blind and deaf, unable to hold up his head, and had poor sucking ability. On December 27, 2006, Emilio was admitted to the pediatric intensive care unit at Children's Hospital of Austin with a collapsed lung. There, he was placed on a ventilator to help him breathe, and a nasogastric tube was inserted to allow the administration of nutrition and hydration. Without the support of the ventilator, Emilio would die within hours. Even with the ventilator support, his neurological status continued to worsen as his brain atrophied. It was clear to his caretakers that Emilio was dying, and in pain. He was semicomatose, unable to move his arms or legs, or to empty his bladder. He was having frequent seizures, and providers had "great difficulty keeping his lungs inflated."[112]

After several months of aggressive treatment, the health care team treating Emilio determined that his condition was irreversible and that continued treatment would only "serve to prolong his suffering without the possibility of cure." They felt that "the burdens associated with his current care plan clearly outweigh[ed] its benefits" to Emilio, and that his "aggressive treatment plan ... amount[ed] to a nearly constant assault on Emilio's fundamental human dignity."[113] In discussions with Emilio's mother, the treatment team recommended that aggressive treatment, including mechanical ventilation, be discontinued in favor of comfort care.

---

[111] Seton HealthCare Network Neonatal/Pediatric Ethics Committee, *Ethics Committee Report Form for Patient Emilio Lee Gonzales* 2 (2007), *available at* http://www.northcountrygazette.org/documents/PediEthicsCommitteeReport.doc.

[112] Lifeethics.org, *Leigh's Disease (Long Post on End of Life and Baby Emilio Gonzales)*, March 19, 2007, *available at* http://www.lifeethics.org//2007/03/leighs-disease-long-post-on-end-of-life.html.

[113] June Maxam, *Saving Emilio*, N. Country Gazette, March 18, 2007, *available at* http://www.northcountrygazette.org/articles/2007/031807SavingEmilio.html.

Emilio's mother, Catarina, refused to consent to the withdrawal of life-sustaining treatment. Instead, she demanded that providers continue the aggressive treatment plan. She insisted that Emilio's providers maintain him until "Jesus takes him," and that "every moment of life he has to spend with her is of inestimable value."[114] Treatment continued, as did discussions between Emilio's providers and his mother. They could not reach consensus about Emilio's condition and care plan. In February 2007, Catarina met with the hospital's Neonatal/ Pediatric Ethics Committee. Again, no consensus could be reached. The providers were determined to terminate treatment they felt was harming Emilio. His mother was fighting to make sure he got that treatment to extend his life. There was a true impasse.

At that point, the hospital invoked the Texas Advance Directives Act (TADA).[115] TADA authorized it to withdraw life support if an ethics committee determined that further life support was medically inappropriate, and the hospital was unable to transfer the patient to another provider willing to comply with the surrogate's treatment request in the ten days following notice of the committee's decision. Emilio was clearly qualified under the statutory definition. His condition was terminal, which is defined under the statute as "an incurable condition caused by injury, disease, or illness that according to reasonable medical judgment will produce death within six months."[116] His condition was also "irreversible," which is defined by Texas law as "a condition, injury or illness:

(A) that may be treated but is never cured or eliminated;
(B) that leaves a person unable to care for or make decisions for the person's own self; and

---

[114] Verified Complaint at Ex. B to Ex. 1, Gonzales v. Seton Family of Hospitals, No. A07CA267 (W.D. Tex. filed Apr. 4, 2007), at 27.
[115] Texas Advance Directives Act
[116] Texas Health and Safety Code § 166.001 (13).

(C) that, without life-sustaining treatment provided in accordance with the prevailing standard of medical care, is fatal."[117]

The question in Emilio's case was whether continued treatment was medically appropriate.

The hospital provided Catarina with the statutorily required notice that a meeting with the ethics committee would be held on March 9. She was invited to attend, which she did with her legal advisors and several family members. Emilio's attending physician testified as to Emilio's medical condition and clinical condition. Members of the treatment team noted that they had contacted other children's hospitals in Texas, but none were willing to accept Emilio as a patient. Members of the ethics committee, Catarina, and others in attendance asked questions of the treatment team, and the committee convened in private to deliberate.

On March 12, the hospitals' ethics committee provided Emilio's mother with written notice that she had ten days to find another facility or physician to treat the child, during which time Emilio would be given life-sustaining treatment. The notice further stated: "If a provider cannot be found who is willing to give the requested treatment within the 10-day period, then all aggressive care measures (including, without limitation, the use of the ventilator) may be withdrawn and the patient's treatment plan may be modified to allow for only comfort care measures."[118]

Unable to find a facility willing to admit Emilio, Catarina Gonzalez filed the first of two lawsuits against the Children's Hospital and individual providers. She was able to convince a judge to extend the time she had to find a facility willing to accept Emilio. She could find none. She then filed a second lawsuit against the hospital seeking a declaration that the Texas law was unconstitutional and demanding that

---

[117] Texas Health and Safety Code § 116.001 (a).
[118] Maxam, *supra* note 113, at 2.

life-sustaining treatment be continued. While these suits were pending, clinical staff continued to provide the treatment that they considered medically inappropriate. The treatments did not save Emilio. He died in his mother's arms on May 19, 2007, before the judge in the second lawsuit ruled in the case.

A. Views from the Disability Community

Just as they did in Sydney Miller's case, disability advocates demanded aggressive treatment for Emilio Gonzalez. Unlike in the Miller case, however, where the advocates questioned the right of parents to make medical decisions for children, advocates rested their arguments in Emilio's case, at least in part, on Catarina Gonzalez's right to make decisions for her own child. For example, Diane Coleman, President of Not Dead Yet, remarked:

> [T]he hospital and the doctors are going against the stated wishes of the legally responsible person, the mother, who has stated her opposition to their "godlike" position. The disability rights movement was founded on the fundamental concepts of "choice and control." Our medical diagnosis shouldn't allow the medical community to override our wishes or the wishes of our legally authorized representative.[119]

Coleman also objected to the lack of legal process provided the Gonzalez family by TADA: "A person on death row in Texas gets more protections than the child in Austin is allowed by Texas' 'futile care' law. The hospital ethics committee has met and the 10-day death clock is ticking. Ten days and you're dead!"[120] At the very least, Coleman argued, Emilio's mother should have been afforded a court hearing before her child's life-saving treatment was withdrawn.[121]

[119] *Id.*
[120] *Id.*
[121] *Id.*

A letter written by a feminist disability rights group to the governor of Texas during the final days of Emilio Gonzalez's life also framed the issue in terms of parental rights:

> Dear Governor Perry,
>
> This coming Friday, 23 March 2007, 16 month old Emilio Gonzalez, against the wishes of his mother, is going to be taken off the respirator that is keeping him alive. We, the undersigned individuals and organizations, join disability rights activists and feminist disability rights activists across the country in denouncing this action as cruel and inhumane.
>
> Under the provisions of The Texas Futile Care Law, the doctors treating Emilio for Leigh's Disease have overridden the wishes of his mother, Catarina Gonzalez, that he be given more time to live. With the backing of the hospital's ethics committee, doctors have determined that treatment is "medically futile" and that if another hospital cannot be found for Emilio by Friday, then they will remove his ventilator and feeding tube, which will result in his death.
>
> It is not the severity of Emilio's illness that is at issue here. Rather, we are opposed to the state-sanctioned removal of Emilio's life support and the violation of his human and civil rights and protections. We also join his mother, Catarina Gonzalez, in her condemnation of doctors "godlike position," and believe her fight for the right of Emilio to live is life-sustaining and life-affirmative. Counter to the perspective of doctors, we do not believe it is undignifying to be on life support.[122]

The feminist disability advocates were part of a large coalition of state and national disability rights groups that intervened in the case to provide legal support and draw media attention to the plight of the Gonzalez family. The advocacy was intense and hostile. A bioethicist who worked in the Austin area during Emilio's hospitalization told me

---

[122] Posting of Amber FRIDA to Feminist Response in Disability Activism (F.R.I.D.A.), http://fridanow.blogspot.com/2007/03/online-petition-for-emilio-gonzalez.html (March 20, 2007, 20:28 EST).

❀

in a personal conversation that the activists were "out of control," venting anger at the doctors, at the ethics committee, and at bioethicists who support TADA.

The angry reaction to application of TADA in Emilio's case reflects an abiding distrust of medically based policies that shorten the lives of people with disabilities that permeates disability scholarship. Cases like Emilio's are commonly referred to as "futility cases." In contrast to run-of-the-mill "end-of-life" cases, which typically involve an effort by a patient or patient's surrogate to stop or prevent treatment, futility cases involve a refusal by a medical provider to provide care sought by the patient or patient's surrogate based on an assertion that the care sought would not achieve reasonable therapeutic goals. Futility is, in a sense, the physician's trump card. Physicians are under no ethical obligation to provide futile care,[123] and as a practical matter deny requested care on futility grounds every day. Some states have specific laws, and some institutions specific policies, that exempt doctors from providing care that is ineffective or inappropriate.[124] Most do not. Where there is no law or policy in place, the meaning of futility, and the application of futility as a tool for decision making, varies widely from hospital to hospital and even physician to physician. Laws like TADA, the Texas law at play in Emilio's case, attempt to impose some process on futility determinations. More importantly, they give physicians legal cover when they refuse to provide desired treatment. They also ensure patients and families are notified before life support is withdrawn on futility grounds.

[123] "Physicians are not ethically obligated to deliver care that, in their best professional judgment, will not have a reasonable chance of benefiting their patients." American Medical Association, *AMA Policy on End-of-Life Care*, Opinion E-2.035 Futile Care, *available at* http://www.ama-assn.org/ama/pub/physician-resources/medical-ethics/about-ethics-group/ethics-resource-center/end-of-life-care/ama-policy-end-of-life-care.shtml.

[124] Va. Code Ann. § 54.1–2990; N.M. Stat. Ann. § 24–7A-7; Md. Health-General Code Ann. § 5–611; Cal. Prob. Code § 4735; Tex. Health & Safety Code Ann. § 166.046 (Vernon 2007).

❦

Futility laws and policies make disability experts very nervous. The belief is that "[f]utility policies are a real and present threat to people with disabilities today – offering concrete proof, it seems, that activists' worries are real: that life with serious disabilities and costly care is indeed considered an economic burden – and the solution, from the healthcare system's standpoint, is death. Which is called 'withdrawal of treatment' or 'withholding treatment.'"[125] Inherent in the disability critique of futility are three concerns explored in more depth by disability scholars: physician bias, the role of money, and equal protection under the law.

Disability scholars lament the role physician bias necessarily plays in futility judgments. Their research suggests that medicine's own "horror of handicap"[126] works to disadvantage people with disabilities when they are the subject of inherently subjective assessment of futility. Scholar James Werth, for example, reviewed the available data on the role of physician bias in futility judgments and concluded that futility "poses the largest threat to persons with disabilities,"[127] more significant even than the assisted suicide laws that have long garnered the attention of disability advocates. With futility, Werth explains, "the power of the physician is maximized and that of the person with disabilities and her or his advocates is minimized,"[128] thus allowing the values of the physician to "determine whether the person lives or dies."[129]

---

[125] *Why Disability Rights Activists Oppose Physician Assisted Suicide*, RAGGED EDGE ONLINE, Jan. 18, 2006, http://www.raggededgemagazine.com/departments/closerlook/000749.html.

[126] Martha A. Field, *Killing "the Handicapped" – Before and After Birth*, 16 Harv. Women's L. J. 79, 88 (1993).

[127] James L. Werth, *Concerns about Decisions Related to Withholding/Withdrawing Life-sustaining Treatment and Futility for Persons with Disabilities*, 16 J. DISABILITY POL'Y STUD. 31, 33 (2005).

[128] *Id.* (citing Ann Alpers & Bernard Lo, *When is CPR futile?*, 273 J.A.M.A. 156–8 [1995]).

[129] *Id.* at 31.

According to Werth, compelling evidence associates provider's beliefs about life with disability with their clinical futility judgments to the detriment of people with disabilities. Previous studies have already shown that physicians make negative social judgments about disability.[130] After reviewing the data, scholar Carol Gill concluded that "health professionals significantly underestimate the quality of life of persons with disabilities compared with the actual assessments made by people with disabilities themselves. In fact, the gap between health professionals and people with disabilities in evaluating life with disability is consistent and stunning."[131]

According to Werth, efforts to remove value judgments from futility decisions do not work. Werth reviews a series of studies that show that "even when decision trees and policies are in place in hospitals," or when futility decisions are cloaked in medical language and clinical speak, futility decisions are not consistent in practice.[132] One of the studies he reviewed showed that in almost a third of cases, "immobility was a predictor of qualitative futility."[133] In another, the researchers noted that "physicians who project their own values onto their judgments of what quality of life is not worth living may make inconsistent, arbitrary, and unfair decisions. They also noted the link between futility and resource allocation. Thus, even if safeguards are in place, the physicians' values are the deciding factor."[134] Although many medical decisions may be affected by values, Werth argues, the fact is that futility decisions may be based on ableism or another form of prejudice to a greater degree than any other so-called medical decision, because the decision-making power is in the hands of people proven time and again to act on unproven social judgments.

---

[130] *Id.* at 32.
[131] *Id.*
[132] *Id.*
[133] *Id.* at 33.
[134] *Id.*

The potential for biased assessment of futility is especially alarming, according to disability experts, given relationship between futility and resource allocation. Disability advocates remember well Oregon's effort to ration health care. In the early 1990s, Oregon embarked on a groundbreaking effort to expand Medicaid to cover more people through a process of explicit health care rationing based on a prioritization scheme.[135] More particularly, Oregon officials engaged in a multilayered process of public discussion and surveys to create a priority list for services that should be covered. The process involved, among other things, a "Quality of Well-Being scale derived from a telephone survey ranking six functional impairments and twenty-three symptomatic conditions."[136] As it was proposed, the Oregon plan would have excluded from Medicaid coverage 122 of 709 services otherwise covered by Medicaid, based on the priority list.[137] The plan gave priority to those services "that would 'return the patient to an asymptomatic state of health'"[138] – a medical priority that does not apply to chronic conditions and permanent disabilities.

To implement the plan, Oregon sought approval from the Department of Health and Human Services, but that approval was denied in 1992 because, in the Department's view, the Plan discriminated against people with disabilities. The Department said that the Quality of Well-Being data "'quantifies stereotypic assumptions about persons with disabilities' by giving heavy weight to the responses of persons who had not experienced such conditions."[139] The danger in the Oregon plan, then, was that people whose Quality of Well-Being

---

[135] For details about the Oregon plan and the process used in its design, see the November–December 1992 Hastings Center Report, which provides both factual details and ethical analysis.

[136] Paul T. Menzel, *Oregon's Denial: Disabilities and Quality of Life*, 22 HASTINGS CENTER REP., Nov.–Dec. 1992, at 21.

[137] *Id.*

[138] Daniel M. Fox & Howard M. Leichter, *State Model: Oregon. The Ups and Downs of Oregon's Rationing Plan*, 12 HEALTH AFF., at 66, 68 (1993).

[139] Menzel, *supra* note 136, at 21.

was ranked low did not agree with the low assessment, but the assessment would nonetheless be used to limit their care. In other words, the plan was "based in substantial part on the premise that the value of the life of a person with a disability is less than the value of the life of a person without a disability."[140] That bias was deemed incompatible with the Americans with Disabilities Act's (ADA) prohibition against discrimination in the provision of health care,[141] and is thought to be at work in futility cases, where people with disabilities will be deemed "too expensive to treat."

Like the Oregon plan, futility determinations have the potential to give priority to services that would return a patient to asymptomatic health, thereby giving less importance to people with permanent disabling conditions and chronic illness. In efforts to contain costs, futility policies aggravate what disability scholars deem an alarming trend toward "restricting services" for people with disabilities. Carol Gill explains:

The notion that people with "permanent" conditions do not always merit the same type, quality, or amount of health care as less "hopeless" patients has taken root in medical training and clinical practice over the last two decades. Every week, I hear another person with a disability recount a disturbing interaction with a physician, nurse, or other health professional who clearly transmitted the view that life with a disability is inherently burdensome. It does not feel safe to have one's life in the hands of someone who views that life as unfortunate, maybe even tragic or unfair. As doctors increasingly engage in withdrawing ventilators, stopping antibiotics, and withholding food and water in cases of nonterminal disability as well as

---

[140] Fox & Leichter, *supra* note 138.

[141] For an accessible explanation of the complicated relationship between health care and the ADA, see, Sara Rosenbaum, *The Americans with Disabilities Act in a Health Care Context, in* INSTITUTE OF MEDICINE: THE FUTURE OF DISABILITY IN AMERICA 426 (Marilyn Jane Field & Alan M. Jette eds., National Academies Press 2007), *available at* http://www.ncbi.nlm.nih.gov/bookshelf/br.fcgi?book=nap11898 &part=a2001315cddd00239.

terminal illness, it is understandable that their attitudes may deteriorate toward those of us who use technology and significant human support to live.[142]

The problem of bias in the health care system is further magnified, according to Gill, by cost-saving measures.

As nurses are given more responsibilities, more monitors to tend, and less time to personally engage with patients in the managed care setting, patients with disabilities who need more time and assistance become *personae non gratae*. Arguably, health professionals have always viewed life with extensive disabilities as burdensome, given their trained commitment to health and normative functioning. However, they have never expressed it as consistently and as openly as they do now. It is as though a threshold has been lowered in the culture of health care, thus permitting freer expression of skepticism about the viability of our lives.[143]

A final disability rights argument against futility policies comes from legal experts who specialize in disability. Harvard Law Professor Martha Fields, for example, argues that "[a] statute that actively promotes the nontreatment of newborns ... violate[s] the Equal Protection Clause."[144] Although futility laws do not specifically target disabled newborns, they give doctors the power to decide on nontreatment based on a newborn's disability status. In Field's view, equal protection jurisprudence does not support such statutes because their discriminatory impact cannot be justified by the state. In her view, "more justification would be required of state discrimination against newborns with handicaps than a mere rational basis or a financial saving to the state."[145]

---

[142] Carol J. Gill, *No, We Don't Think Our Doctors Are Out to Get Us: Responding to the Straw Man Distortions of Disability Rights Arguments against Assisted Suicide*, 3 DISABILITY & HEALTH J. 31, 36 (2010).

[143] *Id.*

[144] Martha A. Field, *Killing "The Handicapped" – Before and After Birth*, 16 HAR. WOMEN'S L. J. 79, 100 (1993).

[145] *Id.*

Other legal scholars argue that the ADA prohibits the disability discrimination inherent in futility policies.[146] The ADA forbids the use of "standards, criteria, or methods of administration that have the effect of discrimination on the basis of disability."[147] Medical care clearly falls under the ADA's operation, and at least some cases hold that a person with disabilities is entitled to all the medical care that would be provided a nondisabled person, and refusal by a medical provider to honor a request for treatment can constitute discrimination under the ADA. For example, a lower court was persuaded by the ADA argument in a case involving an anencephalic baby.[148] The application of the ADA to medical treatment decisions is complicated, however, and the courts have not uniformly agreed that the consideration of disability in medical decision making can constitute illegal discrimination. Futility cases incorporating quality-of-life judgments would present the strongest case to test the viability of the legal arguments, but few such cases end up in court, and even fewer result in decisions owing to the death of the patient before an opinion is rendered.[149]

Regardless of legalities, concerns about bias and resource allocation apply to TADA. Although the qualifying criteria rule out unilateral decisions against treatment based on most disabilities, the statute allows for unilateral withdrawal based on some disabilities. Specifically, the statute allows a provider to withdraw treatment only from "qualified" patients, that is, patients with a terminal or irreversible condition. Although many disabilities are "irreversible," most are not irreversible within the meaning of the Texas statute.

---

[146] See Mary A. Crossley, *Medical Futility and Disability Discrimination*, 81 IOWA L. REV. 179, 182 (1995); Philip G. Peters, *When Physicians Black at Futile Care: Implications of the Disability Rights Laws*, 91 NW. U. L. REV. 798, 817 (1997).

[147] 42 U.S.C. § 12112(b)(3)(A).

[148] *In re* Baby K., 832 F. Supp. 1022, 1028–1029 (E.D. Va. 1993).

[149] *See, e.g.*, Betancourt v. Trinitas. Hosp., 2010 WL 3186158 (N.J. Super. Ct. App. Div. 2010).

To be considered a qualifying irreversible condition, it must be "a condition, injury, or illness:

(A) that may be treated but is never cured or eliminated;
(B) that leaves a person unable to care for or make decisions for the person's own self; and
(C) that, without life-sustaining treatment provided in accordance with the prevailing standard of medical care, is fatal."[150]

A condition like blindness or mental retardation would meet condition A but neither B nor C. On the other hand, quadraparisis with ventilator dependence or cerebral palsy with developmental impairments and a need for medically administered nutrition and hydration might meet all three. "With so broad an approach to what constitutes 'futile care,' [disability experts argue, the] current Texas law is an open invitation to withhold or withdraw life-support from patients with severe disabilities on 'quality of life' grounds"[151] as determined by providers.

Thus, TADA is subject to the disability critique, but that critique has less resonance in Emilio's case than it would, for example, if TADA had been used to justify unilateral treatment withdrawal in Sydney Miller's case. Emilio qualified because he was terminally ill, not because of a permanent but survivable disability. Because his imminent death was inevitable, questions about the quality of his life took a backseat to questions about the best care for a baby in the final days of a fatal illness and, at least potentially, about the financial cost of aggressive care (a charge denied by the Texas hospital). Questions about how to treat dying babies, and the role of money in those treatment decisions, trouble bioethicists, who vigorously debate the best course to take

---

[150] TEX. HEALTH & SAFETY CODE ANN. § 166.002(9) (Vernon 2007).
[151] National Catholic Partnership on Disability, *NCPD BOARD STATEMENT ON "FUTILE CARE"*, Aug. 22, 2008, http://www.ncpd.org/policy/church/ncpd/ statements/futilecare [hereinafter *NCPD BOARD STATEMENT*].

when there is an intractable dispute between the health care team and a patient or surrogate.

B. Views from Bioethics

Although there is widespread consensus in bioethics that physicians have no ethical obligation to provide inappropriate or futile medical care[152] – for example, a doctor can refuse to provide antibiotics to someone with a viral infection without running afoul of moral, legal, or ethical obligations – there is intense debate about what constitutes futile care, and if the concept of futility is helpful at all (the "utility of futility" debate).[153] "The futility debate began as a reaction to the widespread use of [CPR]" after studies that showed that certain groups of CPR patients "rarely survived to discharge from the hospital."[154] The question became whether it was appropriate to administer CPR to patients who were unlikely to benefit from it, and then more broadly,

---

[152] "Physicians are not ethically obligated to deliver care that, in their best professional judgment, will not have a reasonable chance of benefiting their patients." American Medical Association, *AMA Policy on End-of-Life Care*, Opinion E-2.035 Futile Care, *available at* http://www.ama-assn.org/ama/pub/physician-resources/medical-ethics/about-ethics-group/ethics-resource-center/end-of-life-care/ama-policy-end-of-life-care.shtml.

[153] For a review of the futility debate, *see* TOM L. BEAUCHAMP & JAMES F. CHILDRESS, PRINCIPLES OF BIOMEDICAL ETHICS 167–8, 220–1, 278 (6th ed., Oxford University Press 2009); Crossley, *supra* note 146 at 182–203; Judith F. Daar, *A Clash at the Bedside: Patient Autonomy v. a Physician's Professional Conscience*, 44 HASTING L. J. 1241, 1248–9 (1993); Peters, supra note 146, at 801–804.

[154] Peters, *supra* note 146, at 801. *See, e.g.*, Susanna E. Bedell et al., *Survival after Cardiopulmonary Resuscitation in the Hospital*, 309 NEW ENG. J. MED. 569 (1983); Leslie J. Blackhall, *Must We Always Use CPR?*, 317 NEW ENG. J. MED. 1281 (1987); William A. Gray et al., *Unsuccessful Emergency Resuscitation – Are Continued Efforts in the Emergency Department Justified?*, 325 NEW ENG. J. MED. 1393 (1991); George E. Taffet et al., *In-Hospital Cardiopulmonary Resuscitation*, 260 J. AM. MED. ASS'N 2069 (1988).

whether physicians had an obligation to offer other treatments that were unlikely to achieve desired results or whose benefits were outweighed by expected burdens.[155] The debate resulted in a flurry of literature; hundreds of articles, books, and position statements debate the definition and utility of futility.[156] Rather than attempt to summarize that literature here, I will touch on the definitional debate, set forth the major arguments in the utility debate, and explain more specifically how those arguments affect the bioethical response to Emilio's case.

No discussion of the bioethical perspectives on futility would be complete without some overview of the great debate that has long captivated the more conceptual bioethicists, namely about how to define the term "futility." At least three definitions of futile treatment have been advanced. The first is very narrow: A proposed treatment is futile only when "incapable of producing the desired physiologic effect in a patient."[157] Physiological futility exists only in a small number of cases,[158] such as in the antibiotic example mentioned earlier. Proponents of the narrow definition of futility assert that the limited definition is necessary to prevent providers from using subjective value judgments as reasons for withholding treatment.[159] For example, New York's Task Force on Life and the Law, a state-funded bioethics body, rejected the incorporation of quality-of-life judgments in its analysis of futility, explaining that doing otherwise would be detrimental to the trust necessary for good medical decision making.[160]

---

[155] Peters, *supra* note 146, at 801.

[156] *See, e.g.,* Crossley, *supra* note 146; Lisa L. Dahm, *Medical Futility and the Texas Medical Futility Statute: A Model to Follow or One to Avoid?,* 6 HEALTH LAW. 25 (2008); Peters *supra* note 146; Thaddeus M. Pope, *Involuntary Passive Euthanasia in U.S. Courts: Reassessing the Judicial Treatment of Medical Futility Cases,* 9 MARQ. ELDER'S ADVISOR 229 (2008).

[157] Crossley, *supra* note 146, at 187; *see also* Peters, *supra* note 146, at 802.

[158] Crossley, *supra* note 146, at 187–8.

[159] *Id.* at 188.

[160] Alicia R. Ouellette, Timothy Quill, Robert Swidler, Thaddeus Mason Pope, & Nancy Dubler, *A Conversation About End-of-Life Decisionmaking,* 14 NYSBA HEALTH L.J., Fall 2009, at 91.

A second, broader, conception of futility involves qualitative futility.[161] Under this conception, a proposed treatment is futile if the proposed treatment fails to offer "any benefit to the patient as a whole person."[162] The test is "not simply whether the treatment will produce discrete physiological effects," but whether "the patient as a person [will] achieve and appreciate a benefit from the treatment."[163] The typical example of futile treatment under this conception is the use of a gastrostomy tube for an elderly and severely demented woman.[164] "Although the tube would prolong the woman's survival, it would not provide any benefits that she [could appreciate.]"[165] Adherents to the conception of qualitative futility would argue that providers are under no obligation to offer the tube.

A third conception of futility is quantitative futility.[166] A treatment is said to be quantitatively futile when the likelihood that an intervention will benefit the patient is exceedingly poor.[167] "In other words, even if a treatment offers a possible benefit, the probability of achieving that benefit may be so slight that the treatment is properly deemed futile."[168] An example of quantitative futility would include a bone marrow transplant on a patient with otherwise incurable type of cancer that has proven effective only one in one thousand times and is extremely expensive. Some ethicists posit formulas to define quantitative futility. For example, Schneiderman and Jecker proposed a definition "that a treatment should be considered futile when it has not worked once in the last 100 times it was tried."[169]

---

[161] Crossley, *supra* note 146, at 188.
[162] *Id.*
[163] *Id.*
[164] *Id.*
[165] *Id.*
[166] *Id.*
[167] *Id.*
[168] *Id.*
[169] Howard Brody, *Medical Futility: a Useful Concept?, in* MEDICAL FUTILITY AND THE EVALUATION OF LIFE-SUSTAINING INTERVENTIONS 1, 3 (Marjorie B. Zucker & Howard D. Zucker eds., Cambridge University Press 1997).

Because a physician does not need to provide a futile treatment, it would appear critical that a definition of futility be agreed on, either as a matter of practice or by policy or law. Efforts to that effect were made in the 1990s, but as clinical practice was studied by empiricists, it became clear that such efforts did not yield uniform clinical practice.[170] Variability in futility determinations continued from institution to institution, even doctor to doctor. Recognizing the conceptual and practical difficulties in defining futility, but still convinced that physicians should be able to restrict alternatives offered to patients for the sake of physician integrity,[171] some bioethicists turned to arguments for a predefined and fair process that introduces transparency and consultation with ethics committees as a means of preventing abuses of power and protecting patients.[172] Procedural rules allow professional judgments to guide futility determinations but provide checks and balances necessary to ensure against erroneous or biased clinical judgments. The Texas statute at play in Emilio Gonzalez's case works on this model.

In enacting TADA, the Texas legislature neatly sidestepped the definitional debate by applying the concept of futility without using the word itself. That is, the Texas legislature has abandoned efforts to define the specific circumstances under which providers can refuse to provide treatment, and leaves it to a medical assessment of whether treatment is medically appropriate. TADA safeguards against abuse by requiring the use of a multitiered process whenever a provider determines that the continuation of life-sustaining treatment is medically

---

[170] *Id.* at 3.
[171] Tom Tomlinson & Howard Brody, *Futility and the Ethics of Resuscitation*, 264 J. AM. MED. ASS'N 1276, 1278–1279 (1990).
[172] Brody, *supra* note 169; Council on Ethical and Judicial Affairs, American Medical Association, *Medical Futility in End-of-Life Care*, Council Report, 281 J. AM. MED. ASS'n 937 (1999); Robert L. Fine & Thomas W. Mayo, *Resolution of Futility by Due Process: Early Experience with the Texas Advance Directives Act*, 138 Annals Internal Med. 743 (2003).

inappropriate.[173] The process gives the patient or her surrogate an opportunity to be heard by an ethics committee whenever a provider refuses to honor a patient or surrogate's request for continued life-sustaining medical treatment. Life-sustaining medical treatment must be provided during this review process.[174] However, TADA does not define "medically inappropriate" or apply standards for the ethics committee review. In this way, the statute defers entirely to professional medical judgment and allows – even anticipates – that different providers will reach different conclusions about what is medically inappropriate or futile in a particular case: "The statute does not ask the courts to make a determination of medical futility either, reserving that judgment to the medical profession checked by the process of consultation with an ethics or 'medical' committee."[175]

Because the Texas legislature used a pure process mechanism to avoid the definitional conundrum, the more important issue raised by its application in the Gonzalez case is whether the concept of futility is useful or appropriate. Given the reams of bioethical writing on the definition of futility, one might think that there was consensus in the field that the concept was a useful one, but that assumption would be mistaken. Bioethicist Art Caplan succinctly summarized the utility of futility debate as pitting the integrity of the medical professionals against the autonomy rights of patients:

> [P]roponents of the utility of futility (aptly described as futilitarians) foresee nothing less than the demise of the profession of medicine if physicians continue to provide care that is futile. According to this group, professional integrity requires that physicians know and inform their patients that evidence, expertise, and clinical experience have shown certain medical interventions in certain situations

---

[173] TEX. HEALTH & SAFETY CODE ANN. § 166.046.

[174] *Id.* §166.046(a).

[175] Robert L. Fine, *Medical Futility and the Texas Advance Directives Act of 1999*, 13 BAYLOR U. MED. CENTER PROC., April 2000, at 144, 146, *available at* http://www.ncbi.nlm.nih.gov/pmc/articles/PMC1312296/pdf/bumc0013–0144.pdf.

to be pointless, useless, and meaningless. The critics retort that integrating medical futility into clinical practice is immoral at best because physicians have no grounds for imposing their personal values about what ends are worth pursuing at what odds. Even worse, according to these critics, such decisions are misleading because statistical information about classes of patients frequently cannot be used to forecast the outcome for a particular patient.[176]

Caplan's summary correctly identifies the fundamental disagreement between proponents and opponents of futility: "[W]hether, and on what basis, a physician enjoys the moral and legal authority to make unilateral decisions limiting medical treatment deemed futile"[177] (or, under TADA, "inappropriate"[178]). The debate comes down to the relative importance of physician autonomy or professional integrity versus the "patient's right of self-determination, or autonomy" (often as expressed by surrogates).[179] "Thus, while other interests and factors figure into the debate, the fundamental conflict concerns who – patient or physician – ultimately exercises decisional authority with respect to treatment that the patient desires, but the physician judges to be nonbeneficial."[180] TADA answers the question definitively in favor of professional autonomy. That is, the Texas legislature determined that patient requests, or request of patient's surrogates, should not be sanctioned when they violate professional integrity. The resulting legislation gave providers the authority they attempted to assert in Emilio's case.

The bioethical debate over futility played out in Emilio's case. Art Caplan sided with the Hospital: "There are occasions when family members just don't get it right," he said, and "[n]o parent should have

---

[176] Arthur L. Caplan, Editorial, *Odds and Ends: Trust and the Debate over Medical Futility*, 125 ANNALS INTERNAL MED., Oct. 15, 1996, 688.

[177] Crossley, *supra* note 146, at 190.

[178] TEX. HEALTH & SAFETY CODE ANN. § 166.046(e).

[179] Crossley, *supra* note 146, at 190–1.

[180] *Id.* at 190.

the right to cause suffering to a kid in a futile situation."[181] In such cases, Caplan argues, physicians have a moral obligation to override the wishes of the family to prevent unwarranted suffering or contributing to an undignified death.[182] Lainie Ross, a pediatrician and medical ethicist at the University of Chicago, disagreed.[183] She argued that Emilio's mother, not the doctors, should be able to decide whether Emilio's life is worth living: "Who am I to judge what's a good quality of life?" she said, "[i]f this were my kid, I'd have pulled the ventilator months ago, but this isn't my kid."[184]

Harvard ethicist and physician Robert Truog also argued against unilateral withdrawal in Emilio's case.[185] Truog systematically addressed arguments that could support unilateral withdrawal in some cases to assess their strength in Emilio's case.[186] For example, he said that suffering could justify unilateral treatment in some cases, but not in Emilio's. According to Truog, suffering was not an issue in Emilio's case, because "patients who require mechanical ventilation can always be made comfortable."[187] Nor are cost considerations weighty in cases like Emilio's, argues Truog: "Even if life support were consistently denied to patients whose situations met common definitions of futility, the monetary savings would be trivial. This counterintuitive finding results from the facts that such cases are relatively rare ... and that the patients usually die within a short period, even when the requested life support is continued"[188] (as was the case for Emilio). Finally, Truog argues, "[t]he claim that continued life support for Emilio was morally

---

[181] Elizabeth Cohen, *Fight over Baby's Life Support Divides Ethicists*, CNN, April 25, 2007, http://www.cnn.com/2007/HEALTH/04/25/baby.emilio/index.html.

[182] *Id.*

[183] *Id.*

[184] *Id.*

[185] Robert D. Truog, *Tackling Medical Futility in Texas*, 357 NEW ENG. J. MED. 1 (2007).

[186] *Id.* at 1.

[187] *Id.*

[188] *Id.* at 2.

objectionable was nothing more than an assertion that the values of the clinicians were correct while those of Ms. Gonzalez were wrong."[189] The clash of values should have been resolved in favor of Emilio's mother if it could not be resolved by aggressive medication. Like many ethicists, Truog believes that most futility disputes can be resolved by mediation, although he acknowledges that some – like the one over Emilio – are simply intractable.[190] In those cases, and in Emilio's specifically, Truog argues that physicians "should seek to enhance our capacity to tolerate the choices of others, even when we believe they are wrong."[191]

III. OBSERVATIONS

The thing that strikes me most in thinking about cases like Sidney Miller's and Emilio Gonzalez's is how unconnected the theoretical debates about the meaning of disability and the utility of futility must seem to the reality experienced by Mark and Karla Miller, Catarina Gonzalez, and other parents of critically ill babies.[192] In reading the words of Catarina Gonzalez ("I love my kid so much, I have to fight for him," "That's your job – you fight for your son or your daughter. You don't let nobody push you around or make decisions for you."[193]) and the words of Mark Miller ("we opted for compassionate care ... humane care"[194]), I am reminded of the sage observations of disability

---

[189] Id.

[190] Id. at 3.

[191] Id.

[192] For a compelling account of one family's story, see Barbara Farlow, When What Seems Broken is Perfect, at www.livingwithtrisomy13.org/entry.php/381-Essays-by-Barbara-(Annie's-Mom)-Trisomy-13-Parents.

[193] Cohen, *supra* note 181.

[194] Mark Miller, *Neonatal Care for Premature Infants*, Letter to the Editor, 35 HASTINGS CENTER REP., Jan.–Feb. 2005, at 4.

scholars Philip Ferguson and Adrienne Asch that "[t]he most important thing that happens when a child with disabilities is born is that a
child is born. The most important thing that happens when a couple
becomes parents of a child with disabilities is that a couple becomes
parents."[195] The fact is, these cases are about parents of sick babies who
are doing their best to do the right thing for their children. Regardless
of how one thinks about parental autonomy, resource allocation, suffering, the good death, the sanctity of life, conceptions of disability,
disability bias, or even whether babies Sydney and Emilio should be
thought of as children with disabilities, it seems clear that even the
most loving parents would struggle to make the best decisions concerning babies facing grave, potentially fatal medical crises. To be sure,
some decisions could be infected by disability bias, as well as rescue
fantasies that will waste resources and cause real pain to babies. But
unless one adopts the strictest sanctity-of-life approach, it is hard to
argue that there is only one right answer. It is no more unreasonable
for a parent to want to prevent a child from suffering than to want to
have every moment possible with a beloved but dying baby. Decisions
of any sort are open to charges of parental selfishness – nontreatment
serves the parents by relieving them from a lifetime of caregiving obligations; decisions for aggressive treatment indulge the parent's rescue
fantasy or desire to hold on to a dying infant at the cost of his pain and
suffering. They are also defensible. The cases are complicated on so
many levels that they do not lend themselves to formulaic solutions.

The Texas solution in both *Miller* and *Gonzalez* was to rely on
the professional judgment of doctors. In the Miller case, that meant
allowing doctors to resuscitate in the moments following birth against
the express wishes of the parents. In the Gonzalez case, that meant
allowing doctors to terminate treatment against the express wishes of

---

[195] Philip M. Ferguson, *Mapping the Family: Disability Studies and the Exploration of
Parental Response to Disability, in* HANDBOOK OF DISABILITY STUDIES 373, 375
(Gary L. Albrecht et al. eds., Sage Publications, Inc. 2001).

the mother (although Emilio died before the decision to terminate was implemented). Texas may have strong arguments for trusting doctors to exercise professional judgment – doing so protects professional integrity, guards against wasteful misuse of limited resources, and helps minimize moral distress of health care providers forced to participate in treatment protocols they find morally objectionable – but assurances that we can and should trust doctors to exercise professional judgment based on training, experience, and (presumably) sound verifiable evidence and best practices is small comfort to disability experts. In fact, the argument that medical judgment is an objective, reliable measure that can be counted on to ensure against disability bias runs directly counter to the teaching of disability scholars. And it is the perceived failure of medicine and bioethics to take seriously the evidence of disability bias in decision making by medical professionals that has given rise to the "toxic and contentious environment"[196] that surrounds many bioethical cases.

The head-to-head comparison of the disability response to Sidney Miller and Emilio Gonzalez's cases may help explain why some bioethicists fail to take seriously the disability critique. The disability position appears riddled with internal contradictions that undermine the credibility of argument. For example, the calls to support parental choice in Emilio's case ring hollow in the aftermath of Sydney Miller's case, where the wishes of the parents were deemed irrelevant. The inconsistencies give rise to the charge that the advocacy is unprincipled and result-oriented: Parental rights matter, but only if they are exercised in the way disability advocates say they should be. I've been told by more than one philosophically trained ethicist that disability advocacy should be dismissed without serious consideration precisely because of this internal inconsistency. Moreover, the form of "discussion" is problematic. A well-regarded bioethicist, who is remarkably disability-conscious

---

[196] Mark Kuczewski & Kristi Kirschner, *Bioethics and Disability: A Civil War?*, 24 THEORETICAL MED. & BIOETHICS 455, 455 (2003).

in practice, told me in a recent conversation that no one in the field of bioethics will take seriously people who interrupt academic conferences and hospitals in deliberately disruptive protests.

I think dismissal of the disability critique is a mistake. It is important to remember that disability scholars have communicated through traditional academic channels in traditional academic language. They have presented compelling empirical evidence to support their claims. They have collected and published narrative accounts. They have participated at academic conferences, senate hearings, and in legal cases. The problem is, except in the courts, they are not heard or taken seriously. So they shout and protest to get attention in the press. I would hope that even my philosophy-trained colleague could look beyond the form of the message to ask why in the world are the people so angry. In fact, I would argue that it is incumbent upon bioethicists to ask that question and then to act to address it. The fact that members of a historically disenfranchised and abused population must shout to be heard is reason for alarm, not disdain. Respectful debate is possible only when all sides are heard and all concerns acknowledged.

I also think that it is a mistake to make too much of the inconsistencies in the advocacy positions. In my view, the inconsistency in advocacy is more a function of context than a lack of principle. Unlike bioethics, which as a field that eschews issuing "positions on substantive moral and policy issues"[197] and "carrying on of propaganda, or otherwise attempting, to influence legislation,"[198] the disability community forthrightly embraces legal advocacy. Many leaders in the disability community are trained in law, and that training shows in the positions taken on particular cases where lawyers put forward whatever arguments best serve a client in a particular case. Lawyers are trained to provide zealous representation on a case-by-case basis, which means emphasizing the particular argument that best serves the

---

[197] *Bylaws of the American Society for Bioethics and Humanities*, Article III, Section 4.1, *available at* http://www.asbh.org/about/bylaws.pdf.
[198] *Id.* at Article III, Section 2.2.

particular client in a particular case. Emphasizing different threads of an argument in different cases is part of good legal practice. And for the most part, the ethical rules permit lawyers to take directly inconsistent positions in unrelated matters so long as doing so poses no substantial risk of adversely affecting another client.[199] As a matter of legal practice, then, it is hardly surprising that disability advocates argued in favor of respect for parental choice in Catarina Gonzalez's case and for a bright-line rule requiring treatment in the Miller case. The cases are factually distinguishable, and the argument made in one does not directly undermine the argument made in the other; the desired result – continued life – is the same in both. Thus, the inconsistencies between cases can be understood as a function of classic legal practice.

Underlying the advocacy rhetoric in imperiled-newborn cases is a consistent and core assertion at the heart of the disability critique. The central claim of disability experts is that misperceptions about life with disability have a detrimental effect on people with disabilities, particularly in the medical setting, where people with disabilities – especially babies with disabilities – have been isolated, victimized, and left to die based on incorrect assumptions about the potential for quality of life. The claim is historically accurate, and its currency is supported by sound empirical data and compelling theoretical analysis. The perception that disability bias continues in medical practice and is supported by decision-making frameworks posited by bioethicists who focus on quality-of-life concerns generates fear, distrust, and anger within the disability community. That fear, distrust, and anger manifest on a public level as angry rhetoric and protest. On a more private level, the fear and distrust may interfere with the ability of some parents to engage in thoughtful, informed decision making because of outright skepticism of information provided by physicians. For that reason, it seems important to me that anyone concerned with good medical decision making take seriously the studies that provide evidence showing a disability

[199] MODEL RULES OF PROF. CONDUCT R. 1.7 cmt. 9 (2007).

bias deeply embedded in medical culture. To be sure, the role of bias in medical decision making needs further study, and the data relied on by Carol Gill and others needs updating. Even with these limitations, however, the evidence generated by disability advocates should give bioethicists, especially those bioethicists who claimed that good ethics requires good facts, reason to reexamine decision-making frameworks and educational practices to guard against decision making based on unproven assumptions about disability.

This is not to say that bioethicists should adopt the one-size-fits-all, aggressively-treat-all-babies-till-the-end approach sometimes advocated by disability advocates. Long experience counsels against prolonging the suffering of dying babies. In this respect, bioethicists have a distinct advantage in their understanding of the complexity of cases like Sidney Miller's and Emilio Gonzalez's. Bioethicists have a place on the hospital floor. They are insiders, and as such, have access and experience unavailable to outsiders. As participants in real cases, bioethicists are forced to understand that these cases involve real babies, as well as real parents and real doctors who are struggling to make the best decisions that they can in light of highly uncertain medical prognoses. As bioethicist and pediatrician John Lantos observed:

> The focus on particular decisions for particular children, rather than on general questions about the fascinating philosophical, legal, or financial principles that ought to guide decisions, changes the moral focus of the decision. It is one thing to develop a philosophical rationale, a practice guideline, a legal framework, or sophisticated cost-effective analysis. It is quite another to watch a tiny baby struggle for breath, trying to decide whether particular treatments are likely to be more beneficial than harmful and trying to understand what it might mean for the baby and the family, or what it might tell us about ourselves, to make one choice over the other.[200]

[200] JOHN D. LANTOS & WILLIAM L. MEADOW, NEONATAL BIOETHICS: THE MORAL CHALLENGES OF MEDICAL INNOVATION 7 (Johns Hopkins University Press 2006).

Inside access on the hospital floors and close involvement with clinicians also allows bioethicists to understand that the fear expressed by disability advocates that nondisabled parents are likely to wish their disabled children dead is simply not the case. Clinicians report that "when parents are given the choice between trying a desperate treatment that has a small chance of short-term success or withholding treatment ... most parents choose treatment most of the time."[201] "The cases in which *either* a physician or a parent wants to withhold treatment are rare,"[202] and as a practical matter most cases are decided by consensus. "[I]f consensus is not achieved, treatment continues."[203] Were disability experts given a place on the hospital floor, they might be comforted by the rarity of cases involving unilateral decisions to terminate treatment. As they watched babies struggle and suffer under aggressive treatment, and doctors and parents struggle to do the right thing, some disability advocates might come to realize that the charge that every treatment-withholding decision is a form of disability discrimination is factually inaccurate.

Fair or not, disability advocates hold bioethicists accountable for perpetuating physician bias in the nontreatment of newborns. The focus of this strand of argument tends to be on Peter Singer's utilitarian position.[204] I was at a conference recently where Tom Koch, a scholar with disabilities who works in bioethics, repeatedly asserted that the utilitarian views of Peter Singer are part and parcel of bioethical thinking.[205] The implication was that bioethicists teach physicians that it is morally acceptable to allow parents of babies with disabilities

---

[201] *Id.* at 7.

[202] *Id.*

[203] *Id.*, at 120.

[204] *See, e.g.,* Tom Koch, *The Difference That Difference Makes: Bioethics and the Challenge of "Disability"*, 29 J. MED. & PHIL. 697 (2004) (arguing the Peter Singer's utilitarian ethos is the dominant thread in a bioethics focused on autonomy).

[205] *See also,* Tom Koch, *The Difference That Difference Makes: Bioethics and the Challenge of "Disability"*, 29 J. MED. & PHIL. 697, 700–703 (2004) (tracing theoretical roots of bioethics to Singer).

to allow their newborns to die. Koch repeated this assertion in a published piece, where he accused mainstream bioethics of assuming:

> ... the superiority of persons whose physical attributes and cognitive abilities are at least normal, if not superior. Those with physical or cognitive limits lose a measure of their personhood to the degree their autonomous participation in society is limited. From this perspective, extreme limits (negative deviations from the norm) result in a duty not to care for the individual so restricted.[206]

In the article, Koch equates bioethical thinking with Peter Singer's thinking. Koch is not alone in asserting that Peter Singer's position on newborns with disabilities plays an important role in mainstream bioethical thinking.[207]

In this respect, bioethics has a Peter Singer problem. Peter Singer no more represents bioethics than the 9/11 hijackers represented Islam. As previously detailed, bioethicists are engaged in a rich and nuanced debate about the treatment and nontreatment of imperiled newborns. This debate would be enriched by inclusion of disability scholars who could bring to bear their expertise in these difficult cases. This discourse seems impossible, though, so long as the notion persists that Singer's utilitarian views are on the table. Whereas disability expert Harriet McBryde Johnson was willing to go toe to toe with Singer, most disability experts understandably recoil at the thought of engaging in a debate about whether their own parents would have been better off had they allowed them to die. It seems important to me that bioethicists regularly, loudly, and forcefully renounce Singer's radical position in favor of killing disabled babies. Babies are not replaceable. They are independent human beings, even when they were born too early, or born with a fatal illness, and will not survive for long. The loss of even one of these tiny sick frail humans is tragic, as is recognized by parents,

---

[206] *Id.* at 698.

[207] *See, e.g.*, Posting by Wesley J. Smith, *Peter Singer Values Thriving*, http://bioethics. com/?p=5618 (Oct. 31, 2008).

medical staff, and anyone involved with the baby. I'm not a philosopher, but I know an offensive and discriminatory argument when I see it. I challenge the philosophers among bioethicists to take on Peter Singer's argument and explain why the argument fails. Perhaps a concerted effort to distance bioethics from the academic thought experiments played by Singer will help remove an impediment to productive dialogue informed by disability experts.

Toward the end of engaging disability experts to ferret out and remove disability bias from decision making about imperiled newborns, it is important to consider the effect of futility policies and laws like the one from Texas applied in Emilio Gonzalez's case. The Texas law depends on professional judgments respecting outcome-based medicine and gives decisive weight to those professional judgments. Such a scheme will never be acceptable absent trust in physicians to assess potential outcomes without bias. Absent trust, assertions that we can rely on data about medical futility are met with skepticism by disability advocates, who remember too well the medical pronouncement made in the course of the Baby Doe cases ("some people with Down Syndrome are 'mere blobs'"[208] for whom "the possibility of a minimally adequate quality of life was nonexistent."[209]). Regardless of how much attitudes in medicine have actually changed, the wounds caused by the Baby Doe cases are too deep and raw to have fully healed.

For this reason, I tend to agree with Nancy Dubler and other bioethicists who argue that mediation is the better way to resolve disputes than club-like futility laws.[210] Dubler and others suggest that in the

---

[208] GREGORY E. PENCE, CLASSICAL CASES IN MEDICAL ETHICS: ACCOUNTS OF CASES THAT HAVE SHAPED MEDICAL ETHICS, WITH PHILOSOPHICAL, LEGAL, AND HISTORICAL BACKGROUNDS 220 (McGrawll-Hill, 4th ed, 2004) (quoting the referring obstetrician, Walter Owens).

[209] Id. (quoting the testimony of the referring obstetrician Walter Owens, which repeated his prognosis).

[210] See Nancy Neveloff Dubler & Carol B. Liebman, Bioethics: Mediating Conflict in the Hospital Environment, 59 DISP. RESOL. J. 32 (2004).

very few intractable cases, the better course in terms of building trust between vulnerable and fearful populations and medical culture is to provide the requested care. Of course, the view that we do not need futility policies for cases involving newborns may be unrealistic given the limited resources available for health care and the nation's focus on health reform. But I think that the inevitability of health reform and the desperate need for fair process for allocating limited resources actually makes the strongest case for putting futility policies on hold at least for the time being in a few intractable cases involving extremely premature newborns and dying babies. The cases are simply too volatile, and the history of the mistreatment of the so-called "Baby Does" too fresh.

Perhaps by putting aside the philosophical debates about futility for the time being would help make room for the very necessary, thoughtful, deliberately inclusive conversation about how best to allocate scarce resources. That conversation can only take place if there is trust, and getting to that trust will be hard because it will require compromise and transparency. At the end of the day, however, if people with disabilities are involved in policy making and the disability position is taken seriously, it seems possible that we can reach a solution that achieves widespread consensus. Such consensus has, after all, been reached on policies for allocating donated organs, another scarce resource. Organs are allocated according to a scheme that includes consideration of health and potential benefit but excludes irrelevant, disability-related factors. The distribution scheme is also reasonably noncontroversial within the disability community. In theory, a similar consensus could emerge over when to use aggressive treatment to preserve the lives of newborns.

Cases involving imperiled infants are hard. They should be a matter of debate. In the face of so much uncertainty about science and each individual specifically, bright-line, one-size-fits-all rules are inappropriate. But frameworks allowing for individualized assessments, especially those that involve subjective assessments and value judgments, require trust. Including disability experts in internal, nuanced debate taking place within bioethics about extremely premature new-borns might help build that trust. At the very least, the debate would be richer if all of the stakeholders were brought into the conversation and all the evidence was considered.

Conflict may be inevitable. Just as bioethicists may never agree on how to define futility – or even if it is a useful concept – bioethicists and disability experts may never agree on what constitutes "quality of life" or a "life worth saving," or even if those concepts are useful. On the one end will be those who take the sanctity-of-life position and on the other those who argue that the determination requires consider-ation of an individual family's values and needs. But the fact of conflict should not stop conversation and cross discipline learning. The reality is that the conflict is not nearly as deep as the rhetoric in the "civil war" suggests. A vast majority of bioethicists agree with disability advocates that everything should be done to save those infants who have cogni-tive or physical disabilities, at least those with disabilities that do not extinguish the possibility for meaningful relationships or symbolic thought.[211] But even where this is conflict, it should be apparent that disability experts have something to teach parents and medical profes-sionals about the potential for quality of life of many people with many kinds of disabilities. If nothing else, there would be value in considering how to make those conversations a regular part of care in the NICU.

---

[211] JOHN LANTOS & WILLIAM MEADOW, NEONATAL BIOETHICS: THE MORAL CHALLENGES OF MEDICAL INNOVATION, 10, 92 (Johns Hopkins University Press 2006) (describ-ing an approach of treating until the baby "declares self").

4

Childhood

THE EXPERIENCE OF CHILDREN WITH DISABILITY IN THE clinical setting is as varied as any other human experience. Many children with disabilities lead rich, full lives in which they attend school, play with friends, participate on sports teams, and come into contact with physicians for little other than routine well-child care visits. Other children with disabilities, particularly developmental disabilities, may be physically healthy but limited in their capacity for mental and social development. Still others may face disability-related or other health problems that bring them into regular contact with the health care system.[1] Like all parents, parents of children with disabilities are the primary decision makers for their children. They make decisions about whether, when, and how to treat illness or use technology to correct or improve functionality. They also make decisions about whether, when, and how to manage the particular physical manifestations or social needs resulting from disability. As with most medical decision making for children, the process by which parents make medical decisions for children with disabilities is mostly unremarkable. The parents consult

---

[1] *See* Federal Interagency Forum on Child and Family Statistics, *Children with Special Health Care Needs*, http://www.childstats.gov/americaschildren/special1.asp.

with the child's doctor, weigh the risk and benefits of medically reason-able alternatives, and then make the decision that is, in their estimation, in the best interest of their child.

The deference given parental decisions in the health care setting is more than a matter of convenience or custom. A parent's right to make medical decisions for his or her child is protected by the Due Process Clause of the Fourteenth Amendment.[2] This right is not abso-lute, but it is well established.[3] So long as parents are fit, "there will normally be no reason for the State to inject itself into the private realm of the family to further question the ability of that parent to make the best decisions concerning the rearing of that parent's children."[4] The constitutional protection afforded fit parents clothes them with a presumption that they "act in the best interests of their children"[5] in making choices, including medical choices, for their children.[6] The presumption that parents act in their child's best interests effec-tively shields most parental decisions about a child's health care from

---

[2] Parham v. J.R., 442 U.S. 584 (1979).

[3] *Id. at* 604 (finding a "presumption that parents possess what a child lacks in maturity, experience, and capacity for judgment required for making life's difficult decisions," and that "natural bonds of affection lead parents to act in the best interests of their children," but also that this presumption only exists "absent a finding of neglect or abuse"); *see also* Prince v. Massachusetts, 321 U.S. 158, 166 (1944) (claiming that "[i]t is cardinal with us [the Court] that the custody, care and nurture of the child reside first in the parents").

[4] Troxel v. Granville, 530 U.S. 57, 68, 69 (2000); *see also Parham,* 442 U.S. at 602 (stating that "our constitutional system long ago rejected any notion that a child is 'the mere creature of the State'") (quoting Pierce v. Soc'y of Sisters, 268 U.S. 510, 535 [1925]). Where a parent is deemed unfit, or neglectful, the state may intervene more freely. *See, e.g., In re* Sampson, 278 N.E.2d 918 (N.Y. 1972) (ordering that a child undergo facial surgery and receive blood transfusions despite the mother's reli-gious objection).

[5] *Parham,* 442 U.S. at 602.

[6] *Troxel,* 530 U.S. at 68–9.

scrutiny or limitation. Whereas a court may occasionally override a parent's decision to *refuse* treatment if the choice puts the child's health or life at risk,[7] courts almost never intervene when a parent chooses a medically approved alternative to treat a child.[8] Thus, the law generally leaves the tough decisions to parents.

This chapter presents two cases in which the legality, ethics, and morality of health care decisions made by parents of children with disabilities were called into question. The first involved a parental decision to forgo the use of technology to ameliorate disability. The second involved a parental decision to use aggressive surgical and medical interventions to shape the body of a young child with profound disabilities. The first triggered judicial scrutiny; the second did not. But the second case, the case of Ashley X, is one of the most controversial in bioethics and the disability rights movement (and thus the source of much better developed arguments than many of the case studies in this book). Both cases – that of Lee Larson's boys and of Ashley – illustrate with stunning clarity how differing perspectives about the role of medicine and meaning of disability can affect one's view of a particular case.

---

[7] *See, e.g.*, Jehovah's Witnesses v. King County Hosp. Unit No. 1 (Harborview), 390 U.S. 598 (1968), *aff'd per curiam*, 278 F.Supp. 488 (W.D. Wash. 1967) (overriding parental refusal to provide blood transfusion where death would result without the transfusion); Custody of a Minor, 379 N.E.2d 1053 (Mass. 1978) (ordering a child to undergo chemotherapy over the parents' objections because the treatment had inconsequential side effects and would save the child from certain death).

[8] *See, e.g.*, Tenenbaum v. Williams, 193 F.3d 581 (2d Cir. 1999); *In re* Hofbauer, 393 N.E.2d 1009 (N.Y. 1979) (holding that the court would not interfere with parents' decision to forgo conventional chemotherapy for their eight-year-old son who suffered from Hodgkin's disease and treat him with laetrile and a special diet instead); *In re* Hudson, 126 P.2d 765 (Wash. 1942) (holding that a mother was free to refuse surgery to remove her child's deformed arm despite the recommendation by two physicians that it should be removed for the child's health because both courses of action entailed risk).

I. LEE LARSON'S BOYS

Lee Larson's two boys, Kyron and Christian,[9] were two and three years old, respectively, in 2002. Larson was a deaf single mother.[10]

Like their mother, both Kyron and Christian were profoundly deaf. The family's native language and primary mode of communication was American Sign Language (ASL). Larson took great pride in the family's deaf identity and participation in Deaf culture.[11] Deaf culture is tight-knit social structure whose members share ASL as a common, visual language.[12] Culturally Deaf individuals "characteristically think it is a good thing to be Deaf.... [E]xpectant Deaf parents characteristically hope to have children with whom they can share their language, culture, and unique experiences – that is, Deaf children."[13]

The school Kyron and Christian attended did not share Larson's enthusiasm for Deaf culture. Because there was no room for them in the school district's ASL-affirmative program, Lee Larson's boys were enrolled at Shawnee Park Elementary School, which offered only an oral-aural program for deaf children. The program used no signing; it relied on oral communication. Because the boys were unable

---

[9] Michigan Protection and Advocacy Service, Inc.'s Amicus Curiae Memorandum of Law Asserting No Jurisdiction, In the Matter of Kyron & Christian Robinson, No. 01–0702–00 NA at 5 [hereinafter *Amicus Curiae Memorandum of Law In the Matter of Kyron & Christian Robinson*].

[10] Cal Montgomery, *The Cochlear Implant Trial*, RAGGED EDGE ONLINE, Oct. 4, 2002, *available at* http://www.ragged-edge-mag.com/extra/deaftrial1.html [hereinafter *The Cochlear Implant Trial*].

[11] Theresa D. Mcclellan, *Deaf mom gets the 'no' she wants*, THE GRAND RAPIDS PRESS, Oct. 5, 2002, at A1, *available at* http://www.bridges4kids.org/articles/2002/10–02/GRPress10–5–02.html.

[12] The film "Sound and Fury" is an excellent introduction to the Deaf culture. The film traces the stories of two brothers – one deaf and one hearing – as they and their wives struggle to make decisions about cochlear implants for their hearing children.

[13] Harlan Lane & Michael Grodin, *Ethical Issues in Cochlear Implant Surgery: An Exploration into Disease, Disability, and the Best Interests of the Child*, 7 KENNEDY INST. ETHICS J., Sept. 1997, at 231, 234.

to communicate with teachers, staff, or other children, officials at Shawnee Park Elementary became concerned that the boys were falling behind their peers. They urged Larson to have her sons surgically implanted with cochlear implants.[14]

Cochlear implants are a form of technology that allows deaf people to obtain various degrees of hearing. Cochlear implants function differently from hearing aids, which simply amplify sound. A cochlear implant transforms speech and other sounds into electrical energy that is used to stimulate surviving auditory nerve fibers in the inner ear. The implant is embedded within the skull, near the ear, and has external and internal components. One part of the device is a microphone that resides outside the ear while the other part processes sounds captured by the microphone. A transmitter sends the processed signals to a receiver implanted under the skin. The receiver converts the signals into electrical impulses that are then delivered to the auditory nerve. The stimulation of the auditory nerve allows the user to experience representations of sound and might help the user develop spoken language ability. The degree to which cochlear implant recipients develop spoken language ability varies depending on the age at which the recipient is implanted (younger recipients are more likely to develop spoken language ability than older recipients) and the amount of spoken language training provided to the recipient. Indeed, audiologists strongly recommend that upon activation of the implant recipients be totally immersed in oral/aural communication at home and in school. In other words, a deaf child's success with an implant depends on close interaction with parents for constant monitoring, feedback, and reinforcement of good oral speech patterns. The recommendation is that families that choose cochlear implants make a total commitment to oral-only communication (no ASL) for the best cochlear implant results.[15] In 2000,

---

[14] Mcclellan, *supra* note 11.

[15] *See* Lane & Grodin, *supra* note 13, at 235–6; *See, e.g.*, Harlan Lane, *Ethnicity, Ethics, and the Deaf-World*, 10 J. DEAF STUD. & DEAF EDUC., Summer 2005, at 291, 299–300; Adam B. Zimmerman, *Do You Hear the People Sing? Balancing Parental Authority*

the Food and Drug Administration (FDA) lowered the acceptable age for implantation of one such device to twelve months.[16] According to the FDA, as of April 2009, approximately 188,000 people worldwide had received implants, and in the United States, roughly 41,500 adults and 25,500 children had received them.[17]

Although they are commonly used, cochlear implants are not risk-free. They cost thousands of dollars, there are efficacy problems, and they require surgery, which always entails risks.[18] Reports of complications are not infrequent. They include injury to the facial nerve, meningitis, cerebrospinal fluid leakage, perilymph fluid leak, infection, attacks of dizziness or vertigo, tinnitus, and loss of residual hearing.[19] Cochlear implants also do not turn a deaf child into a hearing child. The degree to which they facilitate speech and the ability to understand oral speech varies tremendously from person to person. Children of hearing parents who communicate with oral language or a combination of oral language and sign language tend to develop far better oral speaking skills than children of deaf parents. Despite these risks and questions about efficacy, audiologists strongly recommend cochlear implants for deaf children who cannot hear with the amplification of hearing aids.[20]

In considering the school's suggestion that the boys be implanted, Larson researched and spoke with people about implants. Ultimately she decided that the disadvantages of implantation outweighed any possible advantages. Although she concluded that the boys could

---

and a Child's Right to Thrive: The Cochlear Implant Debate, 5 J. HEALTH & BIOMED. L. 309, 317–18 (2009).

[16] National Institute on Deafness and Other Communication Disorders, *Cochlear Implants*, Aug. 2009, *available at* http://www.nidcd.nih.gov/health/hearing/coch.

[17] *Id.*

[18] Lane, *supra* note 15, at 299–300; Zimmerman, *supra* note 15, at 318.

[19] Food & Drug Admin., *Benefits and Risks of Cochlear Implants*, *available at* http://www.fda.gov/MedicalDevices/ProductsandMedicalProcedures/ImplantsandProsthetics/CochlearImplants/ucm062843.htm.

[20] *See, e.g.*, Baylor College of Medicine, *Cochlear Implants*, *available at* http://www.bcm.edu/oto/jsolab/cochlear_implants/cochlear_implant.htm (last visited July 8, 2010).

make the decision to get implanted when they got older, at that time she wanted them "to grow up with a strong self-esteem, not trying to be something they are not."[21] She also wanted them to be "part of the Deaf culture" and continue to communicate in ASL.[22] The boys' father, from whom she was separated, agreed with Larson's decision against implants, which she communicated to school officials.[23]

In 2002, Larson traveled out of town and left the boys in the care of a friend who was also deaf. Unfortunately, the friend apparently abused the boys. School officials charged Larson with neglect for leaving them in her care. The state issued charges, and a court found that Larson neglected the children by leaving them with care providers who physically abused them.[24] The court declared the children temporary wards of the state and, with Larson's consent, placed the boys in foster care while Larson took parenting classes with the aim of regaining custody.[25] The foster parents who had temporary custody of the boys did not speak ASL and communicated with the boys through oral speech.[26]

The court appointed a guardian ad litem for the boys. The guardian, who was in touch with the foster parents and school officials, sought to have the boys surgically implanted with cochlear implants.[27] He filed a Motion for Court to Order Cochlear Implants, claiming that it was in the children's best interests "... that they receive cochlear implants in order for them to realize their full potential in life" and that time is of the essence given "... the 'window of opportunity' ... is from birth through age 4."[28]

---

[21] Mcclellan, *supra* note 11.

[22] *Id.*

[23] *Id.*

[24] *Amicus Curiae Memorandum of Law In the Matter of Kyron & Christian Robinson,* *supra* note 9, at 5.

[25] Mcclellan, *supra* note 11.

[26] *Id.*

[27] *Id.*

[28] *Amicus Curiae Memorandum of Law In the Matter of Kyron & Christian Robinson,* *supra* note 9, at 9.

The guardian's petition was unusual. Under state law, Larson retained the clear right to make medical decisions for her children, including decisions to refuse elective (non-life-saving) treatments. The boys' placement in temporary foster care did not diminish that right, and cochlear implants are not life-saving. No state agency supported the guardian's request. In fact, the Michigan Family Independence Agency, which oversees the children's foster care, explicitly advised the judge its policy is to allow parents to "decide whether or not a child in foster care should have elective surgery."[29] Nonetheless, the state prosecutor joined the guardian to argue that Larson's decision against cochlear implants was a form of medical neglect, and Lee Larson's refusal to consent to implantation the cause of a medical emergency.

After a preliminary hearing, the judge agreed to consider the guardian's petition and scheduled a trial. She also ordered the boys to be evaluated in preparation for surgery.[30]

The case caused considerable consternation within the disability and Deaf communities. Activists came out in force to protest against the real possibility that the court would find the mother's refusal to ameliorate deafness with cochlear implants a form of medical neglect.[31]

The judge heard testimony for several days in a courtroom packed with Deaf and disability rights activists.[32] The state prosecutor questioned the guardian who testified that the boys should get implants because they would benefit from the acquisition of oral language and the opportunities for education and employment that would insure the boys could lead a "healthy, happy, normal life."[33] The state's expert

---

[29] Jon Hall, *Michigan Judge Rules Deaf Boys Needn't Undergo Surgery*, BOSTON GLOBE, Oct. 5, 2002, at A3, *available at* http://www.bridges4kids.org/articles/2002/10–02/ Globe10–5–02.html.

[30] Mcclellan, *supra* note 11.

[31] Cal Montgomery, *Ripples, A Tide, An Ocean*, RAGGED EDGE ONLINE, Nov. 2002, http://www.raggededgemagazine.com/1102/1102ft3.html.

[32] *The Cochlear Implant Trial, supra* note 10.

[33] Montgomery, *supra* note 31.

testified that being deaf will prevent the boys from reaching their full potential because without the implants, the language-processing areas of their brains wouldn't reach full development. The guardian argued that time was of the essence because the window in which the boys would receive the most benefit from the implants was rapidly closing. Multiple expert witnesses testified that implants are crucial for a deaf child's language development.[34]

Larson and her lawyer countered. Larson testified that she made a thoughtful and careful decision to decline surgery for her boys after considering the risks, benefits, and alternatives to treatment. The Michigan Deaf Association produced evidence that speech is not the equivalent to language and that it is access to a language, not access to sound and speech, that ensures proper development of the brain. Sign language – a visual language used in the Larsen home – is sufficient to allow the brain to develop fully.[35] Deaf studies specialist, Robert Hoffmeister of Boston University, told the court that there was no guarantee the implants would benefit the Larson boys in their language acquisition or schoolwork. According to the research, "it's all a roll of the dice, actually," and in most cases involving children who are born deaf, the benefits of cochlear implants are minimal.[36]

Also supporting Larson was the Michigan Protection and Advocacy Services (MPAS), which submitted an amicus brief framing the case as one about parental rights. MPAS argued that the decision of whether to consent to or refuse implants was Larson's alone. The brief confirmed that Larson was not alone in her belief that cochlear implants were not in the best interest of her children. That position, MPAS argued, is widely agreed on within the disability community. Washington Protection and Advocacy System (WPAS) also emphasized the importance of family autonomy: "ALL families are special and unique, but families who have children with disabilities regularly encounter barriers that impact

---

[34] *Id.*
[35] *The Cochlear Implant Trial, supra* note 10.
[36] *Id.*

on the family and require them to form a different view of how 'normal' is defined within their family, and how they interact with the world around them. Second-guessing by outsiders is a regular part of that life, and contributes to the development of the family's culture."[37]

The judge ultimately, but grudgingly, ruled in favor of Larson. She stated, "[t]he court has no doubt it would be in the boys' best interest to have implants, [but] has paid close attention to [Larsen's] adamant right to decide and not to participate in after care"[38] needed if the implants had been ordered. The judge stated that the law was clear that courts cannot intervene in parental decisions about medical treatment for their children absent an emergency, and the refusal to consent to implants did not qualify as an emergency.[39]

A. Views from the Deaf and Disability Communities

Deaf and disability advocates came together in fierce and unanimous support of Lee Larson. The legal petition to require implants threatened to make a reality what the disability and Deaf communities had long feared: that the medical view of disability would take root in law. If the petition had been granted, the court's decision would have created legal precedent deeming medical neglect a parent's failure to ameliorate traits like deafness based on "proof" that individuals with disabilities need medical fixes to participate meaningfully in society.[40]

The notion that deafness is a defect that needs fixing runs directly counter to beliefs and teachings of the Deaf and disability

---

[37] *Amicus Curiae Memorandum of Law In the Matter of Kyron & Christian Robinson*, *supra* note 9, at 4.

[38] Mcclellan, *supra* note 11.

[39] *Id.*

[40] *See, e.g., Amicus Curiae Memorandum of Law In the Matter of Kyron & Christian Robinson*, *supra* note 9, at 12–13 (2002). *See also* Montgomery, *supra* note 31 (explaining how if the petition was granted it would set a precedent that would have a significant impact on parents of children with disabilities in the future).

communities.[41] As discussed in Chapter 2, disability scholars and activists reject the notion that the problem of disability is located in the individual whose body deviates from species-normal. The problem, assert the scholars, lies in society's failure to accommodate all its members. The solution to the problem of disability, under this view, is not to modify the person with the physical difference, but to make social, legal, educational, or other accommodations to ensure full participation in society. Indeed, disability and Deaf scholars often use the example of deafness on Martha's Vineyard, an island off the coast of Massachusetts, to make the point that overcoming social barriers to participation in the life of a community can in fact eliminate the disabling aspects of impairment. Historically, hereditary deafness was so prevalent on Martha's Vineyard that everyone spoke sign language.[42] As a result, the deaf were fully integrated and successful in community life. Deaf islanders were not identified as a distinct group by other islanders, and they were equally successful in terms of work and social lives. The one exception was with respect to school, where the deaf children tended to *outperform* hearing children.[43] The lesson Deaf and disability experts take from the experience of Martha's Vineyard is that deafness is not disabling in a society that appreciates difference and makes a deliberate effort to include fully people of different abilities.

[41] For more information on Deaf culture, *see* Lane, *supra* note 15. *See, e.g.*, Margaret Usha D'Silva et al., *Deaf is Dandy: Contrasting the Deaf and Hearing Cultures*, 13 INTERCULTURAL COMM. STUD. 111 (2004); Tingting Gao, *A Neglected Culture: How Cochlear Implants Affect Deaf Children's Self-Esteem*, 6 DIALOGUES@RU 79, 87 (2007), http://dialogues.rutgers.edu/vol_06/essays/documents/gao.pdf; Claire L. Ramsey, *Ethics and Culture in the Deaf Community Response to Cochlear Implants*, 21 SEMINARS HEARING 75 (2000); Claire L. Ramsey, *What Does Culture Have to Do with the Education of Students Who Are Deaf or Hard of Hearing?*, *in* LITERACY AND DEAF PEOPLE: CULTURAL AND CONTEXTUAL PERSPECTIVES 47 (Brenda Jo Brueggemann ed., Gallaudet University Press 2004); Robert Sparrow, *Defending Deaf Culture: The Case of Cochlear Implants*, 13 J. POL. PHIL., May 2005, at 135.
[42] *See generally* NORA ELLEN GROCE, EVERYONE HERE SPOKE SIGN LANGUAGE: HEREDITARY DEAFNESS ON MARTHA'S VINEYARD (Harvard University Press 1985).
[43] *Id.*

This social model of disability argument is clearly evident in activist Cal Montgomery's response to Lee Larson's case:

> ... I am certain that if all participants in the case viewed deafness as just another kind of diversity, the situation would never have arisen.
>
> If the boys' present and future disadvantages were attributed to our hearing-dominated society rather than to their own deafness (and their deaf parents' acceptance of their deafness), teaching them pride in who they are and the skills to struggle would make more sense. Many people who do hold the institutions of the hearing majority responsible (including some who regard cochlear implants as a good thing in some cases) are vehemently opposed to [the state expert's] position.
>
> But because the people who brought the case forward blame these disadvantages on the boys' inability to hear rather than on society's insistence on hearing as a prerequisite to full memberships, cochlear implants are seen by many people as a solution to disability. Denying the children implants looks like condemning them to a lesser life.[44]

Another activist explained: "The medical establishment has continually told us that being Deaf is a tragedy. It refuses to admit that American Sign Language is wholly sufficient to allow the development of the language center of a deaf child's brain and to allow the deaf child to develop full linguistic and cognitive competence, given each individual's potential. It refuses to admit that there are viable options other than a cochlear implant."[45]

Indeed, cochlear implants are particularly controversial within the Deaf community. Although many deaf adults choose implants for themselves and their children, many others, especially Deaf activists

---

[44] *The Cochlear Implant Trial, supra* note 10.

[45] Equal Access Communication, Inc., *2002 Grand Rapids Cochlear Implant Case,* Oct. 4, 2002, *available at* http://www.equalaccesscommunication.com/2002Grand RapidsRally/index.htm.

and their supporters, vehemently oppose their use in all cases. The arguments against cochlear implants vary. Some argue that there is an intrinsic value in being deaf. They view deafness as a defining feature of identity as important as race or gender, an essential component of personhood. In their view, using implants deprives children of that essential piece of themselves. Under this view, denying children their deafness deprives them of the key to entry to a rich culture, ripe with language, arts, and tradition.[46] This argument often compares Deafness to other characteristic central to identity such as race, gender, or sexual orientation. Consider, for example, this comment, made by a former president of the National Association of the Deaf:

> I'm happy with who I am ... and I don't want to be "fixed." Would an Italian-American rather be a WASP? In our society everyone agrees that whites have an easier time than blacks. But do you think a black person would undergo operations to become white?[47]

Other opponents of cochlear implants argue that treating deafness as an illness needing cure is insulting and demeaning because of its message that the deaf are of lesser worth than the hearing. Others argue that widespread use of cochlear implants constitutes a form of cultural genocide.[48] For example, Harlan Lane argues:

> [W]hile surgical programs that implant large numbers of Deaf children do not have as their intent the destruction of Deaf-World culture, both the U.N. Declaration [of the Rights of Persons Belonging to National or Ethnic, Religious and Linguistic Minorities] and the Convention [on the Prevention and Punishment of the Crime of Genocide] express humankind's interest in preserving and fostering minority languages and cultures and thus, once the minority

---

[46] *See, e.g.*, Lane, *supra* note 15, at 292–294; Lane & Grodin, *supra* note 13; Sparrow, *supra* note 41.

[47] Roslyn Rosen, as quoted in Edward Dolnick, *Deafness as Culture*, THE ATLANTIC MONTHLY, Sept. 1993, at 38, *available at* http://gallyprotest.org/atlantic_monthly.pdf.

[48] *See, e.g.*, Sparrow, *supra* note 41, at 135–6.

language and culture of the Deaf-World is recognized, alert us to the conflict of values arising from those surgical programs.[49]

The arguments against cochlear implants have not convinced most parents against implantation. Most deaf children are born to hearing parents,[50] and most of those parents choose implants for children who are eligible.[51] Many deaf adults also choose implants for themselves and their deaf children. In fact, the two Deaf parents of a Deaf child whose decision against cochlear implants for their daughter Heather was the subject of the award-winning documentary "Sound and Fury" ultimately had a change of heart and got implants not just for their daughter, but for another deaf child and themselves.[52]

Although some members of the Deaf and disability communities would argue against cochlear implants in all cases and others elect implants for themselves and their children, there is widespread agreement on one thing: A decision to use cochlear implants is ethically fraught and should be made with great care and caution. Deaf and disability experts suggest that anyone considering the use of implants for their children be advised, in no uncertain terms, not only of the known risks of implantation (nerve damage, infection, meningitis, even death) but also the cultural and psychological costs.[53] For example, Clair Ramsey cautions: "[I]f we take the child as a whole person rather than 'a broken ear with a child attached' we are obligated to consider the effects of an implant on the child's psychological development

---

[49] Lane & Grodin, *supra* note 13, at 238.

[50] National Institute on Deafness and Other Communication Disorders, *Quick Statistics*, *available at* http://www.nidcd.nih.gov/health/statistics/quick.htm ("Nine out of every 10 children who are born deaf are born to parents who can hear").

[51] *See, e.g.*, Gao, *supra* note 41, at 84 (noting that most hearing parents of deaf children "invariably choose cochlear implants for their deaf child in order to facilitate his or her assimilation into the hearing world").

[52] Karen Putz, *'Sound and Fury' Update: A Family Comes Together Again*, HANDS & VOICES (2005), http://www.handsandvoices.org/articles/misc/V8–4_soundfury.htm.

[53] Ramsey, *supra* note 41, at 77–8.

(especially identity formation), educational progress, and social life."[54] Thus, parents should have reasonable expectations. Cochlear implants will not make congenitally deaf children into hearing children. Parents "should be made aware that an implant may augment the patient's ability to detect sound, but that the patient will still have severely impaired hearing" and limited speech proficiency. [55]

Moreover, and perhaps most importantly, parents must be advised that implanted children may experience psychological distress. Implanted children "often find themselves in limbo" as they become independent of their families: "[T]hey are not deaf people because they do not sign. Yet, ... they find that they are not hearing people either."[56] As one undergraduate reported, "it is emotionally exhausting to pretend to be a regular, hearing person."[57] It is only when deaf people raised with oral-exclusive education learn to sign as adults that they develop strong self-esteem and experience the end of the psychological distress caused by the deprivation of their most natural and comfortable form of communication.[58] For this reason, Deaf and disability activists urge parents who choose implants for their children to be sure to expose the children to Deaf culture and Deaf people throughout their lives, and to teach the children ASL from an early age.[59]

Given the varied views on cochlear implants within the Deaf community itself, it is not surprising that the community focused on a more

---

[54] *Id.* at 78.

[55] *Id.*

[56] *Id.* at 79.

[57] Gao, *supra* note 41, at 87.

[58] Andrew Restuccia, *Michael Schwartz: Multiple Communication Methods Assist Deaf Law Professor in and Outside of the Classroom,* THE DAILY ORANGE, Mar. 7, 2010, http://www.dailyorange.com/2.8691/michael-schwartz-multiple-communication-methods-assist-deaf-law-professor-in-and-outside-of-the-classroom-1.1237578; Mary C. Holte & Maria C. Dinis, *Self-Esteem Enhancement in Deaf and Hearing Women: Success Stories,* 146 AM. ANNALS DEAF, Oct. 2001, at 348, 352–53; Gao, *supra* note 41, at 87–88.

[59] Gao, *supra* note 41, at 87.

unifying issue in its advocacy for Lee Larson: parental rights. For example, Claudia Lee of the Deaf Community Advocacy Network explained that the case is about "the *rights of parents* and not whether we agree or disagree with cochlear implants or the choices that parents make."[60] In an amicus brief, MPAS argued: "Michigan and federal constitutional and statutory law and practices honor and embrace the family unit as the centerpiece of the fabric of America. Taking Ms. Larson's right to make this core medical decision on behalf of her children would rip that fabric, and imperil her ability to reunify her family."[61] Moreover, MPAS argued, "[a] decision allowing 'outsiders,' including this Court, to invade the family core by second-guessing parental decisions about how and by whom their children's disabilities will be treated takes a challenging family environment and threatens its very core."[62]

The focus on the right of parents of kids with disabilities to make medical decisions for their children is consistent with the official position of the National Association for the Deaf (NAD).[63] The NAD recognizes the right of parents to make informed decisions on behalf of their children for or against implantation. To ensure decision making is truly informed, "the NAD strongly urges physicians, audiologists, and allied professionals to refer parents to qualified experts in deafness and to other appropriate resources so that parents can make fully informed decisions – that is, decisions that incorporate far more than just the medical-surgical. Such decisions involve language preferences and usage, educational placement and training opportunities, psychological and social development, and the use of technological devices and aids."[64]

---

[60] Montgomery, *supra* note 31.

[61] *Amicus Curiae Memorandum of Law In the Matter of Kyron & Christian Robinson, supra* note 9, at 4 (2002).

[62] *Id.*

[63] National Association of the Deaf, *Cochlear Implants, available at* http://www.nad.org/issues/technology/assistive-listening/cochlear-implants. Reprinted in Addendum, *Infra,* at 188.

[64] *Id.*

B. Views from Bioethics

Whereas the case of Lee Larson's boys mobilized the disability community, it appears to have gone largely unnoticed within bioethics. That is not to say that bioethicists have not considered the question of cochlear implants – they have – but they have not responded in public commentary or academic writing to the particular case. Despite the lack of specific commentary on Larson's case, the available commentary on cochlear implants and pediatric ethics is abundant.[65] That commentary indicates that Lee Larson's choice to refuse cochlear implants for her boys would cause debate within bioethics. Many bioethics scholars and clinicians would support Larson's choice as a matter of parental autonomy, but some would agree with the state's attorney and the guardian that Larson's choice to refuse to implant deaf children is so ethically problematic that intervention is or could be warranted.

Within bioethics (as in medicine in general), respect for parental choice runs deep. A bedrock principle of law and bioethics is that medical treatment must be provided or withheld only on the basis of a legally valid consent or refusal. To be legally valid, a consent or refusal of treatment must be informed and free. It must also be made by a person with decision-making capacity – that is, someone who is capable of understanding the proffered treatment, its goals, consequences, and attendant risks, and the alternatives to treatment. At law, children lack the capacity to make their own health care decisions in most instances, so it is up to parents to decide whether or not to consent to treatment. Bioethicists recognize that children should have an increasingly

---

[65] *See, e.g., The Cochlear Implant Trial, supra* note 10; Mcclellan, *supra* note 11, at A1; Lane & Grodin, *supra* note 13, at 234–236; Lane, *supra* note 15, at 291, 299–300; Zimmerman, *supra* note 15, at 317–18; National Institute on Deafness and Other Communication Disorders, *supra* note 16.

important voice in medical decision making as they mature,[66] but young children, like Lee Larson's boys, cannot participate meaningfully in medical decision making. For this reason, parents are presumed to be the appropriate decision makers for young children.

As decision makers for children, parents are expected to weigh all relevant factors – such as the risks, benefits, and alternatives of treatment, a particular child's pain tolerance, her medical and social history – and proceed in accordance with whatever course is, all things considered, in the child's best interests. Deciding whether a particular course of treatment or nontreatment is in an individual child's best interests requires an assessment of the relative importance of each factor. Clinicians and ethicists who place primary emphasis on the principle of respect for autonomy tend to conceive the assessment as a subjective one belonging to the parent, who is free to consider religious, familial, or other values in deciding among treatment options. In other words, the commitment to autonomy is expressed through value neutrality – an obligation not to interfere with the choice of another – regardless of whether the decision maker is the principal or a surrogate. Except in the rare circumstance in which the decision will have devastating consequences for the child,[67] the commitment to autonomy requires deference to parental choice. Parents, after all, are in the best position to know what is best for a child. Clinicians and ethicists will thus presume their choices to be in the best interests of the child.

The commitment to parental autonomy expressed through value neutrality is evident in many legal cases in which courts have refused to second-guess parental choices about a child's medical care despite medical recommendations for a different course of action.[68] Physician ethicist Douglas Diekema explains that the real question in medical

---

[66] *E.g.*, Rachel Bulford, *Children Have Rights Too*, 314 BMJ 1421–2 (1997); Wilma C. Rossi et al., *Child Assent and Parental Permission in Pediatric Research*, 24 THEORETICAL MED. & BIOETHICS, March 2003, at 131–8.

[67] *E.g.*, *Custody of a Minor*, 379 N.E.2d 1053.

[68] *See, e.g.*, *In re* Hofbauer, 393 N.E.2d 1009.

cases involving children is not identifying which medical alternatives represent the best interests of the child, but rather "identifying a harm threshold below which parental decisions will not be tolerated."[69] For many, that harm threshold is reached only when the treatment refusal directly threatens the life of a child, such as in the case of the refusal of a simple blood transfusion. When there are questions about medical efficacy of a particular treatment, or reasonable disagreement about the therapeutic value of an intervention, bioethics teaches that both intervention and avoidance of intervention are permissible alternatives.[70]

Cochlear implants certainly are not life-saving treatment. Although they are often touted as "miraculous," the current state of implant technology is such that their use exposes a child to substantial risks, including infection, meningitis, and nerve damage. Furthermore, their efficacy for prelingually deaf children is questionable at best. For these reasons, the therapeutic value – the ability of the particular intervention to cure or prevent illness or impairment – is questionable. Given the state of cochlear implant technology, their use in children would be deemed a matter of parental choice under this type of standard autonomy-based bioethical inquiry.

Other bioethicists take a different view. Adopting a more objective best interests inquiry, some argue that all deaf children for whom cochlear implants would be medically appropriate should be implanted. For example, Australian bioethicist Julian Savulescu argues:

> [W]hen a couple deny an existing child a cochlear implant, they deny that child the opportunity to hear speech, sound, music and to participate in the dominant culture, as well as being able to participate in a signing community. They make that child worse off. This

---

[69] Douglas S. Diekema, *Parental Refusals of Medical Treatment: The Harm Principle as Threshold for State Intervention*, 25 THEORETICAL MED. & BIOETHICS, July 2004, at 243, 244.

[70] David Benatar, *Non-Therapeutic Pediatric Interventions*, in THE CAMBRIDGE TEXTBOOK OF BIOETHICS 127, 128 (Peter A. Singer & Adrian M. Viens, eds., Cambridge University Press 2008).

is analogous to a deaf couple with a hearing child who, wanting that child to be like them, deafen that child. That would be child abuse.

[D]enying a child a cochlear impact can have a similar outcome. It is a[s] neglectful as denying a child with an amputation a limb prosthesis, on the grounds that the child can walk well enough on crutches.

In the case of competent adults, we can leave it to them to decide for themselves whether they have a cochlear implant or remain deaf, or even if they choose to become deaf. I have vigorously defended the liberty individuals to make controversial choices.[71] But when it comes to parents making choices for their children, there are two plausible principles. Firstly, the intervention must plausibly be in the child's interests. In this case, the use of a cochlear implant is likely to make a child's life go better than remaining deaf.

Secondly, we should protect the child's right to decide for herself. In this case, being able to hear has one advantage over deafness. The hearing can easily become deaf, while the deaf cannot easily become hearing later in life. So a child given a cochlear implant could always choose to have it removed later in life, or turned off somehow. A child, unhappy with the hearing culture, can reject it as an adult. She can be made deaf. But a deaf child cannot easily hear later in life.

To my knowledge, no hearing adult has ever freely chosen to become deaf. But it would be easy to achieve. So the cochlear implant affords the deaf child an extra option: to be deaf or hearing later in life.

Both respect for liberty/autonomy and beneficence argue in favour making the provision of cochlear implants a legal requirement.[72]

Savulescu's argument reflects an understanding of the best-interest inquiry as an objective one based on standardized norms and common goals. One of those goals, he argues, is preserving the child's right to decide for herself.

---

[71] *See* Julian Savulescu, *Autonomy, the Good Life and Controversial Choices, in* THE BLACKWELL GUIDE TO MEDICAL ETHICS 17–37 (Rosamond Rhodes et al. eds., Oxford: Blackwell Publishing 2007).

[72] Posting of Julian Savulescu to Practical Ethics, *available at* http://www.practicalethicsnews.com/practicalethics/2009/07/refusing-cochlear-implants-is-it-child-neglect.html (July 13, 2009).

Ethicist Dena Davis shares Savulescu's view that parents have a moral obligation to preserve future options for their children. Adopting Joel Feinberg's conception of a "child's right to an open future," Davis argues against deference to parental autonomy in favor of protecting a child's potential autonomy.[73] Davis and Feinberg divide rights into four categories. First, there are rights that adults and children have in common, such as a right not to be killed.[74] Second, there are rights that are generally possessed only by children and "childlike" adults, which derive from the child's dependence on others for such basics as food, shelter, and protection.[75] Feinberg calls these dependency rights, and they include the child's right to be fed, nourished, and protected. Third, there are rights that can be exercised only by adults, such as the free exercise of religion.[76] Finally, Feinberg identifies a category of "rights-in-trust" – rights to be "saved for the child until he is an adult."[77]

Rights-in-trust, Feinberg argues, include "anticipatory autonomy rights"[78] that will eventually belong to the child when she becomes a "fully formed self-determining adult":[79]

> An example is the right to choose one's spouse. Children and teen-agers lack the legal and social grounds on which to assert such a

---

[73] Dena S. Davis, *Genetic Dilemmas and the Child's Right to an Open Future*, 28 RUTGERS L. J. 549 (1997).

[74] Joel Feinberg, *The Child's Right to an Open Future, in* WILLIAM AIKEN, WHOSE CHILD? CHILDREN'S RIGHTS, PARENTAL AUTHORITY, AND STATE POWER 124, 125 (1980); *see also* Philip Fetzer & Laurence D. Houlgate, *Are Juveniles Still 'Persons' Under the United States Constitution? A New Theory of Children's Constitutional Rights*, 5 INT'L J. CHILD. RTS. 319 (1997) (emphasizing the difference between having a right and enjoying it).

[75] Feinberg, *supra* note 74, at 126.

[76] *Id.*

[77] *Id.* at 125–6. Laurence D. Houlgate makes a similar argument in *Three Concepts of Children's Constitutional Rights: Reflections on the Enjoyment Theory*, 2 U. PA. J. CONST. L. 77 (1999).

[78] JOEL FEINBERG, HARM TO OTHERS: THE MORAL LIMITS OF THE CRIMINAL LAW 38 (Oxford University Press 1984) (explaining that a person has an interest in something when he "stands to gain or lose" depending upon the outcome).

[79] Feinberg, *supra* note 74, at 126.

right, but clearly the child, when he or she attains adulthood, will have that right. Therefore, the child *now* has the right not to be irrevocably betrothed to someone.[80]

According to Feinberg, rights-in-trust can be violated before the child is in a position to exercise them:

> The violating conduct guarantees *now* that when the child is an autonomous adult, certain key options will already be closed to him. His right while he is still a child is to have these future options kept open until he is a fully formed self-determining adult capable of deciding among them.[81]

Parents are morally obligated to protect a child's rights-in-trust now so that the child can exercise them as an adult. When a parent seeks to violate a right held in trust, Feinberg argues, the state should step in: "Children are not legally capable of defending their own future interests against present infringement by their parents, so that task must be performed for them...."[82]

Applying the open-futures approach to cases involving the use of genetic screening to ensure the birth to a Deaf child, Davis argues that a parental choice for deafness causes children moral harm. Whether one views deafness as a disability or as a culture, Davis contends that a choice for deafness violates the child's right to an open future:

> If deafness is a disability which substantially narrows a child's career, marriage, and cultural options in the future, then deliberately creating a deaf child counts as a moral harm. If Deafness is a culture, as Deaf activists assert, then deliberately creating a Deaf child who will

---

[80] Dena S. Davis, *The Child's Right to an Open Future: Yoder and Beyond*, 26 CAP. U. L. REV. 93, 94 (1997).

[81] Feinberg, *supra* note 74, at 126.

[82] *Id.* at 128.

have only limited options to move outside of that culture also counts as a moral harm.[83]

Under Davis's reasoning, no health care provider should acquiesce to a parental choice "that confines [a child] forever to a narrow group of people and a limited choice of careers...."[84]

To be clear, Davis has not explicitly argued in favor of cochlear implants for all children. It is quite possible that she would oppose any legal or other rule requiring cochlear implants, especially given the current state of the technology. That said, Davis clearly supports parents who choose to consent to implantation.[85] Indeed, with the exception of papers published by disability and Deaf scholars in bioethics publications, all the academic writing in bioethics suggests strong support for the right of parents to mitigate deafness with technology.

Neil Levy, for example, argues that no parent should be deprived of an opportunity to use cochlear implants for a deaf child.[86] Levy considers but ultimately rejects what he calls the disability argument, the argument that any disadvantage caused by deafness should be addressed by altering society because that disadvantage is caused by society. Although he acknowledges that much of the disadvantage caused by deafness could be addressed through social adjustments, Levy asserts that the deaf are at least in part "... naturally disabled. They are, for example, disadvantaged by the fact that sound is widely relied upon as a means of alerting people to dangers, from car horns to sirens to fire alarms."[87] No social fix, including flashing lights on alarms, could fully redress this disadvantage. Levy also concedes that

---

[83] Davis, *supra* note 73, at 575.
[84] *Id.*
[85] Dena S. Davis, *Cochlear Implants and the Claims of Culture? A Response to Lane and Grodin*, 7 KENNEDY INST. ETHICS J., Sept. 1997, at 253–8.
[86] Neil Levy, *Reconsidering Cochlear Implants: The Lessons of Martha's Vineyard*, 16 BIOETHICS 134 (2002).
[87] *Id.* at 140.

Deaf culture is real and valuable, and the cochlear implants threaten its continued existence. Nonetheless, he argues that hearing parents of deaf children have no special obligations to Deaf culture that would require them to commit their children to Deaf culture – something that is not required of Deaf adults. Balancing the competing values, he concludes:

> [W]hatever internal restrictions on the Deaf themselves might be justified by the need to preserve that culture, Deaf activists and their supporters have no right to impose the burdens of deafness on hearing-impaired children. So long as Deaf culture survives, the costs associated with it will be relatively high, in that the deaf will remain an effectively isolated and underprivileged minority.[88]

In sum, there is no consensus about the case of Lee Larson's boys in bioethics.

The many ethicists who apply a value-neutral autonomy principle to support parental choice in medical decision making would agree with disability experts that Lee Larson had the right to decide against cochlear implantation for her boys. Others would disagree on the ground that a parent has a moral obligation to ensure an open future for a child. The one issue about which bioethicists appear to have reached consensus is that a parental choice *to use* cochlear implants is ethically and morally defensible. Interestingly, the divided Deaf and disability communities have also reached consensus on the affirmative use of cochlear implants, but the position of Deaf and disability advocates is at odds with that of bioethicists. Whereas bioethicists agree that parents have the moral authority to *use* cochlear implants and few would question a parental decision to use the technology, disability and Deaf activists view the affirmative use of cochlear implants as ethically fraught.

The next case study also tests the limits of parental choice to mitigate the effects of disability with technology.

---

[88] *Id.* at 152.

II. THE CASE OF ASHLEY X

Ashley X[89] was a six-year-old white female patient at the Children's Hospital of the University of Washington in 2004.[90] Ashley had profound developmental disabilities of unknown etiology.[91] For reasons the doctors could not explain, her mental development had never advanced beyond that of an infant.[92] Her doctors described her condition at the time the case presented as follows:

> At the age of 6 years, she cannot sit up, ambulate, or use language. She is gastrostomy-tube dependent for nutrition … [S]he clearly responds to others – vocalizing and smiling in response to care and affection. The combined opinion of the specialists involved in her care is that there will be no significant future improvement in her cognitive or neurologic baseline.[93]

Ashley's college-educated parents cared for their daughter at home where doctors described Ashley as an "integral, and much loved, member of the family."[94] Her parents called Ashley their "pillow angel" because "she is so sweet and stays right where we place her – usually on a pillow."[95] They also described what Ashley's presence at home means to them:

> Ashley brings a lot of love to our family and is a bonding factor in our relationship; we can't imagine life without her. She has a sweet

---

[89] Much of the material in this section first appeared in Alicia R. Ouellette, *Growth Attenuation, Parental Choice, and the Rights of Disabled Children: Lessons from the Ashley X Case*, 8 HOUS. J. HEALTH L. & POL'Y 207 (2008) (copyright © Alicia R. Ouellette).

[90] Daniel F. Gunther & Douglas S. Diekema, *Attenuating Growth in Children with Profound Developmental Disability: A New Approach to an Old Dilemma*, 160 ARCHIVES PEDIATRIC & ADOLESCENT MED. 1013, 1014 (2006).

[91] *Id.*

[92] *Id.*

[93] *Id.*

[94] *Id.*

[95] Ashley's Mom and Dad, *The "Ashley Treatment," Towards a Better Quality of Life for "Pillow Angels," available at* http://ashleytreatment.spaces.live.com (last visited June 19, 2008) [hereinafter Parents' Blog].

demeanor and often smiles and expresses delight when we visit with her, we think she recognizes us but can't be sure. She has a younger healthy sister and brother.... As often as we can we give her position changes and back rubs, sweet talk her, move her to social and engaging places, and manage her entertainment setting (music or TV). In return she inspires abundant love in our hearts, so effortlessly; she is such a blessing in our life![96]

Like many children with profound disabilities, Ashley showed signs of early puberty.[97] At age six, she had begun to develop pubic hair and breast buds.[98] Her parents were concerned about the onset of puberty.[99] The doctors noted that "it was clear that the onset of puberty had awakened parental fears for their daughter's long-term future."[100] Future growth would, the parents feared, make it impossible for them to care for their daughter at home.[101] Ashley's parents wanted her to stay at home. They did not want her care "in the hands of strangers."[102]

The parents consulted Ashley's physicians about their options.[103] Together, they developed a plan for growth attenuation and surgical stunting of Ashley's sexual development.[104] The plan had three main components. The doctors would perform a hysterectomy, a mastectomy,[105] and administer to Ashley high doses of estrogen to

[96] *Id.*
[97] Gunther & Diekema, *supra* note 90, at 1014.
[98] *Id.*
[99] *Id.*
[100] *Id.*
[101] *Id.*
[102] *Id.*
[103] *Id.*
[104] *See id.*
[105] The parents refer to this part of the interventions by the more benign-sounding "breast bud removal." Parents' Blog, *supra* note 95; The "Ashley Treatment," *Towards a Better Quality of Life for "Pillow Angels,"* available at http://pillowangel. org/Ashley%20Treatment%20v7.pdf (last visited Dec. 30, 2007). The Children's Hospital Ethics Committee, however, described the protocol in its ethics opinion regarding this intervention as a "mastectomy." *See* DAVID R. CARLSON & DEBORAH

stunt her growth permanently.[106] The hysterectomy would prevent Ashley from menstruating; the mastectomy would prevent Ashley from developing mature breast tissue; and the estrogen therapy would prevent Ashley from reaching her projected adult height and weight.[107] The goal of the procedures was to keep Ashley in a child-sized body to allow the parents to continue to take care of Ashley at home.[108] Ashley's parents explained:

Ashley will be a lot more physically comfortable free of menstrual cramps, free of the discomfort associated with large and fully-developed breasts, and with a smaller, lighter body that is better suited to constant lying down and is easier to be moved around.

Ashley's smaller and lighter size makes it more possible to include her in the typical family life and activities that provide her with needed comfort, closeness, security and love: meal time, car trips, touch, snuggles, etc. Typically, when awake, babies are in the same room as other family members, the sights and sounds of family life engaging the baby's attention, entertaining the baby. Likewise, Ashley has all of a baby's needs, including being entertained and engaged, and she calms at the sounds of family voices. Furthermore, given Ashley's mental age, a nine and a half year old body is more appropriate and provides her more dignity and integrity than a fully grown female body.[109]

The physicians supported the parents' choice but recognized that the intervention was unprecedented.[110] As a result, they referred the case to the hospital's ethics committee.[111] The ethics committee at

A. DORFMAN, DISABILITY RIGHTS WASHINGTON, INVESTIGATIVE REPORT REGARDING THE "ASHLEY TREATMENT" 6, 7, 19 (2007) (describing Special CHRMC Ethics Committee Meeting/Consultation [May 4, 2004] and the ethics opinion given by the Children's Hospital Ethics Committee).

[106] *Id.* at 7.
[107] *Id.*
[108] Gunther & Diekema, *supra* note 90, at 1014.
[109] Parents' Blog, *supra* note 95.
[110] Gunther & Diekema, *supra* note 90, at 1014.
[111] *Id.*

Children's Hospital (hereinafter "Committee") is made up of health care providers from across disciplines, community members with training in medical ethics, and one of the hospital's attorneys.[112] It issues "non-binding recommendations to practitioners and family members looking for guidance regarding procedures or practices that appear to raise ethical concerns."[113] The Committee met with Ashley, her family, and her doctors "for over an hour."[114] The Committee's written report notes that the discussion of risks and benefits of the proposed interventions was "thorough, painful and occurred with considerable initial division of the members as to whether or not to support the proposal."[115]

The Committee considered the potential risks and benefits of each of the three main components of the proposed intervention. As to the administration of high-dose estrogen, it identified the potential risks as "increased potential for deep vein thrombosis, possible weight gain, [and] possible nausea."[116] The Committee identified the potential benefits of growth attenuation as facilitating Ashley's care "by a smaller rather than a larger size, i.e. moving in/out of bed, wheelchair, car, bathtub, and changing position to avoid pressure sores, etc."[117] The Committee noted a concern that "this intervention is not a standard of care and would in all likelihood be 'new territory' in the management of profoundly retarded juvenile patients."[118]

The Committee identified the risks of a hysterectomy as "anesthesia, surgery, and post-operative recovery period, with the

---

[112] Mission Statement for the Ethics Committee of the Children's Hospital & Regional Medical Center, *in* CARLSON & DORFMAN, *supra* note 105, at exhibit H.

[113] CARLSON & DORFMAN, *supra* note 105, at 13.

[114] Special CHRMC Ethics Committee Meeting/Consultation 2 (May 2004), *in* CARLSON & DORFMAN, *supra* note 105, at exhibit L [hereinafter Committee Meeting].

[115] *Id.* at 3.

[116] *Id.* at 2.

[117] *Id.*

[118] *Id.*

additional short term discomfort and suffering."[119] The potential benefits included avoidance "of the menstrual cycle, physical discomfort, hygienic issues, confusion and anxiety in an individual unable to understand what is going on."[120] An additional benefit of the surgery, said the Committee, "would be to totally exclude the possibility of the patient being sexually assaulted and impregnated."[121] The Committee noted that Washington law required court review of the hysterectomy.[122]

As to the mastectomy, the Committee identified the potential risk as "minimal at this time with the patient's breast development being rudimentary."[123] The potential benefits of removing Ashley's breast tissue were "comfort/quality of life improvement; there is a family history of large breasts with fibrous cystic disease and breast cancer."[124] The Committee also noted that "the restraint strap that holds Ashley in the wheel chair goes right across the area of her body where the breasts would be if they develop," and a concern that this part of the proposal "is clearly not the standard of care for a minor patient with developmental delay and would, like the limitation of linear growth, be 'new territory' in the management of such a patient."[125]

After deliberating privately, the Committee reached consensus that the administration of high-dose estrogen, hysterectomy, and mastectomy were all ethically appropriate. It was "the consensus of the committee members that the potential long term benefit to Ashley herself outweighed the risks; and the procedures/interventions would improve

[119] *Id.*
[120] *Id.*
[121] Committee Meeting, *supra* note 114, at 2–3. This conclusion appears to be poorly worded. Obviously, a hysterectomy would do nothing to totally exclude the possibility of a person being sexually assaulted.
[122] *Id.* at 3.
[123] *Id.*
[124] *Id.*
[125] *Id.*

her quality of life, facilitate home care, and avoid institutionalization in the foreseeable future."[126]

Having received the blessing of the Committee, the treatment was implemented without judicial or further review.[127] The surgeons removed Ashley's uterus and her breast buds in an "uneventful" surgery.[128] They also removed her appendix.[129] They then began a course of high-dose hormones administered through patches placed on Ashley's skin.[130] The treatment continued for more than a year and was terminated when Ashley's growth was permanently halted.[131] She reached a final height of four feet, five inches, and a weight of seventy-five pounds. On their internet blog, Ashley's parents reported that the "Ashley treatment," the hormones, hysterectomy, and mastectomy, cost about 30,000 dollars, and that all costs were covered by insurance.[132]

Two physicians involved in Ashley's case, Doctors Daniel Gunther and Douglas Diekema, published a paper on the case that received widespread media attention.[133] In their paper, Gunther and Diekema

---

[126] Id.

[127] The hospital later admitted that it erred by failing to seek judicial review of the decision to remove Ashley's uterus. Carol M. Ostrom, *Children's Hospital Says It Should Have Gone to Court in Case of Disabled 6-year-old*, SEATTLE TIMES, May 8, 2007. The physicians involved asked specifically about the part of the Committee's report that noted the need for judicial review of that part of the proposed interventions, but were advised that such review was unnecessary because the procedure was not being preformed to sterilize Ashley but for other purposes.

[128] Gunther & Diekema, *supra* note 90, at 1014.

[129] Parents' Blog, *supra* note 95 ("The surgeon also performed an appendectomy during the surgery, since there is a chance of 5% of developing appendicitis in the general population, and this additional procedure presented no additional risk. If Ashley's appendix acts up, she would not be able to communicate the resulting pain. An inflamed appendix could rupture before we would not know what was going on, causing significant complication").

[130] *See* Gunther & Diekema, *supra* note 90, at 1014.

[131] Id.

[132] Carlson & Dorfman, *supra* note 105, at 15 (citing Parents' Blog, *supra* note 95).

[133] Gunther & Diekema, *supra* note 90.

hailed the intervention as "a new approach to an old dilemma" and "a therapeutic option available to [profoundly disabled] children should their parents request it."[134] Interestingly, the paper discussed the physicians' use of the estrogen therapy and the hysterectomy, but it did not report on or explain the removal of Ashley's breast buds or her appendix.[135]

Gunther and Diekema considered the ethical issues raised by the interventions.[136] In particular they considered whether growth attenuation and hysterectomy offered benefits and did any harm to the patient.[137] Their discussion tracks the report of the Committee, but it also evaluates some alternatives to the proposed interventions. For example, Gunther and Diekema discussed the possibility of using oral medication or injections to control menses as an alternative to surgical removal of the uterus, but concluded that "in these profoundly impaired children, with no realistic reproductive aspirations," hysterectomy has the advantage of sparing "the individual and her caregivers the expense, pain, and inconvenience of a lifetime of hormone injections."[138] In addition, hysterectomy eliminates the need to give progesterone during administration of high-dose estrogen for growth attenuation, which decreases the risk of thrombosis.[139]

In a media interview, Doctor Diekema further explained why he agreed the procedures were in Ashley's best interests:

When you look at the growth attenuation, the primary benefits are by being a smaller girl, it will be easier for people to lift her, and will allow her to receive a more personal level of care from her parents for a longer period of time. They really want to be able to pick up their daughter and give her a hug and put her in a chair. It will be

---

[134] *Id.* at 1013.
[135] *Id.* at 1014.
[136] *Id.*
[137] *Id.* at 1014–16.
[138] *Id.* at 1015.
[139] *Id.* at 1015–16.

easier for them to move her to the car and go on outings rather than thinking about leaving her behind with a caretaker when they go on vacation. As far as removing her uterus with a hysterectomy, there are many profoundly disabled children who are traumatized by menstruation. They don't understand why there is blood coming from that part of their body, and it's impossible to make them understand. Unlike a normal 11- or 12-year-old, you can't explain to them this is a normal part of your development. The family wanted to spare Ashley that drama. Ashley's a little girl who already had experienced being terrified of blood.[140]

Following publication of the doctors' paper, the parents published a blog on which they celebrated the "Ashley treatment" and the doctors who helped Ashley by performing it.[141] In it, they repeated much of the discussion from the Gunther paper. They also elaborated on their decision to remove Ashley's breasts, something the Gunther paper did not address:

Ashley has no need for developed breasts since she will not breast feed and their presence would only be a source of discomfort to her. This is especially true since Ashley is likely destined to have large breasts, given her maternal and paternal female lineage. [For example, an] aunt had a breast reduction operation at age 19.[142]

Moreover, they claim, "[l]arge breasts could 'sexualize' Ashley towards her caregiver, especially when they are touched while she is being moved or handled, inviting the possibility of abuse."[143]

The blog and paper generated considerable controversy and media attention.[144] Of particular note is the number of people who reported

---

[140] Amy Burkholder, *Ethicist in Ashley Case Answers Questions*, CNN.COM, Jan. 11, 2007, http://www.cnn.com/2007/HEALTH/01/11/ashley.ethicist/index.html.

[141] *Id.*

[142] Parents' Blog, *supra* note 95.

[143] *Id.*

[144] *See generally id.* (posting excerpts and links to various media articles regarding their case).

Childhood

on the blog that they have sought and received similar interventions to manage their child's disabilities.[145] At least a dozen children had reportedly received similar treatment as of 2008.[146]

A. Views from the Disability Community

The publication of Ashley's case and her parents' blog triggered a national debate. The most vocal opponents to the interventions used on Ashley were members of disability rights groups.[147] The reaction of these groups was understandable given the poor track record of the medical establishment in dealing with people with disabilities. Past practices such as involuntary sterilization, life-long institutionalization, and experimentation on people with disabilities were so abusive that many people in the disability rights community are frankly distrustful of medical management of disability.[148] As stated by one disability advocacy group, "'[b]enevolence' and 'good intentions' have often had

[145] *See id.* (posting several of the "thousands of private emails that were sent to PillowAngel@hotmail.com").

[146] *Id.* (reporting correspondence from a dozen parents who used growth attenuation on their children and an e-mail from a physician attendee at a pediatric ethics conference in Hawaii in May 2008 reporting disclosure of "about a dozen or so" cases.).

[147] *E.g.*, Elizabeth Cohen, *Disability Community Decries "Ashley Treatment"*, CNN. COM, Jan. 11, 2007, *available at* http://edition.cnn.com/2007/HEALTH/01/11/ashley.outcry/.

[148] For a more extended discussion of the disability perspective on the medical establishment, *see* JAMES A. CHARLETON, NOTHING ABOUT US WITHOUT US: DISABILITY OPPRESSION AND EMPOWERMENT (University of California Press 1998); HANDBOOK OF DISABILITY STUDIES 351–514 (Gary L. Albrecht et al. eds., Sage Publications, Inc. 2001) (documenting the experience of disability); MARY JOHNSON, MAKE THEM GO AWAY: CLINT EASTWOOD, CHRISTOPHER REEVE, AND THE CASE AGAINST DISABILITY RIGHTS (The Advocado Press, Inc. 2003); HARRIET MCBRYDE JOHNSON, TOO LATE TO DIE YOUNG: NEARLY TRUE TALES FROM A LIFE (Henry Holt and Co. 2005); JOSEPH P. SHAPIRO, NO PITY: PEOPLE WITH DISABILITIES FORGING A NEW CIVIL RIGHTS MOVEMENT 12–40 (Three Rivers Press 1993) (classifying the treatment received by people with disabilities as either "Tiny Tims" or "Super Crips").

disastrous consequences for the disability community. Throughout history, 'for their own good' has motivated and justified discrimination against us."[149] It is not surprising, then, that news of Ashley's case triggered bitter accusations, alarm, and protests by members of the disability rights community.

Some disability activists criticized the motivations of Ashley's parents.[150] For example, a spokesperson from the disability rights group Not Dead Yet said, "This is an issue of basically subjecting a child to drastic physical alterations to fit the convenience of her caregivers."[151] Steven Taylor, director of Syracuse University's Center on Human Policy, stated, "It is unethical and unacceptable to perform intrusive and invasive medical procedures on a person or child with a disability simply to make the person easier to care for."[152]

Others argued that the management of Ashley's disabilities through growth attenuation and surgery denied her basic rights in a way that dehumanized her and others like her.[153] For example, one advocate wrote:

> This is the denial of a child's basic right as a human being to be free from the unwarranted and unnecessary manipulation of [her] basic biological functions merely to satisfy the needs of a third party … Children with severe developmental disabilities are, first and foremost, human beings. The manipulation of a child's physical development relegates those receiving such treatment to a less than human category.[154]

---

[149] Dave Reynolds, *Advocates Speak Out and Call for Investigations Over "Ashley Treatment,"* INCLUSION DAILY EXPRESS (Jan. 12, 2007), *available at* http://www.inclusiondaily.com/archives/07/01/12/011207waashleyx.htm.

[150] *Id.*

[151] *Id.*

[152] *Id.*

[153] *Id.*

[154] *Id.* (quoting a letter to the editors of the *Archives of Pediatrics and Adolescent Medicine* by TASH board president Lyle Romer).

Another lashed out, "The message is very clear: disabled people are not human – they are profoundly flawed and extreme measures will be taken to transform their bodies."[155]

Some activists questioned the efficacy and safety of the procedures. The procedures do not ensure that Ashley would be cared for at home, they said, "because the future development of any six year old child will depend on many factors, [and as a result,] the medical, social and programmatic needs of the adult Ashley will become cannot be anticipated with certainty."[156] Others noted the unknown risks of the use of estrogen in the profoundly disabled.[157]

Other activists argued that the case is a dangerous precedent that could be used to justify additional invasive elective procedures on people with disabilities. "What is next?" asked a blogger, "Amputate the legs of paralyzed people because they are at risk for skin problems and blood clots?"[158] In a similar response, a disability rights position paper argues that under the rationale used to support the modification of Ashley:

> [If] weight ever becomes a difficulty due to age-associated loss of strength for the parents (rather than obesity of the child), then …

[155] William Peace, *The Ashley Treatment and the Making of a Pillow Angel*, COUNTERPUNCH (Jan. 18, 2007), *available at* http://www.counterpunch.org/peace01182007.html (discussing the ethics and social aspects of mutilating disabled people).

[156] Position Statement, Bd. of Directors of the Am. Assoc. on Intellectual & Developmental Disabilities, *Unjustifiable Non-therapy: A Response to Gunther & Diekema (2006) and to the Issue of Growth Attenuation For Young People on the Basis of Disability*, http://www.aamr.org/Policies/board_positions/growth.shtml [hereinafter AAIDD Board Position Statement].

[157] *Id.*; Jeffrey P. Brosco & Chris Feudtner, *Growth Attenuation: A Diminutive Solution to a Daunting Problem*, 160 ARCHIVES PEDIATRIC & ADOLESCENT MED. 1077, 1077–8 (2006).

[158] William Peace, *Protest from a Bad Cripple – Ashley Unlawfully Sterilized*, COUNTERPUNCH, May 26, 2007, *available at* http://counterpunch.org/peace05262007.html.

bariatric surgery or severe restriction in caloric intake would be a form of therapy. If that proves insufficient, the goal of reducing the size of the child could be addressed by "amputation-therapy," justified by the fact that the patient would never be ambulatory in any event.[159]

Based on these arguments, disability rights groups across the country called for a moratorium on growth attenuation and surgery in children with disabilities.[160] A statement from the American Association on Intellectual and Developmental Disabilities represents the views of the groups:

> It seems painfully obvious that medical practice for an individual can rapidly degenerate if the anxieties of the parents regarding as yet unclear future issues replace the medical best interest of the child as the primary focus, even with the noblest of intentions of all parties involved…. [W]e believe that this practice, if judged acceptable, will open a doorway leading to great tragedy. This door is better left closed.[161]

At the same time disability activists and groups were reacting to Ashley's case, the WPAS, a federally funded watchdog agency with authority to investigate allegations of abuse and neglect of persons with disabilities in Washington, initiated an investigation of "what

---

[159] AAIDD Board Position Statement, *supra* note 156.

[160] *See, e.g., id.; Chicago Area Advocacy Groups Meet with AMA to Voice Opposition to "Ashley's Treatment"*, CATALYST (Coalition of Citizens with Disabilities in Illinois, Springfield, IL), (Mar. 2007), *available at* http://www.ccdionline.org/newsletter. php?article_id=32& (reporting that Feminist Response In Disability Activism, Not Dead Yet, and Chicago ADAPT had demanded a moratorium on the performance of future "Ashley Treatments"); F.R.I.D.A., Feminist Response In Disability Activism, http://fridanow.blogspot.com/search?q=Ashley%27s+Treatment (search "Search Blog" for "Ashley's Treatment") (listing articles relating to FRIDA's position on "Ashley Treatments"); Not Dead Yet, http://notdeadyetnewscommentary. blogspot.com/search?q=Ashley%27s+Treatment (search "Search Blog" for "Ashley's Treatment") (listing articles relating to FRIDA's position on "Ashley Treatments").

[161] AAIDD Board Position Statement, *supra* note 156.

happened to Ashley."[162] Its report concluded the hysterectomy violated Ashley's constitutional and common law rights because it was conducted without a court order as required under Washington law.[163] The report further concluded that surgical breast bud removal and hormone treatment "should require independent court evaluation and sanction before being performed on any person with a developmental disability."[164]

WPAS also negotiated a plan for the future with Children's Hospital. In light of the WPAS report, Children's Hospital conceded error in failing to seek a court order before allowing its doctors to remove Ashley's uterus.[165] Children's Hospital also agreed to obtain a court order prior to any other medical interventions to attenuate growth or remove the sexual organs in children with developmental disabilities,[166] and to notify WPAS about any cases in which growth attenuation procedures were requested.[167] Although the agreement applies to Children's Hospital only, the WPAS report urges global adoption of the procedures.[168]

B. Views from Bioethics

Bioethicists struggled with Ashley's case. Art Caplan, often the public face of bioethics, was among the first to take a public position. Caplan, who had polio as a child, is often conscious of the disability

---

[162] CARLSON & DORFMAN, *supra* note 105, at 1.

[163] *Id.* at 27.

[164] *Id.* at 1.

[165] Press Release, David Fisher, Children's Hosp. Med. Dir., Growth Attenuation Press Conference (May 8, 2007) [hereinafter Hospital Press Release] (on file with author), *available at* http://www.seattlechildrens.org/home/about_childrens/press_releases/2007/05/002039.asp.

[166] CARLSON & DORFMAN, *supra* note 105, at exhibit T.

[167] Hospital Press Release, *supra* note 166, at 2.

[168] CARLSON & DORFMAN, *supra* note 105.

critique in his work. That consciousness was evident in his commentary on Ashley's case, which echoed that of members of the disability community:

> The key point the parents make is that they decided to keep their child permanently as a child for her own good. I understand the parents' logic. And I can even understand how a medical team might come to agree that a person who cannot move will have a better life small than big. But I think the Peter Pan option is morally wrong.
>
> I believe it is true that it is easier to move Ashley about if she is the size of a 6-year-old. But I also believe that a decent society should be able to provide appropriately sized wheelchairs and bathtubs and home-health assistance to families like this one. Keeping Ashley small is a pharmacological solution for a social failure – the fact that American society does not do what it should to help severely disabled children and their families.
>
> True, it may be better if Ashley does not become sexually developed in terms of protecting her from attack. But that can be said of any woman. To surgically remove her breasts is simply to maim her in a way that ought not be done. She needs a safe environment at home and if the day comes, a safe environment in an institution. Lopping off her breasts to keep her safe cannot be the right or the only answer.
>
> There are many parents and families who deal with severely disturbed children and adolescents. More than once a parent of a child with severe autism has told me they do not know if they can physically manage their child. Others worry about their children harming themselves or others due to their mental illnesses or disorders.
>
> The problems Ashley and her parents face are terribly real. But permanently freezing a person into childhood is not the solution. Families like Ashley's need more help, more resources, more breaks from the relentless pressure of providing care and some hope that their daughter can be somewhere safe and caring after they are gone.

America has not yet made that promise to Ashley or her parents or the many other parents and kids that face severely disabling mental illness and impairment. We should.[169]

A handful of others within bioethics agreed with Caplan or offered other critiques of the handling of Ashley's case, but as time passed and the case was analyzed in greater depth, initial condemnation gave way to substantial (if not majority) support for the decisions of Ashley's parents and the actions of the doctors and the ethics committee involved in her care. Ethicists around the United States expressed the same sentiment as pediatric ethicist Ben Wilfond who admitted that he "was a little startled" when he first learned of Ashley's case, but later came to understand the parents' position.[170]

The tide began to change with the publication of the first paper on the Ashley case in the influential Hastings Center Report.[171] In it, S. Matthew Liao, Julian Savulsecu, and Mark Sheehan argued that careful analysis of the case required separate consideration of each of the interventions used on Ashley, not global consideration of the package of treatments that had come to be called "the Ashley Treatment" as proffered elsewhere. Applying a traditional best-interest inquiry to the use of high-dose estrogen to stunt Ashley's growth, the authors concluded the intervention was ethically acceptable "given her likely natural and social circumstances." In effect, they accepted the argument that Ashley's parents would be better able to take care of Ashley and to include her in family activities if she were small. They next acknowledged that her

---

[169] Arthur Caplan, Commentary, *Is 'Peter Pan' Treatment a Moral Choice?: Debate Over Stunting a Disabled Child's Growth Pits Comfort Against Ethics*, MSNBC, http://www.msnbc.msn.com/id/16472931

[170] *Surgery to Stunt Girl's Growth Sparks Debate: Parents Say Drastic Treatment Allows Them to Take Better Care of Their Child*, MSNBC, http://www.msnbc.msn.com/id/16473471

[171] S. Matthew Liao et al., *The Ashley Treatment: Best Interests, Convenience, and Parental Decision-Making*, 37 HASTINGS CENTER REP., Mar.–Apr. 2007, at 16.

parents may not have acted solely on Ashley's behalf, but for their own convenience, but they concluded that the motivation of parents is essentially irrelevant to moral and ethical analysis of medical decision making for children. "[A]cting out of the motive to convenience the caregivers or otherwise promote their interests is not necessarily wrong," they said, because "motives may only form part of the justification of the treatment of children, [and because] moral obligations should typically not be so demanding that one must make enormous sacrifices in order to fulfill them."[172] The question to focus on, they argued, is not the motive of parent, but whether the procedure promotes the interests of the patient. As to the interests of children with disabilities like Ashley's, they concluded, "[t]he benefits of being cared for at home by one's family may warrant imposing some burdens on incompetent dependents to enable them to remain at home and to make it possible for care to be delivered there."[173] Although they acknowledged the possibility that Ashley could have been cared for at home had more resources been available, they concluded that "[t]hose who defend the Ashley Treatment are right to respond that because these resources are not now adequately provided, Ashley's parents may be taking the only option open to them. Indeed, to deny her both the necessary social resources and medical treatment is to doubly harm her."[174]

Liao and colleagues reached a different conclusion about the mastectomy and hysterectomy performed on Ashley. They rejected as premature and overstated the parents' justifications for the interventions – that the hysterectomy would allow Ashley to avoid the pain of menstruation and eliminate the possibility of pregnancy and uterine cancer, and the mastectomy would eliminate the possibility that Ashley would develop large uncomfortable breasts, fibroid tumors, breast cancer, and problems with securing Ashley in her wheelchair

[172] *Id.* at 17.
[173] *Id.* at 18.
[174] *Id.* at 19.

because of the position of the strap on her chair. Focusing on the both the physical risks of the surgeries and the affront to dignity caused by what they term "gender *elimination*," Liao and colleagues argued that measures less invasive than surgery, such as painkillers for cramps or modifications to the wheelchair, should have been tried before Ashley's body was surgically modified.[175]

The distinction made by Liao's group between the estrogen treatment and the surgical interventions used on Ashley resonated with pediatric bioethicist John Lantos.[176] Unlike Liao and colleagues, Lantos focused on the legality of performing a hysterectomy on a child without court review, as well as the lack of transparency in the process used to decide how to handle Ashley's parents' request for intervention. Lantos correctly pointed out that Children's Hospital admitted it made a legal error when it allowed the doctors to remove Ashley's uterus without the court permission required under Washington law and requested by the ethics committee.[177] This procedural lapse, he argued, caused the case to be "an example of arrogance and secretiveness by doctors and hospitals [that] reinforces, rather than challenges, the strong societal prohibitions on sterilization for children like Ashley."[178] Lantos further argued that the secrecy was only compounded by the fact the authors of the initial paper failed to mention that Ashley's breast buds were removed, and repeated that omission in subsequent papers that focused only on the estrogen treatment.[179] Lantos suggested the omissions were purposeful because the justification finally offered by Diekema for the

---

[175] *Id.* at 18–19.

[176] John Lantos, *It's Not The Growth Attenuation, It's The Sterilization!*, 10 AM. J. BIOETHICS 45 (2010).

[177] Press Release, David Fisher, Children's Hosp. Med. Dir., Growth Attenuation Press Conference (May 8, 2007), *available at* http://www.seattlechildrens.org/home/about_childrens/press_releases/2007/05/002039.asp.

[178] Lantos, *supra* note 176, at 45.

[179] *Id.* at 45–46. *See, e.g.*, David B. Allen, et al., *Growth-Attenuation Therapy: Principles for Practice*, 123 PEDIATRICS, June 2009, at 1556; Douglas S. Diekema & Norman Fost, *Ashley Revisited: A Response to the Critics*, 10 AM. J. BIOETHICS 30 (2010).

mastectomy was specious. Diekema claimed that breast bud removal was not experimental because it had been performed in boys. Lantos issued a challenge in response: "I'd like them to find even a single reference to a case in which prophylactic mastectomy was performed in a prepubertal girl because of the fear that large breasts would cause discomfort. Even one."[180] Diekema and other bioethicists could not answer Lantos's challenge. Nonetheless, a consensus of sorts has emerged at national bioethics conferences and in the bioethics literature that the use of medical and surgical interventions to stunt the growth and sexual development of children with profound cognitive disabilities is ethically acceptable.[181] For example, in an article that was published in *Pediatrics*, two pediatric endocrinologists and two bioethicists concluded:

---

[180] Lantos, *supra* note 176, at 46.

[181] *See* Seattle Growth Attenuation and Ethics Working Group Report, *Evaluating Growth Attenuation in Children with Profound Disabilities: Interests of the Child, Family Decision-Making and Community Concerns*, http://www.seattlechildrens.org/ research/initiatives/bioethics/events/growth-attenuation-children-severe-disabilities. In a symposium about growth attenuation hosted by the Treuman Katz Center for Pediatric Bioethics at the University of Washington in January 2009, Dr. Douglas Diekema stated that ethics committees in two major Children's hospitals have investigated growth attenuation thoroughly and concluded that there are no ethical issues with the treatment when provided to a child with similar conditions to Ashley's. In an article titled "Ashley Revisited: A Response to the Critics," published in the American Journal of Bioethics, January 2010, two bioethicists concluded:

"Many individuals and groups have been critical of the decisions made by Ashley's parents, physicians, and the hospital ethics committee that supported the decision. While some of the opposition has been grounded in distorted facts and misunderstandings, others have raised important concerns. The purpose of this paper is to provide a brief review of the case and the issues it raised, then address 25 distinct substantive arguments that have been proposed as reasons that Ashley's treatment might be unethical. We conclude that while some important concerns have been raised, the weight of these concerns is not sufficient to consider the interventions used in Ashley's case to be contrary to her best interests, nor are they sufficient to preclude similar use of these interventions in the future for carefully selected patients who might also benefit from them."

Our analysis suggests that growth attenuation is an innovative and sufficiently safe therapy that offers the possibility of an improved quality of life for nonambulatory children with profound cognitive disability and their families. Pediatricians and other care providers should include discussion of these options as part of anticipatory guidance around the age of 3 years so that, if elected, potential clinically meaningful benefits of growth-attenuation therapy can be realized.[182]

The arguments supporting the use of the cluster of interventions used on Ashley take at least two forms. One strand of argument emphasizes parental rights and value neutrality. This argument essentially casts the cluster of interventions used on Ashley as run-of-the-mill medical decisions made by parents of children with disabilities every day. In responding to critics of the Ashley treatment, for example, Diekema and Fost repeatedly compare growth attenuation, mastectomy, and hysterectomy in a six-year-old child to appendectomies, surgeries to remove tonsils and tumors, the insertion of a gastronomy and tracheotomy tubes, fundoplication, spinal fusion, and tendon release used in management of children with disabilities.[183] They argue that as with ordinary medical interventions, "parents should be able to weigh [the] potential benefits and burdens and make a decision for their child in collaboration with qualified physicians."[184] Pediatric bioethicist Dr. Benjamin Wilfond agrees:

In this case, being short is a benefit to the child....There are other parents that make decisions to make their children taller because that may be a benefit to the child. And so I think what all these cases have in common is an intention to help the child.[185]

---

[182] Allen, *supra* note 179, at 1556.
[183] *See* Diekema & Fost, *supra* note 179, at 34–7.
[184] *Id.* at 40.
[185] *Surgery to Stunt Girl's Growth Sparks Debate: Parents Say Drastic Treatment Allows Them to Take Better Care of Their Child*, MSNBC, http://www.msnbc.msn.com/id/16473471

According to this argument, deference to parental choice for interventions of the type used on Ashley is appropriate so long as there is a plausible argument the interventions will benefit the child. The benefits can be medical or social:

> The tools of medicine are used commonly to treat disorders or conditions that are commonly defined as social. Consider laser treatment for facial hemangiomas, braces for crooked teeth, drug prescriptions for acne, and drugs to improve fertility.... The insistence on "medical" indications is not sufficient to help us distinguish why some interventions are appropriate and others are not. The relevant question is whether medical interventions were likely to be safe and effective in providing benefit to the patient and improving her quality of life.[186]

According to this argument, it is up to the parent to make this assessment, with the help of the health care provider. The provider's role "is to create an environment for parents to raise their child according to their values and beliefs."[187] The bioethicist should remain value-neutral in the handling of the case. As a bioethicist explained at a symposium on growth attenuation therapy, "We don't tell doctors what to do ... [w]e simply advise how it should be done."[188] Nor should bioethicists interfere with parental choices, argues pediatric ethicist Lanie Friedman Ross, who insists that doctors should respect family choices for growth attenuation: "These are families committed to doing what is best for their children....While outcome data would be useful, the presumption should be to respect parental autonomy."[189]

[186] Diekema & Fost, *supra* note 179, at 37.

[187] Benjamin S. Wilfond, *The Ashley Case: The Public Response and Policy Implications*, 37 HASTINGS CENTER REP., Sept.–Oct. 2007, at 12–13.

[188] Emi Koyama, *Why I Am Suspicious of Bioethics*, HASTINGS CENTER: BIOETHICS FORUM, Feb. 18, 2010, http://www.thehastingscenter.org/Bioethicsforum/Post.aspx?id=4492#ixzz0rgCNeTPz

[189] Lainie Friedman Ross, *Growth Attenuation by Commission and Omission May Be Ethically Justifiable in Children with Profound Disabilities*, 161 ARCHIVES PEDIATRICS & ADOLESCENT MED., Apr. 2007, at 418.

The second thread of argument supporting the decisions made for Ashley and the use of similar interventions on other children rests on disability status and the effect that status has on caregivers. Diekema and Fost, the staunchest proponents of growth attenuation, mastectomy, and hysterectomy as viable options for children with disabilities, make very clear that the interventions are appropriate only because of Ashley's disabilities.[190] They dismiss as inapplicable in Ashley's case concerns about dignity, autonomy, the right to reproduce, and the right to have female body parts that might make the interventions problematic for what they call a "normal child."[191] Merle Spriggs agrees: "[D]ue to the state of Ashley's cognitive and neurological abilities, discussion of her interests is limited to whether Ashley experiences pain and suffering."[192] Peter Singer too argues that Ashley lacks dignity. He posits that neither a very young child nor an older human with comparable intellectual capacities can have dignity. A baby is cute, he says, not dignified. So too dogs and cats, "though they clearly operate at a more advanced mental level than human infants." If we do not attribute dignity to dogs and cats, why should we attribute dignity to infants or those who have an infant's intellectual capability?[193]

Given Ashley's status, proponents argue, and the demands that status puts on caregivers, the interventions are acceptable because they make Ashley easier to care for. Her parents would not have to bring strangers into the home, modify the wheelchair, or install lifts in their home. I call this the familial-best-interests argument. The familial-best-interest argument rejects what bioethicist Hilde Lindemann

---

[190] Diekema & Fost, *supra* note 179.
[191] *Id.* at 39.
[192] Merle Spriggs, *Ashley's Interests Were Not Violated Because She Does Not Have the Necessary Interests*, 10 AM. J. BIOETHICS 52, 53 (2010).
[193] Peter Singer, *A Convenient Truth*, N.Y. TIMES, Jan. 26, 2007, *available at* http://www.nytimes.com/2007/01/26/opinion/26singer.html?_r=1&scp=1&sq=A%20Convenient%20Truth&st=cse.

deems "the romance of the family," the notion that parents are morally obligated to act in the best interests of their children.[194]

> [I]n the case of Ashley X, the romance of the family expresses itself in the demand that her parents may justify medical interventions only by appealing to Ashley's best interests. Neither the parents' own needs nor their worries about the burden of care that Ashley's siblings might one day have to assume are allowed to be voiced, much less taken seriously.[195]

According to Lindemann, the romance is fiction. As participants in a lifetime relationship, parents cannot be expected to make every decision for the sake of their children. In fact, she argues, "parental motives for actions involving their children need not have *any* regard for their children's best interests, in even the most ordinary circumstances. Instead, … we bring children into a world where we all have to accommodate each other and where no one, not even the youngest or most helpless character in the romance, can expect the family to revolve solely around her needs."[196] According to Lindemann, "[e]thical thinking [would] be improved if we simply scuttle the family romance and its attendant fantasies of unconditional welcome and best-interests principles, and begin instead to ask concrete questions – for example, about the amount of net harm to which parents can defensibly expose their children. Or more speculatively, about the ethical significance we attribute to certain notions of the integrity of the human form…."[197] Acknowledging how families actually work, and the burdens faced by parents of kids with significant disabilities, will, according to Lindemann, allow for a more honest discussion of why parents who lack social and financial support seek solutions like growth attenuation

---

[194] Hilde Lindemann & James Lindemann Neslon, *The Romance of the Family*, 38 HASTINGS CENTER REP., July–Aug. 2008, at 19.

[195] *Id.*

[196] *Id.* at 21.

[197] *Id.*

for managing children's disabilities, and why it may be morally acceptable for them to do so.[198]

III. OBSERVATIONS

The issues raised in the cases of Lee Larson's boys and Ashley X
are a matter of intense debate within and between the disability and
bioethics communities. For the most part, bioethics supports parental choice for interventions like cochlear implants and growth attenuation that ameliorate physical impairments or the impact of these
impairments on caregivers. Disability experts view such interventions
as flawed and indicative of inherent social inequality. Some disability
experts would go so far as to prohibit the use of cochlear implants
in children, whereas some bioethicists would insist on implants for
all. Most disability experts would prevent parents from using growth
attenuation, mastectomy, and hysterectomy to manage a child with
profound disabilities, whereas a substantial number of bioethicists
believe growth-attenuating interventions to be an ethically appropriate
choice. I don't need to repeat the different arguments or point out the
different values driving the analyses. I do think it worthwhile, however,
to highlight several points that will be useful to keep in mind for use in
developing a disability-conscious bioethics.

First, within the debates on cochlear implants and growth attenuation, there is some consensus. For example, both disability and bioethics experts support the right of parents to make decisions for their
own children in most cases. Disagreements arise about when, whether,
and how to limit parental choice. But respect for informed parental
choices is a threshold principle and a starting point for discussion
across the disability and bioethics communities. There is also agreement that parents of children with disabilities need social support

[198] *Id.*

and education about life with disability and options for their children. Again, the details differ. Disability experts stress social support and exposure to disability experts, especially those with conditions similar to those of the child in question. Bioethics experts stress medical alternatives, their physical risks and attendant benefits, and defer largely to medical experts in defining alternatives that should be made available to parents. Both communities, however, appear to recognize that parents of children with disabilities may need more support and education in guiding their children through the medical system than do other parents.

The consensus on these two critical issues – that parents should, in most cases, be trusted to make decisions for their children, and that parents of children with disabilities need education and outside support to ensure their children are given opportunities for a good life – suggests a starting point for reconciliation and common work. However, any effort at reconciliation requires trust between the groups. In my view, trust can be achieved only if all concerned acknowledge and understand the alliances, fears, and values at play in the conflict. When it comes to acknowledging their own alliances, fears, and values with respect to disability issues in children, it seems to me that bioethics experts have some work to do.

Disability experts have long voiced fear and skepticism of medicine, medical providers, and the medical technologies designed to ameliorate disability. That fear and skepticism was on full display in the responses to the Larson and Ashley cases. Disability experts characterized both cases as new examples in the long, well-documented tradition of cases in which health providers participated in negative, even abusive treatment of persons with disabilities based on serious misconceptions about the realities of life with disability. Having acknowledged this antimedicine bias, they have not let it drive the agenda.

In their internal debate surrounding cochlear implants, for example, we saw disability experts wrestle quite expressly with their fear and skepticism of medicine. They argue that whatever benefits implanted children may derive, the children suffer a cost. Despite this cost, all but a handful of disability scholars and activists accept and support the right of parents to choose implants for their children. Indeed, the mainstream position of disability experts is not that technology is bad or should be avoided, but that decisions to use technology are ethically fraught and should be made with care and consultation with disability experts who can help parents understand the child's need for visual language as a complement to whatever oral/aural skills the child will develop via the implants. They advocate specific strategies for educating parents about cochlear implants and protecting the well-being of implanted and nonimplanted children that ensure truly informed decision making and better outcomes for children whose parents elect implantation.[199] To be sure, many disability activists have called for a moratorium on growth attenuation, but the Disability Rights Washington reached a more moderate conclusion. After close study of the Ashley case, they called for a cautionary approach involving close monitoring and court oversight of growth attenuation interventions to prevent abuse of children with disabilities.

In contrast to disability experts who wrestle with their biases, bioethics experts have been far less forthright about – or at least less cognizant of – their alliance with medicine as an institution. Once populated by philosophers and theologians who offered theoretical constructs that challenged the then-prevailing doctor-knows-best culture of medicine, bioethics is now embedded within medical institutions. Clinical ethicists have a (hard-earned!) place on the hospital floor: They make rounds on patients, write chart notes, and respond to requests for consultations by other providers. Academic ethicists teach medical students alongside other medical specialists. Ethics committees play pivotal roles in determining hospital policy and reviewing difficult cases. In other words, bioethicists are part of the health care team. They are insiders. And

---

[199] *See* Addendum, National Association for the Deaf Position Statement on Cochlear Implants.

health care providers – doctors and nurses – are equally embedded in bioethics. Indeed, many bioethicists, including the pediatric ethicists who have most staunchly defended the use of growth attenuation, mastectomy, and hysterectomy on Ashley, are physicians.

As part of the health care team, today's bioethicists have a role to play in the provision of medical care, but they leave the medicine to the medical specialists. They rarely challenge medical orthodoxy. Instead, bioethicists focus on issues of informed consent and respect for patient's choice; they will support patients who make informed choices against particular interventions, and they stand ready to analyze any emerging technology in anticipation of possible ethical dilemmas. Once an intervention is deemed "standard of care" or "medically appropriate" by their medical colleagues, however, choices for the intervention are rarely a concern of bioethics. In the last two decades, the instances in which bioethicists have challenged the voluntary, affirmative use of treatments deemed medically acceptable are few and far between.[200]

The reluctance of bioethics experts to challenge medical orthodoxy shows in cases involving cochlear implants and growth attenuation. Rather than challenge medical perspectives, bioethics experts incorporate them or defer to medical expertise. With respect to cochlear implants, the bioethics literature assumes that because their affirmative use is standard medical treatment, their use raises no ethical issues. When bioethics experts write about cochlear implants, they focus on the reasons why children should not be denied implants. They worry about "confin[ing] forever [a child] to a narrow group of people,"[201] or dooming a child to a life of disability.[202] The arguments for implantation incorporate the medical understanding of disability and reflect the medical justification for implantation: The benefits of "fixing"

---

[200] The most notable challenge to medical orthodoxy from bioethics in the last two decades was the so-called genital normalizing surgery performed on newborns with ambiguous genitalia.

[201] Davis, *supra* note 73, at 575.

[202] *Id.*

the child outweigh the medical risks of intervention. Clearly, those points should be discussed, but the absence from bioethical debate on cochlear implants of any concern about the problems faced by child recipients of cochlear implants raised without visual language (ASL) is troubling. Recall that the case of Lee Larson's boys generated no interest within bioethics.

The same deference to medical perspectives explains the bioethical debate about growth attenuation, hysterectomy, and mastectomy in Ashley's case. Initial challenges to the novel use of the interventions gave way to calls for deference to medical and parental judgment. The arguments made in support of the interventions are indistinguishable from the arguments made in support of these and other interventions in the medical literature. It comes down to a cost-benefit analysis: "whether medical interventions were likely to be safe and effective in providing benefit to the patient and improving her quality of life."[203] Concerns that the use of the interventions would be deemed abusive but for the disabled status of the child are dismissed with a medical justification: In medicine, physical difference justifies differential treatment. No ethical issues there.

Likewise, bioethicists have distanced themselves from the cautionary approach to future growth attenuation cases accepted by the hospital where Ashley was a patient. The emerging consensus among bioethicists who support growth attenuation is that courts and regulators should have no role in decision making by parents about growth attenuation, hysterectomy, or mastectomy for children with disabilities. This position also aligns closely with that of medical professionals, who tend to treat law and lawyers as a threat to their professional integrity and job performance.

In my view, the deference given the medical perspective in bioethics leaves gaps in bioethical analyses. If bioethics experts are at all committed to becoming allies of disability experts in ensuring respect for

---

[203] Diekema & Fost, *supra* note 179, at 37.

all people in the health care setting, they must be willing to challenge medical orthodoxy. So long as bioethicists continue to see disabilities as medical problems, "the medical remedy will likely make most sense."[204] The trouble is that medical remedies do not always make sense. As evidence generated by Deaf and disability experts shows, even medically acceptable means of ameliorating disability may be problematic, even traumatizing, for a child. For example, people who have grown up with cochlear implants, like members of the Deaf community who grew up passing as hearing, report psychological trauma if they were not taught to sign or exposed to deaf culture. Hearing parents have no way to know they may be harming their children if they chose cochlear implants at the expense of sign language, which is exactly what medical professionals recommend. Should not bioethics concern itself with ensuing that parents are aware of harms caused by interventions used to ameliorate disability, even if those interventions are medically acceptable? Does not a commitment to informed consent require at least that much?

ADDENDUM: NATIONAL ASSOCIATION FOR THE DEAF POSITION STATEMENT ON COCHLEAR IMPLANTS[205]

Professional Training

Medical professionals have historically been the first point of contact for parents of deaf children. Their expertise is valuable but is primarily limited only to their medical areas of expertise. They should not be viewed as, nor should they function as, experts with regard to larger issues such as the educational, psychological, social, and linguistic needs of the deaf

---

[204] Sara Goering, *Revisiting the Relevance of the Social Model of Disability*, 10 AM. J. BIOETHICS 54, 55 (2010).

[205] National Association of the Deaf, *Cochlear Implants*, http://www.nad.org/issues/technology/assistive-listening/cochlear-implants.

child. Medical professionals may be experts regarding the mysteries of the inner ear, but they are not experts regarding the inner lives of deaf children and adults. Psychological, social, educational, cultural and communication aspects of deafness, including the wellness model, must be a significant part of every medical school curriculum, especially within the specialty of otolaryngology. In-service training programs should be implemented for all interdisciplinary staff at cochlear implant centers that would include guidance and counseling methods with parents of deaf children and adults considering cochlear implants. These training programs should be conducted by professional counselors who are trained, qualified, and competent to work and communicate with deaf and hard of hearing children and adults and their families.

Early Assessment of Hearing Aid Benefit

It is widely understood and accepted that a trial period of hearing aid use is necessary prior to cochlear implantation. Advanced digital hearing aids should be explored. The NAD encourages that this effort be earnest and of appropriate duration for adequate assessment by objective testing and skilled observation of behaviors and communication skills. This assessment is complicated by the child's lack of prior auditory experience, and inability to communicate what s/he is hearing. The length of this trial period will vary with the individual. Further research by the medical and educational communities regarding objective hearing assessment and hearing aid trials is strongly encouraged.

Cochlear Implant Team

Candidacy assessment and surgery must be performed in a medical setting that has a close working relationship with a team of professionals that will provide ongoing long-term support to implant recipients. To be a responsible implant center, caution must be taken when describing the potential benefits of implantation, including risks, limitations, and long-term implications. Parents of deaf children and adults must be assisted in developing realistic and appropriate expectations. Critical to both pediatric and adult cochlear implantation and the long-range medical, audiological, psychological, social, emotional, educational, and vocational adjustment is access to implant centers fully complemented by an interdisciplinary staff, including rehabilitation specialists, psychologists and counselors. Implant center personnel must also work with and involve deafness professionals in education and in the helping professions. It takes a coordinated team of specialists, parents, educators and counselors to raise an implanted child and to support an implanted adult over an extended period of time. The implant team is also morally obligated to recognize when the implant experience has been unsuccessful and provide alternate strategies for language training.

Habilitation

An essential component of the cochlear implant process is habilitation. Parents and professionals must make a long-term commitment to integrating listening strategies throughout the child's day at home and at school. It is important to recognize that a newly implanted child is unable to understand spoken language through listening alone. Therefore parents and professionals should continue to use sign language to ensure age-appropriate psychological, social, cognitive, and language development.

Insurance Coverage

The NAD recommends that medical insurance carriers also provide fair and equitable coverage for hearing aid devices and associated support services.

Media

Reporters, journalists, anchors and directors of newspapers, television networks and film are encouraged to research and prepare their material more carefully and without bias. There is a serious need for a more balanced approach to fact-finding and reporting.

Research

Longitudinal research is critically needed, including a more thorough analysis of those for whom the implant is not working. Future research should involve highly controlled, manufacturer-independent and unbiased research on the long-term outcomes of childhood implants on auditory and communicative development, academic and intellectual development and achievement, psychological, social and emotional adjustment, and interpersonal relationship functioning. Comparative research on children without implants receiving parallel support services should also be conducted, especially those for whom sign language is the primary form of communication. Research findings relative to children with and without cochlear implants in educated lay terms must be made available and disseminated to deaf individuals, to parents of implanted children, to those in the helping professions, and to those contemplating implants.

Parents

The NAD knows that parents love and care deeply about their deaf children. Since the decision to perform implant surgery on the deaf child is made for the child, it is necessary for parents to become educated about cochlear implants – the potential benefits, the risks, and all the issues that they entail. During this critical education process, parents have both the need and the right to receive unbiased information about the pros and cons of cochlear implants and related matters. The NAD knows that parents want to make informed decisions. Parents also would benefit by opportunities to interact with successful deaf and hard of hearing adults, as well as with parents of deaf and hard of hearing children.

Deafness is irreversible. Even with the implant and increased sound perception, the child is still deaf. Cochlear implants are not a cure for deafness. The most serious parental responsibility from the very beginning is total commitment to, and involvement with, their child's overall development and well-being. Throughout the developmental years, the deaf child – implanted or not, mainstreamed or not – should receive education in deaf studies, including deaf heritage, history of deafness and deaf people, particularly stories and accounts of deaf people who have succeeded in many areas of life.

Support Services

Parents must understand that, after suitability testing and the decision-making process, the actual surgical procedure is just the beginning – a prelude to a lifetime proposition for the child and years of commitment by the parents. Implanted children are still deaf and will continue to require educational, psychological, audiological assessment, auditory and speech training, and language support services for a long period of time. Services for families and children should be provided in a manner that is consistent with standards set by the Individuals with Disabilities Education Act (IDEA), with focus on the whole child and the family. It is imperative that psychological support be available, including counseling services. Such services are to be available throughout the child's developmental years, often until adulthood.

Visual Environment

The NAD has always and continues to support and endorse innovative educational programming for deaf children, implanted or not. Such programming should actively support the auditory and speech skills of children in a dynamic and interactive visual environment that utilizes sign language and English. In closing, the NAD asserts that diversity in communication modes and cultures is our inherent strength, and that mutual respect and cooperation between deaf, hard of hearing, and hearing individuals ultimately benefit us all.

5

The Reproductive Years

IN 2005, AN 11.5-FOOT-TALL, 13-TON SCULPTURE ENTITLED "Alison Lapper Pregnant" by British artist Marc Quinn was unveiled on the fourth plinth of Trafalgar Square.[1] Subject and model Alison Lapper was cast in the nude when she was seven months pregnant with her son Parrys, whom she has raised since his birth in 1999. Lapper was born without arms and with shortened legs as a result of a medical condition called phocomelia. Brought up in British institutions for children with disabilities, Lapper is an artist in her own right. Her work focuses on her lived experience in her particular body. The public display of the Quinn's representation of Lapper's nude pregnant body ignited a public furor.

Among the reactions to "Alison Lapper Pregnant" were surprise, dismay, and revulsion at the notion that a woman with disabilities was a sexual being who was raising a child. Despite the fact that millions of people with disabilities of all types enjoy healthy sexual relationships

---

[1] For a thoughtful analysis of the sculpture's representation of disability, *see* Ann Millett-Gallant, *Sculpting the Body Ideals: Alison Lapper Pregnant and the Public Display of Disability, in* THE DISABILITY STUDIES READER (Lennard J. Davis ed., Routledge 2010). For additional information about Lapper, and the public's reaction to the statue, *see* Cahil Milmo, *The Woman on the Plinth: The Story of Alison Lapper*, THE INDEPENDENT (March 17, 2004), and Lapper's autobiography, LIFE IN MY HANDS (Simon & Schuster Ltd. 2005).

and successfully parent children,[2] a belief that people with disabilities are asexual or somehow incompetent to parent a child persists. People with disabilities of all kinds are "seen as child-like, asexual or over-sexed, dependent, incompetent, passive, and genderless and therefore considered inadequate for '*nurturant, reproductive roles....*'"[3] The belief may be the result of what social scientists deem the "spread" of stigma: "[A]n impairment of one capacity is perceived by others to spread to an impairment of all areas."[4] That belief translates to prejudice.

Historically, prejudice against disability was codified in eugenics-inspired laws that required the sterilization of people with cognitive and physical disabilities.[5] Primarily aimed at preventing "feebleminded" persons from procreating, compulsory sterilization laws were enacted by states across the United States to "protect" society from perceived burdens of supporting people who were thought to be necessarily dependent and antisocial, as well as to protect offspring from the misery thought inevitably associated with being raised by presumptively unfit parents. Under laws that remained on the books as recently as 1971, more than 60,000 people were subjected to compulsory sterilization in the first part of the twentieth century.[6]

[2] In the United States alone, parents with disabilities make up 15% of all families. See ABILITY MAG., *New National Center for Parents with Disabilities*, http://www. abilitymagazine.com/news_NCPD.html (last visited Sept. 17, 2010). Parents with psychiatric disabilities have had less success than parents with physical disabilities in maintaining custody of their children. Susan Stefan, *Accommodating Families: Using the Americans with Disabilities Act to Keep Families Together*, 2 ST. LOUIS U. J. HEALTH L. & POL'Y 135, 140 (2008).

[3] Women With Disabilities Australia (WWDA), *Parenting Issues for Women with Disabilities in Australia: A Policy Paper by Women With Disabilities Australia*, May 2009, at 11 (citing eight studies).

[4] Adrienne Asch, *Foreword* to *Disability, Reproduction & Parenting*, 2 ST. LOUIS U. J. HEALTH L. & POL'Y 1, 7 (2008) (citing BEATRICE A. WRIGHT, PHYSICAL DISABILITY: A PSYCHOLOGICAL APPROACH [HarperCollins 1960]); ERVING GOFFMAN, STIGMA: NOTES ON THE MANAGEMENT OF SPOILED IDENTITY (Touchstone 1986).

[5] *See* Chapter 1, *supra*, for a more in depth discussion of the history.

[6] *See* N. C. Ass'n For Retarded Children v. North Carolina, 420 F. Supp. 451, 457–458 (M.D.N.C. 1976); Cook v. State, 495 P.2d 768, 771–772 (Or. Ct. App. 1972); Erika

Despite the eventual condemnation and abolition of compulsory sterilization laws,[7] the passage of laws against disability-based discrimination[8] and recognition of constitutionally protected zone of privacy surrounding procreation and parenting,[9] people with disabilities continue to encounter equipment, social, financial, attitudinal, and legal impediments to reproduction and parenting. Modern-day incarnations of the prejudice behind eugenic sterilization laws persist to discourage or deny people with disabilities, especially women, the opportunity to bear and raise children. It starts in childhood, explains disability advocate and scholar Barbara Faye Waxman: "The message for disabled kids is that their sexuality will be realized through their sexual victimization ... I don't see an idea that good things can happen, like pleasure, intimacy, like a greater understanding of ourselves, a love of our bodies."[10] Disability expert Carol Gill explains, "women with disabilities are stripped of our roles. We are not expected to be workers, romantic partners, caregivers, or mothers. Socially, we are in limbo – not quite children, but not adults; not men, but not real women either.

T. Blum, *When Terminating Parental Rights Is Not Enough: A New Look at Compulsory Sterilization*, 28 GA. L. REV. 977, 989–990, 1000–1005 (1994). *See also In re* Simpson, 180 N.E.2d 206, 208 (Ohio Law Abs. 1962).

[7] *See* Skinner v. Oklahoma, 316 U.S. 535 (1942) (discussing that state law which allowed forced sterilization of habitual criminals violated the Fourteenth Amendment's Equal Protection rights).

[8] *E.g.*, Section 504 of the Rehabilitation Act of 1973, 29 U.S.C. § 794 (2000); Fair Housing Act, 42 U.S.C. § 3601 (2000); American with Disabilities Act of 1990, 42 U.S.C. § 12101 (2000).

[9] *See, e.g.*, Meyer v. Nebraska, 262 U.S. 390 (1923); Pierce v. Soc'y of Sisters, 268 U.S. 510 (1925); Prince v. Massachusetts, 321 U.S. 158 (1944); *Skinner*, 316 U.S. 535 (1942); Griswold v. Connecticut, 381 U.S. 479 (1965); Eisenstadt v. Baird, 405 U.S. 438 (1972); Roe v. Wade, 410 U.S. 113 (1973).

[10] Anne Finger, *Forbidden Fruit*, NEW INTERNATIONALIST, July 1992, *available at* http://www.newint.org/issue233/fruit.htm. For a powerful first-hand account of one paraplegic woman's hunt for medical advice before becoming pregnant, see HEATHER KUTTAI, MATERNITY ROLLS (Fernwood 2010).

It is difficult to get your bearings and struggle out from under that kind of unremitting yet subtle oppression, because it steals from you the very sense of self you need in order to fight."[11]

Negative attitudes toward sexuality and parenting affect people with cognitive and physical disabilities differently. People with cognitive disabilities, mental retardation, and mental illness face a presumption of unfitness to parent that historically has resulted in the immediate loss of custody of children who are born. Also people who lack capacity to make their own decisions are sterilized, isolated, and directly prevented from engaging in sexual relationships or becoming parents for their own protection. People with disabilities confront the attitude that people with disabilities are not sexual and should not become parents in medical offices. Doctors are far less likely to ask women with mobility and other physical impairments routine questions about reproductive health than they are other women,[12] and explicit requests for routine reproductive health services like pap smears and mammograms are sometimes denied. For example, a woman with post-polio syndrome who uses a power wheelchair reported:

> My primary physician and several specialists I respect all practice at a major university medical center fairly close to my home. Recently, though, when I requested a gynecology referral there, I was told that I would not be seen unless I could bring my own assistants to help me get on the examining table. This is a huge world-renowned hospital. This is the era of [the] ADA. Still I am treated as though I don't belong with the other women who seek services in OB/GYN unless I can make my disability issues go away. This news makes me weary. I know it means once again that I can't simply pursue what

[11] Carol J. Gill, *Becoming Visible: Personal Health Experiences of Women with Disabilities, in* WOMEN WITH PHYSICAL DISABILITIES: ACHIEVING AND MAINTAINING HEALTH AND WELL-BEING 5, 6 (Danuta M. Krotoski et al. eds., Paul H. Brookes Pub. Co. 1996).

[12] *See id.* at 8–9; Barbara Faye Waxman, *Up Against Eugenics: Disabled Women's Challenge to Receive Reproductive Health Services*, 12 SEXUALITY & DISABILITY, June 1994, at 155.

I need as an ordinary citizen. I can't be just a woman who needs a pelvic exam; I must be a trailblazer.[13]

The lack of accessible medical equipment necessary for basic women's health screening has real consequences for women with disabilities. In a law review article well worth reading,[14] law professor Elizabeth Pendo documents cases in which treatable cancers were left undiagnosed to fatal effect because women with disabilities were unable to find a provider with accessible screening equipment. Antidiscrimination laws have failed to solve the problem. As Pendo documents, twenty years after the ADA required the removal of architectural barriers to health care, providers have not installed accessible examining tables or mammography equipment that can be used by women with mobility impairments – except when subjected to lawsuits that forced the issue.[15]

The medical understanding of disability plays a role in the continued denial of reproductive health services to people with disabilities: "When disability is equated with illness, all of the associations made with illness are called into play. Persons who are ill, for example, are exempt from normal responsibilities, are not expected to be productive, are perceived as victims of a horrible disease process, and are expected to comply with the orders of persons who are experts in that disease process. For women this has the effect of neutralizing their femininity, creating the perception that they are gender-free, have no need for intimacy and sexual expression, are incapable of being a sexual

---

[13] Excerpted from Elizabeth Pendo, *Disability, Equipment Barriers, and Women's Health: Using the ADA to Provide Meaningful Access*, 2 ST. LOUIS U. J. HEALTH. L. & POL'Y 15, 16 (2008); Isaacson Kailes, *The Patient's Perspective on Access to Medical Equipment*, in MEDICAL INSTRUMENTATION: ACCESSIBILITY AND USABILITY CONSIDERATIONS 3, 5 (Jack M. Winters & Molly Follette Story eds., CRC Press 2006).

[14] Pendo, *supra* note 13.

[15] *Id.* at 33–41 (documenting ADA cases challenging lack of accessible medical equipment). Equipment barriers do not just affect access to reproductive health. *See* Kristi Kirschner, *Structural Impairments That Limit Access to Health Care for Patients with Disabilities*, 297 J.A.M.A. 1121 (2007).

partner, and have no need for reproductive Health Care Services. One woman with a severe physical disability who was interviewed for a study commented, 'I always felt like the neutral sex. It's like I'm not a woman, not a man, I don't know what I am because I was never approached like a woman.'"[16]

Parents with disabilities are also told they cannot parent their children. Some, especially parents with cognitive and psychological disabilities, are literally stripped of custody by the State.[17] For others, the message is more subtle. Scholar and activist William Peace, who uses a wheelchair to get around, described his experience, which is, by all accounts, fairly typical of a parent with visible disabilities:[18]

At the time my son was born I was flagrantly violating social norms associated with disability: I was highly educated, articulate, employed, married, and a father. None of these ordinary life experiences were or are associated with disability despite the fact there are an estimated 8 million families that include a parent with a disability. But fatherhood made me stand out (pun intended). As a parent,

---

[16] Margaret A. Nosek, *Wellness among Women with Physical Disabilities, in* WOMEN WITH PHYSICAL DISABILITIES: ACHIEVING AND MAINTAINING HEALTH AND WELL-BEING, *supra* note 11, at 17–18.

[17] Indeed, Professor Laura Rothstein has convincingly argued that there is "a judicial presumption of unfitness in many cases involving child custody for handicapped parents." LAURA F. ROTHSTEIN, RIGHTS OF PHYSICALLY HANDICAPPED PERSONS 185 (McGraw-Hill 1984). Rothstein observes that "this judicial presumption of unfitness often manifests itself in different guises for different types of disabilities: deaf parents are thought to be incapable of effectively stimulating language skills; blind parents cannot provide adequate attention or discipline; and parents with spinal cord injuries cannot adequately supervise their children." *Id. See also* Michael Ashley Stein, *Mommy Has a Blue Wheelchair: Recognizing the Parental Rights of Individuals with Disabilities*, 60 BROOK. l. REV. 1069 (1994) (documenting cases in which fit parents with physical disabilities have lost custody of children due to their disabilities); Stefan, *supra* note 2 (documenting cases in which people with psychiatric disabilities have lost custody of their children due to their disabilities).

[18] For some remarkably moving narratives, *see* BIGGER THAN THE SKY: DISABLED WOMEN ON PARENTING (Michele Wates & Rowen Jade eds., Women's Press, UK 1999).

I suddenly became public property. Anonymity was not possible. Strangers, friends, family, and all those I encountered had an opinion about my ability to parent and care for a child. No one hesitated to express their opinion and the questions directed at me were stunning. I was shocked by my loss of privacy and the utter lack of trust in my ability to care for another human being. The message sent via this constant assault on my abilities was crystal clear: paralyzed people such as myself were not parental material. My disability precluded parenting a child.[19]

Medical providers often make it worse. At a conference I recently attended, Peace described an experience that typifies what happens when a disabled parent seeks emergency medical treatment for a child. Peace's son fell and lacerated his arm when he was in middle school. Peace drove the boy to the emergency room, where staff, intake nurses and treating physicians looked to the young child for answers about who they should call about his medical care and how to contact his parents. They all assumed that Peace, who sat beside his son in a wheelchair, was just another patient.

Peace's story is typical and troubling. It suggest how thoroughly indoctrinated medical providers are in the belief that people with disabilities are patients, not people. That said, it is important to acknowledge that in some cases, especially cases involving profound cognitive disabilities, a person's impairment may in fact interfere with his or her ability to parent. In other cases, physical impairments can impact fertility or make pregnancy medically complex. Distinguishing cases in which physical or cognitive impairments actually affect a person's ability to reproduce or parent from cases in which barriers arise because of misbegotten social and attitudinal presumptions is no small task. This chapter presents two cases that struggle with that task. The first is an older but seminal case involving involuntary sterilization of a

---

[19] Posting of William Peace to Bad Cripple, http://badcripple.blogspot.com/2010/05/being-parent-with-disability.html (May 13, 2010, 9:16 EST).

woman with cognitive disabilities. The second is a hypothetical drawn from anecdotal stories related by people with disabilities who have sought the assistance of fertility clinics to become pregnant. The issues raised in the two cases are completely different in some ways because of the nature of the disabilities involved. Still, in many important ways, the stakes are the same.

I. THE CASE OF VALERIE N.

When the Supreme Court of California decided her case in 1985, Valerie was twenty-nine years old.[20] Born with Down syndrome, Valerie lived at home with her mother and stepfather, as she had her entire life. Valerie's cognitive impairments were severe. With an IQ of 30, she was not able to read or write and appeared unable to understand even basic mechanisms of voter registration or court proceedings. Valerie showed no understanding of the events that swirled around her when her parents petitioned the courts to be named her conservators so they could authorize doctors to sterilize Valerie by means of a tubal ligation. She only expressed a desire to continue living at home with her parents.

Valerie's parents sought sterilization because they believed it would improve the quality of Valerie's life; they did not contend that the sterilization was in any way therapeutic. Her mother testified that she and her husband were trying to prepare Valerie "for the time when they can no longer care for her, and to broaden her social activities as an aspect of this preparation."[21] Those efforts were stalled, however, because Valerie was interested in sex but physically and emotionally unprepared for pregnancy. As a result, her parents were not able to enroll her in new social situations with less than constant supervision. They felt her life was unduly limited by the threat that she would initiate

[20] *In re* Valerie N., 40 Cal.3d 143, 707 P.2d 760, 219 Cal. Rptr. 387 (1985).
[21] *Id.* at 148.

sexual contact and become pregnant. Sterilization would allow Valerie to lead a fuller life. Her mother explained that "Valerie had not been sexually active, apart from masturbation, because she had been closely supervised. She was aggressive and affectionate toward boys. On the street she approached men, hugged and kissed them, climbed on them, and wanted to sit on their laps."[22] The parents attempted therapy and behavior modification to address Valerie's aggressive sexual advances toward men, but the therapy was unsuccessful. They also tried other means of contraception for their daughter. Her mother testified that "Valerie had been given birth control pills in her early teens, but she rejected them and became ill. Her doctor then recommended the tubal ligation. Valerie was unable to apply other methods of birth control such as a diaphragm, and would not cooperate in a pelvic examination for an intrauterine device...."[23]

Valerie's personal physician supported her parents' petition. He testified that a tubal ligation procedure was "advisable and medically appropriate in that a potential pregnancy would cause psychiatric harm to Valerie."[24] A family and child counselor who had worked with Valerie on a weekly basis for a year submitted a written declaration that a tubal ligation was "an appropriate means of guarding against pregnancy," and that she had observed Valerie acting affectionately and inappropriately toward adult men. The counselor "was of the opinion that because Valerie's parents had found it necessary to be overly restrictive in order to avoid a possible pregnancy which would have 'severe psychologically damaging consequences' to Valerie, close monitoring had severely hampered Valerie's ability to form social relationships. She also believed that the level of Valerie's retardation meant that no alternative birth control methods were available that would ensure against pregnancy."[25]

[22] *Id.* at 149.
[23] *Id.*
[24] *Id.*
[25] *Id.*

A lawyer was assigned to represent Valerie. He offered no evidence, but argued "that less drastic alternatives to sterilization should be used...."[26] Valerie's lawyer also raised the issue that became central to the case: whether any California court had legal authority to authorize sterilization of nonconsenting conservatees. His negative answer to that question was supported by legislation. In an effort "to discontinue the longstanding, but discredited, practice of eugenic sterilization, and to deny guardians and conservators authorization to have the procedure performed on their wards and conservatees,"[27] California lawmakers had enacted a legislative scheme that absolutely prohibited the sterilization of "incompetent developmentally disabled persons." The trial court considering Valerie's case applied the legislation as written and dismissed the parents' petition on the ground that it lacked the power to grant the parents the relief they sought, namely permission to have Valerie's tubes tied. The parents appealed to the Supreme Court of California.

After engaging in extensive statutory analysis, the appellate court determined that the legislature's intent was clear: "[N]either the probate court, nor state hospital personnel were to retain authority to permit a nontherapeutic sterilization of a conservatee who is unable to personally consent to the procedure."[28] That conclusion, said the court, raised another issue: whether the legislative scheme prohibiting surgical sterilization of people with profound disabilities was constitutional.

Valerie's parents argued that the prohibition against sterilization deprived Valerie of her right to reproductive choice. Counsel for Valerie argued that the California legislative scheme protected her against sterilization forced on her by the will of others. The California Supreme Court framed the case differently from both parties. "The sad but irrefragable truth," said the court, "is that Valerie is not now

[26] *Id.* at 150.
[27] *Id.* at 143.
[28] *Id.* at 155.

nor will she ever be competent to choose between bearing or not bearing children, or among methods of contraception. The question is whether she has a constitutional right to have these decisions made for her, in this case by her parents as conservators, in order to protect her interests in living the fullest and most rewarding life of which she is capable."[29] The court noted that Valerie's parents, as conservators, had clear legal authority to make many choices for Valerie. They could, for example, choose to "impose on her other means of contraception, including isolation from members of the opposite sex. They are precluded from making, and Valerie from obtaining, the advantage of, the one choice that may be best for her, and which is available to all women competent to choose – contraception through sterilization."[30]

Emphasizing the constitutional protections afforded marriage and procreation, the court explained that "[a]n incompetent developmentally disabled woman has no less interest in a satisfying or fulfilling life free from the burdens of an unwanted pregnancy than does her competent sister."[31] "If the state withholds from her the only safe and reliable method of contraception suitable to her condition, it necessarily limits her opportunity for habilitation and thereby her freedom to pursue a fulfilling life."[32] The court therefore concluded that the legislative scheme, "which absolutely precludes the sterilization option, impermissibly deprives developmentally disabled persons of privacy and liberty interests protected by the Fourteenth amendment to the United States constitution, and article I, section 1 of the California constitution."[33]

Despite its agreement with the parents on the critical issue of access to sterilization, the court did not grant the parents' petition. Instead it

[29] *Id.* at 160.
[30] *Id.*
[31] *Id.* at 163.
[32] *Id.*
[33] *Id.* at 160–161.

204

placed strict limits on the ability of guardians to make a decision for sterilization. It would not permit guardians to opt for sterilization without evidence that sterilization was necessary for the betterment of the individual's life, and that no less intrusive means of contraception was available. In Valerie's case, the court found insufficient evidence on the record that sterilization was necessary given the absence of evidence that Valerie could in fact become pregnant, and a dearth of evidence that no less intrusive alternatives was available. The court was dissatisfied with the testimony by Valerie's mother that some form of birth control pill or other method of contraception would not be appropriate for Valerie. The court therefore remanded the case to the trial court for additional fact finding.

Three judges dissented. One would have deferred to the state legislature because it had studied "the sad historical reality pertaining to sterilization of developmentally disabled" and engaged in "prudent and constitutionally permitted legislative action."[34] Another of the dissenters objected to the majority's invocation of procreative choice for the developmentally disabled and the fiction of "substituted consent."[35] In the dissenter's view, the testimony offered in support of sterilizing Valerie reflected nothing more than the same values and assertions that had justified wholesale sterilizations in the past. Those justifications were found insufficient to maintain past practices:

> [T]here is no specific basis given for the conclusion that Valerie would be psychologically harmed by pregnancy. If the harm is the same as that which would occur to any similarly disabled person, then the specter of wholesale sterilization of such persons looms more concrete. Indeed, there is absolutely nothing in the medical evidence presented that significantly differentiates Valerie's medical and psychological condition from that of any other severely developmentally disabled woman in similar circumstances.[36]

[34] *Id.* at 170.
[35] *Id.* at 171.
[36] *Id.* at 172.

The third dissenter argued that choice and consent are meaningless concepts when applied to incompetents, and that the state has a compelling interest in protecting the fundamental rights of its citizens to bear children, which it properly exercised when it prohibited the sterilization of people who are unable to consent to sterilization.[37]

A. Views from Bioethics and the Disability Community

Although the court itself was divided over Valerie's case, the majority opinion and the issues decided are no longer particularly divisive. In the years after the case was decided, state courts and legislatures consistently followed the California court's lead and devised some procedure by which a court can authorize sterilization in individual cases.[38] In addition, disability and bioethics experts appear comfortable with the result. In fact, the responses to the issue of involuntary sterilization are consistent enough that it is not necessary to treat their reactions to Valerie's case in separate sections. Unlike with many of the issues raised in the cases in this book, there is a great deal of consensus around Valerie's and other cases of involuntary sterilization.

As a threshold matter, compulsory sterilization laws are uniformly condemned by the bioethics and disabilities communities. Whether as a matter of respect for people with disabilities or as a matter of respect for the principles of autonomy and beneficence, it is agreed that no class of people should be subjected to sterilization absent some form of consent. Disability scholars provide plentiful evidence that people with disabilities, including cognitive disabilities, can be excellent parents,

---

[37] *Id.* at 174–175.

[38] Indeed, all states but Colorado provide some procedure by which an adult with profound cognitive disabilities can be sterilized. In a strange pre-Valerie decision, the Colorado Supreme Court held that although a Colorado statute prohibits the sterilization of adults absent their consent, parents may consent to the sterilization of their disabled children. *See In re* A.W., 637 P.2d 366 (Colo. 1981).

and equally compelling equality and humanitarian-based arguments that all people should be afforded the same opportunities to become parents, regardless of impairment.[39] Bioethics experts concur, offering scathing scholarly attacks on compelled sterilization laws and their application in cases like those of Carrie Buck.[40]

With respect to Valerie's case, which of course involved a request for permission to sterilize, not application of a compulsory sterilization law, bioethics and disability experts also appear to agree on a number of points. First, no one appears to dispute that Valerie's cognitive impairments made it impossible for her to consent to surgical or other sterilization. Had there been disagreements as to Valerie's capacity to make her own decisions about the surgery, bioethics and disability experts would have agreed that "all efforts must be made to communicate the procedure and intent of the planned intervention to the patient," so that informed consent should be attained to whenever and to whatever extent possible.[41] To the extent there are disputes about Valerie's case, the disputes concern whether and under what circumstances someone other than Valerie could consent to sterilization on Valerie's behalf.

Moreover, the majority view among disability experts, and the apparently universal view of bioethics experts, is that the California court was correct to strike down the state's ban on sterilization. Among disability experts, an initial impulse to create bright-line rules against nontherapeutic sterilization of people too incapacitated to make their own reproductive choices has given way to a widespread recognition that "access to sterilization [is] an important right, and one that should be preserved for individuals who have retardation – even those deemed incapable of giving informed consent – along with the freedom to preserve one's

---

[39] *See, e.g.*, Stein, *supra* note 17, at 1085.

[40] *E.g.*, Paul A. Lombardo, *Taking Eugenics Seriously: Three Generations of ??? Are Enough?*, 30 FLA. ST. U. L. REV. 191, 201–205 (2003).

[41] Committee on Bioethics, American Academy of Pediatrics, *Sterilization of Women Who Are Mentally Handicapped*, 85 PEDIATRICS, May 1990, at 868.

reproductive capacity."[42] Reconsidering his initial reflexive opposition to involuntary sterilization, for example, disability scholar William Peace now allows that in some cases, the sterilization of people with profound cognitive disabilities "is permissible but only after it is determined that 'less intrusive and temporary methods for contraception or control of menstruation are not acceptable alternatives, and procedural safeguards have been implemented to assure a fair decisonmaking process.'"[43]

Although disability experts remain cautious about the use of sterilization on people with disabilities absent the consent of the person involved, only a handful would bar its use.[44] Most advocacy groups and scholars currently advocate laws that would allow *courts* – not parents or guardians – to permit involuntary sterilization so long as "a court order determines that the ward cannot consent, *and* sterilization is in the ward's best interest."[45] "To take away the right to obtain sterilization from persons who are incapable of exercising it personally is to degrade those whose disabilities make them wholly reliant on other, more fortunate, individuals."[46]

[42] MARTHA A. FIELD & VALERIE A. SANCHEZ, EQUAL TREATMENT FOR PEOPLE WITH MENTAL RETARDATION: HAVING AND RAISING CHILDREN 80 (Harvard University Press 2000).

[43] William J. Peace, *Ashley and Me*, HASTINGS CENTER: BIOETHICS FORUM, June 22, 2010, http://www.thehastingscenter.org/Bioethicsforum/Post.aspx?id=4742.

[44] Women With Disabilities Australia put out a white paper in May 2009, titled "Parenting Issues for Women with Disabilities in Australia," that advocates a ban on sterilization of the incompetent except when medically necessary. Unlike the other positions taken in the paper, the call for a ban on sterilization is unsupported by argument or explanation.

[45] Posting of Disabled Politico to Disaboom, *available at* http://www.disaboomlive.com/Blogs/disabled_politico/archive/2009/03/02/indiana-house-bill-2290-would-bar-involuntary-sterilization-of-people-with-disabilities-in-indiana.aspx (Mar. 2, 2009, 15:15 EST). *See also, e.g.*, Equip for Equality and F.R.I.D.A. (Feminist Response in Disability Activism), advocating such a law in Illinois, http://www.ourfrida.org/uncategorized/anti-sterilization-bill-needs-you/.

[46] Eric M. Jaegers, Note, *Modern Judicial Treatment of Procreative Rights of Developmentally Disabled Persons: Equal Rights to Procreation and Sterilization*, 31 U. LOUISVILLE J. FAM. L. 947, 976 (1993).

Calls for court oversight of medical decision making usually meet resistance in bioethics, but that has not been the case with respect to involuntary sterilization. In fact, Peace's statement directly quotes pediatric ethicist Douglas Diekema – the main proponent of the so-called Ashley treatment – in stating his position. In a paper published three years before he became embroiled in the Ashley case, Diekema published a paper titled "Involuntary Sterilization of Persons with Mental Retardation: An Ethical Analysis" in *Mental Retardation and Developmental Disabilities Research Reviews*. In the paper, Diekema argued that as opposed to other medical interventions, "sterilization requires a higher level of justification because of the greater harm that can result."[47] He also argued that in order to sterilize someone with mental disabilities, there had to be clear and convincing evidence that sterilization was in the best interests of the person, and that there were no less intrusive alternatives available to achieve the best interest of the person. Thus, he urged providers to consider "a range of options without the invasiveness or irreversibility of sterilization,"[48] such as oral contraceptives, intramuscular injections, Norplant, transdermal contraceptive patches, and long-term progesterone-releasing intra-uterine devices.[49] Consideration of less invasive and nonpermanent alternatives was important, said Diekema, because there's always a possibility that some more novel contraceptive means will be developed in the future. Thus, a person should not be sterilized before it becomes actually necessary. Diekema's paper emphasized the importance of incorporating a fair decision-making process in any case in which a person might be sterilized without his or her consent. He urged that the person in question be evaluated by an independent professional and insisted on the importance of abiding statutory

---

[47] Douglas S. Diekema, *Involuntary Sterilization of Persons with Mental Retardation: An Ethical Analysis*, 9 MENTAL RETARDATION & DEV. DISABILITIES RES. REV. 21, 26 (2003).

[48] *Id.* at 23.

[49] *Id.*

requirements of any particular jurisdiction, including requirements for court authorization.

Bioethicist Norm Cantor advocates a similarly cautionary approach to nonconsensual sterilization. He presents a powerful argument that constitutionally protected liberty rights, often equated with autonomous choice, require access to sterilization for people with disabilities, even those who cannot make their own autonomous choices:

> Liberty in the sense of autonomous choice is not the only aspect of liberty important to profoundly disabled persons. Even a constitutional prerogative that normally involves autonomous choice has constitutionally cognizable elements that are highly relevant to a profoundly disabled person. Consider the right to refuse medical intervention. That right is now established as a fundamental aspect of liberty under the Fourteenth Amendment. The right has at least three components: an interest in self-determination (that is, in making a choice about treatment), an interest in well-being (that is, in having net interests advanced by a decision about treatment), and an interest in maintenance of bodily integrity (that is, freedom from unnecessary bodily invasion).... While the profoundly disabled person cannot exercise the self-determination component, the other two personal interests that underlie a right to reject treatment – well-being and bodily integrity – are still present for the profoundly disabled patient. And while the disabled person's self-determination is not exercisable by a surrogate acting for a never competent person, a surrogate can meaningfully implement the other two elements within the right to refuse treatment. A conscientious surrogate can seek to determine whether a medical intervention will promote the net interests (well-being) of a profoundly disabled patient and whether the patient's bodily integrity (or dignity) will be needlessly compromised by the contemplated medical procedure.
>
> The same analysis applies to ... sterilization decisions. Never competent persons have important potential interests (bodily integrity, physical well-being, and procreative capacity) in these medical options even if self-determination is an impossibility.[50]

[50] Norman L. Cantor, Making Medical Decisions for the Profoundly Mentally Disabled 37–38 (MIT Press 2005).

For this reason, says Cantor, wholesale exclusion of sterilization from the list of options available to surrogate decision makers is impermissible. Quoting the court in Valerie's case, Daniels insists that "the interests of the incompetent which mandate recognition of procreative choice as an aspect of the fundamental right to ... liberty do not differ from the interests of women able to give voluntary consent to [sterilization]."[51] When sterilization would "promote a disabled person's long-range happiness, dignity, and a fuller life,"[52] it must be an option.

Making sterilization available, Cantor adds, avoids causing "dignitary harm" to people with disabilities:

> A dignitary harm occurs to profoundly disabled persons when a state categorically excludes a potentially beneficial class of medical decisions from the range of surrogate decision-making authority. It is dehumanizing to the affected disabled person when surrogates are required to preserve the medical status quo rather than weigh the potential benefits and detriments associated with possible medical responses.... The disabled individual is treated like an inanimate object in contrast to the competent patient who would be entitled, in comparable medical circumstances, to exercise the potentially beneficial option.[53]

Even though he argues that "profoundly disabled persons should be given a right to have critical medical decisions made by conscientious surrogates acting according to the interests of the disabled person,"[54] Cantor emphasizes the need for substantive and procedural safeguards against abuse:

> In a constitutional framework assuring beneficial surrogate choice, the state would have to do more than simply articulate a limiting

---

[51] *Id.* at 38 (citing *In re* Valerie N., 707 P.2d 760, 772 [Cal. 1985]); Wentzel v. Montgomery Gen. Hosp., 447 A.2d 1244, 1258 (Md. App.1982).

[52] *Id.* at 65.

[53] *Id.* (citing Philip Peters, *The State's Interest in the Preservation of Life: From* Quinlan *to* Cruzan, 50 OHIO ST. L. J. 891, 960–961 [1989]).

[54] Norman L. Cantor, *The Relation Between Autonomy-Based Rights and Profoundly Mentally Disabled Persons*, 13 ANNALS HEALTH L. 37, 79 (2004).

standard, such as best interests, to protect the disabled person from abuse by surrogates. A state would be required to allow surrogate choice on behalf of a profoundly disabled person, but would have a concomitant obligation to protect the dependent person against surrogate abuse.... States would use criminal law to punish serious deviations from acceptable guardianship standards, and civil machinery to actively intervene and supplant surrogate decisions inconsistent with the well-being of the ward. Many states already have agencies that oversee child protection and adult guardianship that could readily assume oversight of medical surrogate decision-making....

In addition to carefully articulating a standard for surrogate decision-making, a state can develop procedural safeguards to ensure that the standards are enforced. A surrogate decision made by a parent or guardian can be subjected to mandatory independent review, such as by an institutional ethics committee. That mechanism can scrutinize both the underlying facts and the surrogate's application of the relevant decision-making criteria to those facts. In the case of sterilization decisions, decision-making authority can be vested in a judge charged with deciding after fair hearing processes. Typical hearing requirements for a sterilization decision include appointment of a guardian ad litem to represent the incapacitated person's interests and appointment of independent medical experts. Another possible safeguard is to adjust the standard of proof utilized by the surrogate decision-maker. For example, end-of-life and sterilization determinations have often been subject to a standard of clear and convincing evidence that the incapacitated patient's interests dictate a particular medical course. These kinds of safeguards provide alternative means to curb abusive treatment of disabled persons short of preventing all access to a possibly beneficial surrogate medical decision.[55]

Martha Field, an expert in disability and constitutional law, also emphasizes the importance of court review. "[I]t is accepted," she says, "that parents, guardians, and caretakers cannot decide on sterilization

---

[55] *Id.* at 69–71.

themselves, without obtaining judicial approval. This might be considered the most fundamental procedural protection prerequisite to forced sterilization today."[56] Judicial involvement is imperative, says Fields, because "[w]ithout it, standards and limitations on nonconsensual sterilization might be enunciated, but no disinterested decisionmaker could determine whether or not they were actually satisfied. Judges usually are without direct interest in the particular controversy and can supervise the decisions of parents, guardians, or caretakers to assure that they follow the rules."[57]

However, Fields also recognizes that judges "have their prejudices and their shortcomings."[58] She would curtail the discretion afforded judges by imposing on them strict standards. Like Cantor, who insists that "in the context of sterilization, best interests could be broken down to include focus on the physical and mental needs of the disabled patient ... as well as on the availability of alternative contraceptive techniques,"[59] Fields would require that that "only the needs of the patient ... be considered"[60] in sterilization decisions. She explains:

> Family interests and societal interests could defensibly play a role in procreative decisionmaking for *all* persons, but our lawmakers have not pursued that policy. Perhaps a first wife with two children to support should be able to object before her ex-husband brings more children into the world; perhaps a look at the whole family would dictate that his sterilization was in the family's and society's interest. But that approach has been definitively rejected, as it has consistently been held that procreative decisionmaking is a matter of individual choice. Indeed, the doctrine extends so far that a husband does not have any say in his wife's abortion decision; the state cannot even impose a requirement that he be notified.

[56] FIELD & SANCHEZ, *supra* note 42, at 90.
[57] *Id.*
[58] *Id.*
[59] CANTOR, *supra* note 50, at 59.
[60] FIELDS & SANCHEZ, *supra* note 42, at 101.

The choice whether to abort belongs to the individual woman whose body is involved.

Because this is the clearly adopted policy for procreative decision-making by other people, there is no room for argument that persons with retardation should be subject to decisions made for the family's or the public's good. On this question, at least in theory, the law has recognized that persons with retardation should not be treated differently from all other persons. To do so would reflect our tradition of eugenic sterilization for the public good, and it would be inconsistent with our constitution's guarantees of equal treatment.[61]

Until Ashley's case (See Chapter 4) became front-page news, bioethicists appeared to agree with Fields and other disability experts that equal treatment of people without decision-making capacity required the best-interest inquiry to focus only on needs of the person for whom sterilization was in question, not her caregivers. The paradigm shift seen in Ashley's case has not yet affected bioethical analysis of involuntary sterilization cases.

Questions about equal treatment of people with different types of disabilities are also raised in the next case.

II. THE CASE OF BOB AND JULIE EGAN

Two preliminaries before I begin this case study. First, the case is a hypothetical. Unlike the others in this book, this "case" presents a fictional scenario that is an amalgam of the experiences I've heard described at conferences and phenomena regularly alluded to in literature on access to assisted reproductive technologies (ART).[62] The

---

[61] *Id.*

[62] *See, e.g.*, Carl H. Coleman, *Conceiving Harm: Disability Discrimination in Assisted Reproductive Technologies*, 50 UCLA L. REV. 17 (2002); Judith F. Daar, *Accessing Reproductive Technologies: Invisible Barriers, Indelible Harms*, 23 BERKELEY J. GENDER L. & JUST. 18 (2008); Andrea D. Gurmankin et al., *Screening Practices and Beliefs of*

reason I am using a hypothetical case is simple: There is no published account of a specific case from which I can draw.[63]

Second, I am purposefully setting up the case to avoid raising issues about creating or destroying fetuses with disabilities. My purpose in structuring the case this way is to focus affirmatively on the role medicine plays in the reproductive lives of people with disabilities without getting mired in issues about harm to the unborn, the moral status of the embryo, abortion politics, the non-identity problem, and the like. As I explained in the introduction to the book, those issues, although of tremendous importance to disability and bioethics experts, are both distracting and overwhelming. Treating them in any depth would consume this book and distract attention from other areas of equal (or greater) importance to adults with disabilities. Call it prudent or call it cowardly, but I intend to leave those issues for another day. Now, the "case."

Julie and Bob Egan met in college. Owing to complications of a condition called retinopathy of prematurity that sometimes affects the eyes of children born before thirty weeks gestation, Julie was blind. She used a cane and a guide dog to get around, lived on her own, and was a successful student. Bob was less successful academically, but he was a terrific athlete. Immediately after graduation, Bob and Julie got married. At times during college and her marriage to Bob, Julie experienced clinical depression for which she sought treatment. She has taken tricyclic antidepressants and various selective serotonin reuptake inhibitors for extended periods over the years.

Assisted Reproductive Technology Programs, 83 FERTILITY & STERILITY, March 2005, at 61; Kimberly Mutcherson, *Disabling Dreams of Parenthood: The Fertility Industry, Anti-discrimination, and Parents with Disabilities*, 27 LAW & INEQ. 311 (2009); Richard F. Storrow, *The Bioethics of Prospective Parenthood: In Pursuit of the Proper Standard for Gatekeeping in Infertility Clinics*, 28 CARDOZO L. REV. 2283 (2007).

[63] My research has located only one case that went to court that raised the issue of disability-based discrimination in access to ART. The case was dismissed on procedural grounds, and the plaintiffs did not actually allege that they had any specific disabilities. They simply refused to answer the question on the screening form. *See* Sheils v. Univ. of Pa. Med. Ctr., 1998 WL 134220, at 2 (E.D. Pa. 1998).

After several years of marriage, the Egans tried to start a family. For reasons they could not figure out, their concerted efforts over a six-month period did not result in pregnancy. Julie consulted her primary care doctor, who ran some preliminary tests. Finding nothing obvious impeding her ability to become pregnant, she referred Julie to the only fertility specialist in the region where they live. Julie and Bob set up an appointment, but their plans were interrupted when Bob had a diving accident in which he sustained a C6 spinal cord injury.

As a result of the accident, Bob's legs were completely paralyzed. He has limited use of his arms and even more limited use of his hands. Writing with pen and paper and other fine motor tasks are difficult for him. In other respects, Bob has adjusted to his disabilities. He uses a motorized wheelchair for mobility, and has had his car modified so he can drive himself and Julie without assistance. After a period of rehabilitation, he returned to work for the State of Massachusetts.

Two years after the accident, Julie and Bob decided to resume their efforts to start a family. Bob is able to have sex, and produce viable sperm, but like many paralyzed men, he is not able to ejaculate.[64] Knowing they would need medical assistance to retrieve Bob's sperm, and remembering the fertility issues they faced before the accident, Bob and Julie made an appointment with the same fertility specialist they planned to see before Bob was injured. When they arrived for their appointment, an intake worker asked them to fill out some forms. Julie asked if it would be possible to fill in the forms using a computer. The couple had worked out a system for filling out forms with a computer – Bob would read and position the mouse; Julie would type – but neither Julie nor Bob could fill in a form using pen and paper. Because a computer was not available, the intake worker

---

[64] For statistics on the physical effects of spinal cord injury on sexuality and repro-duction, *see* Dan DeForge et al., *Sexuality and Reproductive Health Following Spinal Cord Injury*, Summary, Evidence Report/Technology Assessment: Number 109. AHRQ Publication Number 05-E003–1, AGENCY FOR HEALTHCARE RESEARCH AND QUALITY, Dec. 2004, http://www.ahrq.gov/clinic/epcsums/sexlspsum.htm.

filled in the forms for them. The forms asked a number of questions about their fertility history, current health status, and health histories. The Egans described their impairments, disclosed Julie's history of depression, and reported that they were otherwise healthy. Their impairments were not heritable; the couple simply needed help getting pregnant.

After the forms were completed, Julie and Bob expected to meet with the doctor. Instead, the receptionist told them that the doctor would review their records and be in touch if he decided to take their case. Hearing nothing for several days, Julie called the office. She spoke with a nurse who told her the doctor had decided against taking their case. Julie asked if it was a question of insurance, because she and Bob had good insurance and enough money saved to pay any uncovered costs of in vitro fertilization (IVF) treatments. The nurse said no. Julie asked if the doctor's decision meant she could never become pregnant. Again, the nurse said no. The nurse explained only that Julie and Bob would need to find another care provider.

The nurse did not tell the Egans that the fertility doctor had struggled with his decision against assisting the couple. His review of the medical records gave him every reason to believe that Julie and Bob were good candidates for IVF. Nonetheless, something about treating the Egans made him profoundly uncomfortable. Quite simply, he was concerned that a future child would be at risk in their care. He could imagine all kinds of ways a baby or toddler could get hurt if left in the care of a blind mother with a history of depression and quadriplegic father. The doctor had colleagues who did not provide ART treatment to people who would be single parents or to women older than fifty because of concerns that children born to single parents or older women would be at a disadvantage from the outset. Surely, the doctor thought, a baby born to this couple would face at least as many disadvantages.

The doctor had been taught in medical school that physicians may decide which patients to take on, but he was also aware that it was illegal to discriminate against patients on the basis of race or disability. There had been a lot written in the professional literature about a California court ruling that found a fertility clinic's decision to deny services to a lesbian couple to be a form of unlawful discrimination.[65] But he was not sure that case applied to the Egan's situation.

Cautious by nature, the doctor called his lawyer to ask if any law required him to enter into a doctor-patient relationship with the Egans. The lawyer asked whether the doctor was considering whether to turn away the Egans because Julie was blind and Bob quadriplegic. The doctor said "No. I am concerned about the child we would be creating. I would treat a blind woman who was married to an able bodied man, or even a quadriplegic parent if there were a healthy parent to ensure the child was safe. But with this couple, there seem to be real risks. What if the child were to run into traffic, for example, or if there were a fire in the house? Could either parent get the child outside to safety? What if Julie goes into depression following the pregnancy? How will Bob change the baby's diapers or lift it out of a crib? He can't even hold a pen. I just don't see how this could possibly be safe for a child."

The lawyer confirmed the doctor's understanding that the physician-patient relationship is a voluntary and personal one that the physician may choose to enter, or not, for a variety of reasons, except those prohibited by law, including disability.[66] The lawyer further explained that it is not at all clear that turning Bob and Julie away would amount to disability discrimination under the law. With respect to medical treatment, the courts have been very reluctant to find

---

[65] North Coast Women's Care Med. Group, Inc. v. San Diego Superior Court, 44 Cal. 4th 1145, 189 P.3d 959 (Cal. 2008).

[66] Coleman, *supra* note 62, at 31–32 (noting that "the most important constraint on physicians' discretion over patient selection decisions is Title III of the ADA, which prohibits disability discrimination in places of public accommodation, including private physicians' offices"). *See also* 42 U.S.C. § 12181(7)(F) (2000) (including "professional office of a health care provider" in the definition of public accommodations).

discrimination by physicians, who must, after all, take into account physical and mental status when providing treatment. Unless a physician engages in discriminatory conduct that is entirely unrelated to the patient's need for care, such as turning away a patient who is seeking treatment for diabetes because a patient is deaf, or refusing to provide in-office dental care because someone is HIV-positive, it is not discrimination under the statute.[67] In the Egan's case, Bob's spinal cord injury contributed to his need for services. As such, his disability is related to and a proper thing for the doctor to consider in deciding on the services in question.

More importantly, explained the lawyer, even if one could argue that turning away the Egans was disability-based discrimination, the doctor could use the "direct threat" defense should anyone question his decision, which was unlikely in any event. The "'direct threat" defense allows doctors to engage in conduct that would constitute disability discrimination under the ADA if necessary to avoid "a direct threat to the health or safety of others."[68] The "direct threat defense" reconciles the "importance of prohibiting discrimination against individuals with disabilities" with the need to "[protect] others from significant health and safety risks."[69] The defense applies to threats to the patient, third parties, other providers, and to potential future children.[70] In the Egan's case, said the lawyer, the doctor was concerned about a direct threat to a potential child. A decision to turn them away was therefore defensible.

Feeling that he was on solid legal ground, and unaware of any applicable professional rules that required him to take on any patients, the doctor decided to decline the Egan's case.

---

[67] *See* Bragdon v. Abbott, 524 U.S. 624 (1998); Coleman, *supra* note 62, at 144.

[68] 42 U.S.C. §12182(b)(3) (2000).

[69] *Bragdon*, 524 U.S. at 649.

[70] *See* Coleman, *supra* note 62 at 43–44 (discussing the "direct threat" defense application to future children).

A. Views from Bioethics and the Disability Community

Although the Egan's case is hypothetical, disability and bioethics literature suggests a strong consensus on the most important issue raised by the case, namely that the imposition of barriers to ART based on disability status of the parent is ethically and legally problematic. Some bioethics experts might tentatively defend the actions of the doctor in the Egan's case out of deference to professional autonomy, but those who have written – and the bioethics experts trained in law have done most of the writing on issues related to access to ART[71] – would appear to agree that the fertility doctor described in the Egan's case violated ethical and legal obligations when he denied the couple access to assisted reproductive technology. Before exploring the positions in any detail, let us consider some background information.

ART providers employ a range of screening tools, some of which directly or indirectly include disability status of the prospective parent, to determine their willingness to work with a potential patient or provide a requested service. In an effort to "ensur[e] a prospective child's safety and welfare and [avoid] risking the welfare of the prospective mother,"[72] fertility providers routinely screen patients – and their partners when relevant – for various health-related conditions including sexually transmitted infections, HIV status, illness, transmissible disease, and transmissible genetic conditions.[73] The health-related screenings give prospective parents and providers information about special risks of treatment and pregnancy necessary for informed decision making and treatment planning. Providers also screen for factors more tangentially related to the welfare of the prospective child: a history

---

[71] *See, e.g., id.* at 31–43; Daar, *supra* note 62; Storrow, *supra* note 62.

[72] Gurmankin, *supra* note 62 at 64–65.

[73] *Id.* at 63.

of familial abuse, mental illness, suicide attempts, cognitive impairments, physical fitness, marital status, sexual orientation, and physical disability.[74]

The screening criteria used by practitioners are not uniform. One study of screening practices used in ART programs revealed the haphazard nature of the process:

> [f]ifty-nine percent of responding program directors would be very or extremely likely to refuse service to an HIV-positive woman, while 55% felt the same regarding a diabetic woman with a 10% chance of dying as a result of her pregnancy. Eighty-one percent of programs indicated that they would be very or extremely likely to turn away a couple where the man has been physically abusive to an existing child. Fifty-three percent would be very or extremely likely to turn away a man who does not have a wife/partner, and 48% would turn away a gay couple seeking to use a surrogate to become pregnant.... Sixty percent of the clinics would be not at all likely or slightly likely to turn away couples where the woman has a history of attempted suicide, and 68% answered similarly regarding a couple where both members have limited intellectual ability. Finally, 66% would work with a woman with bipolar disorder, and 91% would work with a couple where both members had become blind from a car accident.[75]

The survey data reflect the prevailing consensus in the fertility industry that providers have a professional obligation to ensure not just the health of the patient who would become pregnant, but also the welfare of the child that would be born if treatment is undertaken and successful,[76] and a belief that the welfare of the child is dependent on the perceived ability of the prospective patient to parent a child. What

---

[74] *Id.* at 63, 65.

[75] Mutcherson, *supra* note 62, at 316–317 (summarizing the findings of the survey reported by Gurmankin, *supra* note 62, at 62–65).

[76] Gurmankin, *supra* note 62, at 63 (indicating 64% of directors surveyed "believe in their responsibility to consider a parent's fitness before helping them conceive").

else would explain the overwhelming number of providers who would turn away a couple based on one partner's history of abusing a child, or the small but significant number of clinics that would not work with a couple rendered blind in a car accident (not by heritable condition)? The variance in response to the surveyed scenarios reveals the stark reality that assessment of the likely fitness of a prospective parent is overwhelmingly subjective and may involve unexamined assumptions that disability impairs child-rearing ability.

In the United States, neither laws nor professional organizations provide authoritative guidance on how fertility doctors should fashion selection criteria.[77] The only authoritative limits on the ability of fertility providers to screen out patients on the basis of disability come from state and federal antidiscrimination laws. The most important of these, the ADA, prohibits private health clinics and practitioners, including fertility specialists, from discriminating on the basis of disability, but the statute

---

[77] Law professor Kimberly Mutcherson suggests that:

[T]his lack of clarity starkly contrasts with the United Kingdom, where the Human Fertilisation and Embryology Authority (HFEA), a regulatory agency, specifically mandates that healthcare providers consider the potential welfare of the child before providing fertility services to prospective parents. This assessment includes considering factors that "are likely to cause serious physical, psychological or medical harm, either to the child to be born or to any existing child of the family." The HFEA requires that providers factor in "any aspect of the patient's (or, where applicable, their partner's) past or current circumstances which means that either the child to be born or any existing child of the family is likely to experience serious physical or psychological harm or neglect." Providers should be concerned about any circumstances that would "likely lead to an inability to care for the child to be born throughout its childhood or which are already seriously impairing the care of any existing child of the family." In this context, the HFEA flags a prospective parent's "mental or physical conditions," "drug or alcohol abuse," or "any aspect of the patient's ... medical history which means that the child to be born is likely to suffer from a serious medical condition."

Mutcherson, *supra* note 62, at 318. Although the regulations cited by HFEA reflect the strict regulation of the fertility industry in the United Kingdom, I am not convinced that they provide fertility specialists any particular specificity as to how and whether a prospective parent's "physical or mental condition" will affect parenting ability.

is riddled with exceptions and ambiguities that arguably allow doctors to treat people with disabilities differently from other people. For example, the law allows a provider to deny access to a requested treatment when such treatment would be outside of the provider's expertise, when an individual assessment of the patient reveals that the treatment would be medically counterindicated because of a patient's disability, and when the provision of treatment would pose a direct threat to a third party. In the medical context, application of these exceptions is exceedingly complex. Disability and medical decision making are unavoidably entangled. Providers must consider a patient's disabilities to assess individual conditions and prognoses, and treatment plans may appropriately depend on a patient's disability status. As a result, ADA claims against health care providers are rarely pursued and even more rarely successful. Absent an admission by a provider that treatment decisions were based on a person's disability status as opposed to individualized consideration of how a patient's disability would affect treatment in the case, courts have consistently rejected discrimination claims lodged against health care providers for their treatment decisions.[78]

Although legal scholars insist that disability-based denials to ART are prohibited under the ADA,[79] the law is having little practical effect on the fertility industry. Law professor and bioethics expert Judith Daar explains: "[I]t will likely be the rare physician who makes a 'smoking gun' admission to the patient that care is being withheld because

[78] *See, e.g.*, U.S. v. University Hosp., 729 F.2d 144 (2d Cir. 1984) (applying section 504 of Rehabilitation Act); *In re* Baby K, 832 F.Supp. 1022, 1028–29 (E.D. Va. 1993), *aff'd* on other grounds, 16 F.3d 590 (4th Cir. 1994); Glanz v. Vernick, 750 F.Supp. 39, 46 (D. Mass. 1990); Lesley v. Hee Man Chie, 250 F.3d 47, 55 (1st Cir. 2001). *Compare* Bragdon v. Abbott, 524 U.S. 624, 649 (1998).

[79] Coleman, *supra* note 62, at 33 (arguing "that courts should interpret 'disability' and 'discrimination on the basis of disability' broadly in the context of ART decisions, in order to facilitate patients' ability to establish a prima facie case. Such an approach would not necessarily lead to a finding of unlawful discrimination, but it would ensure that the physician's reasons for denying the patient treatment are subject to judicial review.").

of the person's race, national origin, marital status, or sexual orientation. Overwhelmingly, treatment denials will be justified on the basis of physician autonomy, unrelated to the personal characteristics of the patient which would amount to impermissible discrimination."[80] Thus, fertility doctors are likely to continue the practice of screening based on perceived ability to parent, at least until a physician makes the mistake of being unusually candid with a person who is willing to pursue a private cause of action, and the courts get involved. Moreover, because no regulatory body is charged with overseeing the fertility industry or enforcing the ADA in the health care context, even discriminatory denials will likely continue unchecked.

Although professional organizations in the United States have played a significant role in ensuring compliance with law and ethical principles in other fields, they have not played the same role in the fertility industry. Professional organizations do not demand that certified fertility doctors provide equal access to fertility treatments for patients regardless of disability status. Existing professional guidelines do suggest equal access, but they have no teeth. For example, an ethics opinion published by the American Society of Reproductive Medicine's Ethics Committee calls into question the ethics and morality of using subjective assessments about fitness to parent in screening potential patients.[81] Published in 2009 by a committee of prominent bioethicists and fertility specialists, the report concludes that fertility providers "may withhold services from prospective patients on the basis of well-substantiated judgments" that the child would not be adequately provided for, but singles out parents with disabilities as a group to whom services should not be denied "except in rare cases."[82] The opinion is merely aspirational, however.

---

[80] Daar, *supra* note 62, at 65.
[81] The Ethics Committee of the American Society for Reproductive Medicine, *Child-Rearing Ability and the Provision of Fertility Services*, ASRM Ethics Committee Report, 92 Fertility & Sterility, Sept. 2009, at 864 [hereinafter Committee Report].
[82] *Id.*

As such, it is more telling about the application of bioethical analysis to access issues than meaningful in terms of reigning in discrimination in screening practices by fertility specialists.

Given the understanding by fertility specialists that they are obligated to promote the welfare of prospective children and the lack of legal or professional limitations on the screening practices of fertility doctors, Julie and Bob Egan's case is not far-fetched. Should a similar case come to the attention of disability and bioethics experts, however, one can expect widespread disapproval of the actions of the doctor.

The disability perspective on the issue of access to ART is quite clear. Medical, social, and legal screening for parental ability has long been a concern in the disability community. It is not just mandatory sterilization laws that are an issue. People with disabilities lose custody of their children at alarming rates based on widespread assumptions that disabilities impair child-rearing ability. For example, in a California case, a trial court decided that after he was injured in a jeep accident that left him a quadriplegic, William Carney should lose custody of the boys he had raised on his own in favor of an ex-wife who had not visited or contributed in any way to their support.[83] In transferring custody, the court based its ruling on Carney's physical disability and its presumed adverse effect on his capacity to be a good father. The trial judge reasoned that "because of William's physical disability, he could not 'do anything for the boys except maybe talk to them and teach them, be a tutor, which is good, but it's not enough.' After all, the judge reasoned, wouldn't it be better if the boys had a parent who could 'take them places, play little league baseball, go fishing?'"[84] Although the decision was overturned on appeal, the trial court's decision encapsulates the common understanding, contested by the disability community, that a parent with a disability is unable to provide care, unable to provide love, and unable to be a parent.

---

[83] Carney v. Carney, 598 P.2d 36 (Cal. 1979).
[84] Stein, *supra* note 17, at 1083.

Disability experts counter this perception. They often quote the decision of the California Supreme Court, which reversed the lower court in *Carney*, to offer a more expansive understanding of the parent-child relationship that one dependent on physical care. The stereotype that disabled parents cannot parent "is false because it fails to reach the heart of the parent-child relationship. Contemporary psychology confirms what wise families have perhaps always known that the essence of parenting ... lies in the ethical, emotional, and intellectual guidance the parent gives to the child throughout the formative years, and often beyond."[85] Through narrative after narrative and study after study, disability experts demonstrate that people with disabilities are excellent parents, and that children raised by parents with disabilities are stable, educated, and safe.[86] Based on this evidence, disability experts argue that people with disabilities should be afforded the same presumptions of fitness to parent as any other adult. From a disability perspective, then, people with disabilities should have access to ART on an equal basis with anyone else. Presumptions about child-rearing abilities should have no place in the process because they are an unfair barrier to the ability of people with disabilities to "found a family."[87]

---

[85] *Carney*, 598 P.2d at 44.

[86] *See, e.g.*, BIGGER THAN THE SKY: DISABLED WOMEN ON PARENTING, *supra* note 18; RICHARD OLSEN & HARRIET CLARKE, PARENTING AND DISABILITY: DISABLED PARENTS' EXPERIENCES OF RAISING CHILDREN (Policy Press 2003); Stein, *supra* note 17; WOMEN WITH PHYSICAL DISABILITIES: ACHIEVING AND MAINTAINING HEALTH AND WELL-BEING, *supra* note 11; WWDA, *supra* note 3, at 15–16, 19–20.

[87] WWDA, *supra* note 3, at 23 (citing Universal Declaration of Human Rights art. 16, G.A. Res. 217A (III), at 71, U.N. Doc A/810 [Dec. 10, 1948]); International Covenant on Civil and Political Rights art. 23, March 23, 1976, 999 U.N.T.S. 171; International Covenant on Economic, Social and Cultural Rights art. 10, Jan. 3, 1976, 993 U.N.T.S. 3; Convention on the Elimination of All Forms of Discrimination Against Women art. 16, Sept. 3, 1981, 1249 U.N.T.S. 13; Standard Rules on the Equalization of Opportunities for Persons with Disabilities Rule 9, G.A. Res. 48/96, Annex, 85th plen. mtg. Dec. 20, 1993; Convention on the Rights of Persons with Disabilities art. 6, 23, May 3, 2008, 189 U.N.T.S. 137.

Bioethicists are also troubled by the imposition of barriers to ART for people with disabilities, but they debate what, if any, restraints on access to ART are justified by disability-related health concerns for mother or child. In bioethical debate, the question is what, if any, weight should be given three interests implicated by access questions: "[t]he interest of future children in having a healthy home environment and minimally competent rearing parents ... the interest of infertile persons in receiving the treatment services they need to reproduce and the provider's own sense of moral responsibility in deciding what patients to treat." [88]

The ASRM ethics committee concluded that some weight must be afforded to each of these interests. In reaching a compromise position, it debated whether, and then concluded that, "the well-being of offspring is an overriding ethical concern that should be taken into account in determining whether to provide infertility services."[89] The committee rejected philosophical arguments that harm to a child from assisted reproduction can never be a valid reason to withhold services because the alternative is that the child will never be born as "too narrow a view of the relevance of offspring welfare in determining ethical conduct":[90]

> Although a child may not strictly speaking be "harmed" as a result of fertility procedures that made its birth possible, we think that concerns about future harm to offspring validly may be taken into account in making ethical assessments about those treatments. For some persons the diminished welfare of the child alone is sufficient to justify this conclusion. Others might point to the significant costs and burdens that children with greatly diminished welfare impose on others. In addition, it is difficult to understand how a person's interest in reproducing and rearing offspring is rationally served in cases in which there is a high risk of injury to a prospective child from conception or the rearing situation into which the child will be born.

[88] Committee Report, *supra* note 81, at 865.
[89] *Id.*
[90] *Id.*

These are not easy judgments to make, and providers or policy-makers should be very cautious in making them. A wide range of social situations are compatible with a child thriving and having a meaningful life and persons having a rich and responsible parenting experience. For concerns about the welfare of offspring to be relevant to ethical assessment or policy choice, they would have to be very large deviations from normal health and social situations, with such assessment made only after careful consideration of relevant factors.[91]

The committee further concluded that "[p]rofessional autonomy ... entitles physicians to choose *not to treat* persons whom they think will be inadequate child-rearers (as long as they comply with anti-discrimination laws)."[92] Balancing the interests of future children and professional autonomy against the interests of infertile people in repro-ducing, the committee concluded that "physicians in private practice might legitimately, when a clear case of a substantial risk of harm to offspring is shown, choose not to provide services that make such a birth or rearing situations possible."[93] The committee noted that "[m]ost persons with disabilities are able and well-qualified to rear children, and should not be disqualified from doing so merely because of their disability."[94] Indeed, the committee noted that the ADA prohibits fer-tility providers from denying services to persons with disabilities "if the denial is based on ill-founded doubts or stereotypes about their ability to rear and parent."[95] According to the ASRM committee, examples of "substantial, non-arbitrary basis for concern about parental ade-quacy" include "uncontrolled psychiatric illness, a history of child or spousal abuse, or drug abuse."[96]

[91] *Id.* at 865–866.
[92] *Id.* at 866–867.
[93] *Id.* at 866.
[94] *Id.*
[95] *Id.*
[96] *Id.* at 865.

Judith Daar, Carl Coleman, and other legal experts who work in bioethics would give providers less room to deny access ARTs to people with disabilities than would the ASRM Committee.[97] Daar, for example, would give less deference to provider autonomy:

I agree that physician discretion to deny ART is warranted in certain situations, but on grounds different than those articulated by the ASRM. Basing a physician's ability to deny ART services on his or her prediction about the child-rearing abilities of a prospective parent is speculative and leaves too much opportunity for masking pure discrimination with concern for offspring. Instead, providers should be able to deny ART services if they believe the patient's well-being will be negatively affected by the treatment. Just as intensive care physicians should have the right to refuse to provide non-beneficial care to irreversibly ill patients, ART providers should be able to withhold services they reasonably believe would cause harm to a person. Admittedly, this window of refusal is decidedly narrow, but it is not nonexistent. For example, it may be reasonable for an ART provider to conclude that a woman with uncontrolled psychiatric illness or a history of drug abuse would not fare well during pregnancy. She may be unable to manage the physical and psychological burdens of pregnancy, causing harm to herself or others. Likewise, a woman who is the subject of spousal abuse might be an even greater target of violence, as studies show that abused women report higher levels of violence during pregnancy.[98]

Unlike Daar, Coleman would permit physicians to take into account the implication of ARTs for resulting children, but he argues against allowing providers "to consider the full range of factors that prospective parents consider in deciding whether to reproduce."[99] "As licensed professionals, they should be limited to rational considerations that

---

[97] *See also* Storrow, *supra* note 62 (concluding that bioethical principles limit the rights of fertility providers to act as gatekeepers to ART services for people with disabilities).

[98] Daar, *supra* note 62, at 67–68.

[99] Coleman, *supra* note 62, at 60.

society is prepared to recognize as fair,"[100] such as health implications for children directly attributable to a parent's impairment. Health concerns are different from concerns about the impact of a patient's disabilities on her ability to care for a child, says Coleman. The inability of a person to parent would have to be "truly extraordinary to justify a decision to withhold ARTs," says Coleman, because "[p]redictions about the parenting ability of patients with disabilities are especially prone to error and bias. Even when patients' disabilities affect their ability to parent effectively, they may be able to compensate for any deficiencies with the assistance of family members, friends, or other support networks."[101]

Notwithstanding the differences between their approaches, application of the bioethical analyses proposed by the ASRM committee, Daar, and Coleman yield the same conclusion with respect to Julie and Bob Egan's case. The denial of care was ethically problematic. The physician's vague feelings about the kind of parents the Egans might make do not even meet the most relaxed of these standards. Even those most concerned about physician autonomy reject the notion that providers can deny access based on biased assumptions about the ability of people with disability to parent. Thus, on the concededly narrow issues raised by the Egan case, bioethics and disability experts are on the same page.

III. OBSERVATIONS

Many of the issues confronting people with cognitive and physical disabilities in their reproductive years stretch well beyond the scope of this book. How to provide and who should pay for parenting support, what that support should look like, and how to resolve custodial

---

[100] *Id.*
[101] *Id.* at 60–61.

disputes are just some of the issues that are outside the realm of bioethics, even if bioethics is broadly defined. Some of the issues raised in this chapter, however, attitudinal and equipment problems in exam rooms, sterilization of people who lack decision-making capacity, and access to technologies that assist in reproduction – fall squarely within the realm of bioethics expertise. What struck me most in considering these case studies is how little attention bioethics has given to what appear to me the most pressing, and easily resolved, of the issues: equipment barriers, attitudinal problems, and educational gaps in medical training that allow health care providers to treat parents like William Peace as nonpersons. Bioethics literature is full of debate about the ethics of terminating fetuses with disabling conditions[102] and the use of cutting-edge technologies like preimplantation genetic screening and manipulation.[103] Issues about access to ART, another new technology, have gotten attention, but the literature is oddly silent on the experiences of people with disabilities who seek reproductive health care or become parents. Instead, bioethics experts tend to focus attention – at least in published work and in scholarly conferences – on the new and innovative technologies and dramatic end-of-life cases.

This myopic focus of bioethics seems to me especially troubling when it comes to reproductive issues and people with disabilities. It is almost cliché to talk about the rewards and challenges of parenting. The onset of fertility, the entry into sexual relationships, the desire to avoid pregnancy, the desire to become a parent, the moment of conception, the course of pregnancy, the transition to parenthood, and daily life of caregivers of children are all fundamental parts of the human experience. The importance of the right to create a family has

---

[102] For reasons I explained in the introduction, I am purposefully leaving discussion of prebirth issues for another day.

[103] *See, e.g.,* Judith F. Daar, *Embryonic Genetics*, 2 St. Louis U. J. Health L. & Pol'y 81 (2008).

been recognized by the U.S. Supreme Court[104] and codified in international treaties.[105] Despite that, things as simple as a nonaccessible examination room tables or the failure of physicians to understand the reproductive and parenting capacities of persons with disabilities impede the ability of thousands of people to get the care needed to fully exercise their reproductive rights. Surely, bioethicists could work together with disability experts to eliminate these barriers. Bioethics' stunning lack of interest in addressing such easily removable barriers suggests a problem of priorities. Putting the bioethicists to work with disability experts to break down these barriers might go a long way toward building trust between the groups.

I'll propose specific areas for collaborative work after I make a second, related observation about the cases in this chapter. As I noted throughout the chapter, access to reproduction and reproductive health services is an area about which disability and bioethics experts agree more often than they disagree. To be sure, there is some debate about the role of family issues, provider autonomy, and court involvement in reproductive cases. Unlike with other case studies, however, the sides are not calling for absolute positions (always deny access to X; always allow access to X). Instead, the debates are about balancing competing concerns – recognized by all constituencies as real and relevant. We see

---

[104] *See* Eisenstadt v. Baird, 405 U.S. 438, 453 (1972) ("If the right of privacy means anything, it is the right of the individual, married or single, to be free from unwarranted governmental intrusion into matters so fundamentally affecting a person as the decision whether to bear or beget a child").

[105] *See* Universal Declaration of Human Rights art. 16, G.A. Res. 217A (III) at 71, U.N. Doc. A/810 (Dec. 10, 1948); International Covenant on Civil and Political Rights art. 23, March 23, 1976, 999 U.N.T.S. 171; International Covenant on Economic, Social and Cultural Rights art. 10, Jan. 3, 1976, 993 U.N.T.S. 3; Convention on the Elimination of All Forms of Discrimination Against Women art. 16, Sept. 3, 1981, 1249 U.N.T.S. 13; Standard Rules on the Equalization of Opportunities for Persons with Disabilities Rule 9, G.A. Res. 48/96, Annex, 85th plen. mtg. Dec. 10, 1993; Convention on the Rights of Persons with Disabilities art. 6, 23, May 3, 2008, 189 U.N.T.S. 137.

all constituencies working to ensure access where appropriate without risking the health of individuals involved or allowing biased stereotypes to drive the results. We see members of the disability and bioethics communities calling for the education of medical providers to counteract the bias that concededly taints medicine. The conversations are, in my view, where they should be: constructive, forward-moving, and respectful.

The fact of consensus and civil conversation is something to consider in its own right. What makes this conversation different from the other, more contentious conversations? The general agreement about access to sterilization is especially telling. Cases involving involuntary sterilization could easily devolve into the angry shouting matches and reactive posturing that plague debates about end-of-life cases. But they do not, at least in their present incarnations. One explanation may be the passage of time. The initial reaction to the abolition of mandatory sterilization laws was, after all, the enactment of extreme laws that banned the use of sterilization on certain populations – a position that proved untenable with time.[106] All constituencies have had more time to think about involuntary sterilization than genetic modification of embryos or the Ashley treatment. With time, defensiveness abates, flaws in extreme reactionary positions become apparent, and discussions become more nuanced.

Still, I think a more important factor is the simple acknowledgment by all constituencies that the fears and concerns of others should be taken seriously. When it comes to sterilization, medical and bioethics experts do not dismiss as improbable the concerns of the disability community about abusive practices. On their part, disability groups do not dismiss the concerns of medical and bioethics experts that absolute prohibitions against sterilization of groups of people can harm individuals in those groups. The various constituencies show respect

---

[106] Cantor, *supra* note 54, at 51–53 (discussing the history of involuntary sterilization laws).

for one another by acknowledging the legitimacy and need to account for the concerns of others. The mutual showing of respect allows room for constructive conversation that is not available when people are shouting to be heard.

Given the respectful space that exists with respect to access issues in the reproductive years, I see a tremendous opportunity for bioethicists to join forces with disability activists. Disability expert Carol Gill has issued this call to action: "Physicians and other health professionals must receive more information about our value and full lives as women with disabilities so we may all leave clinics feeling like *women* rather than medical *problems*. Gynecologists and obstetricians, in particular, must be trained to affirm our gender and sexuality by offering us more complete information and a full array of reproductive health options."[107] Bioethicists have a role to play in this training. As faculty members in medical schools, bioethicists can shape curriculum and teach about disability issues. Even better, they can bring in disability experts to do the educating.

Nothing educates us about different people better than exposure. The public display of "Alison Lapper Pregnant" challenged assumptions and preconceptions, forced conversations, and facilitated changed attitudes. Would William Peace and his son have had a different experience in the emergency room if health care providers had been exposed as part of their training to parents of different abilities who challenge their preconceptions about what a fit parent looks like? I think so. I know how powerfully my interactions and the friendships I've developed with people with disabilities have changed my understanding of disability over the course of this project.

Even if the collaborative efforts of bioethicists and disability experts do nothing more than address the low-hanging fruit – equipment and attitudinal barriers to reproductive heath – the effort will help ease

---

[107] Gill, *supra* note 11, at 12.

the distrust of people with disabilities toward the medical system. Carol Gill explains:

> Simple changes can make a real difference in the life of woman with disabilities. For example, making the gynecological clinic accessible to women with disabilities, and recognizing women with disabilities, can be empowering. Consider the experience of one woman with physical disabilities who described 20 years of searching for gynecological exams. She finally found a clinic that specialized in access for women with disabilities. She "felt acknowledged as a woman for the first time." She was effusive about the accessible examining chair, the discreet and respectful assistance she received, and the doctor who allowed her to remain in control and who encouraged her to watch the exam in a mirror. She said the most exciting part was being treated like she was not strange, or defective, or a problem. She had never experienced this attitude of acceptance in a gynecological clinic before. She said it would almost be worth getting a yeast infection so she could go back![108]

Clinical ethicists also have a role in this work. Physicians should not be complicit in perpetuating unfair stereotypes. They may not be aware of the "spoiling process" in which impairment "obscure[s] all other characteristics behind that one and swallow[s] up the social identity of the individual within that restrictive category."[109] Clinical ethicists can use their place on the hospital floor to identify and educate about the spoiling process. Furthermore, as Norm Cantor writes:

> [S]urrogates and medical personnel [should be admonished] against allowing common prejudices or stereotypical misconceptions [about disabled persons] to play a role in surrogate decision-making. Medical personnel should also be reminded of their duty to

---

[108] *Id.* at 11.

[109] Irving Kenneth Zolo, *Self, Identity, and the Naming Question: Reflections on the Language of Disability, in* THE SOCIAL MEDICINE READER 77, 80 (Gail E. Henderson et al. eds., Duke University Press 1997).

seek review (from an ethics committee or a court) when a surrogate medical decision seems inconsistent with acceptable standards of patient care.[110]

Using the civil space around access to reproductive health as a starting point for collaborative work between the disability and bioethics communities may pay dividends of good faith and trust that will pay off when the communities turn attention to the next issue. Of course the challenge to the collaborative work I've suggested is putting aside, for the time being, divisive issues like the deliberate destruction of embryos with disabilities. I think it is worth the effort.

[110] CANTOR, *supra* note 50, at 59.

6

The Adult Years

IN THE NINE YEARS BETWEEN THE EQUESTRIAN ACCIDENT that rendered him a ventilator-dependent quadriplegic and his death in 2005, American actor Christopher Reeve focused on a single goal: he was determined to walk again. "The most famous disabled person after Roosevelt,"[1] Reeve became a national spokesman and public symbol of the "fight for the cure." In appearances before Congress, on television news shows, and in an address to the Democratic National Convention, Reeve pleaded for funding for innovative research to cure spinal cord injuries. He engaged in intensive rehabilitation efforts and publicized his accomplishments. Explaining that he was "not that interested in lower sidewalks and better wheelchairs,"[2] he kept his focus on a cure: "It's nice to have good equipment and access while you're disabled but I think all of us with these problems should be allowed to regard them as a temporary setback rather than a way of life."[3]

Reeve's single-minded focus on cure alienated disability activists. Although they acknowledged that finding a cure for spinal cord injuries

---

[1] Mary Johnson, *Christopher Reeve, Rest in Peace*, RAGGED EDGE ONLINE, Oct. 11, 2004, http://www.raggededgemagazine.com/mediacircus/creevedeath.html.

[2] Pat Williams, *Christopher Reeve: What's It Gonna Take?*, RAGGED EDGE MAG., Jan./Feb. 1997, *available at* http://www.raggededgemagazine.com/archive/p16story.htm.

[3] *Id.*

was a "laudable goal,"[4] the activists found Reeve's attitude counterproductive and insulting to "innumerable disabled people who are more concerned with social injustices than a cure for paralysis."[5] In her book *Make Them Go Away: Clint Eastwood, Christopher Reeve & The Case Against Disability Rights*, activist Mary Johnson lamented Reeve's affirmation of the widely held but strongly contested belief "that a disabled person's defining problem is that his body is not 'whole'; that what he needs – the only thing he needs, really – is to be cured. That without this cure, things will never truly be all right for a disabled person. For this is the message one sends when one pushes for cure to the exclusion of rights and access."[6]

Activists would have preferred to see Reeve focus on other issues. They suggested, for example, that Reeve's time would be better spent putting a national spotlight on access issues that plague the thousands of people with disabilities who do not have Reeve's "access to such high-level medical care [or] the financial resources to hire fulltime employees…. In separating himself from other disabled people, Reeve has lost a golden opportunity to raise awareness of the myriad problems disabled people encounter daily."[7] Access issues affect employment, recreation, education, transportation, and reproduction. They also affect health care, as documented in the scholarly work of Deaf law professor Michael Schwartz, who describes experiences of deaf adults who suffer "misdiagnoses, misinformation, incorrect dosages, and poor understanding of their health, in large part because the information from the doctor was either incomprehensible or unavailable

---

[4] William Peace, *Wishing for Kryptonite: A Response to Christopher Reeve's Pursuit of Cure*, RAGGED EDGE MAG., Sept. 24, 2002, *available at* http://www.ragged-edge-mag.com/extra/reevepeace.html.

[5] *Id.*

[6] MARY JOHNSON, MAKE THEM GO AWAY: CLINT EASTWOOD, CHRISTOPHER REEVE AND THE CASE AGAINST DISABILITY RIGHTS 129–130 (Advocado Press 2003).

[7] Peace, *supra* note 4.

… because the lack of effective communication access in an aurally inaccessible office."[8]

Reeve's focus on cure was not unusual in an adult confronted with a sudden-onset disability. Nor was it particularly ethically fraught. Even the disability activists who disagreed with or were disappointed by Reeve's focus on cure did not argue that his individual choices for rehabilitative care were ethically or morally problematic. "People have different reasons for turning to medicine, and will have different reactions to their impairments,"[9] they acknowledged. The disability critique of the "cure agenda" focuses on the unwelcome pressure it exerts on people who do not experience disability negatively or see their bodies as broken, and the practical problems that arise when "new medical research findings are associated with hyperbole and raised expectations that do not translate into benefits" despite their drain on scarce resources.[10]

Some reactions to disability generate more ethical debate than Reeve's choices for rehabilitation. Treatment refusal cases are especially controversial. They arise in a variety of contexts. At this point in our study of disability and bioethics, it should be clear that different people experience disability in different ways. An individual's experience may differ depending on time of onset, type of disability, or a host of other factors. Some adults "for example, people with congenital impairments which are largely static in nature tend to be well-adjusted to their situation, partly because they have known no other state. Impairment is their normality."[11] For such individuals, impairment becomes a part of personal identity, the individual cannot conceive of him or herself without the trait, and the prospect of "cure may

---

[8] Michael Schwartz, *Deaf Patients, Doctors, and the Law: Compelling a Conversation About Communication*, 35 FLA. ST. U.L. REV. 947, 956 (2008).

[9] TOM SHAKESPEARE, DISABILITY RIGHTS AND WRONGS 109 (Routledge 2006).

[10] *Id.* at 110–112.

[11] *Id.* at 106.

be seen as irrelevant or even threatening."[12] Others, especially those who develop static impairments as a result of disease, degenerative condition, or accident, may experience impairment as a devastating loss. For some, loss is so significant that death seems a better option than continued life. Still others may have life-long, or newly developed cognitive impairments that affect identity, self-awareness, and decision-making capacity. People in any of these situations may resist recommended medical treatment (or have surrogates who resist on their behalf) for any number of reasons: a lack of interest in care, an assertion of independence or values, or a desire to hasten death. The last category – the refusal of treatment to hasten the death is the source of fierce debate and conflict between and among the disability and bioethics communities.

This chapter presents three cases that span a variety of experiences of disability. The first concerns a woman with life-long physical disabilities. The second involves a man with sudden adult-onset physical disabilities. The third involves a man with life-long profound cognitive and physical disabilities. The ethical issues raised by each case are as different as the factual situations presented, but the cases share a common thread: Each involves a hard-fought decision to refuse recommended medical treatment for an adult with disabilities. In each, the right of the patient or the patient's surrogate to refuse the proffered treatment was vindicated based on application of basic principles of bioethics. The response to the issues raised in these cases is more complicated from a disability perspective, where the disability critique of life-and-death decisions calls into question application of those basic bioethics principles. These case studies help explain why the issues raised in treatment refusal cases remain so contentious, despite an initial impulse, shared by disability and bioethics experts, to allow individuals with disabilities to control their own lives.

[12] *Id.*

I. MARY'S CASE

"Mary" was a forty-eight-year-old woman from Rochester, New York, who "had been institutionalized since her early childhood and for the first 30 years of her life had been believed to be severely mentally retarded."[13] During that period, she lived in "a custodial facility that paid attention only to her most basic needs."[14] As advances were made in medical understanding of intelligence and cognitive disability, Mary was reevaluated. "It was discovered that, in fact, she had severe cerebral palsy and had high-normal intelligence. She learned to read quickly and was able to communicate using a spelling board."[15]

Even after state officials recognized that Mary was mentally competent, it was determined that Mary needed to remain in a state facility because she had no family and no means to provide the day-to-day care necessitated by her physical limitations. Mary, therefore, was placed in a group home facility under the authority of the state mental health department. There, she made it vividly clear that "she valued her independence and was fiercely protective of her right to control her own body."[16]

During a routine physical exam, Mary's primary care provider, a family doctor, recommended that she have either a barium enema or a flexible sigmoidoscopy for screening purposes. Using her spelling board, Mary explained "that she did not want the procedure and firmly asserted her right to refuse it."[17] The primary care physician, a family doctor, accepted her decision, but the group home director did not.

---

[13] Jane Greenlaw, *Does the Law Interfere with Ethical Patient Care? How It Can and Why It Need Not*, 7 HARV. REV. PSYCHIATRY 361, 363 (2000).
[14] *Id.*
[15] *Id.*
[16] *Id.*
[17] *Id.*

The group home director felt responsible to enforce a mental health department regulation that required that patients in department facilities be provided the full range of health services. The regulation put responsibility for enforcement on the facility director. He read the rule as an absolute requirement that facility residents undergo all recommended screening procedures, and considered himself susceptible to discipline or liability if he did not ensure compliance.

Despite the protestations of the facility director, the family doctor refused to perform the procedure on Mary without Mary's consent. The doctor forced the issue by calling a meeting attended by Mary, the facility director, mental health department officials, and two health law professors. The conversation was heated. During the confrontation, Mary explained her position about the procedure on her spelling board by writing out the words "VIOLATE! VIOLATE!"[18]

Eventually, the group came to a consensus that Mary's wishes should be respected. The state officials acknowledged that the regulation was intended as a "protective measure to prevent medical neglect of institutionalized people, not a means to force institutionalized people to have medical treatment they did not want."[19] Mary was permitted to make her own medical decisions in consultation with her doctor.

A. Views from the Disability Community

Although disability experts have not written about Mary's case specifically, it seems fairly clear that from a disability perspective, Mary's doctor did two things right: She listened to Mary, and she fought a paternalistic institutional policy that would have limited Mary's ability to direct her own life.

From its inception, the disability rights movement has challenged professional domination of people with disabilities. Demanding

---

[18] *Id.* at 363–364.
[19] *Id.* at 364.

self-determination, adults with disabilities and parent advocates for children with disabilities protested assertions of power by government authorities that usurp their decision-making authority. As part of early independent living movements and today's broader disability rights agenda, the disability community stresses the "importance of the right to self-direction and self-determination, the right to informed consent for treatment, right to appoint an agent to make decisions when the individual is unable to make their own decisions, [and] right to refuse treatment"[20]

The support for self-determination is part and parcel of a strong antipaternalism principle that has been central to the disability rights movement. Disability rights activist James Charlton explained: "[P]aternalism lies at the center of the oppression of people with disabilities. Paternalism starts with the notion of superiority: We must and can control these 'subjects' in spite of themselves, in spite of their individual will, or culture and tradition." [21]

In Mary's case, the facility director sought to apply a paternalistic regulation designed to protect people with disabilities by ensuring that they were not deprived of health services because of institutionalization. On paper, the regulation appeared to be a good thing: It would ensure against the medical neglect of people living in institutions. In practice, the regulation had unintended consequences. In Mary's case, application of the regulation would result in a violation of her body, and her will, as she so colorfully and eloquently expressed on her message board. Already a victim of paternalistic policies that gave state officials complete domination over Mary's life – from locking her away in institutions to making incorrect assumptions about her cognitive capacity – Mary had every reason to be suspicious of intrusive tests

---

[20] *E.g.*, Disability Rights California, *Personal Autonomy Principles* (2007), http://www. disabilityrightsca.org/legislature/Principles/102401.htm.

[21] JAMES I. CHARLTON, NOTHING ABOUT US WITHOUT US: DISABILITY OPPRESSION AND EMPOWERMENT 52–53 (University of California Press 2000).

that were alleged to be "for her own good." Disability advocates of all stripes would likely support Mary's right to control her own body and decline an invasive medical procedure.[22] Respecting that single decision would afford Mary a degree of human dignity and independence that had otherwise been denied her.

One could expect a disability critique of Mary's case. That critique would focus not on the treatment refusal, but on the other decisions that were made for Mary throughout her life. Why was she institutionalized for so many years? Why was she not be more integrated than housing in a mental health facility would allow after it was discovered that she was in fact mentally competent? Condemning the tragedy of Mary's past and continuing institutionalization, disability advocates would likely call for her release from institutional care into community and independent living where she would be free to direct the course of her own life on a much greater scale than in one interaction with one physician.

As will be evident in the study of the next case, support for the autonomous choices of individuals with disabilities to refuse treatment is not unqualified within the disability community. When a decision would hasten the death of a person with disabilities, different concerns trump respect for individual choice among many disability activists. In Mary's case, however, there is nothing to suggest that her refusal to have the screening measure was one intended to hasten her death. An assertion of independence and self-direction, Mary's decision was hers to make.

B. Views from Bioethics

From a bioethics perspective, Mary's was an easy case. Jane Greenlaw, the nurse-turned-lawyer-turned-bioethicist who wrote about Mary's

---

[22] Disability advocates recognize the right of individuals to refuse medical treatment. *E.g.*, Disability Rights California, *supra* note 20; ADAPT, *Homepage* (2009), *available at* http://www.adapt.org/index.php.

case, presented the case as an example of inappropriate overinterpretation of a law to require unbending obligations that, in turn, harm the people the law was designed to protect. Greenlaw's ethical analysis was succinct: "To state what may be obvious, adults who live in group residences do not have fewer rights about bodily integrity than do adults who live elsewhere." One would be hard-pressed to find a bioethics expert who would disagree with Greenlaw on this point.

The right of competent adults to make informed refusals of medical care is bedrock in bioethics. Some ethicists might question whether Mary's refusal was informed: Did the doctor give Mary enough information about the purpose of the screening tests? Did she understand the risks posed by her choice? Once satisfied that Mary understood the risks, benefits, and alternatives involved, bioethicists would agree that the choice to refuse the test was Mary's to make. To the extent there is controversy within bioethics about treatment refusal cases involving adults, the debate generally arises with respect to adults who lack the capacity to make their own decisions, and then the debate is about the standards or methods for substitute decision making, not whether to allow treatment refusal in the first place. In Mary's case, there was no reason to suspect she lacked decision-making capacity. That she had physical disabilities was simply beside the point.

Physical disability plays a greater role in the next case. A classic case in bioethics and disabilities studies, the case of Larry McAfee shows a clear rift between the disability and bioethics perspectives on respect for autonomous choices when the choice is for death instead of life with disability.

II. THE CASE OF LARRY McAFEE

Larry James McAfee spent the afternoon of May 5, 1984 picnicking with friends in the mountains of Georgia. An engineering student at

Georgia Tech in Atlanta, who worked full-time at an engineering firm, McAfee planned to become a mechanical engineer. A large man at six-foot-six, McAfee enjoyed hunting and motorcycle riding. As he rode home from the mountain picnic, he lost control of his motorcycle, snapped his neck where his helmet ended, and lost the ability to breathe on his own.[23]

A nurse who had been traveling with him evaluated and treated McAfee on the scene. She administered CPR, and paramedics rushed him to a local hospital, where he was stabilized and then airlifted to Georgia Baptist Hospital in Atlanta. Paralyzed from the neck down, McAfee could not move his legs or hands, and he could not breathe without mechanical ventilation. Doctors drilled "holes … into his skull to attach a brace for traction. Another hole was opened in his throat to insert the plastic tube from the respirator."[24] McAfee would spend the rest of his life on the ventilator.

After his health was stabilized, McAfee was discharged from the hospital and spent the next four years in different living arrangements, including a number of institutions and nursing homes. In January 1989, McAfee was discharged from an Ohio nursing home and admitted to Grady Memorial Hospital in Atlanta, Georgia. Because he was on a respirator, he was admitted to the intensive care unit. In the spring of 1989, after three months in the ICU, McAfee, called a lawyer with a request. "'Help me,' he said, 'I want to die.'"[25]

With his lawyer's help, McAfee filed a petition in Fulton Superior Court seeking a determination that he be allowed to turn off his ventilator, so that he would die. He also requested that he be provided a sedative to alleviate the pain that would occur when the ventilator was disconnected.

---

[23] Michael Mason, *From a Nursing Home Bed, One Patient Sues for the Right to Die*, PEOPLE, Feb. 19, 1990.

[24] JOSEPH P. SHAPIRO, NO PITY: PEOPLE WITH DISABILITIES FORGING A NEW CIVIL RIGHTS MOVEMENT 262 (Three Rivers Press 1994).

[25] *Id.* at 258.

The judge assigned to the case held a bedside hearing. McAfee told the judge that "life as a quadriplegic, sustained by a machine and dependent on attendants for everything from eating to coughing had been, 'intolerable.'"[26]

> He recounted how he had been moved from one far flung nursing home to another and that he no longer foresaw a life out of a hospital bed. 'It is very heartbreaking.... Every day when I wake up there is nothing to look forward to.'

> McAffee ... even told the judge how he planned to end his life. The method had come to him while he had been lying in the ICU. He described the device he invented to kill himself in the same matter of fact tone he would use to explain any other engineering project. It consisted of a time switch, one relay, and two valves. This simple invention would force the air from the respirator to spill ineffectively into the room instead of into his lungs, without setting off the alarm. A friend would assemble it according to McAfee's instruction. Someone else, with permission from the court, would help McAfee swallow a sedative. Then, before he drifted into a deep sleep, McAfee would clench a mouthstick between his teeth and use it to turn on the timer. It would tick off the last seconds of air pumped into his lungs. Death would come – gently, comfortably – in his drug-induced sleep.[27]

McAfee's family supported his decision to refuse medical treatment, as did the doctors who evaluated him and the state attorney assigned to his case. Finding McAfee to be a competent adult, who had been counseled on the issues, the trial court granted McAfee's petition. The trial court found that McAfee's constitutional rights of privacy, liberty, "and the concomitant right to refuse medical treatment outweigh any interest the state has in this proceeding."[28] The trial court concluded that it could not order a medical professional to administer a sedative

---

[26] *Id.* at 259.

[27] *Id.*

[28] Georgia v. McAfee, 259 Ga. 579, at 580, 385 S.E.2d 651, at 652 (1989).

to Mr. McAfee, but held that no civil or criminal liability would attach to anyone who did so.

On appeal, the Supreme Court of Georgia affirmed McAfee's right as a competent adult to refuse medical treatment. The court further held "that Mr. McAfee's right to be free from pain at the time the ventilator is disconnected is inseparable from his right to refuse medical treatment. The record shows that Mr. McAfee has attempted to disconnect his ventilator in the past, but has been unable to do so due to the severe pain he suffers when deprived of oxygen. His right to have a sedative (a medication that in no way causes or accelerates death) administered before the ventilator is disconnected is a part of his right to control his medical treatment."[29]

A. Views from the Disability Community

From the disability perspective, the court got Larry McAfee's case wrong. McAfee's case was not about an individual's right to refuse treatment, but a classic example of the failure of society to ensure that people with disabilities are provided with independent living, equal access to society, and psychological counseling. The court's decision, explained scholar Joseph Shapiro, is best understood "as the story of how this country fails miserably to care for severely disabled people. Instead of getting help to live on his own, McAfee was sentenced to indifferent nursing homes and hospitals and stripped of basic decision-making about his life."[30]

When disability activists talk about Larry McAfee's case, they emphasize a number of facts that were left out of the court's narrative. They point out, for example that McAfee was not despairing over his disability until he had been stuck in nursing homes for years. In

[29] *Id.*
[30] Shapiro, *supra* note 24, at 260.

fact, during the first year of his rehabilitation, McAfee made significant strides toward independent living and planned to start working again:

> In April 1986, McAfee moved into an apartment on Atlanta's north side. His Blue Cross/Blue Shield policy, which had been in effect from the beginning, paid for round-the-clock nursing and most everything else. His parents – Amelia, a clerk in a machine shop; and James, who works in a coal mine – supplemented the insurance money and a Social Security disability check (about $700 a month) with their $20,000 savings. The bills were enormous – nursing alone cost about $7,000 a month. Nonetheless, the McAfees managed to buy a burgundy Dodge van and have it customized with a lift and locks for Larry's wheelchair. For a brief, wonderful time, he rode to the grocery store, the occasional movie or basketball game. Larry McAfee seemed to be rejoining society.[31]

Unfortunately, McAfee's private insurance ran out, and he was forced to search for an institution that would take Medicaid payments. That search proved difficult, as McAfee was healthy but ventilator-dependent, and Georgia's payment scheme for in-patient nursing care was stingy. In November 1987, officials at the rehabilitation center McAfee attended found an institution in Cleveland, Ohio, that would accept him. Hundreds of miles from friend and family, McAfee stayed in the Ohio nursing home for fourteen months. There, "[h]e felt neglected and ignored by the staff":[32]

> There was no longer any talk from optimistic therapists about the possibility of a job. The twenty-bed ventilator unit was made up almost entirely of geriatric residents. Most, says McAfee, had not been taught how to speak over the ventilator tube. McAfee tried to show them. He spent lonely days staring out the window. His roommate was an elderly man in a coma. Growing more and more frustrated, and upset about what he thought was poor care, McAfee filed complaints about his treatment with Ohio health officials.[33]

---

[31] Mason, *supra* note 23.
[32] *Id.*
[33] Shapiro, *supra* note 24, at 266.

Eventually administrators determined that McAfee should be discharged. "Early one Monday morning in January 1989, McAfee was loaded onto a plane and sent back to Atlanta. Administrators at Grady Memorial, the city's huge public hospital, weren't told McAfee was on the way until the plane had taken off."[34]

When McAfee arrived at Grady, doctors were surprised to find him years away from his life-threatening accident. They expected to receive a person in crisis. But McAfee was stable. He did not belong in a hospital at all; he simply needed nursing care. Once McAfee had been admitted, however, the hospital could not discharge him until it found somewhere for him to go. McAfee was placed in the intensive care unit while officials tried unsuccessfully to find a nursing home that would take a young man on a respirator.

Disability experts explain that an ICU was the wrong place for a young man like McAfee: "It was a stopping-off point for patients near death. But McAfee was not dying; he wasn't even sick. Trapped in his hospital bed, he felt as if the weeks were ticking off in slow motion while around him the intensive care unit seemed to whirl at hyperspeed."[35] It was in the ICU that Larry McAfee decided he would rather die than continue without control over his life.

When the court issued its decision and characterized McAfee as sensible and brave, "it was another chilling reminder of how a disabled life was dismissed – by doctors, judges, and the public – as a devalued life. As they viewed it, a judge who saw a man with a translucent plastic coil connecting a hole in his throat to a machine and eagerly ruled this a life not worth living. It did not matter that about 15,000 Americans living outside hospitals use respirators. A nondisabled man who asked the state to help them take his life would get suicide-prevention counseling, but McAfee had not been considered rash or even depressed."[36]

---

[34] Mason, *supra* note 23.
[35] Shapiro, *supra* note 24, at 258.
[36] *Id.* at 260.

Four Atlanta disability rights groups issued a press statement condemning "Georgia's Attorney General and others who supported McAfee's petition for assisted suicide. They declared themselves 'outraged that our state for years left Larry McAfee without enough support for independent living and now steps in willingly to help with his suicide.... The state creates an unbearable quality of life and then steps in and says disabled people should be assisted to die because their quality of life is so poor.'"[37] The view that improving the social support and context for people with disabilities will transform the "intolerable" to tolerable – even rich and fulfilling – seems to have been vindicated by what happened in McAfee's life in the aftermath of the court's decision. Having drawn the attention of disability rights advocates with the publicity that surrounded his court case, McAfee got help from people who moved him out of the ICU to another facility that focused on teaching him the skills he needed to work and live on his own. Larry McAfee changed his mind about dying. He was "offered creative possibilities to regain control of his life and to work in computer engineering. In the end, he testified before the Georgia state legislature, calling upon them to fund independent living."[38] He was able to live in an apartment, equipped with special computers that he could control. "His mood bounced up and down, often paralleling occasional respiratory problems. But on the whole, he pronounced himself happy to be alive, living a 'good' life that had given him 'hope.'"[39]

McAfee's case, like that of Elizabeth Bouvia and David Rivlin – two other people with disabilities who sought and received court permission to end their lives by terminating medical treatment – focused the attention of disability scholars on assertions by bioethicists that decisions to refuse treatment deserved respect as a matter of an individual's right to autonomy, liberty, and self-determination. In the wake of the

---

[37] Paul Longmore, *Essay*, in RAGGED EDGE MAG., Jan./Feb. 1997, http://www.ragged-edge-mag.com/archive/p13story.htm.

[38] *Id.*

[39] Shapiro, *supra* note 24, at 288.

McAfee decision, scholar Paul Longmore, an academic who had physical disabilities that required the use of a ventilator, argued, "[t]his is the sort of 'autonomy, self-determination and liberty' society willingly accords people with disabilities: the freedom to choose death. And then it applauds our 'courage' and 'rationality,' all the while ignoring how society itself has battered us and made our lives unbearable."[40]

Longmore could relate to McAfee. He could easily have been in his place. At the point in time that the court granted McAfee's request to die, Longmore described his situation:

> [I] was still being denied the right to work, and I would have been denied the right to self-determined independent living if I had lived in Georgia or Michigan. I could very well have found my life unendurable. I could have been the one to say, "I would rather be dead." And many people, many civil- liberties lawyers and compassionate judges and humane doctors, would willingly have helped me die. They would have lamented how hard my life had been because of my disability. They would have admired my "courage" in "choosing" death. And they would have congratulated themselves for upholding the "ethical vision in this country" that individuals have a "right to autonomy, self-determination and liberty."[41]

Longmore's critique of the autonomy agenda of bioethics took hold in disability studies, where health care "choices" are not viewed in a vacuum, but as part of a social structure rife with disability bias. Decisions to hasten death are seen "not as an act of personal autonomy, but an act of desperation. It is a fictional freedom, it is phony autonomy. The rhetoric of 'choice' is deployed to hide the realities of coercion."[42] Thus, in the wake of McAfee's case, and others like it, a significant branch of the disability community shifted its attention to laws that allowed people with disabilities to hasten their own deaths. The fight

[40] Longmore, *supra* note 37.
[41] *Id.*
[42] PAUL K. LONGMORE, WHY I BURNED MY BOOK AND OTHER ESSAYS ON DISABILITY 195 (Temple University Press 2003).

for independent living became a fight for life itself. To be sure, there is debate among disability experts about the importance of autonomy, and contradictions of imposing paternalistic protections on competent adults with disabilities who refuse medical treatment,[43] but the notion that the autonomy-based arguments of bioethics are suspect runs deep and is firmly embedded in disability scholarship.

B. Views from Bioethics

McAfee's case is typically presented in bioethics as a paradigmatic example of the "right of a competent patient to refuse customary life-sustaining treatment."[44] In some textbooks, it is also used to exemplify the type of case in which physicians can take actions that will hasten a patient's death without running afoul of the principle of nonmaleficience. For example, until the sixth edition of their classic text was published in 2009, Tom Beauchamp and James Childress included Larry McAfee's case in *Principles of Bioethics*, under the heading "Justified Physician-Assisted Suicide."[45] Contrasting McAfee's case against the reckless actions of Jack Kevorkian, Beauchamp and Childress count McAfee's as first among several "prominent cases of *justified* assisted suicide." Reviewing the facts of the case, they noted that McAfee wanted more than to refuse life-sustaining treatment. McAfee "asked for a physician's assistance in administering a sedative to control pain enough so that he could disconnect himself."[46] They note with approval the court's finding that no criminal or civil liability would be attached to a physician who helped McAfee by administering the sedative, as well as the court's finding that "McAfee's right to have a sedative (a medication that no

---

[43] *See, e.g.,* Shakespeare, *supra* note 9.
[44] TOM L. BEAUCHAMP & JAMES F. CHILDRESS, PRINCIPLES OF BIOMEDICAL ETHICS 150 (5th ed. 2001).
[45] *Id.*
[46] *Id.*

way causes or accelerates death) administered before the ventilator is disconnected is part of his right to control his medical treatment."[47]

Beauchamp and Childress then argued that McAfee should not have been forced to go to court to enforce his autonomy rights. His doctors should simply have acted on his choices. "The right acknowledged is a right that healthcare facilities should recognize without the patient having to meet repeated refusals of assistance from physicians. We do not propose a right that requires coercion of physician's consciences, a troubled area of medical ethics. Instead, we recommend that medical professionals themselves confront these issues and acknowledge that it is permissible to assist some patients in their dying."[48]

Interestingly, the McAfee case was dropped, without explanation, from the most recent edition of *Principles*, which presents a more developed defense of physician-assisted death, with a principal focus on physician-assisted suicide. Beauchamp and Childress explain that a physician's first obligation to a sick patient is:

> [t]o rid the patient's body of its ills. Restoration of health is a morally mandatory goal if a reasonable prospect of success exists and the patient supports the means necessary to this end. However, to stop at this point and confine the practice of medicine to measures designed to cure diseases or heal injuries is an unduly narrow way of thinking about what the physician has to offer the patient. The value of physicians is broader. When, in the patient's eyes, the burdens of continued attempts to cure outweigh their probable benefits, the caring physician, in consultation with the patient, should redirect the course of treatment so that its primary focus is the relief of pain and suffering. For many patients, palliative care with aggressive use of analgesics will prove sufficient to accomplish this goal. For other patients, relief of intolerable distress or suffering will come only with death, which some patients will seek to hasten.[49]

[47] *Id.*

[48] *Id.* at 150–151.

[49] TOM L. BEAUCHAMP & JAMES F. CHILDRESS, PRINCIPLES OF BIOMEDICAL ETHICS 184 (6th ed. 2008).

They explain their view that physician-assisted suicide is not morally different from physicians' other actions that hasten death, which would include the actions sought by McAfee:

> A favorable response by a physician to a request for assistance in facilitating death by *hastening* it through fatal medication is not relevantly different from a favorable response to requests for assistance in facilitating death by *easing* it through the removal of life-prolonging technology... The two acts of physicians are morally equivalent as long as there are no other differences in the cases. That is, if the disease is relevantly similar, the request by the patient is relevantly similar, then the responding to a request to provide the means to hasten death seems morally equivalent to responding to a request to ease death by withdrawing treatment ...[50]

In their most recent edition, Beauchamp and Childress give a nod to the disability critique of their position, but do not appear to be moved by it. They describe the reaction of conference attendees to a clinical presentation of "a case involving the disconnection of a ventilator maintaining the life of a patient with Amytrophic Lateral Sclerosis." Many of the audience members had disabilities and had themselves experienced long-term ventilator use. The clinical speakers had framed the case as an end-of-life case, but the audience members argued "that this was a disability case in which the clinicians should have provided better care, fuller information, and more options to the consumer, particularly to help him overcome his felt isolation after the recent death of his spouse. What to the clinicians was a textbook case of end-of-life decisionmaking was, for their audience, a story in which a life was ended as a result of failure of information and assistance by the presenters themselves."[51] In response, Beauchamp and Childress defend their argument that physicians can and should hasten death in limited situations:

> We clearly need further improvements and extensions of various modes of support for people who suffer from a variety of serious

[50] *Id.*
[51] *Id.* at 185.

medical problems. Control of pain and suffering is now a moral imperative. However, significant progress will not obviate all last-resort situations, in which individuals desire and need to control over their dying in ways that have been denied them.[52]

Others in bioethics have been more cognizant of the social context in which people with disabilities make medical decisions. In reaction to the McAfee case, for example, Art Caplan, who is generally a supporter of the right of people to make informed choices to refuse life-saving treatment, noted that "[m]any disabled people could possibly be cared for at home, but they're left to languish in nursing homes. Money is a bigger obstacle to care for the disabled than technology. Often the technology is quite good, but there's no way to pay for it."[53] Caplan suggested that Medicaid payments be federalized, not left to capricious state legislatures, as a means of addressing the problem, but he did not challenge the court's holding that McAfee had the right to turn off the ventilator.

Other bioethicists have further revised their understanding of cases like Larry McAfee's in light of their emerging awareness of the disability critique. Bioethicist Howard Brody, for example, published an apology for his earlier writings in support of court decisions like that in McAfee's case.[54] Brody explained that such court decisions – he discussed David Rivlin's case, which was strikingly parallel to McAfee's except that Rivlin ultimately did have the ventilator removed – were:

> … somewhat exciting for those of us working on bioethics.… Many physicians in that day refused to accept the patient's right to refuse therapy and continued to insist that they could impose treatment on unwilling, dying patients, because doing anything else was

---

[52] *Id.*

[53] Mason, *supra* note 23.

[54] Howard Brody, *A Bioethicist Offers an Apology*, LANSING CITY PULSE, Oct. 6, 2004, *available at* http://www.dredf.org/assisted_suicide/bioethics.html.

tantamount to killing. I thought myself a champion of patient's rights by agreeing with the decision of the county court in Rivlin's case.

At the time of the Rivlin ruling, a few advocates for persons with disabilities complained about the decision, because Rivlin had never really talked with them to learn what other possibilities besides death and staying in a nursing home existed for a quadriplegic person on a ventilator. At the time I wondered who those busybodies thought they were. Rivlin had not asked for their help. Why were they sticking their noses into his very private and personal decision?

I am now embarrassed to realize how limited was the basis on which I made my decisions about David Rivlin. In hindsight, it has been very well documented that there was no medical need for Rivlin to be effectively incarcerated in a nursing home. If Rivlin had been given access to a reasonable amount of community resources, of the sort that other persons with disabilities were making use of at the time, he could have been moved out of the nursing home and probably could have had his own apartment. He could have been much more able to see friends, get outside a bit, and generally have a much more interesting and stimulating life. The reasons he gave for wanting to die were precisely how boring and meaningless life was for him.

There's every reason to believe in hindsight that David Rivlin died unnecessarily, and that we who claimed to care about his "rights" should have been demanding that services be made available for him rather than that he be allowed to die. As one who argued the wrong thing back then, I apologize for my shortsightedness.[55]

Brody is not alone in positing that bioethicists should not be so quick to demand that people with disabilities be allowed to die, but he is among a small minority. The notion that bioethicists have a role to play in insisting on improved living conditions for people with disabilities has not garnered much support in a field focused on clinical solutions to perceived medical problems.

---

[55] *Id.*

The next case presents another permutation of the treatment refusal case, which raises issues of cognitive impairments, surrogate decision making, and the special problem of feeding tubes.

III. THE CASE OF SCOTT MATTHEWS

In 1996, Scott Matthews was a twenty-eight-year-old man with life-long and profound cognitive and physical disabilities, who resided in a community residence in the Albany, New York area.[56] Scott's parents were deeply involved in his care, as were the caregivers at the group home where he lived. In July, a disagreement about Scott's care came to a head in a lawsuit that pitted Scott's parents against the facility director and disability rights advocates.

Scott had cerebral palsy and profound mental retardation. His physical impairments included a swallowing disorder that made it difficult for him to be fed orally. Even when he was spoon-fed pureed foods, he sometimes choked or aspirated food. During 1996, Scott had been repeatedly hospitalized for dehydration, malnutrition, infections, and aspiration pneumonia. Although his ideal body weight was only "50-plus pounds,"[57] he had dropped to 42.4 pounds in July 1996. At that point, his doctors described Scott as "severely malnourished."[58] His physicians opined that "Scott's malnutrition was life threatening and Scott 'does not and cannot get adequate nutrition and hydration from oral feeding.'"[59] As they had in the past, the doctors recommended

---

[56] *In re* Matthews, 650 N.Y.S.2d 373, 377 (App. Div. 1996). Much of the material on Scott Matthews's case was first printed in a previous article I published in the *Oregon Law Review: Disability and the End of Life*, 85 OREGON L. REV. 123 (2006) ©2006, University of Oregon. It is reprinted here, with minor modifications, by permission.

[57] *In re* Matthews, 650 N.Y.S.2d at 374.

[58] *Id.*

[59] *Id.* at 375.

that a gastrostomy tube or other medically appropriate feeding tube be surgically placed in Scott.

Scott's parents were his court-appointed guardians, and therefore had the authority to make his health care decisions. Over the years, they had repeatedly decided against allowing doctors to place a feeding tube into Scott. Scott's parents objected to the feeding tube because of the possible medical complications of the procedure and "the effect on Scott's emotional well-being if he was denied the social contact that feeding with others [has] provided."[60] Specifically, his mother explained "that Scott, who is quadriplegic, nonverbal and incontinent, makes no other purely voluntary decision than his choice to eat." His parents reported the pleasure Scott took from eating, especially his favorite food, a strawberry cream pie his father brought him for lunches on weekends. Replacing oral feeding with tube feeding would have taken away Scott's greatest pleasure. In July 1996, they again refused to consent to the operation.

The doctors and institutional caregivers became alarmed. The facility doctor reported that "Scott appears to be slowly dying from malnutrition and all the resultant complications."[61] Finding slow starvation of a resident unacceptable, the facility's operator and the executive director of the United Cerebral Palsy Association of the Capital District filed a petition asking a New York Court for permission to implant a gastrostomy tube into Scott's stomach.

Scott's parents opposed the petition. Although they recognized that Scott's life might be extended by use of a feeding tube, they argued that the quality of life would be diminished if he lost the ability to eat orally and the social interaction that came with it.[62] His parents also

---

[60] *Id.*

[61] Holly Taylor, *Feeding Tube Dispute Raises Ethical Questions*, ALB. TIMES UNION, July 14, 1996, at D1.

[62] *See* Janeth L. Eberle, *One-on-One Contact Important to Patient*, ALB. TIMES UNION, Nov. 4, 1996, at A10 ("The one-on-one contact was stimulating for him and putting a feeding tube in Scott will remove that one and only joy of his life.").

argued that Scott's life was not clearly threatened by malnutrition. On this point, they were supported by physician Patrick Caulfield who came to know Scott because of a fortuitous visit that occurred when Scott's regular physician was on vacation. Caulfield testified that it was reasonable to allow Scott to continue oral feedings given his parents' concerns, and recommended an aggressive course of oral feeding that, in his medical opinion, would address Scott's nutrition issues.[63] Three physicians testified to the contrary, opining that Scott would die shortly of malnutrition or infection unless he could be provided additional nutrition through a feeding tube. Those three experts conceded that a feeding tube was no guarantee of a long life for Scott. Even with it, he might succumb to infection or aspiration pneumonia, but they asserted that the tube was the only option for providing Scott adequate nutrition.

The trial court decided against Scott's parents. The judge found that Scott suffered from "profound life-threatening malnutrition"[64] and indicated that because Scott had never been competent to form and express an opinion about the use of a feeding tube, the law required the use of a feeding tube if the tube might extend his life. The feeding tube "will not improve his quality of life, nor has it been shown that it will necessarily extend his life, said the trial judge, but "if an error should occur as to whether Scott would want a gastrostomy (a stomach feeding tube) to sustain his life, it should be made on the side of life."[65]

The New York Appellate Division reversed, finding that because Scott had never had the capacity to make his own medical decisions, the parents' choice should be evaluated using a best-interest standard. The court emphasized that under this standard, New York law does

---

[63] *In re* Matthews, 650 N.Y.S.2d at 375.

[64] *Id.*

[65] Holly Taylor, *Feeding Tube Ordered for Handicapped Man*, ALB. TIMES UNION, Oct. 9, 1996, at A1.

not permit a parent to "deprive a child of life-saving treatment, however well intentioned."[66] Scott's parents, thus,

> ... cannot and should not be permitted to make a decision that would result in Scott starving to death, if such could be medically avoided, regardless of how soon he may or may not succumb from other causes. It further follows that a medical recommendation to effectively deny sustenance to a starving patient would be unreasonable on its face. Thus, the pivotal question in this case is whether petitioner is correct in arguing that respondents are depriving Scott of lifesaving or life-prolonging treatment or whether respondents are within their rights in choosing aggressive oral feedings as a reasonable medical approach to Scott's nutritional difficulties given the risks.[67]

Despite its language favoring the use of feeding tubes and limiting options for parents or guardians of people without decision-making capacity, the court went on to interpret Dr. Caulfield's testimony to support the conclusion that Scott's life could be maintained with oral feedings. The court concluded that as long as Scott could sufficiently maintain his life through oral feedings, overriding the parents to order a more invasive feeding procedure would be premature. The court cautioned, however, that had evidence been presented that Scott was being deprived life-sustaining treatment, it would have granted the request for the tube.[68]

Scott's parents were thrilled with the decision. His father could continue his weekly tradition of feeding Scott his favorite strawberry cream pie for lunch on Saturdays,[69] and his mother was pleased that he could "eat and go to the table with his friends. It means he has some

---

[66] *In re* Matthews, 650 N.Y.S.2d at 377 (quoting *In re* Storar, 438 N.Y.S.2d 266, 420 N.E.2d 64 (1981)).

[67] *In re* Matthews, 650 N.Y.S.2d at 377.

[68] *Id.* at 379.

[69] Taylor, *supra* note 61.

control over his life. It means Scotty can have turkey and pumpkin pie (on Thanksgiving), and I don't have to feel guilty."[70]

However, the Court's decision also meant that Scott's weight and medical condition would be closely monitored. If efforts to feed him orally were unsuccessful, and the matter became one of life or death, the court would reconsider its position. As it turned out, Scott's parents and Dr. Caulfield were able to implement a successful course of oral feeding that included aggressive nutritional supplementation and kept Scott alive for more than decade.

A. Views from the Disability Community

Although Scott's case was not one that garnered national attention, it was one that had the attention of disability rights advocates in New York State. They strongly supported the effort to have a feeding tube placed in Scott by filing an amicus brief on his behalf and making a visible showing at court hearings.[71] Displaying skepticism of bioethics-based arguments, the advocates insisted that if the courts blocked the feeding tube, the result would be "unequal medical care for the disabled."[72] As explained by the director of the Disability Advocates, Inc., the most important issue was preserving Scott Matthews' life: "Some may see Scott Matthews' life as a burden to him, but it is the only life he has ever known, and there is no reason to think that he does not treasure it as much as any other person."[73] Alleged quality-of-life concerns should not, in the advocates' view, have trumped Scott's right to life.

---

[70] John Caher, *Court Refuses to Force Feeding*, ALB. TIMES UNION, Nov. 27, 1996, at A1.

[71] Holly Taylor, *Advocates for Disabled Push for Feeding Tube*, ALB. TIMES UNION, Nov. 5, 1996, at B1 (describing a group of disability advocates, including five wheelchair users, who attended oral arguments before the appellate court in the Matthews case.)

[72] *Id.*

[73] Cliff Zucker, *Man May Have Disabilities, But He Has a Right to Life*, ALB. TIMES UNION, Nov. 13, 1996, at A10.

The arguments made by the disability advocates in Scott Matthews's case foreshadowed the arguments disability advocates would assert in the Terri Schiavo case (see Chapter 7), where it became clear on a national level that feeding tubes are a matter of special concern in the disability community. Essentially, members of the disability community view feeding tubes the same way they view wheelchairs: Both are essential to ensuring full participation in life activities by those who need them. For that reason, neither wheelchairs nor feeding tubes should be denied absent an affirmative choice by the individual who needs them. In a case such as Scott Matthews's, where a person has never had the capacity to make health care decisions, the advocates would agree with the New York appellate court's holding on the law, if not the facts, that Scott's parents "cannot and should not be permitted to make a decision that would result in Scott starving to death, if such could be medically avoided, regardless of how soon he may or may not succumb from other causes."[74] Because the advocates involved directly in his case were convinced that using a feeding tube was necessary to prevent Scott from starving to death, they fought his parents when they sought to deny him that care.

B. Views from Bioethics

Scott Matthews's parents were represented on appeal by law professor Dale Moore, whose scholarly writings[75] and arguments in the Matthews case reflect the widespread agreement within bioethics that a surrogate decision maker for a person who has never had the capacity to make his own decisions should have the option of refusing a feeding tube (or of consenting to one) when doing so is in the individual's best interests, or is a medically acceptable option given the risks and benefits of the available options.

[74] *In re* Matthews, 650 N.Y.S.2d at 377.
[75] Dale Moore, *Afterword: The Case of Daniel Joseph Fiori*, 57 ALB. L. REV. 811 (1994).

Bioethical analysis distinguishes cases involving competent adults from those involving adults who have never had decision-making capacity.[76] In the latter category, the principle of respect for autonomy no longer takes a prominent role. There is, by definition, no autonomous, informed choice of the patient to respect. Instead, the inquiry focuses on who should speak for the patient, and what degree of discretion the surrogate decision maker should have in making decisions. There is widespread consensus in bioethics that family members are, in most instances, the appropriate decision makers for adults who lack capacity, especially those family members with a close relationship to the individual.[77] There is also strong support for the proposition that medical decision making for an adult who has never had decision-making capacity should employ the best interest of the patient standard. A best-interest analysis requires the weighing of the burdens of the proposed intervention on the patient against the benefits to the patient of the proposed intervention. There is debate within bioethical literature about whether the best-interest determination must be based on objective estimates of the benefits and burdens of treatment to the patient,[78] or whether a best-interest inquiry can properly focus on subjective criteria such as the incompetent person's interests and preferences, or even the welfare of the person's family.[79] Under either formulation, few proposed treatments are considered obligatory. Unless the benefits of a proposed treatment unequivocally outweigh its burdens, a surrogate decision maker is generally understood to have the moral and legal authority to choose against intervention. Bioethicists apply the risk/benefit analysis to all

[76] Of course there is a third category of cases, those involving adults who once had but subsequently lost decision-making capacity. A case from the third category will be discussed in Chapter 7.

[77] Beauchamp & Childress, *supra* note 49, at 188.

[78] Robert A. Pearlman, *Substitute Decision Making*, in CAMBRIDGE TEXTBOOK OF BIOETHICS 58 (Peter A. Singer & Adrian M. Viens eds., 2008).

[79] Beauchamp & Childress, *supra* note 49, at 171 (citing President's Commission for the Study of Ethical Problems in Medicine).

types of medical treatment, including medically delivered nutrition and hydration.[80] Robert Veatch explains:

> In many cases providing food [and] fluid ... will be very worthwhile on balance, and, in those cases, they should be provided. In other cases, however, they may actually do no good for the patient – from the patient's perspective. They may even produce burdens that exceed expected benefits. In those cases, according to the proportionality view that now prevails, they are morally expendable. They are "extraordinary" means no matter how routine and simple.[81]

In Scott Matthews's case, a bioethical analysis would allow his parents a range of options with respect to the feeding tube, including the option to forgo its use entirely. The court's appointment of Scott's parents as his guardians was a noncontroversial resolution of the issue of who should speak for Scott, and the presence of a doctor who presented an alternative course of aggressive oral feeding to address Scott's malnutrition issues made the case a fairly straightforward one from a bioethical perspective. But even if the oral feedings did not effectively address Scott's nutritional problems, bioethical inquiry into the benefits and burdens of care does not yield a definitive answer as to whether the use of a feeding tube would be in Scott's best interests. The analysis yields a range of acceptable choices from which the surrogate must choose.

There is no question that placement of the feeding tube in Scott would have entailed risks and burdens. It required surgery that intruded on his bodily integrity. The surgery carried the risks of anesthesia, aspiration of vomit, skin irritation from the tube, ulceration and bleeding into the stomach lining, tube blockage over time, osmotic diarrhea, and that the feeding tube might migrate.[82] And its benefits were dubious. The feeding tube might extend the length of his life, but it might have no such effect. Thus, even those bioethicists who would

---

[80] ROBERT M. VEATCH, THE BASICS OF BIOETHICS 102 (Prentice Hall, 2d ed. 2002).
[81] *Id.*
[82] *In re* Matthews, 650 N.Y.S.2d at 375 n. 3.

employ an objective best-interest test would likely agree that the use of a feeding tube in Scott's case was not morally or legally obligatory. An even more compelling case can be made to support the parents' choice against the feeding tube by bioethicists who employ a best-interest test that includes factors beyond clinical efficacy, such as the effect the feeding tube would have had on Scott's enjoyment of his life. By all accounts, Scott enjoyed oral feedings and the social contact that came with them. With a feeding tube, Scott would have been deprived of one activity that brought him the most pleasure, thereby limiting his enjoyment of his life. Most bioethicists would agree that given the loss he would experience in life satisfaction, the use of the feeding tube was not required in his case, even if it were certain – as some of the clinicians believed – that the feeding tube was the only thing that would possibly prevent Scott's imminent death.

IV. OBSERVATIONS

The cases discussed in this chapter, perhaps more than any other in the book, exemplify how different the experience of disability can be from one person to another. Christopher Reeve refused to accept disability as anything but a temporary setback; his critics view impairment as an essential and central component of identity, not a broken bit that needs fixing. Mary, by no choice of her own, was defined by her impairments in nearly all of her life experiences. Larry McAfee, who had known life without impairment, experienced his newly acquired physical impairments as devastating losses when they caused him to be socially isolated, but adapted to the impairments and incorporated them in a new identity, once the social barriers were broken down. And Scott Matthews's experience of cognitive impairments is almost unknowable, as the impairments themselves necessarily limited his sense of self and ability to define his life experience.

Given how differently each of the individuals involved experienced disability, the question arises whether one response to disability is more acceptable than another. The case studies in this chapter are fascinating for what they tell us about why someone might refuse medical treatment and also about how difficult it is to craft a one-size-fits-all solution to cases involving medical decision making. The progression is interesting.

Mary had been subjected throughout her life to paternalistic laws designed to protect people with disabilities. She had been institutionalized, "relieved" of the obligation to become educated, and the recipient of mandatory medical care. Her two-word explanation of why she would not participate in the screening procedure recommended by her physician, and required by the facility director, "VIOLATE, VIOLATE," elegantly encapsulates the unanticipated but real problem with laws designed to protect people with disabilities by limiting their choices. In the health care setting, what might be appropriate care for one person can be unduly burdensome and intrusive for another. In Mary's case, the proposed screening test was one more in a series of bodily intrusions imposed on her by a system that quite literally denied she had anything of import to say about the direction of her own life. Her doctor's support for her choice – that small showing of respect – may well have been the first instance in which Mary was treated as a full human being by the state system in which she had lived and received care for decades. In my view, the case shows the absolute importance of allowing people to make their own decisions about medical care. Choice about screening procedures is part and parcel of a self-directed life. It also shows how a one-size-fits-all, everyone-must-be-screened-and-treated laws can deprive people of dignity and power, even if drafted with the best intentions.

The second case is a cautionary tale about choice. Bioethics offers an antidote to paternalist laws like the one at issue in Mary's case. The answer: respect individual autonomy by supporting patient choice.

267

Bioethics teaches that competent people, people with decision-making capacity, do not have any moral or legal obligation to follow doctor's orders. Individual choices for or against recommended treatments are to be respected so long as they are informed and do not harm third parties. If the patient says, do not treat me – no treatment is required. Doctors and courts have no moral or legal authority to impose unwanted treatment. Let the patient decide. In Larry McAfee's case, however, the doctors, courts, family, and bioethicists were all too ready to accept his choice to withdraw from ventilator support as reasonable. Respect for autonomy blinded the lawyers and judges involved to the sad reality that McAfee did not really want to escape life – he just wanted out of the ICU and other life-deadening institutions.

People living with disabilities understood McAfee's plea and felt threatened by the people in power who seemed determined to facilitate his death instead of improving his life. In response to his case and others like it, disability rights activists now work for laws designed to protect people with disabilities from themselves, their families, and the authorities who are all too ready to accept pleas for death without question or probing. Focused especially on the medical interventions that are simply a daily part of the lives of so many people with disabilities, including ventilators and feeding tubes, these proposed laws would limit options and require treatment. They are inherently paternalistic, but because they come from within the disability community, the problems with their application appear to go unnoticed. There are also problems with their application. Just as paternalistic rules imposed on people with disabilities, such as the regulation at issue in Mary's case, can harm people with disabilities, paternalistic rules that emerge from within the disability community can also harm people with disabilities. Consider how the paternalistic rules proposed by disability advocates in the wake of Larry McAfee's case would have applied in Scott Matthews's case.

In the Matthews case, disability advocates urged the court to apply a rule that would require the use of medically necessary feeding tubes.

In other words, the advocates urged the court to order the insertion of a feeding tube into Scott on the say-so of his doctors. That trust in doctors is surprising, of course, given the distrust in the medical perspective that permeates disability scholarship. It is also troubling in the Matthews case when it seems so clear – at least with the benefit of hindsight – that the medical opinion that death was imminent if a tube was not used was so clearly wrong.

Further, and in my view this is the most troubling aspect of the Matthews case, the unqualified support for the use of feeding tubes advocated by disability experts ignores the fact that feeding tubes can be misused. In nursing homes across the country, elderly patients and people with disabilities are fed via feeding tubes because oral feeding is labor-intensive and requires one-on-one contact between residents and staff. Oral feeding takes too long and is too messy; feeding tubes make residents easier to care for. But they also deprive residents of one-on-one contact so central and important to the human experience. Thus, there is a movement within the dementia community to end the premature and unnecessary use of feeding tubes for people who enjoy oral feeding.[83] Surely, in Scott Matthews's case, some people with disabilities would see the value in his parents' plan to feed Scott and let him have the pleasure of eating and interacting. Indeed, I can easily envision a scenario where disability advocates would oppose the overuse of feeding tubes. Imagine, for example, the disability critique of a state regulation that required that all residents of nursing homes with swallowing disorders to be fed via feeding tubes. Surely, there would be protest. Nonetheless, in the Matthews case, it was disability advocates who pushed for a rule that would require the use of feeding tubes. The rule was intended to protect Scott and other people with swallowing disabilities from pernicious disability-based discrimination that could threaten their lives. Although protective in the abstract, the proposed

---

[83] Roni Caryn Rabin, *Feeding Dementia Patients with Dignity*, N.Y. TIMES, Aug. 3, 2010, at D6, http://www.nytimes.com/2010/08/03/health/03feed.html?_r=1&emc=eta1.

rule pitted disability advocates against his parents, on the side of the doctors, pressing for a medical intervention that could have hurt Scott and limited his life where a social intervention would do. That same rule could apply in other cases as well – including in nursing homes housing demented patients with swallowing disorders who enjoy oral feedings. Paternalism of that sort – "safeguards" that require or forbid particular treatment options – limits the options available to people with disabilities. This troubles me.

The issues surrounding feeding tubes and surrogate decision making feature prominently in the next chapter, where this discussion continues. My point here is that one-size-fits-all rules for medical treatment of people with disabilities are problematic, whether they come from within or without the disability community.

7

The End of Life

THE END OF A PERSON'S LIFE MIGHT COME IN OLD AGE OR it might come before. The final moments can be sudden and shocking. They may also be anticipated in the wake of a long illness or the slow degradation of the human body. Medical technology has enabled control over the moment of death in some cases. That control gives rise to questions. When, if ever, is death the best outcome? Who should make decisions about when to use, and when to stop using, technology to extend life? What is the role of surrogate decision making? Under what conditions should the withdrawal of life-sustaining treatment be permitted by surrogate decision makers? And how does the removal of life-sustaining treatment relate to other forms of treatment? Depending on one's perspective, these questions might implicate disability-related concerns including the role of societal perceptions about the worth of people with disabilities in medical decision making.

This chapter presents two cases that arose at the end of a person's life. The first captured the public's attention in a way that few medical decision-making cases do. The death of Theresa Schiavo was a media event. It generated state and federal legislation, garnered the attention of state and federal courts, and was the subject of hundreds of scholarly articles.[1] The second case, that of Sheila Pouliot, was less public but no less important. Both cases raised questions about end-of-life decision-making law and its future. Both involved surrogate decisions against medically-administered nutrition and hydration for women with profound cognitive disabilities. And both serve as paradigm cases, but for very different reasons. Terri Schiavo was an able-bodied and fully competent woman who suddenly and permanently lost all abilities, including the ability to experience emotions or feel pain. Sheila Pouliot was never able to make her own decisions or care for herself, but was very much aware of the constant pain and suffering she experienced in the final months of her life.

These cases work in tandem. The first was of great concern within the disability community and the second represents the most troubling kind of case for bioethicists. The juxtaposition clarifies the differences in perspectives about the withdrawal of feeding tubes from patients who are unable to consent to withdrawal. For that reason, I will present the two case studies in full before discussing the reactions of the disability and bioethics communities to each.

---

[1] *See, e.g.,* Kathy Cerminara & Kenneth Goodman, *Key Events in the Case of Theresa Marie Schiavo,* UNIVERSITY OF MIAMI ETHICS PROGRAMS, June 15, 2009, http://www. miami.edu/ethics/schiavo/schiavo_timeline.html [hereinafter UMiami Timeline] (last visited Oct. 9, 2010); Matt Conigliaro, *The Terri Schiavo Information Page,* ABSTRACT APPEAL, May 1, 2005, http://abstractappeal.com/schiavo/infopage.html (last visited Oct. 9, 2010); Joan Didion, *The Case of Theresa Schiavo,* 52 N.Y. REV. BOOKS, June 9, 2005, http://www.nybooks.com/articles/archives/2005/jun/09/the-case-of-theresa-schiavo/ (last visited Oct. 9, 2010); THE CASE OF TERRI SCHIAVO: ETHICS AT THE END OF LIFE (Arthur L. Caplan et.al. eds., Prometheus Books 2006). Many of these facts also appear in a report prepared by Jay Wolfson, Terri's third guardian ad litem. *See* Jay Wolfson, Guardian Ad Litem, *A Report to Governor Jeb Bush and the 6th Judicial Circuit in the Matter of Theresa Marie Schiavo* (Dec. 1, 2003), *reprinted in* Jay Wolfson, *Schiavo's Lessons for Health Attorneys When Good Law Is All You Have: Reflections of the Special Guardian Ad Litem to Theresa Marie Schiavo,* 38 J. HEALTH L. 535 app. A at 552–581 (2005).

I. THE CASE OF THERESA SCHIAVO

Theresa Schiavo's court-appointed guardian told her story:

Theresa and Michael Schiavo had been married for six years, and were living in St. Petersburg, Florida, not far from Theresa's parents and siblings. As a child in Philadelphia, Ms. Schiavo had weighed 250 pounds, but at age eighteen, she decided to lose weight, and had dropped to 150 pounds. It was at this point that she met Michael. They wed and she continued to lose weight, until she suffered a cardiac arrest, in the early morning hours of February 25, 1990, when she weighed only 110 pounds. That night, Ms. Schiavo collapsed at home, her husband called 911, and about 11–12 minutes later the Emergency Medical Technicians arrived. They performed CPR, intubated her, and brought her to a hospital about an hour later, where she was trached and placed on a respirator. She remained in a coma for a month, and when she emerged was diagnosed as being nonresponsive and vegetative. She received physical and occupational therapy for more than three years and was brought to California to have electrodes implanted in an effort to stimulate her brain. Mr. Schiavo and his mother-in-law, Mary Schindler, worked as a tireless team, providing care and nearly full time personal attention to the woman they both loved. Extensive neurological testing determined over and over that she had lapsed into a persistent vegetative state, with no hope of recovery. The brain damage caused by the lack of oxygen following her cardiac arrest was profound.

For about eighteen months prior to her collapse, the Schiavos had sought fertility counseling in an effort to have a child. Subsequent to the accident, Mr. Schiavo initiated a malpractice lawsuit against the treating obstetrician, alleging that a complete and proper history and physical examination had never been performed – and that if they had, Ms. Schiavo's possible eating disorder might have been diagnosed. Many attorneys refused the case, and a reading of the complaint does not offer much promise of success. Nonetheless, three years later, a sympathetic jury awarded Mr. Schiavo $ 300,000 for loss of consortium, and Ms. Schiavo more than $ 700,000, placed in a court supervised trust, intended for her maintenance.

The autopsy performed by the medical examiner in 2005 did not rule out bulimia as a factor causing her cardiac arrest, but no cause of her initial collapse was determined. The final autopsy revealed brain damage even more extensive than had earlier been diagnosed, and the medical examiner emphatically stated that Ms. Schiavo could never have experienced a recovery, though she could have remained alive for some time with artificial nutrition and hydration. Her formal cause of death was dehydration, commonly associated with a "natural" death when food and water are no longer administered....

Within a year of the malpractice settlement, Mr. Schiavo, having been told consistently that there was no hope of recovery, began the process of making the decision to withdraw artificial life support[2] because his wife was in a persistent vegetative state (one of the "end of life" conditions for which artificial feeding could, by law, be removed).[3] At this juncture, there occurred a rift between Mr. Schiavo and his in-laws, the Schindlers. What had been a closely knit family devolved rapidly into a media-fueled feud. Mr. Schiavo had been appointed to serve as his wife's guardian shortly after her accident, without any objection from the family. His decision to remove the feeding/nutrition tube caused her parents to challenge his guardianship powers.

Ms. Schiavo did not have a written advance directive – no health care surrogate and no living will. In these circumstances, Florida law provides for the application of a substituted judgment test by the guardian, in the best interests of the ward.[4] It also provides for the introduction of parol evidence in support of what the incapacitated ward's intentions might have been.[5] Mr. Schiavo introduced what amounted to

---

[2] Florida law defines a "life prolonging procedure," or artificial life support, as "including artificially provided sustenance and hydration." FLA. STAT. § 765.101 (10) (2005).

[3] *See id.* § 765.305.

[4] *See id.* § 765.401 (2).

[5] *See id.*

hearsay evidence, statements made by Ms. Schiavo in the presence of others, on at least two occasions (funerals of relatives) where she allegedly stated that she would never want to be kept alive by artificial means. This evidence was challenged by the parents who also sought to introduce clinical evidence that Ms. Schiavo was not in a persistent vegetative state and that she did have a reasonable medical hope of recovery. Toward this latter end, the Schindlers relied upon the testimony of physicians who were not able to produce any published studies, written by them or anybody else, to substantiate their clinical findings and prognoses given the documented facts in her case history and the contrary testimony of other medical experts.

The bottom line with respect to the clinical evidence was that a panel of medical experts was assembled by the courts. Two were selected by Mr. Schiavo, two by the Schindlers, and one by the court. They each examined Ms. Schiavo and her medical record, and reported to the court. Their reports and their testimony were subjected to the clear and convincing test, per the Florida Rules of Evidence. By this standard, the clinical evidence substantiating the diagnosis of persistent vegetative state was met, and the Shindler's experts failed sorely to counter the medical and scientific evidence presented by Mr. Schiavo.

…

Throughout my tenure as Ms. Schiavo's special guardian ad litem, I was deeply moved by the love and care that both her parents and her husband had for my ward. I was struck by the impossible position of parents faced with a child predeceasing them and with the prospect of standing by and watching their child die. The Shindlers are decent, caring people, who found themselves in a horrible and painful circumstance. Mr. Schiavo sought to fulfill what he believed to be his wife's intentions and did so at the expense of vilification. There was no life insurance policy and no money left in the trust fund from which he would benefit.[6]

The guardian's statement does not do justice to the legal and political drama that surrounded Schiavo's death. When Michael Schiavo sought

[6] Wolfson, *supra* note 1, at 543–547.

court approval for the removal of his wife's feeding tube in 1998,[7] he was essentially asking permission to allow his wife to die by dehydration or starvation. She was unable to orally ingest food or water. Florida Law allows the withdrawal of medically assisted nutrition and hydration from a person in a permanent vegetative state if approved by the lawfully appointed surrogate decision maker (deemed by Florida statute the "health care proxy"[8]) so long as the decision to withdraw is the one that the patient would make or the withdrawal of treatment is in the patient's best interests.[9] By Florida statute, Michael Schiavo was his wife's proxy because she had not designated anyone prior to her incapacity. That law, like that of other states, establishes a hierarchy of family members to step in to make certain medical treatment decisions for patients who are unable to speak for themselves.[10] As lawful proxy, Michael Schiavo was not required to seek court approval of the withdrawal of his wife's feeding tube. He sought court approval in

---

[7] *In re* Schiavo, No. 90–2908 GD-003, 2000 WL 34546715 (Fla. Cir. Ct. Feb. 11, 2000) (order allowing the removal of Terri Schiavo's feeding tube pursuant to Florida statute and Michael Schiavo's directions as Terri Schiavo's proxy) [hereinafter Schiavo Original 2000 Order].

[8] Under Florida law, a health care proxy is a person designated by statute to make decisions for an incapacitated person who has not executed an advance directive appointing someone to serve as surrogate. "This terminology contrasts with that used in other states, in which persons making medical decisions for incapacitated persons without patient appointment to such a position (… those who derive their authority from operation of law) are called surrogates." Kathy L. Cerminara, *Tracking the Storm: The Far-Reaching Power of the Forces Propelling the Schiavo Cases*, 35 STETSON L. REV. 147, 178 n.7 (2005).

[9] FLA. STAT. §§ 765.401(2), (3) (2010).

[10] *Id.* § 765.401(1). The following individuals may act as proxy in the following order of priority:
(a) the judicially appointed guardian of the patient … ; (b) the patient's spouse; (c) an adult child of the patient, or if the patient has more than one adult child, a majority of adult children … ; (d) a parent of the patient; (e) the adult sibling of the patient or, if the patient has more than one sibling, a majority of the adult siblings … ; (f) an adult relative … who has exhibited special care and concern for the patient … ; (g) a close friend of the patient[;] (h) [in some circumstances,] [a] clinical social worker….
Id.

deference to his in-laws, who had made their opposition to that course of action well known.[11]

Circuit Judge George Greer held a hearing on the petition. There, a computed axial tomography (CAT) scan was introduced into evidence. The scan revealed that "to a large extent [Schiavo's] brain had been replaced by spinal fluid...."[12] There was also testimony about statements reportedly made by Terri to her husband, his brother, and his sister-in-law in response to the hospitalization of her grandmother, the funeral of another relative, and television shows about circumstances in which Schiavo would not want to continue living. Following the hearing, Judge Greer determined that Terri Schiavo was "beyond all doubt ... in a persistent vegetative state" and that the medical evidence "conclusively establishes that she has no hope of ever regaining consciousness...."[13] He also found clear and convincing evidence that removal of the feeding tube was the decision Terri Schiavo would make if she were competent.[14] Based on this evidence, Judge Greer ordered that the feeding tube be removed.

The Schindlers' appeal of the original order was unsuccessful,[15] and Terri Schiavo's feeding tube was clamped in April 2001 so that she would stop receiving nutrition and hydration through the tube.[16]

Determined to keep their daughter alive, the Schindlers filed a new legal action before a different state court judge, requesting that the removal of life support be enjoined.[17] The judge granted their request.[18]

---

[11] Lois Shepherd, *Terri Schiavo: Unsettling the Settled*, 37 Loy. U. Chi. L.J. 297, 305–306 (2006).

[12] Schiavo Original 2000 Order, *supra* note 7, at *4.

[13] *Id.*

[14] *Id.* at *6.

[15] *In re* Schiavo, 780 So. 2d 176, 180 (Schiavo I) (Fla. 2d Dist. Ct. App. 2001) (affirming the Schiavo Original 2000 Order), *review denied sub nom.*, Schindler v. Schiavo *ex rel.* Schiavo, 789 So. 2d 348 (Fla. 2001).

[16] *In re* Schiavo, 792 So. 2d 551, 555 (Schiavo II) (Fla. 2d Dist. Ct. App. 2001).

[17] *Id.* at 555–556.

[18] *Id.* at 556.

After a series of hearings, motions, and appeals, the Schindlers were granted the right to a new evidentiary hearing by Judge Greer to determine whether a new medical treatment could possibly improve Schiavo's condition.[19]

At the hearing, five doctors submitted testimony on Terri Schiavo's condition. Two of the doctors were chosen by Michael Schiavo, two by the Schindlers, and one by the court. Following the hearing, Judge Greer found that the evidence that Terri Schiavo remained in a persistent vegetative state was "overwhelming[ ]," and that no evidence supported the Schindler's claim that the proposed treatment would improve her quality of life.[20] The court entered a new order to withdraw Schiavo's feeding tube.

Again, the Schindlers exhausted every possible avenue of appeal. When that failed,[21] they worked with their rapidly growing group of supporters to lobby Florida Governor Jeb Bush. Bush responded and worked with the Florida legislature to pass emergency legislation specifically addressing the situation faced by Terri Schiavo and her parents. "Terri's law" allowed the governor to issue a "stay" of the order allowing the feeding tube to be withdrawn and permitted him to order the feeding tube's reinsertion, which he did.[22]

---

[19] *In re* Schiavo, 800 So. 2d 640, 646–647 (Schiavo III) (Fla. 2d Dist. Ct. App. 2001) (ordering new hearing on medical evidence).

[20] *In re* Schiavo, No. 90–2908-GB-003, 2002 WL 31817960 at * 2–5 (Fla. Cir. Ct. 2002).

[21] *In re* Schiavo, 851 So. 2d 182 (Schiavo IV) (Fla. 2d Dist. Ct. App. 2003*)*, *review denied sub. nom.*, Schindler v. Schiavo, 855 So. 2d 621 (Fla. 2003).

[22] H.B. 35-E, 2003 Leg., Spec. Sess. (Fla. 2003), *available at* http://fl1.findlaw.com/ news.findlaw.com/hdocs/docs/schiavo/flsb35e102103.pdf. "Terri's Law" was invalidated by Bush v. Schiavo, 885 So. 2d 321, 336–337 (Fla. 2004). The law provided:

Section 1.

(1) The Governor shall have the authority to issue a one-time stay to prevent the withholding of nutrition and hydration from a patient if, as of October 15, 2003:

   (a) That patient has no written advance directive;

   (b) The court has found that patient to be in a persistent vegetative state;

It is hard to overstate the public reaction to the unprecedented actions of the Florida legislature and Governor Bush. Disability advocates and others who supported the intervention engaged in a media campaign likening the interventions to a "stay of execution" that saved a severely disabled woman from being "cruelly starved to death."[23] Opponents charged that the legislature and governor had grossly overstepped their roles by intruding on an individual's medical decisions, failing to respect the judicial process, and ignoring Terri Schiavo's constitutional rights to bodily integrity and privacy.[24] Protesters gathered by the hundreds outside Terri's hospital. The media covered every aspect of the case, repeatedly showing videos of a slack-jawed woman whose eyes were open and apparently alert.

In 2004, the Florida Supreme Court declared "Terri's Law" unconstitutional as a violation of the separation-of-powers doctrine.[25] The feeding tube was again removed, but only after a failed attempt by the Florida legislature to pass yet another law that would have made it illegal to remove a feeding tube from a person in a persistent vegetative

(c) That patient has had nutrition and hydration withheld; and
(d) A member of that patient's family has challenged the withholding of nutrition and hydration.
(2) The Governor's authority to issue the stay expires 15 days after the effective date of this act, and the expiration of that authority does not impact the validity or the effect of any stay issued pursuant to this act. The Governor may lift the stay authorized under this act at any time. A person may not be held civilly liable and is not subject to regulatory or disciplinary sanctions for taking any action to comply with a stay issued by the Governor pursuant to this act.
(3) Upon the issuance of a stay, the chief judge of the circuit court shall appoint a guardian ad litem for the patient to make recommendations to the Governor and the court.

[23] Shepherd, *supra* note 11 at 308–309; David Sommer, *Advocacy Group Supports Schindlers in Court Fight,* Tampa Trib., Oct. 31, 2003, at 3. .
[24] Shepherd, *supra* note 11 at 341 n.67 and accompanying text.
[25] Bush v. Schiavo, 885 So. 2d 321, 336–337 (Fla. 2004).

state absent a living will.[26] By this time, Schiavo's case dominated the national news, and the federal government intervened.

The fact of intervention by the federal government was startling. Health matters are generally a matter of state or local law, not national concern, and federal intervention into a particular dispute involving a single patient was unprecedented. Nonetheless, a congressional subcommittee subpoenaed Terri Schiavo and others to testify "under a theory that failing to provide her with artificial nutrition and hydration would constitute an illegal obstruction of the subpoena."[27] The tactic did not work, so Congress passed "An Act for the Relief of the Parents of Theresa Marie Schiavo," which granted the federal courts jurisdiction over Terri Schiavo's case.[28] The assigned federal court conducted a hearing but rejected the Schindler's request for an order to reinsert the feeding tube after finding the Schindlers had failed to show that they had been denied due process in the Florida courts.[29] Appeals of that decision failed.

Florida Governor Jeb Bush then made one last attempt to restore Schiavo's feeding tube. Bush asked the Florida Department of Children and Families (DCF) and the Florida Department of Law Enforcement to "take possession" of Schiavo.[30] Although the legal status of the intervention was in question, a squad of state police and DCF officials arrived at the facility where Terri Schiavo was cared for, where they were confronted by local police who would not allow the state agents to remove the feeding tube without a court order.[31] The scene – police confrontation, massive protests, grieving parents, video

---

[26] H.R. 701, 2005 Leg., 107th Sess. (Fla. 2005); S. 804, 2005 Leg., Reg. Sess. (Fla. 2005).

[27] Shepherd, *supra* note 11, at 310.

[28] An Act for the Relief of the Parents of Theresa Marie Schiavo, Pub. L. No. 109–3, § 1, 119 Stat. 15 (2005).

[29] Schiavo *ex rel.* Schindler v. Schiavo, 358 F. Supp. 2d 1161, 1166–1167 (M.D. Fla. 2005).

[30] Carol Marbin Miller, *Terri Schiavo Case: Plan to Seize Schiavo Fizzles*, MIAMI HERALD, Mar. 26, 2005, at 1A.

[31] *Id.*

clips of a vacant but "awake" Terri Schiavo – made for compelling television footage. When Terri Schiavo finally died on March 31, 2005, she had been in a vegetative state for fifteen years.

II. THE CASE OF SHEILA POULIOT[32]

Sheila Pouliot had lived with mental and physical disabilities for forty-two years after she suffered serious complications from the mumps as an infant. Her disabilities left her wholly dependent on others for all her basic life functions. She had profound mental retardation and severe cerebral palsy, which was manifested by incomplete quadriparesis and partial blindness.[33] Unable to ingest food orally, Pouliot received nutrition through a feeding tube for most of her life. By the time she was in her early forties, Pouliot had become chronically ill. She had a seizure disorder, osteoporosis, several dislocated joints, and widespread flexion contractures in her elbows, knees, and hips.[34] The tube feedings caused aspiration pneumonia, episodes of gastrointestinal bleeding, and chronic, severe constipation.

---

[32] Much of the following discussion first appeared in Alicia Ouellette, *When Vitalism is Dead Wrong*, 79 INDIANA L.J. 1 (2004) (Copyright 2004 by the Trustees of Indiana University. Reprinted with Permission).

[33] Kathy Faber-Langendoen, *Sheila Pouliot's Story*, http://www.familydecisions.org/pouliot.html (last visited Oct. 9, 2010) [hereinafter Faber-Langendoen].

[34] Blouin v. Spitzer, 01-CV-0925 HGM/GJD, 2001 U.S. Dist. Lexis 18243, at *1 (N.D.N.Y. Nov. 5, 2001). In his brief to the United States Court of Appeals for the Second Circuit, Attorney General Eliot Spitzer argued that the medical records do not support a finding that Ms. Pouliot suffered from pneumonia at the time she was admitted to the hospital. *See* Brief for Appellees, Blouin v. Spitzer, No. 02–7997 (2d Cir. docketed Mar. 5, 2003). In addition to the bleeding, Ms. Pouliot suffered "osteoporosis (thinning of the bones), with associate fractures in her right humerus and pelvis; dislocation of her left hip as well as possibly of her right shoulder; widespread flexion contractures involving elbows, knees and hips; and a seizure disorder." Aff. of Kathleen McGrail, M.D., Joint Appendix on Appeal at 1639, Blouin v. Spitzer, No. 02–7997 (2d Cir. docketed Mar. 5, 2003) [hereinafter McGrail aff.].

Pouliot's mother cared for her in the family home for twenty years. At home, Pouliot's older sister and brother doted upon her. When her mother became afflicted with Alzheimer's disease and was no longer able to care for her, Pouliot became a resident of a group home operated by the State of New York, where she lived for the next twenty-two years. Pouliot's family visited with her every Sunday, birthdays, and holidays. Although she was not verbal, Pouliot appeared to enjoy the visits. She also enjoyed listening to music.[35]

Pouliot was acutely ill when she was admitted to University Hospital in Syracuse at forty-two years old.[36] By the time she reached the hospital, she was near death. She was feverish, had low oxygen levels, hypotension, aspiration pneumonia, internal bleeding, severe abdominal pain, and a nonfunctioning intestine.[37] Because of gastrointestinal bleeding, she could no longer tolerate tube feeding.[38] She was in obvious pain and communicated her discomfort by groaning. Pouliot's family met with the medical staff, SUNY Hospital's Ethics Committee, and clergy. All agreed that her condition was terminal, and that the appropriate treatment was the provision of palliative care involving the intravenous delivery of morphine only. The group also agreed that neither nutrition and hydration nor antibiotics would be administered because such treatment would merely prolong Pouliot's suffering.[39] One of Pouliot's treating physicians explained the group's decision in a progress note:

> After 1 hour discussion with team, family, social worker, nursing staff, chaplain and ethics consultant, we are in full agreement that this may be Ms. Pouliot's terminal illness. We agree that the most humane course is to provide comfort in the way of [morphine sulfate] as needed and to refrain from invasive resuscitative and recovery measures.[40]

[35] McGrail aff., *supra* note 34, at 1647–1648.
[36] Blouin v. Spitzer, 213 F. Supp. 2d 184, 186 (N.D.N.Y. 2002).
[37] Blouin v. Spitzer, 356 F.3d 348, 352 (2004).
[38] Faber-Langendoen, *supra* note 33.
[39] Blouin, 213 F. Supp. 2d at 186.
[40] Blouin, 356 F.3d at 352.

With the family's agreement, the treatment team terminated administration of nutrition and hydration and provided comfort care. Pouliot rested comfortably for several days. A week after her admission to the hospital, however, the University Hospital's administration brought the case to the attention of the New York State Office of Mental Retardation and Developmental Disabilities. That agency instructed the hospital to obtain a court-appointed guardian for Pouliot and asked the state Attorney General to intervene to enforce New York law on behalf of Pouliot.[41]

At that time, New York law, like that of some other states,[42] did not allow a family member or surrogate to withhold medically-administered nutrition or hydration from a person like Sheila Pouliot who was never capable of understanding or making a reasoned decision about medical treatment. Whereas the State recognized the fundamental right of *competent* patients to refuse medical treatment of all types, the state courts had steadfastly held that the right to refuse treatment is personal to the patient, and that "no person or court should substitute its judgment as to what would be an acceptable quality of life for another."[43] The only situation in which the courts would permit the termination of life-sustaining treatment for a patient who lacked competence was when "the evidence clearly and convincingly shows that the patient intended to decline the

---

[41] Alicia Ouellette, *When Vitalism is Dead Wrong: The Discrimination Against and Torture of Incompetent Patients by Compulsory Life-Sustaining Treatment*, 79 IND. L. J. 1, 14–15 (2004).

[42] Missouri and Michigan had similar laws to those in place in New York when Sheila Pouliot was dying. Wisconsin, Arizona, Hawaii, Mississippi, Ohio, and Utah also place limitations on surrogate decision makers that may not be warranted by the best interest of the patient. *See* Ouellette, *supra* note 41, for a discussion of the parameters of those laws. In July, 2010, New York radically changed its end-of-life laws by enacting the Family Health Care Decisions Act. *See* 2010 N.Y. Laws ch. 8, §2 (codified at N.Y. PUB. HEALTH LAW art. 29-CC, §2994-a (McKinney 2010)).

[43] *In re* Westchester County Med. Ctr. *ex rel.* O'Connor, 531 N.E.2d 607, 613 (N.Y. 1988).

treatment under [the] particular circumstances" he or she was ultimately facing.[44] Thus the law provided no mechanism to allow a decision to terminate treatment for people who never had competence, or for those formerly competent patients who had failed to express their wishes while competent.

In addition, New York law treated people like Pouliot, adults who have never had capacity to make medical choices, as though they were infants.[45] Specifically, the law allowed the parent or guardian of an infant to give effective consent for medical treatment in the best interest of the child, but did not allow a parent or guardian to deprive a child of life-saving treatment, however well-intended or ethically justified the decision to withhold might have been. New York's policy was to err on the side of life: "Even when the parents' [or guardians'] decision to decline necessary treatment is based on constitutional grounds, such as religious beliefs, it must yield to the State's interests, as *parens patriae*, in protecting the health and welfare of the child."[46] The only way to protect a child's health and welfare, in the view of New York Courts, was to provide nutrition and hydration in all cases. Thus parents and guardians could not make "decision[s] that would result in [the incompetent patient] starving to death, if such could be medically avoided, regardless of how soon [the patient] may or may not succumb from other causes."[47]

Nine days after Pouliot was admitted to the hospital, a New York trial judge held a hearing at the hospital.[48] The court appointed a guardian ad litem, who in turn petitioned the court to terminate all nutrition and hydration. The court heard testimony from Pouliot's doctors. All the providers agreed that providing any nutrition would be difficult because the bleeding in Pouliot's gastrointestinal tract

---

[44] *Id.* (citing *In re* Storar, 52 N.Y.2d 363, 379 (1981)).
[45] *See In re* Storar, 52 N.Y.2d at 380.
[46] *Id.* at 380–381.
[47] *In re* Matthews, 650 N.Y.S.2d 373, 377 (N.Y. App. Div. 1996).
[48] *Blouin*, 213 F. Supp. 2d at 186.

made tube feeding impossible.[49] The doctors also agreed that providing any further treatment to Ms. Pouliot would prolong "her agony without any significant health or medical benefits."[50] Nonetheless, the court ordered the continuing provision of hydration and 900 calories of nutrition a day based on a straightforward application of New York law.[51]

Doctors made efforts to provide Ms. Pouliot with the planned 900 calories a day, but the effort was ineffective.[52] The blood vessels through which the doctors tried to infuse sustenance shut down, and the introduction of protein caused projectile vomiting and intractable hiccups.[53] As a result, the only sustenance that Pouliot could sustain was IV hydration with sugar water. The IV provided 300 calories a day but no protein.[54]

The provision of 300 calories a day without protein devastated Pouliot's body over the next two and a half months. The nutrition contained in the fluids was sufficient to maintain life (heart and lung function), but it could not prevent protein starvation, which caused Ms. Pouliot's body to catabolize, or break down and use energy from her own tissue, damaging her organs and causing her severe pain. Further, it caused her severe edema (swelling), which stretched her skin to the point where it fell off, leaving raw painful areas.[55]

---

[49] *Id.* at 187.

[50] *Id.*

[51] *Id.*

[52] *Id.*

[53] Kathy Faber-Langendoen, M.D., *progress note entered into Shiela Pouliot's medical chart,* February 29, 2000 (on file with author) [hereinafter Faber-Langendoen progress note].

[54] *Id.*; David F. Lehmann, M.D., *progress note entered into Sheila Pouliot's medical chart* (Feb. 29, 2000) (on file with author) [hereinafter Lehmann progress note].

[55] During that time, Ms. Pouliot's skin broke down with "excessive maceration," she was "edemous, with total body bloating from hydration in the absence of protein. Hydration alone ... resulted in severe protein malnutrition, which is typified by skin, peripheral muscle, and cardiac muscle breakdown." Faber-Langendoen progress note, *supra* note 53.

Pouliot's physicians used aggressive efforts to control her pain, but their efforts failed. Sheila Pouliot was in agony, dying inch by inch. She communicated her pain by moaning and crying, by furrowing her forehead, and by flexing her extremities. She got no relief despite the fact that she was on the equivalent of approximately 5,000 mg of oral morphine a day. Her family could console her only by stroking her forehead or placing a musical angel next to her head on her pillow.[56]

The physicians became increasingly convinced that the court-ordered treatment that kept Pouliot alive was actually making her condition worse. On February 29, 2000, more than two months after Pouliot entered the hospital, one of her treating physicians entered the following progress note in her chart:

> [t]he intravenous fluids promote that the patient is kept alive for her own body to consume/eat itself.... [T]his current plan of IV hydration promotes an INCREASE in patient suffering, does not promote life quality and maintains her heart/lung capacity only. And, indeed, therefore this current [treatment] is clearly outside of acceptable medical bounds, in effect worsening her condition since she is consuming herself calorically. It is thus, not medically indicated.[57]

Another of Pouliot's physicians stated in a consultation note, "Sheila is edematous, with total body bloating from hydration in the absence of protein. Hydration ... has resulted in severe ... cardiac muscle breakdown. She will die a slow and lingering death from protein malnutrition."[58] The treating physician also noted that the provision of artificial hydration ordered by the Court was "inhumane and is causing suffering.... From a medical standpoint, it is outside the bounds of ... medically indicated care." [59]

---

[56] McGrail aff., *supra* note 34, at 1646 (emphasis added).
[57] *Blouin*, 356 F.3d 3 at 354–355.
[58] *Id.* at 355 n.4.
[59] *Id.*

Finally, the guardian decided to take action. He went back to court seeking an order that would allow the physicians to withdraw the IV fluids despite New York's laws.[60] At the hearing, Pouliot's physicians testified that "the continuation of hydration for this patient is affirmatively causing significant physical harm to the patient in that it is bringing about unnatural and painful decomposition of her body tissues...."[61] The hearing made clear that further treatment would only make the pain worse, but it would sustain her life. Terminating nutrition and hydration would lessen Pouliot's pain, but it would also cause her death. At this point, Pouliot's life expectancy was approximately two to four months if hydration were continued.[62] She would die within three to fourteen days if hydration was discontinued.[63]

Trial Judge Tormey was therefore faced with a dilemma: apply settled law and continue the treatment because it was technically life-sustaining, or buck the law. At this point, Judge Tormey did an unusual thing; he visited Sheila Pouliot in the hospital. There, he ordered the termination of all nutrition and hydration. He acknowledged that New York law did not allow his order, but he explained: "There's the law, and there's what's right."[64] The State of New York appealed the decision, but the appeal was never heard.[65] Sheila Pouliot died on March 6, 2000, just before the appellate court was to hear oral argument.[66]

---

[60] *See* Joint Appendix on Appeal at 409, Blouin v. Spitzer, No. 02–7997 (2d Cir. docketed Mar. 5, 2003).

[61] Aff. of Kathy Faber-Langendoen, M.D., Joint Appendix on Appeal at 797, Blouin v. Spitzer, No. 02–7997 (2d Cir. docketed Mar. 5, 2003) [hereinafter Faber-Langendoenaff.].

[62] *Id.* at 796.

[63] *Id.* at 797.

[64] Michael D. Goldhaber, *The Law v. What's Right*, NAT'L L. J., Apr. 3, 2000, at A1. *See* Blouin v. Spitzer, 356 F.3d at 355.

[65] Joint Appendix on Appeal at790, Blouin v. Spitzer, No. 02–7997 (2d Cir. docketed Mar. 5, 2003).

[66] *Blouin*, 356 F.3d at 356.

The laws that applied in Sheila Pouliot's case were the most restrictive in the country. New York's top court established the law in a series of cases that came before it during the 1980s. In the cases, the judges purposefully imposed the most rigorous burden of proof available in civil cases out of concern that each individual's "right to life" be protected by a standard that ensures that "if an error occurs it [will] be made on the side of life."[67] But the judges also struggled with their professional and personal roles in deciding the cases. The opinions themselves are replete with calls to the state legislature to set up a statutory framework to allow families and doctors to decide end-of-life cases without court involvement. And the judge who wrote the majority opinion in the seminal *O'Connor* case admitted that a family dispute over his own mother's medical care had convinced him that New York needed strict standards to prevent family members from making the wrong decisions for loved ones.[68]

Sheila Pouliot's family was understandably angry after her death. They sued the State Attorney General and his assistants for constitutional and other wrongs allegedly inflected by them against their sister.[69] The lawsuit was unsuccessful. The Attorney General is protected from lawsuits for enforcing the law.[70] The federal appellate court agreed that the Attorney General's hands were tied by New York's laws. It also

---

[67] *In re* Westchester County Med. Ctr. *ex rel* O'Connor, 531 N.E2d 607, 613 (N.Y. 1988).

[68] Richard D. Simons, *Oral History*, 1 N.Y. LEGAL HIST. 53, 86–87 (2005).

[69] *Blouin*, 213 F. Supp. 2d at 187–188.

[70] *Id.* at 190 (district court holding that defendants were entitled to qualified immunity because the "plaintiff ha[d] failed to allege a violation of a clearly established right [and even if] the court found a violation, it could not be concluded that such a right was so clearly established that it was objectively unreasonable for defendants to believe that their actions did not violate the law). *See* Poe v. Leonard, 258 F.3d 123, 133 (2d Cir. 2002) (the defense of qualified immunity is established where "(a) the defendant's action did not violate clearly established law, or (b) it was objectively reasonable for the defendant to believe that his action did not violate such law.").

288

upheld as constitutional those laws.[71] Thus, the only written precedent that followed from Sheila Pouliot's case upheld laws that limit treatment choices for people with profound disabilities, even when there is consensus on the part of family and medical providers that those choices are medically appropriate and in the best interest of the patient.

Pouliot's doctors were also appalled that New York's laws forced them to inflict what can fairly be characterized as an inhumane and torturous death on Sheila Pouliot. They engaged in a lobbying effort to change New York's law regarding medical decision making for incompetent patients. That effort was mildly successful. In 2002, New York passed the Health Care Decisions Act for Persons with Mental Retardation[72], which allows the duly appointed surrogate of a person with mental retardation to terminate life-sustaining treatment under the very narrow circumstances that Sheila Pouliot faced.[73] The Act might have helped Sheila Pouliot, but it did not change the New York laws for children, formerly competent adults.[74]

III. VIEWS FROM THE DISABILITY COMMUNITY

The issues presented by Terri Schiavo's case were a matter of deep concern to some members of the disability community. The belief is that "Terri Schiavo died on March 31, 2005, not from her 1990 brain injury but because of prejudice, the common assumption that life with a significant disability is not worth living."[75] Of course, there is

[71] See Blouin, 356 F.3d at 348.
[72] 2002 N.Y. Laws 1264, ch. 500 (codified at N.Y. SURR. CT. PROC. ACT § 1750 (McKinney 2003)).
[73] See N.Y. SURR. CT. PROC. ACT § 1750-b (McKinney 2003).
[74] New York finally enacted a more comprehensive law in July of 2010. See Family Health Care Decisions Act, 2010 N.Y. Laws ch. 8, §2 (codified at N.Y. PUB. HEALTH LAW art. 29-CC, §2994-a (McKinney 2010)).
[75] Laura Hershey, Editorial, Killed by Prejudice, THE NATION, Apr. 14, 2005, http://www.thenation.com/article/killed-prejudice.

debate within the multifaceted disability rights community about the Schiavo case and the related issues of choice in dying, as well as about physician-assisted suicide. The public message from the community on Schiavo was clear, however: The laws that allowed the removal of Terri Schiavo's feeding tube must be changed to protect the lives of people with disabilities.

Harriet McBryde Johnson's short commentary titled "Not Dead at All: Why Congress Was Right to Stick Up for Terri Schiavo" succinctly and powerfully presented the disability rights arguments against the withdrawal of Terri Schiavo's feeding tube.[76] In the commentary, McBryde Johnson made ten points that can be summarized as follows: Schiavo was not terminally ill; artificial nutrition and hydration are not life support and are not treatment; because Schiavo was not suffering, her death could not be justified as relieving suffering; no one could determine what Schiavo's wishes were at the time the decision to terminate treatment was made; Schiavo had a federal constitutional right not to be deprived of her life without due process; terminating nutrition and hydration for Schiavo would violate the Americans with Disabilities Act; fear of feeding tubes is a form of disability prejudice; and the federal government did not take sides by passing a law to allow the federal courts to step into the Schiavo case after it had been resolved in the state courts.[77] These arguments resonated with many members of the disability community, who remembered the false claims that Elizabeth Bouvia (see Chapter 2) and Larry MacAfee (see Chapter 5) had no possibility for meaningful life because of their disabilities. To people who had lived all their lives being told their lives were not meaningful, Terri Schiavo was one of their own.

McBryde Johnson's arguments paralleled those made in briefs to the court and in position papers by the disability rights group Not

---

[76] Harriet McBryde Johnson, *Not Dead at All: Why Congress Was Right to Stick Up for Terri Schiavo*, SLATE, Mar. 23, 2005, http://www.slate.com/id/2115208, *reprinted in* Editorial, *Overlooked in the Shadows*, WASH. POST, Mar. 25, 2005, at A19.

[77] *See id.*

Dead Yet. Working together with twenty-five national disability groups, Not Dead Yet took on a prominent and public role during the *Schiavo* case.[78] The activists claimed Terri Schiavo as one of their own. As the group wrote in an amicus brief:

> Ms. Schiavo's fate is intertwined with that of many people with disabilities who must rely on surrogates. If ... Ms. Schiavo's "quality of life" – as determined by others – justifies her death, then one cannot distinguish Ms. Schiavo from anyone else who is "incompetent," including thousands who cannot speak due to developmental or physical disabilities.[79]

Not Dead Yet filed several amicus briefs during the course of the *Schiavo* case, all of which raised three principal arguments: First, that the trial court had failed in its fact-finding role; second, that Terri Schiavo had a substantive due process right to receive treatment; and third, that the denial of medical care because of cognitive disability constituted illegal differential treatment under the Americans with Disabilities Act.[80] The *Schiavo* briefs reiterated arguments made for years by the activists, but it was during *Schiavo* that they got the most attention.[81] Also drawing attention to the disability arguments were Not Dead Yet's lobbying effort to the Florida legislature, Florida Governor Bush, Congress, and the President.

After Terri Schiavo died, disability activists brought their agenda to state legislatures across the country. The new activists proposed legislation that would essentially eliminate the ability of surrogates to

---

[78] *See* Cerminara, *supra* note 8, at 154–155 (noting several public interest groups took part in the *Schiavo* appeal).

[79] Brief for Not Dead Yet et al. as Amici Curiae Supporting Appellants, *In re* Schiavo, 851 So. 2d 182 (Fla. 2d Dist. Ct. App. 2003) (No. 2D02–5394), *available at* http://www.notdeadyet.org/docs/schiavobrief.html.

[80] *Id.*

[81] *See, e.g.*, Diana Penner, *Indiana Tackled Right-to-Die Issue in '91: In Schiavo-Like Case, Parents Agonized, then Chose to Remove Tube; A Legal Battle Followed*, INDIANAPOLIS STAR, Mar. 27, 2005, at 1A.

use substituted judgment as a model for decision making and impose instead a default rule that continued life is the appropriate course. For example, the National Council for Independent Living advanced legislation that would "only allow for withholding of food and water in the presence of 'clear and convincing evidence' of the person's wishes or when the person's medical condition renders them incapable of digesting or absorbing the nutrition and hydration so that its provision would not contribute to sustaining the person's life."[82]

Similarly, the Model Starvation and Dehydration of Persons with Disabilities Prevention Act, a law supported by various disability rights groups, would specifically impose a presumption "that every person legally incapable of making health care decisions has directed his or her health care providers to provide him or her with nutrition and hydration to a degree that is sufficient to sustain life."[83] Thus, the Model Act expressly imposes a substituted judgment about what the person would want, regardless of the individual's values. The presumption could be overcome in very limited circumstances. "No guardian, surrogate, public or private agency, court, or any other person" would have the authority to terminate nutrition and hydration except if expressly provided for in a living will, or if the surrogate could produce "clear and convincing evidence that the person ... when legally capable of making such decisions, gave express and informed consent

---

[82] Nat'l Council on Indep. Living, Position Statement, *Rights of People with Disabilities to Food and Water*, July 14, 2005, http://ncil.org/news/FoodandWater.html (emphasis added). *See also* Ctr. on Human Policy, Position Statement, *A Statement of Common Principles on Life-Sustaining Care and Treatment of People with Disabilities*, http://thechp.syr.edu/endorse/ ("Absent clear and convincing evidence of the desires of people with disabilities to decline life-sustaining care or treatment, such care and treatment should not be withheld or withdrawn unless death is genuinely imminent and the care or treatment is objectively futile and would only prolong the dying process.").

[83] Model Starvation and Dehydration of Persons with Disabilities Prevention Act § 3(A) (Nat'l Right to Life Comm. 2006), http://www.nrlc.org/euthanasia/modeln&hstatelaw.pdf [hereinafter MODEL ACT].

to withdrawing or withholding hydration or nutrition in the applicable circumstances," or if the nutrition and hydration is not medically possible, would hasten death, or would not contribute to sustaining the person's life.[84]

The Model Act reflects the social kinship many disability experts feel with others who use feeding tubes. Harriet McBryde Johnson, for example, explained:

> I watch nourishment flowing into a slim tube that runs through a neat, round, surgically created orifice in Ms. Schiavo's abdomen, and I'm almost envious. What effortless intake! Due to a congenital neuromuscular disease, I am having trouble swallowing, and it's a constant struggle to get by mouth the calories my skinny body needs. For whatever reason, I'm still trying, but I know a tube is in my future.[85]

Because she may need a feeding tube someday, McBryde Johnson feels that no one should be denied one. Instead, she believes it is a piece of equipment, like a wheelchair, which should never be denied.[86]

Although the national disability groups did not intervene in Sheila Pouliot's case, their advocacy for the Model Act suggests that if they had, they would have joined the state agency for people with cognitive disabilities in ensuring that Pouliot continued to receive life-extending nutrition and hydration. The Model Act would not have allowed Pouliot's sister to withdraw nutrition and hydration. Because Pouliot was not competent to make her own health care decisions, the Model Act would have created the presumption that Pouliot had "directed ... her health care providers to provide ... nutrition and hydration ... sufficient to sustain life."[87] None of the exceptions in the Model Act would have helped Pouliot. She had no advance directive, could not give express informed

---

[84] *Id.* §§ 3(B), 4(A), (B), 5(A).
[85] McBryde Johnson, *supra* note 76.
[86] *Id.*
[87] MODEL ACT, *supra* note 83, § 3(A).

consent, and was not receiving treatment that was medically impossible, hastening death, or unnecessary to sustain her life.[88]

Thus the advocacy positions taken in the wake of the Schiavo case would leave some people with cognitive disabilities – those who have never had the capacity to express wishes about medical care, or those who became incapacitated without expressing such wishes – in the same position as Sheila Pouliot.

The advocacy positions are explained by disability scholars. Paul Longmore, for example, has written extensively on the "rampant prejudice" faced by persons with disabilities in the health care system.[89] According to Longmore, the prejudice results in a conflation of disability and terminal illness:

> [D]isability is often equated with terminal illness and even viewed as "living death." In right-to-die court cases involving individuals with significant disabilities – Elizabeth Bouvia in California, Larry McAfee in Georgia, David Rivlin in Michigan – the advocates of their assisted death, the news media, and the courts all described their situations in exactly those terms.[90]

Given this history, explains Longmore, and the pressures to cut costs in the health care system, it is hardly surprising that disability advocates are pressing for paternalistic, one-size-fits-all laws.[91]

Longmore also explains why advocacy for paternalistic laws is not incompatible with the commitment of the disability community to the principle of autonomy. The disability movement, he says,

---

[88] *Id.* §§ 4(A), (B).

[89] Paul K. Longmore, *The Disability Rights Opposition to Assisted Suicide Explained and Critiqued, in* END-OF-LIFE ISSUES AND PERSONS WITH DISABILITIES 144, 151 (Timothy Lillie & James L. Werth eds., 2007); Paul K. Longmore, *Elizabeth Bouvia, Assisted Suicide, and Social Prejudice, in* WHY I BURNED MY BOOK AND OTHER ESSAYS 149 (Temple University Press 2003).

[90] Longmore, *The Disability Rights Opposition to Assisted Suicide Explained and Critiqued, supra* note 89, at 151.

[91] Longmore acknowledges that terminal illness is different from disability, and urges the activists to consider the difference.

... has advocated a significantly different ideal [of autonomy than the "atomistic personal autonomy that is dominant in U.S. culture"]: self-determination within interdependent community. Standing as an alternative to the currently dominant, hyper-individualistic and pathologically competitive cultural and socioeconomic order, this vision ... [sees] social relations as especially pertinent ... because so many of those who have ended their lives have been isolated individuals.[92]

Thus, focusing on removal of social barriers rather than removal of isolated individuals is entirely consistent with a commitment to autonomy.[93]

IV. VIEWS FROM BIOETHICS

Long before the media took note of Terri Schiavo's situation, bioethics had reached consensus on certain issues. For example, there was widespread agreement that competent individuals have a legal right to refuse treatment; incompetent individuals have a right to have treatment refused for them; end-of-life decisions should ordinarily be made in clinical settings and not courts; close family members have the legal authority to act as surrogates and make medical decisions for patients who lack decision-making capacity; surrogates may rely on advance directives to ascertain patients' wishes in end-of-life decision making; and medically-administered nutrition and hydration are medical treatments.[94] Application of these principles in Terri Schiavo's case was straightforward, especially in light of the Florida law that designated

---

[92] Longmore, *The Disability Rights Opposition to Assisted Suicide Explained and Critiqued,* *supra* note 89, at 145.

[93] *Id.*

[94] Alan Meisel, *The Legal Consensus About Forgoing Life-Sustaining Treatment: Its Status and Its Prospects,* 2 KENNEDY INST. ETHICS J. 309, 315 (1992). *See also* ALAN MEISEL & KATHY L. CERMINARA, THE RIGHT TO DIE: THE LAW OF END-OF-LIFE DECISIONMAKING 2–6 (Aspen Publishers, 3d ed. 2004 & Supp. 2005).

Michael Schiavo the surrogate decision maker for his wife and the findings by the trial courts about what Terri would have wanted had she been able to speak for herself. Michael Schiavo's petition should have been granted; in fact, he should not have been forced to defend his decision in court in the first place. Like so many other cases that followed the paradigm cases of Karen Ann Quinlan and Nancy Cruzan – cases in which the previously mentioned principles were settled – Terri Schiavo's case looked like an easy one from the perspective of most bioethicists. The fierce opposition came as a surprise.[95]

That is not to say that Schiavo's case did not generate reflection on settled principles and paradigms within bioethics. It did. Rebecca Dresser, for example, challenged the widely held view that that the "substituted judgment" standard applied under the Florida statute was the best measure in end-of-life cases like Schiavo's.[96] Bruce Jennings, Thomas Murray, and others called for reexamination of the value of living wills, the interests of families and communities in end-of-life decision making, the possibility of misdiagnosis, and the narrow clinical focus of discussion on end-of-life cases in bioethics.[97] At the end of the

[95] *E.g.*, Rebecca Dresser, *Schiavo's Legacy: The Need for an Objective Standard*, 35 HASTINGS CENTER REP., May–June 2005, at 20.

[96] *Id.* at 21 (arguing that:[T]he best response to the conflict over Terri Schiavo would be intensified scholarly and public deliberation about the objective standard and its underlying moral judgments. Treatment decisions based on the objective standard must take into account several considerations. Besides prognosis, the patients' level of conscious awareness and experiential burdens and benefits are basic concerns. Another is the duty to protect vulnerable incapacitated individuals.... The antidiscrimination provisions of our disability laws are also relevant.).

[97] *See Improving End of Life Care: Why Has It Been so Difficult?*,HASTINGS CENTER SPECIAL REP., Nov.–Dec. 2005 (Bruce Jennings et al. eds.), *available at* http://www. thehastingscenter.org/pdf/improving_eol_care_why_has_it_been_so_difficult.pdf; *see also* Joseph J. Fins, *Rethinking Disorders of Consciousness: New Research and Its Implications*, 35 HASTINGS CENTER REP., Mar.–Apr. 2005, at 22, 22–24 (arguing that new findings about brain injuries are reason to reconsider the certainty of the PVS diagnosis); Angela Fagerlin & Carl E. Schneider, *Enough: The Failure of the Living Will*, 34 HASTINGS CENTER REP., Mar.–Apr. 2004, at 30, 30–42 (setting forth compelling evidence that living wills do not serve their intended purpose).

day, however, the general consensus in bioethics remains that choices made by families or loved ones for incapacitated patients should usually be respected. And opposition to laws that "either require or forbid certain types of life-sustaining treatment" is strong.[98]

On this point, Sheila Pouiliot's case is paradigmatic. The concern in Pouliot's case is that the laws that required the continued provision of life-sustaining nutrition and hydration caused Pouliot a horrific and prolonged death that no person with capacity would ever choose. Norman Canter, for example, uses Pouliot's case in strong defense of laws that give surrogates broad decision-making powers for people with profound cognitive disabilities:

> [I]t is inhumane and a denial of respect for persons to exclude the profoundly disabled from potentially beneficial surrogate decisions. A legal approach allowing conscientious surrogate decision making yields "a more just and compassionate result,".... The objectives of justice and compassion surely underlie the elaborate guardianship structures that every jurisdiction now supplies on behalf of profoundly disabled persons. Those structures are consistent with the ancient *parens patriae* principle that seeks to protect the interests of profoundly disabled persons. Legislatures should therefore "promote the human dignity of never competent patients by affording access to beneficial results which competent patients could, and likely would, choose under similar circumstances."[99]

Cantor and others are cognizant of the disability critique of laws that allow for the removal of life-sustaining treatment from persons with disabilities,[100] but conclude that those concerns are better addressed

---

[98] *E.g.*, Thomas H. Murray & Bruce Jennings, *The Quest to Reform End of Life Care: Rethinking Assumptions and Setting New Directions*, in IMPROVING END OF LIFE CARE: WHY HAS IT BEEN SO DIFFICULT?: HASTINGS CENTER SPECIAL REP., *supra* note 97, at S52, S56 (claiming such laws would be at best "premature and imprudent; at worst, tyrannical and unjust.").

[99] NORMAN L. CANTOR, MAKING MEDICAL DECISIONS FOR THE PROFOUNDLY MENTALLY DISABLED 68 (MIT Press 2009).

[100] *See id.*

through procedural protections like heightened evidentiary standards and third-party review than by one-size-fits-all laws like that applied in Sheila Pouliot's case.

V. OBSERVATIONS[101]

I remain deeply troubled by the advocacy positions taken by some disability advocates in the wake of the Schiavo case. The disability rights position responds to important concerns: the possibility of misdiagnosis, disability discrimination, and the devaluing of life with disability. The problem is that the proposed solution – laws that would limit the ability of surrogates to choose against treatment for certain individuals with cognitive disabilities – would have tragic consequences for some of the people they are designed to protect.[102] Sheila Pouliot's is a case on point.

The laws promoted by some disability activists, such as the Model Starvation and Dehydration of Persons with Disabilities Prevention Act, are essentially identical to the laws that victimized Sheila Pouliot. Such laws require the continued provision of nutrition and hydration (and other life-saving treatment) in the absence of expressed wishes by a competent patient to forgo such treatments. The legally mandated

---

[101] This section is an amalgam of materials I've previously published in two prior articles: *When Vitalism is Dead Wrong: The Discrimination Against and Torture of Incompetent Patients by Compulsory Life-Sustaining Treatment*, 79 IND. L. J. 1 (2004); *Disability and the End of Life*, 85 ORG. L. REV. 123 (2006).

[102] *See, e.g.*, MODEL ACT, *supra* note 83; NCIL Position Statement, *supra* note 55 (supporting legislation "that restores and maintains restrictions on surrogate decisions for withholding of food and water via tube");Ctr. On Human Policy, Position Statement, *A Statement of Common Principles on Life-Sustaining Care and Treatment of People with Disabilities*, http://thechp.syr.edu/endorse (last visited Oct. 12, 2010) (stating that for those lacking capacity and a directive, "treatment should not be withheld or withdrawn unless death is genuinely imminent" or continued care "is objectively futile").

treatment was catastrophic for Pouliot. Her skin broke down, she swelled to grotesque proportions, her body began to catabolize its own organs, her muscles rotted, and her heart deteriorated. Moreover, she was in excruciating pain because of the treatment. In contrast, she rested comfortably during the several days that physicians abided her family's request to withhold nutrition and hydration.

Pouliot's experience was predictable. The law required the provision of life-saving treatment because her disabilities prevented her from ever expressing a wish to refuse treatment. It is well established that prolonging a person's life indefinitely can cause unreasonable burdens to the patient.[103] For that reason, the consensus among palliative care specialists is that terminating life-sustaining treatment is an appropriate course of treatment in the final stages of dying.[104] Terminating nutrition and hydration respects the natural dying process and provides pain relief. As death approaches, "[m]ost patients completely lose their appetite and stop drinking."[105] The natural urge

[103] *See* Thomas E. Finucan et al., *Tube Feeding in Patients with Advanced Dementia, A Review of the Evidence*, 282 JAMA 1365 (1999) (concluding that tube feeding should be discouraged in severely demented patients because the risks outweigh the benefits); Christopher M. Callahan et al., *Outcomes of Percutaneous Endoscopic Gastrostomy Among Older Adults in a Community Setting*, 48 J. AM. GERIATRIC SOC. 1048 (2000) (concluding that gastrostomy tubes can burden patients without providing concomitant benefits).

[104] *See* Robert M. McCann et al., *Comfort Care for Terminally Ill Patients: The Appropriate Use of Nutrition and Hydration*, 272 JAMA 1263 (1994) (recognizing that providing nutrition and hydration to terminally ill patients can cause unwanted and painful side effects and finding that terminating the treatment increases patient comfort); Robert J. Sullivan, Jr., M.D., *Accepting Death Without Artificial Nutrition or Hydration*, 8 J. GEN. INTERNAL MED. 220 (1993); BRITISH MEDICAL ASSOCIATION, WITHHOLDING AND WITHDRAWING LIFE-PROLONGING MEDICAL TREATMENT: GUIDANCE FOR DECISION MAKING (BMJ Books 1999).

[105] Frank D. Ferris et al., *Ensuring Competency in End-of-Life Care: Controlling Symptoms*, BMC PALLIATIVE CARE, July 30, 2002, at 10, *available at* http://www.biomed-central.com/content/pdf/1472–684X-1-5.pdf (citing Eduardo Bruera & R.L. Fainsinger, *Clinical Management of Cachexia and Anorexia, in* OXFORD TEXTBOOK OF PALLIATIVE MEDICINE 548, 548 [Derek Doyle et al. eds., Oxford Univ. Press

has direct benefits. "[M]ost experts feel that dehydration in the last hour of living does not cause distress and may stimulate the release of endorphins and anaesthetic compounds that promote the patient's sense of well being."[106] Stopping nutrition and hydration can also prevent harm: "Intravenous lines can be cumbersome and particularly uncomfortable when the patient is cachectic, or has no discernible veins. Excess parenteral fluids can lead to fluid overload with consequent peripheral or pulmonary edema, worsened breathlessness, cough, and orotracheobronchial secretions, particularly if there is significant hypoalbuminemia."[107] Thus, the termination of nutrition and hydration itself provides pain relief and can prevent serious harm to the patient. In other words, terminating treatment is as essential to appropriate palliative care practice as is the administration of opiods.

Laws like those applied in Pouliot's case and those proposed in the wake of *Schiavo* are legally problematic. They create barriers to adequate palliative care medicine that implicate the constitutional and statutory rights of persons with disabilities.

A. Constitutional Implications

Although the U.S. Supreme Court has upheld laws that make it difficult for surrogate decision makers to withdraw life-sustaining treatment from unconscious or permanently vegetative patients,[108] the Court appears to distinguish the rights of patients who can feel pain

1998]); and J. A. Billings, *Comfort Measures for the Terminally Ill: Is Dehydration Painful?*, 33 J. AM. GERIATRICS SOC. 808 (1985).

[106] Ferris et al., *supra* note 105, at 10 (citing J. E. Ellershaw et al., *Dehydration and the Dying Patient*, 10 J. PAIN SYM. & MANAGEMENT 192 [1995]); C. F. Musgrave et al., *The Sensation of Thirst in Dying Patients Receiving IV Hydration*, 11 J. PALLIATIVE CARE 17 (1995); D. R. Musgrave, *Terminal Dehydration: To Give or Not to Give Intravenous Fluids?*, 13 CANCER NURSING 62 (1990).

[107] Ferris et al., *supra* note 105, at 10.

[108] *See* Cruzan v. Dir., Mo. Dep't of Health, 497 U.S. 261 (1990).

and those who cannot. Legal scholars point out the Supreme Court has "effectively required all states to ensure that their laws do not obstruct the provision of adequate palliative care, especially for the alleviation of pain and other physical symptoms of people facing death."[109] Alan Meisel has noted a trend toward the development of an even broader right: "Over the past few years, a concrete right of terminally ill patients to adequate pain control has gradually begun to emerge, first from state legislation and later from decisions of the United States Supreme Court."[110]

The argument for the emerging right to pain control is based on the Court's recognition of a distinction between "prohibiting conduct on

[109] Robert A. Burt, *The Supreme Court Speaks: Not Assisted Suicide but a Constitutional Right to Palliative Care*, 337 NEW ENG. J. MED. 1234, 1234 (1997).

Taking into account the tenor of Justice Souter's opinion, a majority of the Court (Justices Stevens, O'Connor, Souter, Ginsburg and Breyer) clearly accepted that dying individuals have a right to be free of unnecessary pain and suffering at the end of life. Robert Burt concludes from this that "a Court majority has found that states must not impose barriers on the availability of palliative care for terminally ill patients" and that state laws "restricting the availability of opioids for the management of pain are the most likely targets for judicial invalidation by this criterion."

David A. Pratt, *Too Many Physicians: Physician-Assisted Suicide After Glucksberg/Quail*, 9 (no.2) ALB. L.J. SCI. & TECH. 161, 223 (1999); *see also* Yale Kamisar, *On the Meaning and Impact of the Physician Assisted Suicide Cases*, 82 MINN. L. REV. 895, 908 (1998) (stating that five justices appear to accept a liberty interest in pain relief).

[110] Alan Meisel, *Pharmacists, Physician-Assisted Suicide, and Pain Control*, 2 J. HEALTH CARE L. & POL'Y 211, 214–215 (1999) (citing Washington v. Glucksberg, 521 U.S. 702, 736–738 (1997) (O'Connor, J., concurring)); *see also* Larry I. Palmer, *Institutional Analysis and Physicians' Rights After* Vacco v. Quill, 7 CORNELL J.L. & PUB. POL'Y 415, 424–426 (1998) (arguing that Justice O'Connor has opened the door to future litigation regarding barriers to pain relief); Kathryn L. Tucker, *The Death with Dignity Movement: Protecting Rights and Expanding Options After* Glucksberg *and* Quill, 82 MINN. L. REV. 923, 935–936 (1998) (arguing that at least five members of the Supreme Court would likely strike down state legislation requiring life-sustaining treatment if it would force dying people to endure excessive pain).

the part of physicians that intentionally hastens death and permitting conduct that may foreseeably hasten death but is intended for other important purposes, such as the relief of pain" in the physician-assisted suicide cases.[111] The Court's recognition that a physician can validly provide treatment that benefits the patient by relieving pain even though that treatment might hasten death suggests that the same physician can validly deny treatment that would cause pain, even if denying that treatment would cause death. In concurrence, Justice O'Connor also suggests that the avoidance of pain at death is a protected liberty interest under the Fourteenth Amendment. The opinion "refers twice to the allegedly undisputed availability of medication (to alleviate suffering) and palliative care,"[112] and concludes that the Court need not decide "the question whether suffering patients have a constitutionally cognizable interest in obtaining relief from the suffering they may experience in the last days of their lives" because "[t]here is no dispute that dying patients in Washington and New York can obtain palliative care, even when doing so would hasten their deaths."[113] Thus, her concurrence implied that "if a future case were presented to the Court in which there was a 'dispute' about the existence of state barriers to adequate palliative care, then this would be the 'quite different' and 'considerably stronger' argument" for a constitutional right than that presented in the physician-assisted suicide cases.[114] Four other Justices agreed with her assertions. Thus, there is a good argument that the constitution will not allow states to erect barriers to adequate palliative care.

In addition, several decisions of the Supreme Court suggest that states cannot compel inappropriate medical treatment without running afoul of the Fourteenth Amendment. Indeed, the Supreme Court has applied a "medical appropriateness" limitation that requires courts to find that state-compelled medical treatment is in the patient's best

[111] Burt, *supra* note 109, at 1234.
[112] Pratt, *supra* note 109, at 222.
[113] Washington v. Glucksberg, 521 U.S. 702, 737–738 (1997).
[114] Burt, *supra* note 109, at 1235.

medical interests before considering whether the state can justify the imposition of the medication.[115]

The Court has most clearly established the medical appropriateness limitation in cases involving forced treatments of prison inmates. Those cases make clear that involuntary treatment raises questions of clear constitutional importance[116] by recognizing a "'significant' constitutionally protected 'liberty interest'" in avoiding forced medical treatment.[117] The state may override that interest for the purpose of creating competency to stand trial only when the forced "treatment is medically appropriate, is substantially unlikely to have side effects that may undermine the fairness of the trial, and, taking account of less intrusive alternatives, is necessary significantly to further important governmental trial-related interests."[118]

Thus, states may only administer antipsychotic drugs to prisoners after proving the drugs are medically appropriate. The requirement that the treatment be "*medically appropriate*, that is, in the patient's best medical interest in light of his medical condition"[119] is a threshold constitutional protection afforded by the Due Process Clause. The medical appropriateness requirement is, therefore, a fundamental constitutional limitation that may not be overcome by competing state interests.

---

[115] *See, e.g.,* Washington v. Harper, 494 U.S. 210, 222 n. 8 (1990) (stating that forced medication may be administered only after "the inmate's treating physician ... make[s] the decision that medication is appropriate").

[116] *See* Sell v. United States, 123 S.Ct. 2174, 2186 (2003) (requiring State to prove that, in light of all possible alternatives, the need for antipsychotic treatment is medically appropriate and "sufficiently important to overcome the individual's protected interest in refusing it"); *Harper,* 494 U.S. at 221–222 (recognizing that an individual has a "significant" constitutionally protected "liberty interest" in "avoiding the unwanted administration of antipsychotic drugs"); Winston v. Lee, 470 U.S. 753, 759 (1985) (expectation of privacy and security are implicated by the compelled surgical intrusion into an individual's body).

[117] *Sell,* 123 S.Ct. at 2183 (citing *Harper,* 494 U.S. at 221).

[118] *Id.* at 2184.

[119] *Id.* at 2185 (emphasis in original).

The constitutional requirement that forced medical treatment be medically appropriate has not yet been applied in any cases dealing with a refusal of treatment at the end of life. It should be. The discussion of the contours of the liberty interest at stake when the state forces medication on anyone is clearly pertinent in cases like Sheila Pouliot's, where a particular course of treatment is mandated by law.[120] Moreover, like the right to refuse treatment itself, with its "long legal tradition,"[121] the ability to avoid inappropriate medical care has enjoyed historical legal protection. The malpractice laws, the informed consent cases, the regulations prohibiting the dispensation of experimental drugs, and prohibitions on experimental surgery are all part of the tradition that protects people from inappropriate medical care. Furthermore, the notion that the state could force any person to submit to medical care that the medical profession deems inappropriate runs against all notions of fairness and ethical behavior.

In the case of Sheila Pouliot, New York law required doctors to provide hydration and calories to maintain her life for months after it was no longer medically appropriate to do so. The Model Act promoted by disability advocates as a solution to disability discrimination would do the same. In my view, adoption of the Model Act or laws like it would be a mistake. States should no more be allowed to force inappropriate medical care on a dying patient than on a prisoner. To be sure, "the State has an interest in protecting vulnerable groups – including the poor, the elderly, and disabled persons – from abuse, neglect, and mistakes."[122] That interest is undoubtedly important and justifies the use of heightened evidentiary standards to ensure that claims of

---

[120] Indeed, *Cruzan v. Dir., Mo. Dep't of Health*, 497 U.S. 261, 278 (1990), relied on the seminal case of *Washington v. Harper*, 494 U.S. 210, 220–222 (1990), to find a liberty interest in refusing unwanted medication. In *Harper*, the court noted that "[t]he forcible injection of medication into a nonconsenting person's body represents a substantial interference with that person's liberty." 494 U.S. at 229.

[121] Washington v. Glucksberg, 521 U.S. 702, 725 (1997).

[122] *Id.* at 731.

medical inappropriateness are not pretexts for discrimination. It is not so compelling, however, as to justify bright-line rules that require treatment for certain classes of disabled patients despite the harm caused by the treatment.

B. Discrimination

Federal statutes, especially the ADA, provide even broader protection against disability discrimination than that provided by the Constitution.[123] Application of these statutes to cases like those of Terri Schiavo or Sheila Pouliot does not – as claimed by the new disability activists – undermine laws that allow surrogates to choose to withdraw or withhold life-prolonging treatment for persons with disabilities.[124]

---

[123] Two federal statutes protect people with disabilities from improper discrimination. Section 504 of the Rehabilitation Act of 1973, 29 U.S.C. § 794(a) (1994), provides that "no otherwise qualified individual with a disability ... shall, solely by reason of her or his disability, be excluded from the participation in, be denied the benefits of, or be subjected to discrimination under any program or activity receiving Federal financial assistance ..." The ADA's coverage is broader, applying to disability-based discrimination to employers, doctor's offices, and hospitals. 42 U.S.C. §§ 12112, 12131, 12181(7), 12182 (2000). Because the coverage of the ADA is broader, this section focuses on that statute.

[124] *See* Brief for Not Dead Yet et al. as Amici Curiae Supporting Petitioners, Gonzales v. Oregon, 126 S. Ct. 904 (2006) (No. 04–623) [hereinafter *Gonzales* Amici Brief]; Brief for Not Dead Yet et al. as Amici Curiae Supporting Appellants, Oregon v. Ashcroft, 368 F.3d 1118 (9th Cir. 2004) (No. 02–35587) [hereinafter *Ashcroft* Amici Brief]; Brief for Not Dead Yet et al. as Amici Curiae Supporting Respondents, Wendland v. Wendland, 28 P.3d 151 (Cal. 2001) (No. S087265) [hereinafter *Wendland* Amici Brief]; Brief for Not Dead Yet et al. as Amici Curiae Supporting Appellants at 4, *In re* Schiavo, 851 So. 2d 182 (Fla. Dist. Ct. App. 2004) (No. 2D02–5394), *available at* http://www.notdeadyet.org/docs/schaivobrief.html [sic] [hereinafter *Schiavo I* Amici Brief]. To be sure, the activists also challenged factual determinations in the individual cases, such as the finding that Terri Schiavo was in a persistent vegetative state and that there was clear and convincing evidence of her wishes. *See Schiavo I* Amici Brief. Those case-specific challenges are less important than the broader claims of

To the contrary, the ADA requires access to surrogates or some other decision maker to ensure that persons with disabilities have access to the same courses of treatment available to persons without disability.

The purpose of the ADA is to "provide a clear and comprehensive national mandate for the elimination of discrimination against individuals with disabilities."[125] The ADA offers broader protection against disability discrimination than the protection provided by other federal laws. The ADA provides that "[n]o individual shall be discriminated against on the basis of disability in the full and equal enjoyment of the goods, services, facilities, privileges, advantages, or accommodations of any place of public accommodation...."[126] The ADA also forbids "utilizing standards, criteria, or methods of administration that have the effect of discrimination on the basis of disability."[127] Medical care clearly falls under the ADA's operation.[128]

Families of people with disabilities and disability rights activists have successfully turned to the ADA to force health care providers to treat people with disabilities.[129] They have convinced courts that when

disability discrimination that, if successful, would undermine basic legal principles of medical decision making in future cases.

[125] 42 U.S.C. § 12101(b)(1) (2000).

[126] 42 U.S.C. § 12182.

[127] 42 U.S.C.. § 12112(b)(3)(A).

[128] *See, e.g.*, Bragdon v. Abbott, 524 U.S. 624 (1998) (applying ADA in medical treatment case involving a dentist).

[129] The most significant victory came not from the courts, but from a decision by the Health and Human Services Secretary to block the Oregon health care rationing plan on the grounds it would violate the antidiscrimination laws. Letter from Louis W. Sullivan, Sec'y of Health and Human Servs., to Barbara Roberts, Governor of Or. (Aug. 3, 1992) (with accompanying three-page "Analysis Under the Americans with Disabilities Act (ADA) of the Oregon Reform Demonstration"), *reprinted in ADA Analyses of the Oregon Health Care Plan*, 9 ISSUES L. & MED. 397, 409–412 (1994). The advocates have also had some court victories. *See, e.g.*, Henderson v. Bodine Aluminum, Inc., 70 F.3d 958, 960 (8th Cir. 1995) (finding in a case of an insurance denial for a bone marrow treatment that "if the evidence shows that a given treatment is non-experimental – that is, if it is widespread, safe, and a significant improvement on traditional therapies – and the plan provides the treatment for

the family or the patient's surrogate has consented to the care, a disabled person is entitled to all the medical care that would be provided to a nondisabled person.[130] A refusal by a medical provider to honor a request for treatment can constitute discrimination under the ADA.[131] Thus, an HIV-infected woman successfully sued under the ADA to

other conditions directly comparable to the one at issue, the denial of that treatment arguably violates the ADA"); Carparts Distrib. Ctr., Inc. v. Auto. Wholesaler's Ass'n of New Eng., Inc., 37 F.3d 1216 (1st Cir. 1994) (applying ADA to denial of health coverage by employer health plan); *In re* Baby "K," 832 F. Supp. 1022, 1028–1029 (E.D. Va. 1993) (requiring hospital to provide life support to anencephalic infant).

[130] *E.g., In re Baby "K,"* 832 F. Supp. at 1028–1029.

[131] The refusal by a medical provider to give treatment demanded by a patient or a patient's surrogate raises tough questions under the ADA. For further discussion of the role of the ADA in cases where demanded care is refused, *see* Mary Crossley, *Becoming Visible: The ADA's Impact on Health Care for Persons with Disabilities*, 52 ALA. L. REV. 51, 57–68 (2000) (recognizing the ADA's possible application in cases in which an individual is denied care that she sought, and discussing the limits of a statute's applicability in rationing schemes) and Maxwell J. Mehlman et al., *When Do Health Care Decisions Discriminate Against Persons with Disabilities?*, 22 J. HEALTH POL. POL'Y & L. 1385 (1997) (distinguishing the difficult question of the ADA's application to medical treatment decisions made by providers when a patient or patient's legally authorized representative declines treatment). The application of the ADA in cases when providers refuse care due to futility, or where rationing schemes make care inaccessible, are legally distinct from the one posed by the new activists in *Schiavo. See* Crossley, *supra*, at 75–77 (discussing Oregon's rationing scheme); Mary A. Crossley, *Medical Futility and Disability Discrimination*, 81 IOWA L. REV. 179, 202–250 (1995) (arguing that the ADA is an inadequate tool for analyzing the merits of futility policies); Mehlman et al., *supra*, at 1389–92 (1997) (discussing futility disputes); David Orentlicher, *Rationing and the Americans with Disabilities Act*, 271 J. AM. MED. ASS'N 308 (1994); Philip G. Peters, Jr., *Health Care Rationing and Disability Rights*, 70 IND. L.J. 491, 492 (1995) (considering how rationing "can be legally and ethically defended by proof that the excluded treatments are less effective than those which are provided"); Philip G. Peters, Jr., *When Physicians Balk at Futile Care: Implications of the Disability Rights Laws*, 91 NW. U. L. REV. 798, 810–819 (1997) (discussing futility disputes); James V. Garvey, Note, *Health Care Rationing and the Americans with Disabilities Act of 1990: What Protection Should the Disabled Be Afforded?*, 68 NOTRE DAME L. REV. 581, 601–602, 613–616 (1993) (evaluating the Oregon Health Plan's compatibility with the ADA).

force a dentist to fill her cavity in his office instead of in the hospital,[132] and the mother of an anencephalic infant was able to use the ADA to force a hospital to keep her baby alive through ventilation.[133] The courts in these cases reasoned that treatment available to the nondisabled must be available to the disabled.[134]

Applying this reasoning in the case of Terri Schiavo, Not Dead Yet argued that removing Terri Schiavo's feeding tube would deny Schiavo the care that would be provided to people without disabilities because people without her disability would be provided nutrition and hydration.[135] Specifically, the group's amicus brief to the Florida District Court of Appeal in *In re Schiavo* argued:

> Treating people differently based on health or disability status violates the rights of people with disabilities under the ADA. Absent proof that it is truly the person's decision, withholding medical care based on the belief that he or she would rationally want to die because of a disability is discriminatory.... When health care providers deny people with severe cognitive disabilities the health care they need to live, but do not do so for others, they violate Title III of the ADA, governing health care providers and other "public accommodations." When state and local governments establish laws and policies that deprive people with cognitive disabilities of the care granted to "competent" persons, they violate Title II of the ADA.[136]

The argument fails for several reasons. First, it wrongly assumes that Terri Schiavo was denied care that she would otherwise have received because of her disability. She was not. Terri Schiavo could not receive the care because no one with authority to authorize the continuation of artificial nutrition and hydration had consented to it. The U.S. Supreme Court decided the issue in *Bowen v. American Hospital*

---

[132] *Bragdon*, 524 U.S. at 648–654.
[133] *In re Baby "K,"* 832 F. Supp. at 1028–1029.
[134] *See id.* at 1029.
[135] *Schiavo I* Amici Brief, *supra* note 124.
[136] *Id.* at 19.

Association.[137] There, the Court was asked whether the Rehabilitation Act prohibited the withholding of medical treatment to handicapped infants.[138] The Supreme Court found no evidence that the hospitals had denied treatment on the basis of handicap.[139] Rather, treatment was denied because of the absence of parental consent.[140] Accordingly, the Supreme Court concluded, "A hospital's withholding of treatment [from a handicapped infant] when no parental consent has been given cannot violate [the Rehabilitation Act], for without the consent of the parents ... the infant is neither 'otherwise qualified' for treatment nor has he been denied care 'solely by reason of his handicap.'"[141]

The Court's reasoning in *Bowen* applied equally in the case of Terri Schiavo. The case had nothing to do with disability discrimination. A hospital cannot administer medical treatment in the absence of a patient's consent or consent by a legal surrogate because without consent, the patient is not qualified to receive treatment. Under Florida law, Michael Schiavo was Terri Schiavo's legal surrogate. His refusal to consent to treatment on Terri Schiavo's behalf disqualified her for treatment and provided her physicians a reason to withdraw her treatment other than her disability.[142] Thus, *Schiavo* was not a case about treatment refusal based on disability.

---

[137] Bowen v. American Hosp. Ass'n, 476 U.S. 610 (1986).

[138] *Id.* at 612.

[139] *See id.* at 630.

[140] *Id.* at 630–631.

[141] *Id.* at 630; *see also* United States v. Univ. Hosp. State Univ. of N.Y. at Stony Brook, 729 F.2d 144, 161 (2d Cir. 1984) (holding that the Rehabilitation Act did not authorize government intervention overriding the private decision of parents to refuse consent to corrective surgery for a child born with spina bifida and hydrocephalus). Title III of the ADA does not contain the "otherwise qualified" language in section 504 of the Rehabilitation Act.

[142] The real issues in the case were whether Michael Schiavo should be disqualified as a guardian and, if not, whether he had proved what Terri's wishes were by clear and convincing evidence.

Secondly, the laws that gave Michael Schiavo the power to refuse treatment for his wife do not discriminate against people with disabilities; those laws give people with disabilities, like Terri Schiavo, a voice in their medical decision making. Laws that give surrogates the power to make medical decisions are not analogous to a dentist's refusal to fill a cavity for an AIDS patient in a dentist's office.[143] Whereas the dentist's refusal to fill a cavity constituted denial of access to appropriate medical care,[144] the Florida surrogacy laws provided Terri Schiavo with access to medically appropriate options, including the option to refuse treatment.[145]

Terminating treatment is part of good palliative care practice.[146] Like a decision to provide pain-relieving drugs despite the fact that

[143] *See* Bragdon v. Abbott, 524 U.S. 624 (1998).

[144] *See id.* at 641. The dentist did not argue that his desire to treat the patient in a hospital rather than a dentist's office was medically appropriate for the patient. The dentist argued that the option was permissible under the harm exception to the ADA. *See id.* at 648.

[145] Obviously, the ADA does not prohibit medical treatment that is appropriate because of a patient's disability. As the First Circuit Court of Appeals noted:

[S]uch a prohibition would not only be nonsensical; it would be unethical.... "Ethical medical decisionmaking should take into account all medical factors – disability-related or not – affecting a patient's condition and prognosis. Thus, to read the ADA as prohibiting a medical decision-maker from considering medical factors flowing from a disability would put the disabled patient ... in a different, arguably worse, position than the nondisabled patient."

Lesley v. Chie, 250 F.3d 47, 53 n.6 (1st Cir. 2001) (quoting Mary A. Crossley, *Of Diagnoses and Discrimination: Discriminatory Nontreatment of Infants with HIV Infection*, 93 COLUM. L. REV. 1581, 1655 (1993)).

[146] *See* BRITISH MEDICAL ASSOCIATION, WITHHOLDING AND WITHDRAWING LIFE-PROLONGING MEDICAL TREATMENT: GUIDANCE FOR DECISION MAKING (BMJ Books, 2d ed. 2001); Frank D. Ferris et al., *Ensuring Competency in End-of-Life Care: Controlling Symptoms*, BMC PALLIATIVE CARE, July 30, 2002, at 10, http://www.biomedcentral.com/content/pdf/1472–684X–1–5.pdf ("[M]ost experts feel that dehydration in the last hours of living does not cause distress and may stimulate the release of endorphins...."); Robert M. McCann et al., *Comfort Care for Terminally Ill Patients: The Appropriate Use of Nutrition and Hydration*, 272 J. AM. MED. ASS'N 1263, 1265–1266 (1994) (recognizing that providing nutrition and

they might hasten death, a decision to terminate treatment can be made to increase patient comfort, to eliminate pain, or to stop bodily deterioration.[147] The decision might also be made to implement the patient's own judgment about life in her current state. In any of these cases, standard medical care offers all adults the option to choose whether to terminate treatment.

Furthermore, people choose to terminate treatment in hospitals every day. Jehovah's Witnesses refuse blood transfusions. Cancer patients refuse chemotherapy. People in persistent vegetative states refuse nutrition and hydration through advance directives. Because Terri Schiavo had no advance directive and could not make her own health care decisions, she could access treatment options solely through her surrogate. A person with disabilities should no more be denied access to treatment refusal than a person without disabilities. The law that gave Michael Schiavo power to make medical decisions in Terri's stead gave Terri access to appropriate medical care.

In this respect, it seems to me that despite its good intentions, Not Dead Yet's argument turns the ADA on its head. Laws that give people with disabilities access to a choice of medically acceptable treatments protect the rights of people with disabilities – even if one of the choices is the termination of treatment. It is the denial of access to all available options that would violate the ADA. In fact, surrogacy laws ensure that the ADA's demand for access is fulfilled. Substituted-judgment and best-interests-based statutes are reasonable accommodations. They give the people who lack competence to make their own health care decisions access to the same options available to those who have

hydration to terminally ill patients can cause unwanted and painful side effects and finding that terminating the treatment increases patient comfort); Robert J. Sullivan, Jr., *Accepting Death Without Artificial Nutrition or Hydration*, 8 J. GEN. INTERNAL MED. 220, 222 (1993) ("[I]t is likely that prolonged dehydration and starvation induce no pain and only limited discomfort....").

[147] *See* Ouellette, *supra* note 41, at 34, for further discussion on how the option to terminate treatment is essential to palliative care.

competence. In this way, surrogacy statutes can be compared to access ramps installed by building owners after the passage of the ADA. Just as ramps were not the equivalent to stairs (e.g., they might be located in the back of the building and take longer to traverse than stairs), surrogacy laws are not the equivalent to an actual exercise of medical decision making by the disabled person. Nonetheless, both are reasonable accommodations. Just like ramps allow the person with the disability to get into a building, surrogacy laws allow the patient access to all appropriate treatment decisions, including no treatment at all.

So long as a surrogate is choosing between medically acceptable options, the ADA has no role in a medical decision-making case. Palliative care medicine views the termination of treatment, including the withholding of nutrition and hydration, as medically appropriate when a person is terminally ill or permanently unconscious. Like dental treatment, palliative care is a public accommodation available to the general public. The activists' position would limit options for surrogates and thereby deny people who lack the capacity access to an acceptable option in palliative care, thus denying the disabled a public accommodation. The denial of access would be based on the patient's disability, namely the inability to form or express intent.

Given the negative consequences for persons with cognitive disabilities of laws that would limit the ability of surrogate decision makers to terminate treatment, it is difficult to understand why such laws continue to find vocal support in the disability community. The most consistent explanation is a concern that decisions to withdraw treatment is a judgment about the value of life with disability. Although that possibility exists, it simply does not apply in all cases.[148]

---

[148] *E.g.*, Kathy L. Cerminara, *Critical Essay: Musings on the Need to Convince Some People with Disabilities that End-of-Life Decision-Making Advocates Are Not Out to Get Them*, 37 LOY. U. CHI. L. J. 343, 343 (2005) (describing a woman's response to the Schiavo case: "I am not a cabbage, an onion, nor a cob of corn"); Laura Hershey, *Killed by Prejudice*, THE NATION, May 2, 2005, *available at* http://thenation.com/doc/20050502/hershey (claiming that describing feeding tubes and ventilators as

End-of-life decision making is anything but one-dimensional. What might be true for one person might be wrong for another. Physical impairments, permanent vegetative states (PVSs), and terminal illnesses are not the same. Physical impairments that allow sapient life are fundamentally different from PVSs, and paralysis and blindness are fundamentally different from terminal cancer. To be sure, terminal illness can disable a person. But dying people face different questions than people with other physical impairments do.

Likewise, people in PVSs need much of the same care required by quadriplegics, but the conditions are fundamentally different. Unlike other impairments, a PVS is the actualization of a myth of the tragic life with disability. That myth says the person with disability can experience no joy or pleasure in life. For the PVS patient, the myth is reality. A person in a PVS cannot experience pleasure or pain, because the part of the brain that processes those functions is destroyed. The PVS patient is beyond disability. This is not to say that a person in a PVS does not deserve respect or care. My point is merely that the condition of a PVS is different, and individual decisions about a PVS do not reflect on the value of life with other disabilities.

Moreover, decisions to forgo medical treatment, even life-sustaining medical treatment, may have nothing to do with disability. A personal assessment about pain, bodily intrusions, physical limitations, bodily integrity, and freedom from restraint is no more a judgment about the value of people who live with disability than is a decision to take

"life support," disabled people get put in a different legal category "with less reason to live"); Mary Johnson, *After Terri Schiavo: Why the Disability Rights Movement Spoke Out, Why Some of Us Worried, and Where Do We Go from Here?*, RAGGED EDGE MAG., Apr. 2, 2005, at 4, *available at* http://www.ragged-edge-mag.com/focus/ postschiavo0405.html (describing the bigotry of the "better dead than disabled" school); Jenny Morris, *Tyrannies of Perfection*, NEW INTERNATIONALIST, July 1992, at 16, *available at* http://live.newint.org/issue233/tyrannies.htm (arguing that the explicit motivation for court rulings that allow a severely disabled person to choose death over life with disability "is the notion that physical and intellectual impairment inevitably means a life which is not worth living").

a pain reliever for a headache. Those choices are personal and unrelated to the value of other people who live with the impairments, even when the choices involve factors that are central to the lives of many people with disabilities. With respect to feeding tubes, for example, an objection to the use of a feeding tube might have nothing at all to do with disability. Remember Scott Matthews (see Chapter 6). Scott's family asserted the desire to avoid a feeding tube so that he could continue the activity he enjoyed most in his life. The desire to eat, the social enjoyment of a shared meal, and the taste of food are to some so valuable an experience that losing those abilities would be devastating. Scott's parents' decision to avoid the feeding tube reflected values that were inherently personal to Scott; the decision had nothing to do with disability prejudice. The new activists' legislation would deny all of us the ability to decide that the social benefits of eating outweigh the risk of a premature death.

Protecting people with disabilities from unscrupulous surrogates, outright discrimination, and negative social attitudes should be central concerns of a just medical system. Ensuring equal opportunity, providing adequate pain relief, and preventing physical suffering are no less important goals, however. The changes to law sought by some members of the disability community are too blunt a tool to balance all these concerns. Perhaps a disability-conscious bioethics can play a role in revisiting the concerns of the disability community without proposing laws that eliminate choice, disempower families, and cause real harm to people with disabilities.

8

Toward a Disability-Conscious Bioethics

THROUGHOUT THIS BOOK, I HAVE ARGUED THAT
bioethicists have good reason to work with members of the disability
community to resolve ongoing conflicts. The thrust of my argument
is that reconciliation is necessary to the work of bioethics insofar as
bioethics is concerned with facilitating good medical decision making.
Good medical decision making depends on at least three things: trust,
knowledge, and communication. As a field, bioethics has emerged
as a key player in formulation of policy, resolution of disputes, and
creation of educational initiatives that develop trusting relationships,
encourage the reliance on objectively verifiable data, and foster clear
and open communication between by all parties to medical decision
making. Its effectiveness in these roles is undermined at every level
(in individual ethics consultations, in policy making, in educational
initiatives) by indifference to or ignorance about the contribution of
disability scholars to the body of knowledge relevant to good patient
care, as well as the perception by some members of the disability
community that bioethics as a field works against the interests of people with disabilities.[1] Reconciling the conflict will remove a barrier to

---

[1] *See, e.g.,* Diane Coleman & Tom Nerney, *Guardianship and the Disability Rights
Movement,* CENTER FOR SELF-DETERMINATION, http://www.centerforself-
determination.com/docs/guard/GuardianshipDisabilityRightsColemanNerney1.pdf,

this work. True reconciliation will, of course, require engagement of all parties to the conflict. It cannot be forced on any individual. But bioethicists can jump-start the process by developing a deep understanding of the concerns and values of members of the disability community, acknowledging the extent to which bioethics has been insensitive or indifferent to those concerns and the experience of disability, and working to become deliberately conscious of disability-related issues in their work.

Developing disability-consciousness in bioethics will require bioethicists to make the knowledge gleaned by disability experts about the experience of disability central to their work[2] – a project that will invite the development of mutually beneficial relationships between bioethicists and disability experts. The previous five chapters provided the raw materials for the initial steps toward reconciliation. This chapter synthesizes that material with the goal of working toward a disability-conscious bioethics – that is, a bioethics that is mindful of and knowledgeable about the fact of disability in bioethical cases, a bioethics that works for – and with – people with disabilities. The first part of the chapter engages the initial steps necessary for reconciliation; the second part sketches out a skeletal framework for building a disability-conscious bioethics; and the third part revisits the cases to explore how disability-consciousness will affect bioethical debate and achieve better experiences for all people in the health care system.

at 1 (claiming that the "powerful field of bioethics represents the single greatest threat to the welfare of those with significant disabilities in this country. Under the rubric of utilitarian ethics and the language of rights, discrimination against people with disabilities has become enshrined in law and popular imagination."); Christopher Newell, *Disability, Bioethics, and Rejected Knowledge*, 31 J. MED. & PHIL. 269, 275 (2006) (charging that bioethics is a "disabling ... project.").

[2] Toward this end, bioethicists unfamiliar with disability issues should start by turning to their "in house" experts, Adrienne Asch, Anita Silvers, Leslie Francis, and others whose bioethical specialty is disability.

I. WORKING TOWARD RECONCILIATION

Reconciliation is a form of conflict resolution that allows parties to a conflict to build trust and enter into new, mutually enriching relationships.[3] As a process for dispute resolution, it takes various forms. From the formal hearings held by South Africa's Truth and Reconciliation Commission to the "Seeds of Peace" summer camps that bring together Israeli and Palestinian teenagers,[4] reconciliation generally involves bringing parties together to explore and acknowledge the sources of fear and anger behind a conflict, acknowledge and apologize for past wrongs, and build bridges of trust between former adversaries.[5] As compared to other forms of conflict resolution, reconciliation is distinctive for its goal of changing the way adversaries think about one another. It is not an adversarial process in which one side is proven right or wrong, but a search for resolutions that will meet the needs of all involved.

With respect to the conflict between the disability and bioethics communities, I have proposed a fairly informal process of scholarly

---

[3] Charles Hauss, *Reconciliation*, BEYOND INTRACTABILITY, Sept. 2003, http://www.beyondintractability.org/essay/reconciliation/.

[4] *See, e.g.*, SEEDS OF PEACE, http://www.seedsofpeace.org/ (last visited Oct. 4, 2010).

[5] Hizkias Assefa, *The Meaning of Reconciliation*, PEOPLE BUILDING PEACE, http://www.gppac.net/documents/pbp/part1/2_reconc.htm (describing seven core elements of reconciliation:

Reconciliation as a conflict handling mechanism entails the following core elements:

a) Honest acknowledgment of the harm/injury each party has inflicted on the other;
b) Sincere regrets and remorse for the injury done;
c) Readiness to apologize for one's role in inflicting the injury;
d) Readiness of the conflicting parties to 'let go' of the anger and bitterness caused by the conflict and the injury;
e) Commitment by the offender not to repeat the injury;
f) Sincere effort to redress past grievances that caused the conflict and compensate the damage caused to the extent possible;
g) Entering into a new mutually enriching relationship.

reconciliation involving three steps: listening closely to develop a clear understanding of opposing points of view; acknowledging fears, alliances, and values; and working to identify points of agreement on which a preliminary framework for collaboration can be developed. Only so much can be accomplished on paper, but the case studies provide a wealth of information from which the reconciliation process can begin. The following is my take on what can be gleaned by listening to what members of the disability and bioethics communities say about controversial cases, and how a deliberate effort at reconciliation by bioethics might yield new sensitivities and understandings through which a mutually enriching relationship could emerge to improve decision making and medical treatment for all people.

A. Listening and Understanding

Bioethicist Erik Parens describes how powerful the exercise of listening was to his understanding of the perspectives of people with disabilities:

> I am not proud to confess that when I first heard people with disabilities say [that disabling features are a central part of their identity], I practiced some armchair psychoanalysis: "yes, yes, that's very nice. You *say* that the problem is social responses to your disability, not your disability. But let's be honest; you're in denial." The more I heard about people [who] say that the most difficult thing about having a disability was the way temporarily able-bodied people like me treated them, however, the more I began to take them at their word. I became convinced that if, after a process of truly informed decision-making, someone with a disability refuses the use of medical means to improve her social experience, then there is no good alternative to respecting her decision, no matter how surprising I might find it.[6]

---

[6] Erik Parens, *Respecting Children with Disabilities – and Their Parents*, 39 HASTINGS CENTER REP., Jan.–Feb. 2009, at 22, 22.

The study of disability cases across the human life cycle in the preceding chapters was similarly enlightening. "Listening" to disability experts reflect on the cases made one thing perfectly clear: People with disabilities feel devalued in the health care setting. They feel threatened, misunderstood, insulted, marginalized, and scared. The case studies explain the roots of these feelings. From a disability perspective, the health care setting is a dangerous and difficult place. Babies are left to die because they are born with disabling or potentially disabling conditions. Healthy growth is stopped and functioning organs are removed from children with disabilities when such interventions would never be allowed for nondisabled children. Parents are charged with child neglect for failure to cede to social and medical pressure to use medical technologies to cure traits in their children deemed defects by medicine but a valuable human variant by their parents. Women with disabilities are denied their sexuality and gender identities by doctors who fail to ask about their sexual health or even equip their offices to provide basic screening services like pap smears and mammograms. Parents with disabilities are presumed to be incompetent strangers to their own sick and injured children. Fertility specialists deny services based on assumptions about the ability of persons with disabilities to parent. Doctors unquestionably accept as reasonable decisions by adults with disability to die regardless of the surmountable social problems faced by the patient. Finally, components of daily living for adults who live happily with disability – feeding tubes and ventilator support – are deemed artificial and optional by nondisabled surrogates.

Disability experts maintain that bioethics perpetuates the problem.[7] The claim is that in debating when it is appropriate to use medical

---

[7] Disabled Peoples International Europe, *The Right to Live and be Different*, INDEPENDENT LIVING INSTITUTE, Feb. 2000, http://www.independentliving.org/docs1/dpi022000. html (position paper by representatives of disability groups from twenty-seven countries charging that bioethical debates "have had prejudiced and negative views of our quality of life. They have denied our right to equality and have therefore denied our human rights."); Coleman & Nerney, *supra* note1; Newell, *supra* note 1.

technology to promote health or maintain life, bioethicists promote and apply decision-making frameworks that legitimate and even codify the bias that gives rise to mistreatment of people with disabilities in the health care setting.[8] The claim finds some support in the case studies. With respect to newborns, for example, there were bioethicists who supported parental choices to allow disabled babies to die while also proffering and participating in futility policies that limit parental choice for life-extending treatment. Bioethicists were also seen making utilitarian arguments that parents would be better off (and morally justified) if they euthanized "defective" newborns. With respect to the Ashley case, there was bioethical support for the uncritical use of the biomedical risk/benefit model to justify growth attenuation and removal of healthy organs from a child with disabilities. And in positing moral theories to identify the "harm" caused children by their deafness, we saw "non-disabled bioethical commentators ... ignore the cultural and social dimension of bioethical questions articulated from the moral communities of people who use sign language as their first language and who cannot hear."[9] With respect to Larry MacAfee, the autonomy-based arguments offered in support of his choice against mechanical ventilation incorporated the prevailing negative notions about impaired mobility and the other incidents of quadriplegia despite concrete evidence that with social modifications, MacAfee would – and did – have a rewarding life. Despite emerging recognition (including a public apology by prominent bioethicist Howard Brody (see Chapter 7)) that overreliance on the principle of autonomy may have caused too hasty an acceptance of requests for treatment withdrawal based on disability status, respect for autonomy continues to be the defining feature of much bioethical analysis. Indeed throughout the case studies, we saw bioethicists rely on assessments of "health," "medical appropriateness," "quality of life," and familial best interests to justify decision making for people with disabilities, without attention to the role

---

[8] *The Right to Live and be Different, supra* note 7.

[9] Newell, *supra* note 1, at 276.

societal bias may play in such assessments. Given all this, it is no surprise that scholars who specialize in disability view bioethics as a "disabling project" in which "any form of imperfection becomes a moral trump card," and in which "disability becomes the anthesis of choice."[10]

Of course, the case studies also show that bioethical response to disability issues is often more conflicted and nuanced than the characterizations by disability advocates suggest. Indeed, some of the charges lodged against bioethics as a body appear to be unfair when the bioethical debate is considered in any depth. Any claim that bioethics as a project promotes futility laws or stands behind the utilitarian views of Peter Singer (see Chapter 3), for example, is factually inaccurate.[11] Both futility and radical utilitarian views are deeply divisive within bioethics, and even defenders of futility policies would not apply them based on disability status alone. And claims by certain disability activists that the outright disability animus behind the eugenics movement drives bioethics finds no support in the bioethical literature. On the whole, "listening" to the bioethics perspectives on the various case studies reveals bioethics to be an enterprise involving thoughtful, often vigorous debate and careful analysis of complex problems about how best to ensure respect for individual choice, prevent suffering, and justly allocate scarce resources.

That said, the case studies also explain why disability experts demand to be "included in all debates and policy-making regarding bioethical issues,"[12] and argue that "despite the veneer of reason and civility [in bioethical debate], somehow or other non-disabled accounts continue to dominate."[13] Disability experts bring to the conversation knowledge and data that directly challenge traditional understandings

---

[10] *Id.*

[11] Proving a negative is challenging. My support for this assertion lies in the absence of its relevance to clinical practice, its rejection in law, and the fact that it is not part of any discussion taking place in medical or clinical literature.

[12] *The Right to Live and be Different, supra* note 7.

[13] Newell, *supra* note 1, at 272.

of impairment and disability. The information is directly relevant to bioethical debate, yet bioethics is largely indifferent to that knowledge. As scholar Adrienne Asch observed from her unique position as one of a handful of disability experts who works within bioethics:

> [I]n arguing that individuals should not be required to submit to unpleasant medical interventions simply because such technologies had been developed, bioethics was trying to wrest control from what it perceived to be a technology-happy medical establishment and return decisional authority to individuals.... [B]ioethics insists that individuals should be able to determine the situations under which they find life intolerable but has never challenged them to ask themselves what they found intolerable [is it physical pain, or social isolation?].[14]

Except among Asch and colleagues, the cultural and political understanding of the way in which impairments are made disabling by societal failures goes largely unnoticed in bioethics.[15] The case studies are illustrative on this point. Little attention in bioethical debate is given to the notion that many of the conditions associated with the "tragedy" of disability – dependence, incontinence, and lack of mobility – are simply a fact of the highly valued lives of many people with disabilities.[16] They need not be experienced as demeaning or devastating, despite assumptions by the nondisabled to the contrary. This failure of bioethics to take seriously the knowledge of disability experts helps explain why some disability experts are so angry and hostile.[17]

---

[14] Adrienne Asch, *Disability, Bioethics, and Human Rights, in* HANDBOOK OF DISABILITY STUDIES 297, 299 (Gary L. Albrecht et al. eds., Sage Publications, Inc. 2001).

[15] *But see* Howard Brody, *A Bioethicist Offers an Apology*, LANSING CITY NEWS, Oct. 6, 2004, http://www.dredf.org/assisted_suicide/bioethics.html.

[16] *See* Newell, *supra* note 1, at 276–278 (discussing incontinence); Anita Silvers, *Formal Justice, in* DISABILITY, DIFFERENCE, DISCRIMINATION: PERSPECTIVES ON JUSTICE IN BIOETHICS AND PUBLIC POLICY, 95–106 (Rowman & Littlefield Publishers 1998) (contrasting neediness with interdependence).

[17] *See, e.g.*, Coleman & Nerney, *supra* note 1, at 4 ("It appears that bioethics has pretty much dominated end-of-life care movement work in policymaking, imposing a 'lifeboat' approach, deciding who gets thrown out").

Thus far, angry rhetoric has done little to convince bioethicists to listen to disability advocates. Indeed, in my experience, many bioethicists find angry rhetoric so off-putting as to justify dismissal of the disability perspective as a legitimate and central part of bioethical debate. Beyond the angry rhetoric, however, is a body of expert knowledge supporting a perspective well worth considering. The perspective demands respect for and recognition of what people with disabilities know to be true about the value of their own lives, as well as a broader understanding of disability than what medicine offers. Understanding that the priority of disability advocates is ensuring respect for people with disabilities helps explain what might appear to the uninitiated as inconsistencies or contradictions in disability advocacy. For instance, context plays a role in determining the amount of weight given various interests in various cases, as it did in the seemingly contradictory positions on parental rights in cases involving newborns. As advocacy positions offered on a single case, the arguments are not cohesive in the way that philosophical arguments demand. The arguments are not meaningless, however. Parental rights may well be important to disability advocates (the case of Lee Larson suggests that they are), but clearly they are not the only concern at play. The competing interest in demanding respect for people with disabilities and the fear that parents without disabilities will not understand the potential value in a life with disability have a higher priority, meaning that other interests trump parental rights in some cases. In this respect, the field of disability studies is no different from bioethics. Much of bioethical argument involves a weighing of competing concerns or a balancing of factors. Were bioethicists to engage in forthright advocacy, its advocacy positions would likely be plagued with similar superficial contradictions.

It takes more work to understand and accept some of the positions taken by disability advocates that may seem from the outside to be illogical. One such thread of argument is the identification that people with mobility or other physical disabilities feel with people with profound cognitive disabilities. In reaction to Ashley's case, for example, scholar William Peace wrote, "I do not consider myself one iota different from Ashley."[18] Even though Ashley has profound cognitive disabilities, Peace maintained that "the Ashley treatment is about more than one girl in Seattle – it is about all people with disabilities."[19] Similar arguments also cropped up in the cases of Sydney Miller and Terri Schiavo. This claim of affinity perplexed bioethicists who saw obvious and fundamental distinctions between the experts and the individual at the center of the case.[20] Peace, for example, was not a child who would never have developmental capacities beyond that of infant. He is a college professor and published author. By listening to Peace's explanation, one can understand his affinity with Ashley. Peace writes:

> We are the Other, a pervasive and important concept in the social sciences. The Other are strangers, outcasts if you will, people who do not belong. The Other often have fewer civil rights and experience gross violation of those rights.
>
> Thus at a fundamental level there is an us-and-them – those with a disability and those without. This is a false dichotomy, but is a part of the American social structure and dare I say medical establishment. The degree of disability is not important, nor is the type of disability. We people with a perceived disability are the Other.[21]

In other words, so long as the medical and other establishments treat people with disabilities as the Other, people with disabilities of all types are forced to join ranks. What happens to one could happen to all.

Answering claims of affinity with logical argument ("but Professor Peace, you are different from Ashley; you can have meaningful

---

[18] William Peace, *Ashley and Me*, HASTINGS CENTER BIOETHICS FORUM, June 22, 2010, http://www.thehastingscenter.org/Bioethicsforum/Post.aspx?id=4742&blogid=140#ixzz0yEnNJg5f

[19] *Id.*

[20] *See, e.g.*, Anita J. Tarzian, *Disability and Slippery Slopes*, 37 HASTINGS CENTER REP., Sept.–Oct. 2007.

[21] Peace, *supra* note 18.

relationships and engage in symbolic interaction") misses the point. Peace and others who assert affinity arguments acknowledge the differences between themselves and people with profound cognitive impairments. Their point is that because those differences are treated as irrelevant in so many aspects of their lives, they cannot count on the medical establishment or bioethicists to act on such niceties. Consider what Peace experienced as a parent seeking treatment for an injured child in the emergency room (see Chapter 5). Medical personnel dismissed the idea that he could be a competent parent based on nothing more than the fact that he uses a wheelchair. Having been subjected to a presumption that his mobility issues render him incompetent in the health care setting, Peace is naturally concerned with what happens to people who are in fact incompetent. Given his past experience, it is not implausible that he will be treated as though he is incompetent. In other words, his fear of the slippery slope is based on his lived experience. Logic alone will not suffice to eliminate that fear.

Some disability experts argue that the only way to prevent the slippery slope from becoming a reality is to keep the gate locked entirely. For example, in the case studies, we saw disability experts arguing for aggressive treatment of any newborn who might be saved, an absolute prohibition on use of growth attenuation procedures, and a proposed law that would mandate provision of medically administered nutrition and hydration, absent an express directive from a competent patient. Drawing on their experiences in the clinical or hospital setting, bioethicists tend to reject such one-size-fits-all solutions. Bioethicists point out, for example, that aggressive treatment of newborns has resulted in horrendous suffering of terminal babies, and that mandated provision of medically administered nutrition and hydration has caused extraordinary harm and pain to adults who lack capacity to speak for themselves. Thus, bioethicists propose decision-making frameworks that allow for individualized assessment of particular cases. The proposed frameworks are varied: Some give more weight to familial concerns; others defer more to professional judgment; some default in favor of preserving life; others allow surrogates to determine the importance of continued existence. Regardless of their form, one can "hear" in bioethical responses to difficult cases a consistent concern about suffering, whether about the potential suffering that can result from overtreatment or in support for clinical innovations that might prove to relieve suffering in individual patients.

To be sure, some bioethicists recognize the potential for abuse about which disability advocates are so concerned, and some disability advocates recognize the perils of overtreatment and the value in individualized assessment emphasized by bioethicists. Among the proposed solutions to these concerns from both sides are calls for additional procedural steps designed to ensure that strict criteria are in place to ensure against the realization of the slippery slope or biased application. However, even the mutual calls for procedural safeguards reveal substantive differences in the interests of disability and bioethics experts. When bioethicists propose procedural solutions to complex problems, they often propose review by ethics committees as checks against potential misuse of decision-making power. Witness the Texas law at play in Emilio's case, and Diekema and Fost's arguments in Ashley's case. The preference for ethics committee involvement reflects concern for a quick resolution by a decision-making body that has some expertise, and a desire to keeping lawyers out of complex medical cases. By contrast, disability experts express skepticism that ethics committees will impartially assess cases. The view is that ethics committees are biased against people with disabilities because most or all of their members are hospital employees or allies of the medical professionals involved.[22] Disability experts appear more comfortable with court resolution of such cases. Witness the calls for court review – not ethics committee review – in futility, growth attenuation, sterilization, and end-of-life cases. The trust that disability experts put in courts

---

[22] *See* Coleman & Nerney, *supra* note 1, at 4 (stating that the role of the ethics committee is "to persuade [families] that the doctor's decision not to treat is best").

stands in sharp contrast to the strong impulse shown in bioethics to keep the law away from the bedside. Part of the project of reconciliation, then, will be to explore options for a trustworthy process to oversee cases, which takes into account the concerns of both bioethicists and the disability community.

B. Acknowledging Fears, Biases, and Alliances

Listening to members of the disability and bioethics communities yields more than an increased understanding of the perspectives and interests at stake in controversial cases; it also provides insight into the fears, biases, and alliances that affect the positions taken by each constituency. Acknowledging these fears, biases, and alliances may inspire members of each constituency to reconsider their own positions from a new perspective, giving rise to deeper, more advanced understandings of how to facilitate good medical decision making for and by people of all levels of disability.

For the disability community, the fear of practices that devalue lives of people with disabilities is a central driving concern. That fear, in combination with the affinity of people with various kinds of disabilities for one another, manifests in a clear bias toward bright-line rules for maintaining life no matter its quality, as well as a bias against individual assessment based on quality-of-life measures. The inclination for bright-line rules can be problematic, as was eventually recognized by the disability community as it struggled with cases like Valerie's involving involuntary sterilization. There, the initial impulse for a rule barring involuntary sterilizations in all cases gave way to proposals for individualized assessment only after the problematic impact of the prohibitory bright-line rule was felt by the people it was designed to protect. In terms of alliances, disability activists have found themselves working on the same side as various religious and radical right pro-life groups in a series of cases. Although many members of the disability community express discomfort with the alliance and argue that it is a matter of serendipity, not influence, the fact of alignment raises the possibility that radical right groups have some influence on the disability rights agenda,[23] a possibility that merits consideration and internal monitoring.

For bioethics, the fear of a bad death is a driving concern.[24] In case after case, bioethicists have struggled against the perils of overtreatment and asserted autonomy-based arguments to allow individuals and their families to make choices about when to use, and when to stop using, technologies and medicines that prolong life. As bioethicist Howard Brody recognized, the bias against overtreatment and the inclination to support patient's choice may result from a wise and humane initial impulse, but it can also create blind spots that cause bioethicists to accept too quickly assertions by patients that they want to die. As in Larry McAfee's case, a more thorough understanding of the disabling effect of social institutions would have allowed bioethicists to see that the real problem for the person involved is not necessarily the tragedy of physical impairment, but a desire to escape disabling social structures in which the possibility of meaningful life is extinguished. Acknowledging the possibility of blind spots, and taking action to ensure consideration of previously overlooked data, is another step bioethicists could take toward reconciliation.

The case studies also reveal an important alliance between bioethics and medicine.[25] Despite its origins as a field outside of medicine

[23] *Compare* Coleman & Nerney, *supra* note 1, *with* Kathy L. Cerminara, *Critical Essay: Musings on the Need to Convince Some People with Disabilities that End-of-Life Decision-Making Advocates Are Not Out to Get Them*, 37 LOY. U. CHI. L. J. 343 (2006).

[24] Bruce Jennings, *Preface*, *in* IMPROVING END OF LIFE CARE: WHY HAS IT BEEN SO DIFFICULT?: HASTING CENTER SPECIAL REP., Nov.–Dec. 2005, at S2–S4.

[25] I'm certainly not the first to make this observation. *See, e.g.*, HOWARD BRODY, THE FUTURE OF BIOETHICS (Oxford Univ. Press 2009) (criticizing today's bioethics for its neglect of the ethical implications of evidence-based medicine).

that was deeply critical of prevailing medical practices, bioethics is now deeply embedded in medical schools, in hospitals, and on hospital floors. Bioethicists are clinicians and clinicians are ethicists. The importance of this alliance is evident in the responses of certain ethicists to the Ashley case, which uncritically adopt the biomedical model of assessing risk, and in the Gonzales case, where some bioethicists would defer entirely to professional medical judgment about the continuing availability of life-prolonging interventions. Now immersed in the culture of medicine, bioethicists instinctively trust their clinical colleagues to do the right thing, or in bioethics speak, to exercise professional medical judgment. Acknowledging the importance of the alliance between bioethics and medicine, and the potential impact it has on the willingness of bioethicists to challenge medical orthodoxy, might give bioethicists a new perspective on a number of cases in which that medical orthodoxy tends to devalue life with disability.

C. Unearthing Common Ground

Although our study of perspectives on disability-related cases arising at different points in the human life cycle reveals fundamental differences in the approaches taken by members of the disability and bioethics communities, the study also reveals significant areas on which there exists broad agreement. Most fundamentally, disability and bioethics experts share a common interest in promoting a good, just medical system in which all people are treated with respect. Bioethicists and disability experts both favor the just, nondiscriminatory, and nonarbitrary allocation of scarce resources. Both groups also share a commitment to ensuring informed medical decision making by and for people with disabilities.

Disability advocates also share with bioethicists an interest in allowing individuals with disabilities to make autonomous choices and direct their own lives.[26] That commitment to individual autonomy is evident throughout the literature on independent living and in the position statements of many disability groups. The importance of respect for autonomy is evident in Mary's case, where the doctor's respect for her choice against the proposed medical exam afforded her power and self-direction for perhaps the first time in a life in which she had been continually denied independence. Respect for self-determination by people with disabilities is also evident in the cases that arose in the reproductive years, where the consistent thrust of disability argument is that people with disabilities must be permitted to direct their own lives. With Valerie, that meant allowing her parents to consent to sterilization to enable Valerie to engage the world outside her home on her own terms. With the Egans, that meant allowing them to choose parenthood on their own terms. The fact of the common commitment to self-determination or respect for autonomy by disability and bioethics experts is, in my view, more important than the disagreements about limitations on autonomy, because the agreement that people with disabilities should have the same right to control their lives as anyone else provides a broad platform from which to search for mutually agreeable limiting principles.

In addition to these broad areas of agreement, there is consensus on some specific issues, particularly those that arise in the reproductive years. Access issues are important to disability and bioethics experts, and both bioethicists and disability experts have called for increased access to reproductive services, including assisted reproductive technologies, for people with disabilities. There is also general agreement on the question of involuntary sterilization. That is, members of the disability and bioethics communities agree that sterilization should be

---

[26] Ed Roberts, a pioneer in the independent living movement described the goals of the movement. "I'm tired of well meaning non-cripples with their stereotypes of what I can and cannot do directing my life and my future. I want cripples to direct their own programs and to be able to train other cripples to direct new programs. This is the start of something big – cripple power." Ed Roberts, Father of Independent Living, http:www.ilusa.com/links/022301ed_Roberts.htm.

an option for all people, but that it should be used sparingly absent the consent of the individual at issue. Thus, bioethicists and disability experts agree that special procedures and strict criteria are necessary to prevent the use of sterilization for eugenics purposes or for the benefit of anyone but the person to be sterilized.

The fact of consensus on sterilization is important because it provides a road map of sorts for resolving other difficult issues. The agreement that involuntary sterilization cannot be prohibited in all cases without hurting some people with disabilities, and concomitant agreement that careful procedural protections are necessary to ensure that involuntary sterilization be used only in appropriate cases, emerged only with time and experience with extreme rules (involuntary sterilization on demand, absolute prohibitions against sterilization) that proved unworkable in practice. Perhaps the lessons learned in reaching a moderate consensus position on involuntary sterilization might inform efforts to resolve some of the ongoing disputes. At the very least, the experience with involuntary sterilization cases emphasizes the value of procedural protections as tools for building frameworks agreeable to multiple stakeholders.

Given the broad areas of consensus revealed through the direct comparisons of positions taken in response to controversial cases, claims of "civil war"[27] between disability and bioethics experts appear to be exaggerated. Indeed it seems quite possible that bioethicists and disability experts might benefit by working together to address common areas of concern.

II. TAKING ACTION: DEVELOPING DISABILITY-CONSCIOUSNESS IN BIOETHICS

The strained relationship between bioethics and the disability community interferes with collaborative work on areas of common

[27] Mark Kuczewski & Kristi Kirschner, *Special Issue: Bioethics & Disability*, 24 THEORETICAL MED. 455, 455–456 (2003).

concern. At times, the conflict is so heated as to make even civil discourse impossible. On close examination, however, it appears that the conflict is not nearly as deep as some of the rhetoric suggests, and that prospects for reconciliation are viable. With a newfound understanding and acknowledgment of the concerns, interests, fears, biases, and alliances that contribute to the conflict, bioethicists are well positioned to build the trust necessary for successful collaboration. So long as bioethics continues to be perceived as insensitive to or indifferent about the concerns of people with disabilities, however, prospects for reconciliation remain poor. In other words, until bioethicists take action to show a consciousness of disability issues and perspectives as a matter of course in their work, the conflict is likely to persist. As disability scholar Lennard Davis notes, "[T]o be ignorant of disability studies is simply to be ignorant."[28] Bioethicists cannot afford to be ignorant about an issue so critical to medical decision making as the social implications of disability. Developing a disability-consciousness in bioethics will engender trust and prepare bioethicists to recognize when and how negative social perceptions about disability creep into medical decision or policy making. In other words, becoming mindful of disability issues will allow bioethicists to identify and ameliorate the disabling elements of the medical establishment.

This section begins to sketch out a framework for a disability-conscious bioethics. The framework is informed by the study of disability cases and related scholarship. It also incorporates principles enunciated in the UN Convention on the Rights of Persons with Disabilities,[29] an international agreement, generated with extensive participation of disability experts, to ensure the full and equal enjoyment of human rights by persons with disabilities. The model acknowledges

---

[28] Lennard J. Davis, *Preface,* THE DISABILITY STUDIES READER at xii (Routledge, 3d ed. 2010).

[29] Convention on the Rights of Persons with Disabilities, May 3, 2008, 189 U.N.T.S. 137, *available at* http://www.un.org/esa/socdev/enable/rights/convtexte.htm.

the concerns, fears, biases, and points of agreement expressed in conversations between and among bioethics and disability experts, but it is not rigid or determinative on particular cases. Rather, a disability-conscious bioethics is a loose framework for bioethical debate that incorporates disability as a central issue and engages disability experts in the enterprise of bioethics.

A. Principles

Given the importance of moral principles in bioethics,[30] a natural starting point for building a disability-conscious bioethics is consideration of whether and how to incorporate the principles central to the work of disability experts in protecting the human rights of persons with disabilities. As enunciated in the UN Convention of Rights of Persons With Disabilities, those principles are:

(a) Respect for inherent dignity, individual autonomy including the freedom to make one's own choices, and independence of persons; (b) non-discrimination; (c) full and effective participation and inclusion in society; (d) respect for difference and acceptance of persons with disabilities as part of human diversity and humanity; (e) equality of opportunity; (f) accessibility; (g) equality between men and women; [and] (h) respect for the evolving capacities of children with disabilities and respect for the right of children with disabilities to preserve their identities.[31]

The Convention uses these principles to derive general obligations and rules applicable to State parties to the convention. The sweeping obligations imposed on States under the Convention are beyond the scope of this book. Nonetheless, the guiding principles suggest priority areas

---

[30] *See* Chapter 2, *supra*, for an overview of bioethical methodology. *See* TOM L. BEAUCHAMP & JAMES F. CHILDRESS, PRINCIPLES OF BIOMEDICAL ETHICS (6th ed., Oxford University Press 2009) for an extended discussion.

[31] Convention on the Rights of Persons with Disabilities, *supra* note 29, art. 3.

for disability work. To the extent those principles are not already part of bioethical debate, a disability-conscious bioethics will make consideration of the principles a regular part of bioethical analysis.

The Convention's first principle – respect for inherent dignity, individual autonomy including the freedom to make one's own choices, and independence of persons – is already very much a part of bioethical conversation. If anything, bioethics can be fairly accused of emphasizing this principle to the exclusion of others. By contrast, application of the second principle – nondiscrimination based on disability status – is not as well developed. Discrimination takes various forms. It can be overt and purposeful or insidious and unintentional. Overt discrimination exists in policies or practices that deny or grant opportunity based on status alone. Unintentional discrimination results from the application of facially neutral policies or practices that have an adverse effect on members of a particular class. Both purposeful and unintentional types of discrimination subordinate members of the affected class. As such, both are a matter of concern in terms of social policy, justice, and law. As the U.S. Supreme Court noted in the employment context, the "absence of discriminatory intent does not redeem employment procedures or testing mechanisms that operate as 'built-in headwinds' for minority groups and are unrelated to measuring job capacity."[32]

The case studies indicate that although bioethicists oppose overt discrimination, they are less cognizant of unintentional or insidious discrimination.[33] Thus, we see bioethicists rejecting policies that would resolve treatment disputes based on disability status alone,[34] in favor

---

[32] Griggs v. Duke Power Co., 401 U.S. 424, 432, 91 S. Ct. 849, 854, 28 L. Ed. 2d 158, 165 (1971).

[33] Utilitarian Peter Singer is an important exception. I address the need for bioethics to confront its Peter Singer Problem later in the chapter.

[34] *See, e. g.,* BEAUCHAMP & CHILDRESS, *supra* note 30, at 170 ("we should exclude several conditions of patients from consideration altogether. For example, Mental retardation is irrelevant in determining whether a treatment is in a patient's best interests.").

334

of policies that turn on assessments of "medical appropriateness," "medical judgment," "quality of life," "risk/benefit analysis," "familial best interests," and "open futures" – concepts that, according to disability experts, work to the detriment of persons with disabilities. Incorporating the principle of nondiscrimination in bioethics will require bioethicists to take seriously the possibility that such facially neutral policies may operate "as built-in headwinds" for people with disabilities. Taking the possibility of unintentional bias seriously does not mean taking every charge of discriminatory bias at face value, but it does mean considering the existing evidence and engaging in empirical studies designed to determine the degree to which the claims of discriminatory effect of facially neutral policies are grounded in actual practice.

Designing studies to identify practices in the medical and social context that are fair in form but discriminatory in operation is complicated by the fact that a person's impairment may be directly relevant to medical evaluation and treatment. That is, medicine and medical providers may have legitimate reasons to recognize a person's physical or mental condition and alter the course of treatment as a result. The special difficulty in identifying disability discrimination in the provision of health care, then, is in distinguishing when the fact of disability is being considered for legitimate reasons, and when it is being used based on false assumptions about potential quality of life, or as a subterfuge for disability bias. Making this distinction will require frank and potentially uncomfortable discussions about physical and cognitive impairment. What is critical to establishing a disability-conscious bioethics is ensuring that those discussions are informed by reliable data drawn from the experience of people with disabilities, not biased and unreliable assumptions and stereotypes.[35]

---

[35] Having good evidence about the effect of facially neutral policies and practices on people with disabilities will provide a starting point for that debate. Once a disparate impact is proven, bioethicists might incorporate a back-and-forth process modeled on that used in employment discrimination cases to look for proof that the facially neutral policy that has disparate impact on persons with disabilities is in fact justified by

A bioethics that incorporates the Convention's third principle – full and effective participation and inclusion in society – will also have a new focus. For example, application of the principle in cases like Larry McAfee's, in which an individual who is not terminally ill refuses treatment, might inspire (even require) bioethicists to ask what can we as a society do to ensure that this individual is able to participate in meaningful life activities, before asking whether this person has decision-making capacity. It might also require bioethicists to engage in reflection on the practice of bioethics – in hospitals, in medical schools, and on ethics committees – to ensure inclusion of disability experts to both educate about the realities of life with disability and identify barriers and pathways to inclusion in society. Finally, attention to the inclusion principle will require bioethicists to engage in moral and ethical arguments about deinstitutionalization, support for caregivers, and other social tools necessary for full participation in society. In attending this principle, bioethics will ensure that medicine has something to offer persons with chronic conditions or permanent impairment for whom cure is not an option.

"medical necessity." Under Title VII of the Civil Rights Act of 1964, and the Supreme Court's decision in Griggs v. Duke Power Co., 401 U.S. 424 (1971), a person seeking to prove discrimination based on a disparate impact theory must initially prove that the employer has treated classes of people differently using apparently neutral policies. The plaintiff must prove that policies had the effect of excluding persons who are members of a protected class. Once disparate impact is established, the employer must justify that the continued use of the policies or procedures causing the adverse impact is a business necessity. If the employer proves that the requirement of being challenged is job related, the plaintiff must then show that other selection devices without a similar discriminatory effect would not also serve the employer's legitimate interest in efficient workmanship. By analogy, proof that a particular measure has a disparate impact on people with disabilities might be considered sufficient to preclude use of the measure absent some proof that claims of medical necessity are supported by good evidence. Although complicated, the use of an evidence-based burden-shifting approach similar to that used in employment discrimination cases might serve as an agreeable framework for in-depth consideration of the role of non-discrimination based on disability status in bioethical decision making.

Incorporating the Convention's fourth principle – respect for difference and acceptance of persons with disabilities as part of human diversity and humanity – may require a fair amount of work on the part of bioethicists. As an initial matter, bioethicists who are serious about respecting difference and accepting people with disabilities as part of the human condition need to address bioethics' Peter Singer problem.[36] Singer's utilitarian argument on the nontreatment of newborns completely negates the notion of individual worth, and the idea that each baby possesses unique potential, promise, and value. As such, it directly contravenes the principle of respect. Whether the answer to the Peter Singer problem is philosophical argumentation or public distancing depends on one's view of bioethics. Singer argues that "Bioethics, as a field or discipline, should not dedicate itself to advocacy for anyone. Its only commitment, as a field, is to pursue knowledge and understanding with integrity and respect for the views of other scholars in the field."[37] A bioethics that incorporates respect for difference and acceptance of persons with disabilities as a guiding principle will likely have a broader commitment than just to other scholars in the field. It will commit, whether as a matter of academic discourse or practical application, to rebutting arguments that fail to respect the value of persons because of their disability status. But even a bioethics narrowly construed as committed to the "pursuit of knowledge and understanding with integrity" will benefit from wrestling with the evidence that people with persistent disabilities experience a good or excellent quality of life, even when uninformed observers might predict otherwise.[38]

[36] *See* Chapter 3, *supra.*

[37] Peter Singer, *Response to Mark Kuczewski*, 1 AM. J. BIOETHICS, Summer 2001, at 55, 55.

[38] *See*, G.L. Albrecht & P.J. Deulieger, *The Disability Paradox: High Quality of Life Against All Odds*, 48(8) SOC. SCI. & MED. 977 (1999); S. Saigal et. al., *Self-perceived Health Status and Health Related Quality of Life of Extremely Low-Birth-weight Infants at Adolescence*, 276(6) J.A.M.A. 453 (1996); J.R. Bach & M.C. Tilton, *Life Satisfaction*

More fundamentally, a bioethics that respects difference and accepts persons with disabilities as part of human diversity and humanity will also require bioethicists to rethink calls for cure, learn about different ways to parent, and consider whether it is possible to approach physical differences with more than a medical fix. The literature on embodied difference and the value of difference is rich and compelling. It should be required reading for bioethicists, and a tool for use in educating health professionals, families, and people with new-onset disabilities about the value of life with disability.[39]

Having said that, I should emphasize my view that the principle of respect for difference and acceptance of persons with disabilities does not require bioethics to adopt a radical-disability-as-identity position. Just as disability scholars Paul Longmore, Lennard Davis, and Sam Bagenstos recognize the range of responses to disability and negative aspects of impairment (e.g. a propensity to bedsores in quadriplegics, heart problems associated with Down Syndrome), I think bioethicists can show respect for difference and acceptance

and Well-Being Measures in Ventilator Assisted Individuals with Traumatic Tetraplegia, 75(6) ARCH. PHYS. MED. REHABILITATION 626 (1994).

[39] *E.g.,* LENNARD J. DAVIS, ENFORCING NORMALCY: DISABILITY, DEAFNESS, AND THE BODY (Verso 1995); LENNARD J. DAVIS & MICHAEL BERUBE, BENDING OVER BACKWARDS: ESSAY ON DISABILITY AND THE BODY (NYU Press 2002); ROSEMARIE GARLAND THOMSON, EXTRAORDINARY BODIES (Columbia Univ. Press 1996); THE DISABILITY STUDIES READER (Lennard J. Davis ed., 3d ed. 2010); NANCY MAIRS, WAIST-HIGH IN THE WORLD: A LIFE AMONG THE NONDISABLED (Beacon Press 1996); DEVIANT BODIES: CRITICAL PERSPECTIVES ON DIFFERENCE IN SCIENCE AND POPULAR CULTURE (Jennifer Terry & Jacqueline L. Urla eds., Indiana Univ. Press 1995); HARRIET MCBRYDE JOHNSON, TOO LATE TO DIE YOUNG: NEARLY TRUE TALES FROM A LIFE (Picador 2006); ALICE DOMURAT DREGER, ONE OF US: CONJOINED TWINS AND THE FUTURE OF NORMAL (Harvard Univ. Press 2005); DISABILITY/POSTMODERNITY: EMBODYING DISABILITY THEORY (Mairian Corker & Tom Shakespeare eds., Continuum 2002); SURGICALLY SHAPING CHILDREN: TECHNOLOGY, ETHICS, AND THE PURSUIT OF NORMALITY (Eric Parens ed., Johns Hopkins Univ. Press 2008); KATHY DAVIS, DUBIOUS EQUALITIES & EMBODIED DIFFERENCES: CULTURAL STUDIES ON COSMETIC SURGERY (Rowman & Littlefield Publishers 2003).

of persons with disabilities without denying the negative aspects of impairment. The key to application of the respect principle in bioethics is knowledge and validation of the many experiences of disability and development of an inclusive and well-informed discussion about life with disability.

A concrete step bioethicists could take to show respect for difference and persons with disability, for example, would be to pay attention to language and to what disability experts tell us about language. Disability experts explain that certain phrases used to describe disability or aspects of life with disability reflect and promote negative attitudes toward people with disabilities. Use of such terms creates barriers between the speaker and people with disabilities, even where no offense is intended. Although bioethicists avoid terms widely recognized as direspectful ("retard" and "cripple"), the bioethics literature is replete with references to terms that convey more subtle negative and derogatory connotations. For example, the bioethics literature refers to certain children as "abnormal," "normal," "defective," "deformed," "stricken," "afflicted," and "damaged." These terms indicate that certain children are less worthy of respect than others. Likewise, the commonly used term "artificial nutrition and hydration" suggests that the medically assisted nutrition and hydration relied on as an alternative and effective source of food and fluids by thousands of people with disabilities is somehow not real, something lesser, or not as important as food and water relied on by those who consume food by mouth. Disability experts suggest alternative phrases that reflect a positive attitude and respect for difference ("medically assisted nutrition and hydration" instead of "artificial nutrition and hydration," "person who uses a wheelchair" or "wheelchair user" instead of "wheelchair bound" or "confined to a wheelchair"). Although the differences in language are subtle, the less preferred terms convey the messages that some people are the other, a less worthy cousin to their fully functioning relatives. By using language that conveys respect for the dignity of people with disabilities, bioethicists can take concrete steps to show acceptance of variations in mobility, eating, sensing, and otherwise interacting with the world as part of the human condition.

Although the Convention's fifth principle – equality of opportunity – is already embedded in the bioethical principle of justice and very much a part of bioethical debate,[40] the Convention's sixth principle – accessibility – is often overlooked. For example, very little attention is paid in the bioethics literature to equipment and attitudinal barriers that continue to prevent persons with disabilities from accessing health care or having equal opportunities to make autonomous health care decisions.[41] Yet, attitudinal and equipment barriers affect people with disabilities in the health care setting every day. People needlessly die because they do not have or cannot afford access. Attending to accessibility would require bioethics to concern itself with these barriers and the moral and legal obligations, if any, to remove them to the same extent it concerns itself with new medical innovations and other hot topics that tend to dominate bioethical discussion. As explained in the disability literature, the principle of accessibility includes a form of positive obligation. That is, accessibility requires a commitment of resources and action to remove barriers and ensure full participation of persons with disabilities in societal institutions. Philosophically trained bioethicists could help explore the degree to which accessibility supports moral rules of obligation (are hospitals and physicians obligated to replace functional but nonaccessible medical imaging equipment, for example?), and policy-oriented bioethicists could consider accessibility in policy and rule making.

That is not to say that bioethicists are hostile or resistant to accessibility as a guiding principle. Indeed, making all forms of health care accessible to people with cognitive disabilities by empowering surrogate

---

[40] BEAUCHAMP & CHILDRESS, *supra* note 30, at 234.

[41] See, Chapter 5, *supra*. See also, Kirsten Kirschner, *Structural Impairments that Limit Access to Health Care for Patients with Disabilities*, 297(10) J.A.M.A. 1121 (2007).

decision makers to consent to all types of decisions, including palliative care and the termination of treatment, has been a mainstay of bioethical argument since the founding of the field. Ironically, of course, the use of surrogates is one of the points of contention with some members of the disability community. A disability-conscious bioethics does not need to abandon its take on how the accessibility principle applies to support surrogate decision making, but it may need to consider accessibility from other perspectives as well.

The Convention's final principles – equality between men and women, respect for the evolving capacities of children with disabilities, and respect for the right of children with disabilities to preserve their identities – are already recognized in bioethical debate. One might wonder, however, what disability experts could add to the understanding of bioethicists about the right of children with disabilities to preserve their identities.

In sum, whereas some of the guiding principles of disability rights work are already a part of bioethical analysis, some are not of central concern. A disability-conscious bioethics will be cognizant of those less-attended principles. Specifically, a disability-conscious bioethics will concern itself with nondiscrimination, the full and effective participation of people with disabilities in society, respect for difference, and accessibility in new and important ways. Doing so will add a new dimension to bioethical debate. Of course, identifying principles of concern is only the first step in developing a framework for a disability-conscious bioethics. Even assuming the principles are generally agreeable across disciplines, much debate must still take place about how the principles function for the formulation of more specific rules and how they apply in specific cases. Disputes are inevitable. Because disability and bioethics experts bring to bear very different values in assessing the reliability of dispute-resolution processes, part of the project of building a disability-conscious bioethics will concern the role of process in resolving difficult cases.

B. Protecting Against Abuse: The Role of Process

The case studies clarified the reasons why and the degree to which people within the disability community are threatened, devalued, and afraid for their lives in the health care setting. The case studies also revealed that procedural protections – imposition of strict eligibility criteria and oversight by trusted decision makers in appropriate cases – can effectively diffuse distrust and pave the way to reconciliation. The problem, of course, is that the procedural mechanisms preferred by many people in the disability community – prohibitions and court review – are problematic from the perspective of bioethicists who value open access to a full range of medical options and protect the privacy of medical decision making. On the other hand, the procedural mechanisms preferred by many people in bioethics – referral to ethics committees and reliance on profession judgment and medical criteria – are not reassuring to many members of the disability community, who cite historical incidents of biased decision making by medical personnel and institutions, including ethics committees. Developing a means for resolving difficult cases and preventing abuse acceptable to both disability experts and bioethicists will require consideration of two separate issues: when are procedural protections necessary, and what should they look like.

As to the first question, when are procedural protections necessary, there is likely no single answer. Bioethicists and disability activists appear to agree that it is appropriate to make some form of conflict-resolution process available when conflicts arise between stakeholders in an individual case (doctor, patient, among family members, etc.). There is disagreement, however, about when the possibility of abuse based on ignorance about disability or disability bias is so significant as to justify across-the-board procedural protections that interfere with private medical decision making. An answer to this first question might lie in the involuntary sterilization cases. There, persons with disabilities – and only persons with disabilities – were being subjected to involuntary medical interventions that had no direct impact on the disability itself.

That is, sterilizing a person with Down syndrome did not affect the genetic condition responsible for the syndrome or physical or mental manifestations of the condition, nor did it resolve or remediate any physical or cognitive impairment related to the disability. Moreover, the possibility that the intervention would be misused for reasons other than advancing the patient's best interests was supported by verifiable evidence of past practices of unjustified involuntary sterilization. These two factors – the use of treatment options on persons with disabilities not intended to address the physical or cognitive impairment that made the treatment option acceptable ("disability-only interventions"), and evidence of abusive practices – were deemed sufficiently weighty to justify strict procedural safeguards before use of the intervention.

A disability-conscious bioethics might consider whether the presence of either or both factors – a disability-only intervention or evidence of abuse of the intervention – justifies support for across-the-board procedural protections. In the parlance of lawyers, the question would be: Does the use of a disability-only intervention, or evidence of abusive use of a generally applicable intervention, trigger "heightened scrutiny"? When both factors are present, the need for procedural protections seems clear. Where one is present but the other is unknown or absent, the question is more complicated. In such cases – where, for example, a new intervention is proposed for use on persons with certain disabilities for reasons other than correcting or ameliorating impairment, but there is no data on how the procedure has been or will be applied – a disability-conscious bioethics might support a time-limited trial of protective measures and close oversight during which time data are gathered on the use of the procedures to determine whether there is evidence that there is a verifiable risk that they will be used to the detriment of people with disabilities absent protective procedures. Or, where there is verifiable evidence that a generally available treatment option is being used to the detriment of people with disabilities, a disability-conscious bioethics might support across-the-board procedural protections to ensure against misuse or biased application.

Answers to the second issue – what form of process to use – are no more obvious. The challenge for a disability-conscious bioethics is to devise procedural protections against abusive practices, and for efficient resolution of disputed cases, without unduly restricting options in health care for persons with disabilities. Meeting the challenge will require the development of procedural mechanisms deemed trustworthy by disability experts – a process that must involve persons with disability in the formation and makeup of decision-making criteria and decision-making bodies. One solution might be the creation of independent ethics review boards whose members are unaffiliated with institutions involved in care and whose membership includes experts in disability, medicine, ethics, law, and the broader community.[42] Another might be to reconsider broader access to court review for disability-only interventions, or when there is a demonstrated risk of disability bias affecting decisions. Debating, testing, and implementing procedural safeguards that are trusted but not unduly burdensome will be a long-term project in a disability-conscious bioethics.

III. DISABILITY-CONSCIOUS BIOETHICS IN ACTION

Developing a disability-conscious bioethics will take more than agreement on guiding principles and process. The skeletal framework of

---

[42] In Boston, for example, the Harvard teaching hospitals have supported the creation of a community ethics committee, composed of individuals from diverse backgrounds who do not have financial or social ties to the hospitals. This group has already produced white papers on several controversial policy issues, but it is not currently empowered to comment on individual clinical cases. If thoughtfully structured and utilized, however, community ethics committees could be educated around key aspects of medical care at the end of life and could provide a forum for deliberation about such cases that would be much freer from the biases and conflicts of interest that, in my mind, plague the Texas approach.

Robert D. Truog, *Medical Futility*, 25 GA. ST. U. L. REV. 985, 1002 (2009).

principles and procedures sketched out in the previous section needs to be fleshed out on every level for application in specific cases. Even when fully developed, however, a disability-conscious bioethics will not solve problematic cases. What it will do is change the bioethical conversation. A disability-conscious bioethics will incorporate important but overlooked knowledge, evince sensitivity to the values, concerns, and interests of members of the disability community, acknowledge the biases and alliances that affect various parties' perspectives, and focus on principles of importance to disability work that are sometimes overlooked in bioethics – nondiscrimination, full and effective participation and inclusion of people with disabilities, respect for difference, and accessibility. As a result, bioethicists will have the knowledge and tools to identify and redress the disabling elements of the medical establishment.

To explain how disability-consciousness might affect the work of bioethics, it makes sense to revisit each of the cases discussed earlier in the book and explore how application of even a rudimentary framework might change the bioethical conversation. The following discussion does not offer concrete solutions on issues or repeat the observations offered at the end of each chapter about reasons for conflict and pathways for reconciliation. Instead, it identifies how debate and analysis might evolve in a bioethics that is deliberately conscious of disability in all facets of its work.

A. Disability in Infancy: Sydney Miller and Emilio Gonzalez

Sydney Miller's case raised painful questions about suffering and saving, the relative importance of sustaining life in the face of unknowable prognoses, and the responsibilities and burdens of families of marginally viable newborns. In a disability-conscious bioethics, those debates will continue and be supplemented by concern for nondiscrimination and respect for difference. For example, more attention might be placed in empirical study, theoretical debate, and in practical application on identifying, documenting, and addressing disability bias. In this regard, bioethicists might bring to bear the same tools they have used (often in conjunction with experts from various disciplines) with respect to racial disparities in health care[43] to identify, document, and address disparate treatment of newborns with disabilities (or potential disabilities) in the NICU. Further, bioethicists who work in medical schools and in teaching hospitals might work in conjunction with disability experts to ensure that the physicians – who are or will be advising parents such as the Millers on life-and-death decision making – are fully aware of the evidence showing the high value given life with disability by the people who live with difference.[44] As educators, or as part of the informed-consent process, bioethicists might seek to ensure that parents of imperiled newborns are given every opportunity to develop an evidence-based understanding of what it means to live with impairing traits in order to avoid rash, uninformed decision making. This is not to say that disability-conscious bioethicists must agree with Adrienne Asch that the only acceptable course of treatment for a potentially viable newborn is to continue its life. Suffering is real, and physical and mental impairments may cause unavoidable suffering. Still, conversations about and decisions made in consideration of suffering should be based, to whatever degree possible, on accurate and verifiable information.

[43] *E.g.*, COMMITTEE ON UNDERSTANDING & ELIMINATING RACIAL AND ETHNIC DISPARITIES IN HEALTH CARE, UNEQUAL TREATMENT: CONFRONTING RACIAL AND ETHNIC DISPARITIES *in* HEALTH CARE (Brian D. Smedley et al. eds., National Academies Press 2004), *available at* http://www.nap.edu/openbook. php?isbn=030908265X.

[44] Models for disability education in medical schools exist. *See, e.g.*, P. M. Miniham et al., *Teaching about Disability: Involving Patients with Disabilities as Medical Educators*, 24 DISABILITY STUDIES Q. 4 (2004); Kirsten L. Kirschner et al., *Educating Health Care Professionals to Care for Patients with Disabilities*, 302(12) J.A.M.A. 1334 (2009); A. Claxton, *Teaching Medical Students about Disability*, 308 B.M.J. 805 (1994).

In addition to considering nondiscrimination and respect for difference among health care providers, a disability-conscious bioethics might debate how and whether to educate parents of extremely premature newborns about the realities of life with disability. For example, should disability experts be brought into the conversation with parents as soon as it becomes clear that disability might be a factor in decision making for a newborn? Perhaps, but some caution is in order before involving advocates in private decision making. Just as biases and ignorance have a negative impact on bioethical and medical opinion, so they could affect the information provided by disability experts. It might, therefore, be important to ensure that disability experts have first-hand experience with imperiled newborns and their families in the NICU to change the moral focus of the decision from theoretical arguments about the value of life with disability to what should be done for the tiny baby who is struggling for breath and facing innumerable invasive procedures that may be beneficial but may also be harmful. If actual interactions are not possible, the creation of training or educational films might be a worthwhile project of a disability-conscious bioethics.

In thinking about imperiled newborns, a disability-conscious bioethicist might need to reexamine or be transparent when discussing "acceptable outcomes." A bioethics that vests in parents the right to define as unacceptable any outcome other than full functioning and health is one that has not given weight to the principle of respect for difference. Some limits on parental decision making must be in place to ensure that children's lives are not terminated because they are deemed unworthy of medical care based on biased notions of the worthy life. That said, the discussion of decision-making frameworks that turn on a person's ability to interact with others, permanent physical pain, or potential for symbolic relationships need not be abandoned in a disability-conscious bioethics, so long as such discussions acknowledge the affinity many people with physical impairments feel with people with cognitive impairments, and the intent of such discussions is to find an objectively agreeable point of distinction between the life that must be saved and the life that might be better respected if it comes to its natural end.

The bioethical perspectives on the issues raised in the Emilio Gonzales case fell roughly into two camps. Those supporting the Texas law (TADA) that allowed providers to withdraw treatment over the objection of the mother argue that patients and their families have no right to force medical providers to squander resources on hopeless cases to satisfy their irrational wishes. Those opposed argue that doctors have no right to impose their own values on patients and their families in making life-and-death decisions for families. Importing disability-consciousness into the bioethical debate will hardly resolve this fundamental debate. Rather, a debate conscious of disability issues might ask whether such laws and policies – even if morally and ethically defensible – do more harm than good by cultivating a culture of distrust and fear among disability groups.

On the other hand, a disability-conscious bioethicist might be convinced that futility policies or law are appropriate so long as they are consistent with principles of nondiscrimination, respect for difference, and accessibility. From this perspective, two aspects of the Texas law are of concern: its qualifying criteria and its procedural methods. As discussed, the qualifying criteria under TADA are narrow but could still apply to quadriparesis with ventilator dependence or cerebral palsy with developmental impairments and a need for medically administered nutrition and hydration. As such, the law could be applied based on disability status alone despite the evidence that many people with quadriparesis or cognitive disabilities lead valued lives. A disability-conscious bioethics would weigh nondiscrimination and respect for difference in evaluating these possibilities. Such a transparent and inclusive conversation might alleviate the feeling among some disability rights activists that they are under siege, and allow room for drawing distinctions.

The second specific area of concern regarding TADA is the limited procedural process available to patients or families subject to treatment withdrawal decisions. A disability-conscious bioethicist might ask whether that process acknowledges the concerns about fairness and unbiased decision making raised by disability experts, and propose alternative procedures that would better address those concerns. To some extent, that discussion is already happening in bioethics.[45] Robert Truog, for example, argues that under Texas law, the ethics committee is acting:

> ... as a surrogate judge and jury, with the statutory power to authorize clinicians to take life or death actions against the wishes of a patient or family. But whereas the judicial system assures Americans of access to a "jury of peers" or at least an impartial judge, hospital ethics committees are not held to this standard. Although it is true that most committees include one or two members of the community (often grateful patients of the hospital), most members are physicians, nurses, and other clinicians from the hospital staff. Without in any way calling into question their motivations or intentions, one must recognize that they are unavoidably "insiders," completely acculturated to the clinical world and its attendant values. This is hardly an impartial tribunal for many, indeed probably most, of the patients who are subject to these decisions. The TADA thus relies on a due process approach that is more illusory than real and that risks becoming a rubber-stamp mechanism for systematically overriding families' requests that seem unreasonable to the clinicians involved. During a two-year period at Baylor, for example, the ethics committee agreed with the clinical team in forty-three out of forty-seven cases.

Legal and bioethics scholar Thaddeus Pope argues that the reliance Texas puts on ethics committees as the final arbiter of futility disputes does not meet constitutional requirements of due process: "[H]ealth care ethics committees ... don't have the competence[;] they don't

[45] Truog, *supra* note 42, at 1000.

have the neutrality to exercise the sort of decision-making authority that the Texas statute has given them."[46]

A disability-conscious bioethics would add to Truog and Pope's arguments the collective knowledge of disability experts to identify how the lack of neutrality affects people with disabilities in Texas and beyond. Furthermore, it would engage disability experts in developing a more transparent, fair, and neutral decisional process to resolve these difficult cases – a discussion that must reconsider the use of the judicial system for resolution of truly intractable cases.[47]

B. Disability in Childhood: Lee Larson's Boys, Ashley X

Bioethical analysis of issues concerning deaf identity raised in the case of Lee Larson's boys would have a new dimension in a disability-conscious bioethics. In the first place, the specific case would have been a part of the conversation. As noted in Chapter 4, the state's attempt to force surgical implantation of cochlear implants into the boys over the objection of their mother did not get the attention of bioethicists. The lack of attention is curious considering the apparent readiness of bioethicists to comment on controversial cases in media and academic discussions, and the obvious bioethical issues presented by the case. Had the State been successful in its attempt to force implantation in the Larson case, parents of deaf children in Michigan would have been required to implant as a matter of law, regardless of their assessment of a child's best interest. Such a result would surely have troubled many

---

[46] Thaddeus Mason Pope, *Remarks at the Meeting of the President's Council on Bioethics on Medical Futility: Institutional and Legislative Initiatives* (Sept. 12, 2008) (transcript available at http://bioethics.georgetown.edu/pcbe/transcripts/sept08/session5.html).

[47] Truog argues that "[W]e should consider carefully whether the creation of a 'shadow' judicial system through the use of community ethics committees is likely to offer substantial improvements over the mechanisms already in place." Truog, *supra* note 42, at 1002.

bioethicists who argue strenuously that a parent is best situated to assess what course of treatment is in a child's best interests. Of course, there are bioethicists who argue that parents have a moral obligation to ensure their children have opportunities to make choices and engage in a variety of careers as an adult, and that such obligation requires action to avoid deafness where possible. The disability critique of this so-called open-futures debate is fairly obvious and already a part of the bioethical conversation.[48] As such, its inclusion in discussion would not change the debate much, except perhaps to make more vigorous the objection to arguments that equate difference with dysfunction. In the words of a British scholar who works at the intersection of disability and bioethics, "[I]f bioethicists want to be able to say that the *bad thing* about disability, the experienced disadvantage of it, is sufficient grounds for morally serious medical interventions, then we need evidence that the disadvantage is as great as is claimed."[49]

The more important conversational shift to be expected in a disability-conscious bioethics would be the attention given parental decisions to consent to implants for their children. The debate now focuses on opportunities lost for the child whose parents choose deafness. In a bioethics that attends the principles of respect for difference and respect for the right of children with disabilities to preserve their identities, equal attention would be paid to opportunities lost and harms caused children who opt to use cochlear implants or otherwise attempt to "normalize" a child through medical technology. The evidence that Deaf children suffer psychological and identity trauma when denied the opportunity to learn sign language is compelling, at

---

[48] Robert A. Crouch, *Letting the Deaf Be Deaf: Reconsidering the Use of Cochlear Implants in Prelingually Deaf Children*, 27 HASTINGS CENTER REP., July–Aug. 1997, at 14, 17 (arguing that the predominant notion "that the deaf are 'merely and wholly' disabled – is wrong and that we should quickly disabuse ourselves of this ill-begotten notion").

[49] JACKIE LEACH SCULLY, DISABILITY BIOETHICS: MORAL BODIES, MORAL DIFFERENCE 154 (Rowman & Littlefield Publishers 2008).

least with respect to children taught to lip-read and use oral language. As the current generation of cochlear implant users grows up, there is a critical need to collect data on their experience to determine if the same sense of displacement and lack of self-esteem is a known and avoidable risk for implant users.

With respect to Ashley X, we need not speculate about how disability-consciousness might affect bioethical debate. The case has been extensively debated with particular attention to disability issues by a working group of bioethicists and disability scholars and experts at Seattle Children's Hospital, the hospital where Ashley was treated.[50] The working group presented a report addressing the issues of growth attenuation, which is an example of disability-conscious bioethics in action. The report identifies areas of common ground and points of persistent disagreement (including the moral appropriateness of growth attenuation in children with profound cognitive disabilities), and suggests a compromise for the careful and respectful use of growth attenuation in children for whom it might be beneficial. Disability-consciousness is especially evident in the group's recommendations on informed consent and necessary safeguards, which could serve as a model for disability-conscious approaches to other contentious issues.

The working group's recommendations for informed consent are striking in their breadth when compared to the more traditional risks/benefits/alternatives consent process that is mainstay in bioethics. The group's consensus was that although parents are the appropriate decision makers for children, parents must be told that the benefits and risks of growth attenuation are unknown or debatable. The group also

---

[50] *See* Seattle Growth Attenuation and Ethics Working Group Report, *Evaluating Growth Attenuation in Children with Profound Disabilities: Interests of the Child, Family Decision-Making and Community Concerns*, http://www.seattlechildrens.org/research/initiatives/bioethics/events/growth-attenuation-children-severe-disabilities/. *See also,* Benjamin S. Willford, et. al., *Navigating Growth Attenuation in Children with Profound Disabilities: Children's Interests, Family Decision-Making, and Community Concerns*, 40 HASTINGS CENTER REP., Nov.-Dec. 2010, 27–40.

agreed that parents should be required to speak with other parents of children with profound cognitive disabilities before making their decisions, and would require that parents be made aware of the social context of disability, including the history of discrimination against and stigmatization of people with disability. The group would also require parents be told about the objections to growth attenuation raised by members of the disability community, and be provided an informational sheet summarizing arguments for and against growth attenuation and describing various parental experiences and perspectives on the use of the interventions.

The working group also identified a series of safeguards to ensure against misuse of growth attenuation in cases other than those within the very narrowly defined circumstances in which some members felt it morally justifiable. The first recommendation is to ensure that the prognosis of profound, permanent cognitive disabilities is reliable by requiring competent assessment of likely etiology and prognosis of developmental disability, and consultation with a series of specialists. The group would also assure understanding of the interventions and its implications with particular consideration of the perspectives of the disability community, and consider the family's reasoning for requesting intervention.

The working group did not reach consensus on the best form of process for overseeing the use of growth attenuation, but did agree that some oversight is necessary because growth attenuation is an intervention that is unacceptable but for the presence of disabilities in a child (a disability-only intervention). There was agreement that some kind of third-party review is necessary,[51] but there was disagreement over

---

[51] I've argued elsewhere that third-party review with strict qualifying criteria best balances competing concerns in cases like Ashley's:

[T]hird-party review treats people as individuals with unique needs, lives, and values. It balances the competing interests between parents and children, and leaves the medical establishment to decide what treatment options are appropriate. In this way, third-party review ensures adequate protection for vulnerable populations without

the form the review should take. Some members of the group thought court involvement appropriate in all cases, whereas others argued for court involvement only in cases of intractable disputes (and in cases involving hysterectomy where required by state law). Most members of the working group concluded that review by ethics committees was a viable alternative to court review so long as ethics committees included people with experience with disability and experts in disability studies. Finally, the group called for ongoing oversight through research on and monitoring of cases in which growth attenuation is used. Some members of the group supported extensive involvement of institutional review boards because of their authority for continuing oversight and protection of human subjects in research. Others encouraged prospective research protocols to document outcomes, and there was discussion of a national registry to document the incidence of use and outcomes across the county. In other words, the working group engaged the question of procedural safeguards with an understanding of and sensitivity to the concerns and contributions of disability experts. The discussion resulted in creative ideas for resolving difficult issues in a way that addressed the concerns of all stakeholders.

Although the working group's "disability-consciousness" did not resolve difficult moral issues or solve contentious debates, it changed the nature of the conversation from that typical in bioethics, in particular through its emphasis on education about social issues in the informed consent process, inclusion of the disability perspective and

foreclosing access to what might in a particular case be a medically appropriate treatment. It is flexible. It can be structured to curtail the availability of a particular option, or simply to serve as a check on the decision that the proposed intervention serves the particular child's best interest.

Alicia Ouellette, *Growth Attenuation, Parental Choice, and the Rights of Disabled Children: Lessons from the Ashley X Case*, 8 Hous. J. Health L. & Pol'y 207, 241–242 (2008).

disability experts on ethics committees, and agreement that oversight of medical decision making is necessary. It is not clear how, if at all, the expanded informed consent process and procedural safeguards would have affected the outcome in Ashley's case. It does seem clear that the recommended process would have been more transparent, more inclusive, and more trusted than the behind-closed-doors meeting of the ethics committee that so threatened and angered members of the disability community when news of its resolution in Ashley's case was made public. I suspect also that the recommended process would make room for a much needed but difficult discussion about the moral appropriateness of using disability-only interventions for the convenience of caregivers of people with profound disabilities.[52] Engaging in more open conversations about the role of family and family concerns in decision making for children with disabilities might generate new and creative approaches for relieving the burden of caretaking.

[52] As disability-conscious bioethicist Alice Dreger wrote:

The problem I see with Ashley's parents is less their decision than their dishonesty about it. Would menstrual pain and adult breast development really be so painful for Ashley that they warrant hysterectomy and mastectomy? Unlikely. It sounds more like Ashley's parents find they have their hands full enough – literally – and they can't handle any more. They don't *want* to handle any more. I get that. Why not just be honest about that?

Because we're not allowed to be selfish parents and selfish caregivers of people with disabilities, that's why. And yet I can't help but feel that if we were honest about this, then we could have a much more honest discussion about why we might choose for others genital normalizing surgeries, conjoined twin separations, growth hormones for "idiopathic short stature," and "the Ashley treatment." And maybe if we had that more honest discussion, we wouldn't choose them so often. Maybe then we'd do a better job figuring out how we are really weighing best interests, and see that sometimes it isn't the patient whose suffering we're supposedly preventing – that it isn't always the putative patient who needs an intervention.

Alice Dreger, *Ashley and the Dangerous Myth of the Selfless-Parent*, HASTINGS CENTER BIOETHICS FORUM, Jan. 18, 2007, http://www.thehastingscenter.org/Bioethicsforum/Post.aspx?id=332#ixzz0sTtVWjm7

C. The Reproductive Years: William Peace, Valerie, and the Egans

With respect to the cases from the reproductive years disability experts and bioethicists find much common ground. Both support equal access to reproductive services – from sterilization to in vitro fertilization – for persons with and without disabilities. For this reason, issues surrounding access to reproductive health and assisted reproductive technologies might be a strong natural first project for collaborative work between bioethicists and disability experts. These issues also provide plenty of independent work for disability-conscious bioethicists. Two projects seem to me immediately apparent.

As a first project, disability-conscious bioethicists might work to educate health care providers about sexuality and parenting with disability. The principles of respect for difference, full and fair participation of individuals with disabilities in society, and accessibility are incompatible with a medical system that treats people with disabilities as an impairment with a person attached rather than human beings for whom sexuality and parenting are just as important a part of life as they are for any other person. If health care providers developed a kind of disability competency, an understanding that life with disability can include sexual relationships, parenting, and all other aspects of human existence, they would be better prepared to care effectively for their patients with disabilities. Perhaps bioethicists have a role in facilitating that paradigm shift.

As a second project, disability-conscious bioethicists should reconsider provider autonomy in the context of assisted reproductive technologies. Under traditional rules of medical and bioethics, physicians have no moral obligation to enter a relationship with any patient, and physicians may refuse – as a matter of conscious – to provide medical services deemed morally objectionable. As discussed in Chapter 5, people with disabilities are denied fertility services under the auspices of provider autonomy and professional judgment about the well-being

356

of future children. The principles of nondiscrimination, full and effective participation, respect for difference, and accessibility call into question this particular exercise of provider autonomy in the fertility clinic. When access to assisted reproductive technology is denied based on disability status (and presumptions about the ability of a persons with disability to endure pregnancy or successfully parent), autonomous choices of providers come at a cost. They deny people the opportunity to parent based on characteristics (impairments) that cannot be presumed to make a person unqualified to parent given the thousands of examples of successful parents with disabilities. Providers who impose barriers to fertility treatment based on value judgments about prospective patients who are medically and socially capable of bearing children generate distrust and anger among the rejected patients and their supporters, which may have implications for the medical profession generally in addition to the costs to individual patients. At the very least, discussion should be had about the relative importance of protecting provider autonomy when weighed against other principles, and systematic costs of its exercise.

D. The Adult Years: Mary, Larry McAfee, and Scott Matthews

The three cases presented from the adult years raised fundamental questions about a principle of shared importance to bioethics and disability experts: respect for individual autonomy, including the freedom to make one's own choices. Mary chose against an invasive screening procedure; Larry McAfee against life-prolonging mechanical ventilation; and Scott Matthews's parents against using a feeding tube. In each case, the mainstream bioethical response was support for the choice, on the theory that individualized decision making by a patient or appropriate surrogate best respects autonomy and promotes the best interests of individual patients given their unique values, concerns, and conditions. Disability theory adds to the discussion concern for the context in which those decisions are made. For example, disability experts identify systematic failures with health care and health policy that left Mary and Larry McAfee isolated in unduly restrictive and oppressive environments. The emphasis is on fixing the system to promote full and effective participation of individuals with disability in society. In cases like McAfee's, where the systematic failures are so profound as to render meaningless what could be an otherwise meaningful life, disability experts would challenge choices against continued existence on the ground that they represent a hopelessness internalized as a result of social failure and pressure. Viewing the system as so fundamentally flawed, some disability experts would even limit choices available to people with disabilities.

A disability-conscious bioethics would not limit choices, but it would account for systematic failures and work to foster a medical system that addresses the social as well as the medical needs of persons with disabilities. A system that focuses exclusively on cure has little to offer people with permanent disabilities. A greater focus on long-term care and social support could change the reality of existence for people with permanent impairments so they are not left alone in hospitals without any means of achieving their full potential.

Recognizing the role that systematic and social failures play in the lives of people with disabilities may also enable ethicists to better address the question of whether society is too quick to accept as reasonable the decision of a newly disabled person to die rather than to continue to live with a disability.[53] I've called this the Million Dollar Baby problem. In the 2004 film "Million Dollar Baby," the character played by Hilary Swank asked for and received euthanasia shortly after

---

[53] Material in this section is drawn largely from my work *Disability and the End of Life*, which was published by the *Oregon Law Review* and used here with permission.

suffering a catastrophic disability.[54] The disability rights community condemned the movie as perpetuating disability prejudice.[55] As I see it, the problem is not the character's ultimate decision. The problem is that the decision was precipitous. Disability scholarship has produced hard evidence that people who face sudden catastrophic injury might not be able to give informed consent as quickly as previously thought.[56] The studies show that when people are in a "liminal state" – that is, after they have lost their old identity as fully functioning but before they have accepted their new identity as a person with a disability – they may be unable to process information or recognize the potential for a quality life with disability.[57] Thus, they may be inclined to refuse treatment early after the change.

The scholarship also suggests that the notion of what it takes to give informed consent should be revisited in cases of sudden disability. If individuals are truly unable to process information, how can they make informed decisions? Proposals for reforming the informed-consent

---

[54] "Million Dollar Baby" (Warner Bros. 2004).

[55] See, e.g., Daniel Costello, Assisted Suicide at Center Stage Once Again: Award-Winning Movies and Upcoming Legislation Give New Urgency to the Contentious Issue, L.A. TIMES, Mar. 7, 2005, at F1 (noting that disability advocates expressed concerns that the film stigmatizes those with recent disabilities).

[56] See, e.g., Gary L. Albrecht & Patrick J. Devlieger, The Disability Paradox: High Quality of Life Against All Odds, 48 SOC. SCI. & MED. 977, 980 (1999) ("Individuals, families, and communities are unprepared to recognize and seldom ready to accept disability."); Asch, supra note 14, at 312–313 (quoting a 1987 report indicating that the onset of impairment may delay adaptation and comprehension); David R. Patterson et al., When Life Support Is Questioned Early in the Care of Patients with Cervical-Level Quadriplegia, 329 NEW ENG. J. MED. 663, 663 (1993) ("Patients frequently have a diminished capacity to make important decisions during the first several months after an injury....").

[57] Susan Merrill Squier uses this term to characterize unsettled stages of human existence. SUSAN MERRILL SQUIER, LIMINAL LIVES: IMAGINING THE HUMAN AT THE FRONTIERS OF BIOMEDICINE 3–4 (Duke Univ. Press 2004). For a very personal and sensitive description of one family's experience with life in a liminal state, see RICHARD GALLI, RESCUING JEFFREY (St. Martin's Griffin 2001).

process[58] deserve further study, as does the suggestion for "disability consults" as a regular part of medical treatment. [59]

As part of the project of developing the best process for ensuring informed decision making in a case involving disability, disability-conscious bioethics will also guard against perpetuating the myth of the tragedy of life with disability. The criticism of McAfee's decision and others like it is spot on. McAfee's decision to avoid medical treatment should not have been granted because his physical condition foreclosed the possibility of a meaningful life. If his request should have been granted at all, it should have been granted because it was his decision, made after thoughtful deliberation and in full understanding of the alternatives.

Finally, it is my view that disability-conscious bioethics would fully support the decision of Scott Matthews's parents to refuse the feeding tube, despite the arguments made by disability activists that depriving him of a feeding tube was a form of disability prejudice. As lawful decision makers, Scott's parents asserted the desire to avoid a feeding tube so that he could continue the activity he enjoyed most in his life. The desire to eat, the social enjoyment of a shared meal, and the taste of food are to some so valuable an experience that losing those abilities would be devastating. The loss would interfere with a meaningful life. Scott's parents' decision to avoid the feeding tube reflected values that were inherently personal to Scott; the decision had nothing to do with disability prejudice.

---

[58] Arthur Caplan and others argue for an educational model of informed consent that stresses that a patient needs an opportunity to experience the posttraumatic phase of care. The educational model of informed consent allows the treatment team to insist paternalistically on treatment during the initial period following a sudden-onset disability because the patient is not yet fully informed about the potential for a quality life with disability. Arthur L. Caplan et al., *Ethical & Policy Issues in Rehabilitative Medicine*, 17 HASTINGS CENTER REP. SPECIAL SUPP., Aug. 1987, at S1, S11–S14.

[59] Adrienne Asch, *Recognizing Death While Affirming Life: Can End of Life Reform Uphold a Disabled Person's Interest in Continued Life?*, in IMPROVING END OF LIFE CARE: HASTINGS CTR. SPECIAL REP., Mar.–Apr. 2003, at S31 (Bruce Jennings et al. eds.).

E. End-of-Life Decisions: Sheila Pouliot and Terri Schiavo

It is less clear how disability-consciousness will affect bioethical discussions about end-of-life cases like Sheila Pouliot's and Terri Schiavo's. For different reasons, both women were in fundamentally different positions than the adults discussed in the previous chapter, Mary, Larry McAfee, and Scott Matthews. For Mary, Scott, and Larry, the possibility of a meaningful life was alive and well. Disability-consciousness would therefore require a commitment to ensuring every opportunity for allowing the individuals involved to live that meaningful life. Sheila Pouliot and Terri Schiavo's opportunity for meaningful existence had come to an end. Sheila Pouliot was terminally ill, on a downward trajectory toward certain death, and Terri Schiavio's brain had been so badly damaged that she would never again be aware of her surroundings, experience emotion, or feel pain or pleasure. As such, their cases were about certainty in diagnosis, the sanctity of life, the relative importance of a pain-free death, and the proper placement of decision-making power. Debates over those issues will continue regardless of one's knowledge about or consciousness of disability.

The question that might be addressed differently in disability-conscious bioethics is how best to ensure access for all people to a full range of options including palliative or comfort care at the end of life without opening the slippery slope feared by some members of the disability community on which their lives could be involuntarily ended while they still find them meaningful. Ensuring access to the full range of medical options available for people with full decision-making capacity requires some accommodation for persons whose cognitive disabilities impair their ability to make their own medical decisions. Just as a person with a mobility impairment needs a wheelchair to get around, a person with cognitive disabilities (including PVS) needs a surrogate to make medical decisions. If Sheila Pouliot's case teaches nothing else, it teaches that it is inhumane and a denial of respect to deny a person access to a course of beneficial treatment because a disability renders her unable to choose that course. Of course, protecting against abusive surrogate behavior, including decision making based on disability bias, is a legitimate and important concern. As such, surrogate decision-making frameworks must include procedural protections.

It is in crafting, examining, and assessing procedural protections against abusive surrogate behavior that I see a role for disability-conscious bioethicists. Do surrogate decision-making statutes provide safeguards against disability bias? Can we be confident in their qualifying criteria? Do those frameworks that rely on ethics committee review require participation of disability experts on the ethics committee? Do they facilitate consultation by surrogates with disability experts or people who have experience with disability? Are there educational materials that could be developed to ensure surrogates are making decisions based on fact rather than disability bias? What, if any, is the role of court review in these cases? Although there are no clear answers to these questions, and the discussions will not satisfy the members of the disability community who have adopted a strict sanctity-of-life position, the discussions will enrich a bioethics committed to nondiscrimination and respect for all persons.

IV. CONCLUSION – AND A CALL TO ACTION

When I started this project, I planned to defend bioethics from charges that its teachings were responsible for the marginalization and even killing of people with disabilities. The notion that bioethicists are dangerous because they perpetuate prejudice against people with disabilities seemed ludicrous in light of my experiences in bioethics education and my engagement in bioethical conversations and literature. My initial discussions with other people who work in bioethics confirmed that I was not alone in my defensive reaction to charges against bioethics lodged by disability activists. Some people went even further. Behind closed doors, people told me to stay away from "disability people" and disability issues. Not only does disability lack cachet in academic circles, a mentor warned, getting involved with angry activists whose agenda he found suspect would be a waste of time.

I now have a different perspective. Listening to disability experts, reading their scholarship, and discussing contentious points has convinced me that despite my undergraduate and graduate training, I have been ignorant when it came to disability. Even more transformative has been the time I've spent sharing meals, drinking wine, and talking about romance, children, and life in general with friends, colleagues, and students who have disabilities. Meaningful exposure and interaction changes everything. I am now firmly convinced that as a discipline, bioethics has a lot to learn from disabilities experts about the realities of life with disabilities.

The first chapters of this book revealed points of friction about which disability experts and bioethicists tend to disagree. We learned that bioethicists tend to support individual choices to refuse medical care, family decision making, and advanced directives. Members of the disability community are often skeptical of or opposed to these practices. Some disability experts view medically assisted nutrition and hydration as a basic human right. Bioethicists tend to think of medically assisted nutrition and hydration as no different from other medical treatments. Bioethicists support efforts of doctors to fix physical impairments; disability scholars question the need to "fix" the bodies of individual with disability and look instead for societal solutions. Many bioethicists view persistent vegetative state as something entirely different from other disabling conditions; some disability activists deny those differences. Finally, many people in bioethics seek to resolve individual cases without taking into account social and community concerns, whereas social and community concerns are central to the disability community.

The comparative analysis clarifies the genesis and reasons for these differences. It also provides tools for understanding the concerns, interests, fears, and biases that give rise to conflicting perspectives, while identifying the significant areas of common concern. Some of the disputes are likely intractable. Others leave room for compromise and reconciliation. Understanding those concerns, interests, and fears, and acknowledging bias in existing positions, is an important step toward reconciliation, a process that will allow for new, mutually beneficial relationships through which collaborations will become possible. In my view, making room for collaborative work with disability experts will improve the work of bioethics.

In this chapter, I've sketched out a framework for disability-consciousness that emphasizes nondiscrimination, the full and effective participation of persons with disability, respect for difference, and accessibility together with traditional bioethical principles of autonomy, beneficence, justice, and equality of opportunity. Much work needs to be done to fully develop the concept or apply it in particular cases. Nonetheless, the framework is a starting point for debate. And debate will continue. The difference will be the infusion of knowledge and centrality of disability issues to the conversation.

Having developed a disability-consciousness, bioethicists will have work to do. For better or for worse, bioethics has a place in medical schools, on hospital floors, in undergraduate institutions, on governmental commissions, and in governmental agencies. Disability-conscious bioethicists will need to use their positions of power to influence the way we think about disability if they are to eradicate the disabling facets of today's health care system. Of course it would be better if disability experts held the same seats of power, and it may be that part of the project of disability-conscious bioethics is to create or to cede the seats of power to disability experts. At this point, however, it is up to bioethicists to become experts in disability issues so that they can bring that knowledge, as well as the disability experts who generate it, to the medical school classrooms, to the hospital floors, to the pediatrician's office, to the NICU, or any other place where issues involving disability are being discussed. Absent an expertise in disability, bioethics simply is not in a position to advance discussion and include people with disabilities, to recognize the bias inherent in the medical system, or to help patients or families think knowledgeably about the realities of life with disability.

Index

Index

Index

Index

Index

CPSIA information can be obtained
at www.ICGtesting.com
Printed in the USA
LVHW080509050919

630029LV00009B/68/P